THE WISEST FOOL

The Lavish Life of James VI and I

For Sarah

THE WISEST FOOL

The Lavish Life of James VI and I

Steven Veerapen

BIRLINN

First published in 2023 by
Birlinn Limited
West Newington House
10 Newington Road
Edinburgh
EH9 1QS

www.birlinn.co.uk

ISBN: 978 1 78027 816 2

British Library Cataloguing-in-Publication Data

A catalogue record for this book is available from the British Library

Typeset by Initial Typesetting Services, Edinburgh

Papers used by Birlinn Ltd are from well-managed forests
and other responsible sources

Printed and bound by Clays Ltd, Elcograf S.p.A.

Contents

Author's Note

It has become accepted practice to refer to King James's wife as 'Anna' of Denmark, in recognition of both her own preferred spelling of the name and the style which she used herself in diplomatic and private correspondence – and so I have stuck with this name throughout. 'Anna' was also the name which her friends and servants used (her Italian secretary, the scholar John Florio, for example, dedicated his 1611 Italian-English dictionary to her under the title *Queen Anna's New World of Words*). To James, she was always his affectionate 'Annie'. In older studies, her name is given as the anglicised 'Anne'.

Esmé, a favourite who James raised to the dukedom of Lennox, traditionally has his surname spelled in the Scottish style: 'Stewart'. However, I've used the French 'Stuart' for him and his family (and all Stuart/Stewarts of the royal line) so as to separate them from those Stewarts further from the throne. I've also referred to Esmé by his Christian name throughout, despite his elevation to the Lennox title, for the sake of consistency and to differentiate him from Regent Lennox (James's grandfather) and Esmé's son (the 2nd Duke of Lennox). Otherwise, I refer to individuals by their new titles whenever titles changed (for example, Robert Carr is referred to as 'Carr' until, chronologically, he is elevated to the viscountcy of Rochester, after which he is 'Rochester', etc.).

Finally, I'm extremely grateful to the historians Julian Goodare, Kenneth Fincham, Michael Pearce, Leanda de Lisle, and Robert Stedall for providing insightful commentary on early drafts of the text. Any errors are, of course, my own.

The Tudor and Stuart Dynasties

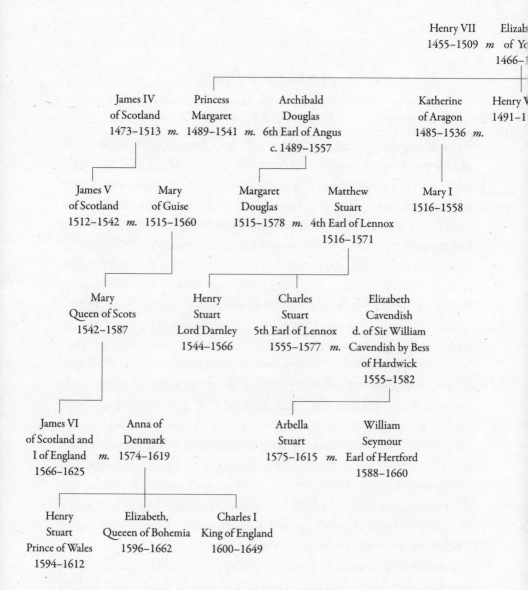

Henry VII
1455–1509 *m*
1466–

Elizab
of Yo

James IV
of Scotland
1473–1513 *m.*

Princess
Margaret
1489–1541 *m.*

Archibald
Douglas
6th Earl of Angus
c. 1489–1557

Katherine
of Aragon
1485–1536 *m.*

Henry V
1491–1

James V
of Scotland
1512–1542 *m.*

Mary
of Guise
1515–1560

Margaret
Douglas
1515–1578 *m.*

Matthew
Stuart
4th Earl of Lennox
1516–1571

Mary I
1516–1558

Mary
Queen of Scots
1542–1587

Henry
Stuart
Lord Darnley
1544–1566

Charles
Stuart
5th Earl of Lennox
1555–1577 *m.*

Elizabeth
Cavendish
d. of Sir William
Cavendish by Bess
of Hardwick
1555–1582

James VI
of Scotland and
I of England *m.*
1566–1625

Anna of
Denmark
1574–1619

Arbella
Stuart
1575–1615 *m.*

William
Seymour
Earl of Hertford
1588–1660

Henry
Stuart
Prince of Wales
1594–1612

Elizabeth,
Queeen of Bohemia
1596–1662

Charles I
King of England
1600–1649

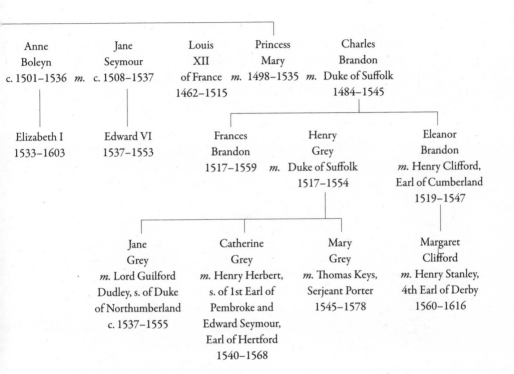

| Anne
Boleyn
c. 1501–1536 | *m.* | Jane
Seymour
c. 1508–1537 | Louis
XII
of France
1462–1515 | *m.* | Princess
Mary
1498–1535 | *m.* | Charles
Brandon
Duke of Suffolk
1484–1545 |

| Elizabeth I
1533–1603 | Edward VI
1537–1553 | Frances
Brandon
1517–1559 | *m.* | Henry
Grey
Duke of Suffolk
1517–1554 | Eleanor
Brandon
m. Henry Clifford,
Earl of Cumberland
1519–1547 |

| Jane
Grey
m. Lord Guilford
Dudley, s. of Duke
of Northumberland
c. 1537–1555 | Catherine
Grey
m. Henry Herbert,
s. of 1st Earl of
Pembroke and
Edward Seymour,
Earl of Hertford
1540–1568 | Mary
Grey
m. Thomas Keys,
Serjeant Porter
1545–1578 | Margaret
Clifford
m. Henry Stanley,
4th Earl of Derby
1560–1616 |

Introduction:
Triumphus Jacobi

Hidden away in England's National Portrait Gallery is a nineteenth-century engraving titled *James I and His Royal Progeny*. It depicts James, looking somewhat like a deflated Father Christmas, wearing his imperial crown and bearing his sceptre in his right hand. To his right sits his wife, the willowy Anna of Denmark. Before and around them is ranged their sprawling family: their sons, King Charles I and Henry, Prince of Wales; their daughters, Elizabeth, Queen of Bohemia, and the little Princesses Mary and Sophia; their grandsons, Princes Frederick Henry, Charles, Maurice, Rupert, and Louis; and their granddaughter, Princess Louise. The engraving is modelled on William de Passe's grandly titled 1623 work, *Triumphus Jacobi Regis Augustaeq*, commissioned by James himself.[1] But these artworks were, and are, fantasies.

If you look a little closer at either, the oddities will catch your eye. Queen Anna, for example, is resting her hand on a skull – that favourite early modern symbol of death. Princesses Mary and Sophia, too – diminutive figures who look more like shrunken little women than children – each rest their elbows on skulls. As ever in the period's paintings and portraiture, death lurks everywhere.

The reasons are obvious. By the time the original image was created, plenty of its sitters were already long dead. Anna of Denmark had died in 1619; Henry, Prince of Wales in 1612; Mary had died at two years old in 1607; and Sophia had not lived long after her birth in 1606. Further, although the increasingly sentimental king became

1

fond of having other people's little children caper about his feet in his dotage, he never, in fact, laid eyes on any of the grandchildren posed around him in the imperious images. The engravings are therefore akin to the great dynastic portraits of Henry VIII, created during and after the 1540s; they convey images of stable, fruitful dynasties which are belied by the often short, frequently sad lives of the individual family members depicted. The intention behind James's commission, particularly, was to press his credentials, influence, and success as a European leader and dynast.

These were the perceptions of James VI and I which the king himself wished to pass into the history books: a family man, a patriarch, and the father and grandfather of sovereigns who would dominate Europe. He was well equipped with the material trappings and the imperious attitude required of 'majesty'. What he lacked (amongst Presbyterians in Scotland and, occasionally, amongst the emerging body of cynical satirists in England) was majesty's most crucial component: 'common' folk consistently willing to buy into the concept. James certainly venerated his own status, and he loved the glamour, glitz, and authority that it bestowed; however, he wanted these things on his terms rather than the public's. He was a man consistently eager to prove his worth as a beacon of stability and peace: a man for whom the provision of a settled and secure royal family was a central plank in his bid to unite the crown of Scotland with that of England following the near forty-five-year reign of the childless Queen Elizabeth.

Yet James the family man is hardly what springs to most people's minds when they imagine the first Scottish King of England.

Casual readers of history will likely have a remarkably vivid image of James VI and I. They will be able to describe a slobbering, slovenly oddball, loping around his privy chambers, wearing heavily padded doublets out of fear of an assassin's blade, and forever pawing lasciviously at a bevy of handsomer, younger men. This is the picture – the frustratingly enduring picture – attributed to the courtier Sir Anthony Weldon:

[James] was of a middle-stature, more corpulent through his clothes than in his body, yet fat enough, his clothes ever being large and easy, the doublets quilted for stiletto proof, his breeches in great pleats and full stuffed. He was naturally of a timorous disposition, which was the reason of his quilted doublets: his eyes large, ever rolling after any stranger [who] came in his presence, insomuch, as many for shame have left the room, as being out of countenance. His beard [was] very thin, his tongue too large for his mouth, [which] made him drink very uncomely, as if eating his drink, which came out of the cup of each side of his mouth. His skin was as soft as taffeta sarsenet, which felt so, because he never washed his hands, only rubbed his finger ends slightly with the wet end of a napkin. His legs [were] very weak, having had (as was thought) some foul play in his youth, or rather before he was born, that he was not able to stand at seven years of age, this weakness made him ever leaning on other men's shoulders, his walk was ever circular, his fingers in that walk ever fiddling about his codpiece.[2]

As notorious is Weldon's claim that the king had earned the unenviable sobriquet of 'the wisest fool in Christendom . . . wise in small things but a fool in weighty affairs'.[3] So influential have these sketches been that they have even – along with James's medical reports – constituted modern-day diagnoses of his health, from the debunked theory that he suffered porphyria (a rare type of blood disorder) to recent suggestions that he had Asperger's syndrome and Lesch-Nyhan disease (a genetic deficiency which can cause behavioural abnormalities).[4] As interesting as these ideas are, the problem is that the accuracy of the original descriptions is in doubt; James's lavish lifestyle, as will be seen, is probably sufficient to account for the collapse of his physical health in his final years.

Less well known is that the slobbering, codpiece-fiddling king came from a narrative which elsewhere offers him a measure of praise, and that the author (whoever it truly was) was certainly prejudiced against James and his court. The vicious description therefore seems more an attempt at snide humour than a realistic determination to capture James's likeness – and, further, it simply became part of a general anti-royalist campaign in the conflict-driven years of the mid-1600s.[5]

What is often ignored by those who reuse the text's image is that the king spoke well and often, albeit he began dogmatically insisting that his native Scots – which was being anglicised and diluted by some writers – was the same language as English (the differences probably accounting for problems English contemporaries had understanding him, without requiring the supposed overly large tongue, which is not mentioned in any other sources). Indeed, he grasped every opportunity for public speaking that presented itself. A highly literate student of rhetoric and poetry, he spoke frequently, studding his speeches with fine phraseology. If anything, he was too fond of the sound of his own voice and certainly never learned the maxim 'less is more'. Consequently, his propensity to show off and drown his hearers in his knowledge of any and every given subject was apt to result in their polite exasperation (or boredom) rather than in delight at his smooth tongue. A dribbling fool who could barely speak he was not; a garrulous, imperious know-it-all he could be.

As for his overstuffed doublets and suspicious fears – these were eminently sensible given the violence of the period. In dress, James had to appease (often Puritanical) critics whilst retaining the politics of display. His solution was to dress soberly as a rule (with a concession to exquisite jewels) and on state occasions to indulge in displays of diamond-encrusted splendour which would have put Henry VIII to shame. Indeed, it is no surprise that the image of Bluff King Hal, fond of earthy humour, made its way onto the stage in James's reign, as it was the Scottish king who – when it suited him – cultivated an image of bluff bonhomie.

Forgotten, too, is that medical opinion of the time, as exemplified by Thomas Moulton's influential *This is the myrrour or glasse of health*, held that bathing was a dangerous means of opening the pores to infection, and hand washing with cloths was a recommended alternative. The idea often recounted – and drawn from the satirical text attributed to Weldon – is that James was filthy and smelly; in truth, the king would have had the best laundresses available to refresh his linens and keep him clean and pleasant-smelling. Bathing in medicinal waters, indeed, was an activity reserved for sufferers of various illnesses (amongst those who could afford to own baths or travel to respectable ones). The joke in the satire, which has been long misconstrued, was not that James was dirty, but that he was a cowardly man who was too frightened to rigorously wash even when, in his later years, his failing health invited the practice. The more serious consequence – and the period encouraged readers to make connections and correspondences – was this: if the king had no regard for his health and well-being, what hope for the nations he and his dynasty embodied? As satires do, the narrative exaggerates the practice of careful, selective washing – standard amongst the upper classes of the period – into the humorous and grotesque.

Familiar to those conversant with stories of James, too, is the idea of his addiction to hunting, which is accurate; he was devoted to the sport. However, the popular image of him gleefully dipping his hands and feet in the blood of his kills, which is often presented as an idiosyncrasy, is neither novel nor unique. The ritualistic practice of 'first blood' (dipping hands and smearing faces with the blood of slaughtered prey), gruesome though it is, far predates the king and was popular amongst hunters. As for him eventually dipping his feet in carcasses, this was amongst the less bizarre remedies recommended for sufferers of what was ascribed to gout, which James endured increasingly in his last decade. On the face of it, Weldon's attempt at making something sinister of the king's engagement in these rituals was a crude effort at reviving xenophobic myths about Scotsmen being barbarous, blood-drinking brutes.

Others might link the king inextricably with the image of a hectoring, lecturing schoolmaster, puffed up with self-importance, firing off tedious, precedent-heavy, classically inspired treatises to the royal printers, warning against the dangers of tobacco and trumpeting the divine right of kings. This is, admittedly, a fairly accurate image – although it should be noted that a scholar-king was a genuine boon in the context of early modern Europe (the young Henry VIII, for example, is still lauded as a magnificent Renaissance prince because of his early intellectual endeavours). Still, it is only a partial picture. An incorrigible know-it-all James was, but this was of a piece with one of the predominant aspects of his character: the desire, which remained with him until his death, to give, to teach, to instruct – always in the style of a firm but loving father.

Problematic, too, was that James was unfortunate enough to live and reign during a period – in both his kingdoms – which coincided with a flowering of scurrilous lampoons and railing verses. In Scotland, the king was fair game for censure by those who held that monarchs were subjects to a theocratic Kirk and thus acceptable objects of attack, and by those secular-minded classicists who looked to the ancient world for their gubernatorial models. In England, despite a raft of laws designed to silence negative public opinion – occasionally through brutal means – the genie had escaped the bottle: the arrival of a Scottish king and his entourage proved too irresistible a subject for dissidents and malcontents to avoid lampooning. By virtue of his nationality, James was unable to harness the English nationalism with which propagandists had fuelled the images of Henry VIII and Elizabeth I – and as a proponent of a single Great Britain, he had no wish that they should. Thus, the king has, historically, suffered a reputation governed by the pens of his enemies.

The fact that cultural representations of James – who remains far less popular amongst dramatists and novelists than his mother, Mary Queen of Scots, or cousin, Elizabeth – tend to fixate on the more prurient image of the king has likely not helped matters. One finds the rough-mannered, bow-legged, witch-hunting fool, complete with that apparently irresistible codpiece-fiddling, in innumerable novels, and played – with wonderful abandon – by Bill Paterson in 1978's inventive *Will Shakespeare*. Always, the bluff, tempestuous, foul-mouthed Scottish king is presented as a counterpoint to the respected, domineering Queen Elizabeth. In this way, modern treatments, particularly fictional ones, have tended to ape a phenomenon apparent in the early seventeenth century: then, as now, a misty-eyed nostalgia for the old queen (well attested in Michael Dobson and Nicola J. Watson's 2002 work, *England's Elizabeth: An Afterlife in Fame and Fantasy*) and her era arose, and a collective amnesia fell over the facts that she (unlike James) had suffered noble rebellions, had sworn like a sailor, and had, according to Bishop Goodman, left England 'weary of an old woman's government'.[6] One can only wonder how novelists and popular historians would treat Good Queen Bess had the writings of her critics or even those of her godson – who wrote an unflattering account of the elderly Elizabeth wandering the halls of her palaces, carelessly dressed, in mortal terror and thrusting a rusty sword into arrases – been allowed to colour the image even of her earlier years. Yet this is the case with James; hostile accounts of him in the last few years of his reign have come to form the root of nearly all cultural and popular depictions, despite the laudable efforts of academics and authors such as Jenny Wormald, Caroline Bingham, Robert Stedall, Alan Stewart, and Julian Goodare to reassess his reigns.

Far less well known than the unhygienic, cowardly caricature is the fair-haired, venturous young king who risked his life on stormy seas to claim his young bride, and who barged into the Old Bishop's Palace in Oslo, still booted and spurred, to steal a kiss. Unfamiliar, too, will likely be the youthful sovereign who rode north with his army to subdue his Scottish rebels, all traces of that infamous cowardice apparently subdued. Yet this is the king who waits to be discovered in the voluminous letters, papers, contemporary histories, and poetry on which our understanding of the period rests. This is the romantic, loving, often emotionally needy monarch obscured by the cartoonish figure who has cut such an enduring – and awkward – dash through the pages of history.

In truth, James's was a colourful, elusive character, hampered in the main by an almost bottomless capacity for hypocrisy. One finds him, for example, issuing dire warnings against the ostensible vice of 'sodomy' and can set them against a note written by his last male favourite, which dates one sexual encounter to 1615 (although it should be noted that locating two people in bed does not tell us precisely what acts they undertook there). We find numerous accounts of him using bad language despite his injunctions against profanity. We can juxtapose his warnings to hold wives 'at the oeconomicke rule of the house' against both his and Queen Anna's lavish spending and occasional, quixotic attempts at economy (which were about as efficacious as applying a course of leeches to a dagger wound).[7] A champion of marriage and chastity – at least outwardly – the king has been accepted by modern scholars as having been actively bisexual, with a strong preference for men. The phrase 'do as I say, not as I do' might well have been coined for King James.

How, then, to make sense of such a character? The answer lies in what was his overriding goal: his quest to fashion himself as a wise and loving patriarch. Love – in various forms – came into James's life four times, each time having significant political ramifications. His first love, his polished and sophisticated cousin Esmé Stuart, 1st Duke of Lennox, was undoubtedly the most significant in shaping the king's character. Unpopular amongst the extreme Calvinist fraternity in Scotland (despite his conversion), Esmé did not set the pattern for James's future lovers but did give the young king a model to aspire to. Throughout the rest of his life, the ageing James attempted to fashion himself in Esmé's mould: an older man who lavished affection and attentions on younger ones. In a curious echo of Elizabeth I, who had been preyed upon by the ambitious Thomas Seymour at thirteen, the thirteen-year-old boy-king found himself groomed (to borrow the modern term) by a man in his late thirties. James, however, would in time assume the role of the loving elder himself, not so much giving his heart away as hurling it with great force at those he fell for.

However, it is important not to become too blinded by twenty-first-century attitudes towards sex and interpersonal relationships. The existence of same-sex activities in the period is not in doubt – though, as Michael B. Young has noted in his seminal *King James and the History of Homosexuality*, scholars have shied away from exploring the king's homosexual relationships in depth (or, worse, they have drawn a veil over them, even in recent years). Certainly, the term 'homosexual' did not yet exist; but those practices we would now call homosexual and bisexual certainly did, and they played a key role in the perceptions of James's ostensibly 'effeminate' penchant for peace and the often-sneering condemnations of the licentiousness and lewdness of the Jacobean court. So too did the king's sexual tastes prove to require amelioration, not least in his desire to display himself as a fruitful father and sovereign. This he was quite prepared to do, even if his romantic and emotional needs proved far more dependent on males.

Anna of Denmark, his wife, represented a watershed, as the king embarked wholeheartedly on a self-fashioning exercise, eager to portray himself on the continental stage as an ardent, courtly wooer. Like James, she has suffered from a historically poor reputation, too often being presented as callow and vacuous, over-fond of dancing and entertainments and far too intellectually lightweight to hold her bookish husband's attention. Even in modern accounts, one finds her variously disregarded as 'petulant and sulky . . . of limited intellect and natural indolence'; even, indeed, 'vacuous and shallow'.[8] The opposite, ironically, is the case. It is likely that the king was genuinely stirred by passion for the gamine fifteen-year-old princess – though that cooled rapidly when he realised that the strong-willed girl was not the empty vessel for his lessons which he had expected and desired. The problem, for James, was that his wife was altogether too fond of her own opinions and ideas, too independently minded, for an autocratic spouse to master. Still, he had sufficient emotional maturity to allow his disappointment and dashed hopes of lasting passion to develop into a deep, mutually felt affection. If Queen Anna failed to maintain her husband's passion, she never lost his goodwill, and the two continued producing children until, curiously enough, the year before he next fell in love.

More infamous was his next great lover, the fresh-faced Robert Carr (or Kerr, in Scots), with whom one of the king's favoured

May-to-December romances sprang up. In an echo of Henry VIII's sudden desire for Anne Boleyn, James gradually, over the course of several years, raised up his younger lover only to drop him – thankfully without the use of a Calais swordsman. Yet, during their romance, the king attempted, as always, to educate and instruct Carr, desirous as ever of finding someone to fit the dual role of lover and child. For his part, however, Carr proved himself unable to be what his king demanded: a provider of constant, loving, familial attention. With his passion having cooled, it is unsurprising that James was receptive to a likelier prospect.

In his last love, the king had more success. The athletic George Villiers, who was deliberately dangled before James – when he was weary of Carr's increasing stroppiness – proved to be exactly what the lovelorn monarch had always sought: a young and attractive receptacle for learning and a willing bedfellow combined. Their sexual relationship did not last long, as the king rapidly gained weight and lost teeth, but this final relationship brought him closest to finding the emotional outlet that had eluded him throughout his life. Yet so too did it help sow the seeds for James's son's downfall, as rumours – which should be considered in their context – persisted that his final lover, acting in concert with the future Charles I, had poisoned him.

Unlike other monarchs, the discussion of whose private lives has expended much ink, James's has tended to be brushed over, treated obliquely, or recognised but deemed largely irrelevant to his rule and public actions. He is, however, entirely the wrong monarch for a strictly political assessment. His style of government was inherently personal, and so often based on affections or idiosyncratic dislikes. Further, his gender allowed him to govern in that way without attracting quite the opprobrium – or as many false rumours – which his female predecessors in both Scotland and England had endured. A king did not face the same level of avid interest – investigation of bedsheets for evidence of sex or pregnancy – as a queen. Despite his life being lived largely publicly, James was able to fill his bedchamber with trusted men and indulge himself accordingly with a degree of licence not afforded female sovereigns. This he did. But not everyone in his life – be it wife, mistress, bedchamber attendant, or favourite – excited in him the same interest.

Around his celebrated great loves – and during the course of them – James had an array of flirtations, affairs, and minor passions, differing in romantic and sexual intensity. He could be found smothering dead-end companions in kisses before marrying them off when they failed to meet his expectations, and he wrote erotically charged poetry to both women and men (long before the mysterious Fair Youth was a glint in William Shakespeare's eye). Yet he has not gone down in history as a monarch driven by either passion or inordinate lusts. Nor was he. Rather, he was governed always by a curious obsession with living out a fantasy of family life, with himself at the head. Indeed, this obsession was so all-consuming that it crossed from his interpersonal relationships into his political rhetoric; one finds him, for example, championing his chimeric dream of uniting England and Scotland by stating, 'What God hath conioyned then, let no man separate. I am the Husband, and all the whole Isle is my lawfull Wife; I am the Head, and it is my Body . . . I hope therefore no man will be so vnreasonable as to thinke that I that am a Christian King vnder the Gospel, should be a Polygamist and husband to two wiues; that I being the Head, should haue a diuided and monstrous Body.'[9]

His vision of union never came to be (even the 1707 Treaty of Union between England and Scotland fell short of uniting, as James had wished, the two nations' Churches and laws), but nevertheless, throughout his life, the king fell back on familial imagery as a crutch for both his ideological and dynastic goals. In his personal life, he routinely cast himself as the father and mentor to his wife, and in a similar role to the young men who became his lovers. Indeed, to Villiers, whom he elevated to the dukedom of Buckingham, he would – uncomfortably – address his letters to 'my sweet child and wife' and sign off 'your dear dad and husband'.[10] This often-hopeless search for a mutually loving sense of family, in both his private and public lives, is perhaps what makes James so endearing; he had a sentimental streak as wide as the Thames and, notwithstanding his arranged marriage and the tepid but genuine affection he came to share with his wife, he was seldom malicious, even to those lovers he cast off. The power of his personality and image – both in terms of praise and satire – ensured his reign became an era: the Jacobean period was one of spectacle and splendour, artistic development and religious balance, domestic peace and royal decadence, and rollicking, railing satire.

In considering King James's colourful life, it is thus possible to see the first British monarch's reign in a new light. The king's passion for building himself a loving family was the driving force in his creation of a public persona, the pursuit of his monarchical agenda, and the selection of the men and women who warmed his pillows.

1

Baptism of Fire

If there is one thing all can agree on about Mary Queen of Scots, it was that the glamorous, French-educated sovereign knew how to put on a show. And that, during the chilly December of 1566, was exactly what she intended to do.

The occasion was the baptism of her son and heir, Charles James Stuart, whom she expected to succeed her as James VI of Scotland and, if she had her way, James I of England, assuming her own claim to the English Crown was duly recognised. As he was the putative heir to both British nations, it was important that the world should be aware of the baptism. Accordingly, the invitations had gone out the previous August: to England, France, Savoy; the black velvet gowns (black being a particularly expensive colour) had been ordered to outfit the prince's nurses; a cradle had been especially carved and covered in a cloth-of-silver blanket; and, less charmingly, £12,000 Scots had been chiselled out of the Scottish people.[1] As it had under earlier Renaissance monarchs, such as James IV and James V, a little bit of continental flair was coming to Scotland.

Stirling Castle, perched on its craggy rock overlooking the royal burgh of Stirling, was the venue. Accordingly, the night sky above the town came to life with the novel spectacle of fireworks. Below, the baby prince was carried to the courtyard's chapel by the French ambassador, who walked through an avenue of Scottish barons and was followed by the country's Catholic noblemen, bearing the accoutrements of baptism. Soldiers were clad in 'Moorish' costumes, the better to entertain the visiting dignitaries as they laid siege to a mock castle. A banquet – then a term denoting rich sweets and drinks

13

— was given in the hammerbeam-roofed Great Hall, which rocked with music and pulsed with torchlight. Latin verses composed by the leading humanist George Buchanan were sung, followed by Italian songs and masques. The festivities carried on over three days, from the 17th to 19th, in a blaze of bonfires, fireworks, hunts, and cannon blasts. The ambassadors were suitably impressed and eager to play their part, distributing their gifts of a solid gold baptismal font (from England, but too small to baptise a six-month-old), jewelled fans, and earrings for the prince's mother.

This frenzy of revelry was, however, an example of the beleaguered Queen of Scots protesting too much — an attempt to paint a little gold leaf over the deepening cracks within the political nation. Conspicuous by his non-appearance was the baby's father, Henry, uncrowned King of Scots — more often known by his lesser title of Lord Darnley. Though provided with a suit of cloth-of-gold, the supposed king remained immured in his chambers at the castle, preferring not to face the contempt of foreign ambassadors, who were all too aware of the division between him and his wife and sovereign. Most irritating of all was that Elizabeth of England, sovereign of the country in which he had been born and raised, had expressly forbidden her ambassador, the 2nd Earl of Bedford, from acknowledging him at all.

This suited Queen Mary. Legends have abounded over the centuries about her whirlwind romance with Darnley, and they have rather tended to obscure what really went on in 1565. Then, the Englishman had been given leave by Elizabeth to leave his homeland to travel north, where Mary intended to rehabilitate his troublesome father, the exiled Matthew Stuart, 4th Earl of Lennox. This had suited both sovereigns, as well as the earl. Mary, having been widowed when her first husband, the French king, Francis II, died, was actively seeking a husband on the continent. Lennox had Scottish royal blood and his ambitious wife was descended, like his cousin the Scottish queen, from the elder sister of Henry VIII; thus, their son had a good claim to both the thrones of England and Scotland. This Queen Mary knew. Elizabeth knew it too, and it seems likely that she hoped to throw a spanner in Mary's marital plans by letting the handsome Darnley intrude on her life. What the English queen did not expect, however, was that her Scottish cousin would realise that marriage with the Infante of Spain, Don Carlos, was a dead letter, and that she might instead woo the hapless Darnley. In doing so, Mary could bring under her own aegis a presumptive (and presumptuous) heir to Scotland and a rival for the English succession. Darnley, who was only a teenager, and one inflated with a grandiose sense of self-importance by his parents, could hardly believe his luck. When the chance of a crown was dangled before him – and a beautiful, willowy, and willing bride offering it – he leapt at it, and the pair had been wed on 29 July 1565, in the teeth of a panicked Elizabeth's commands that he cease his sudden relationship and return to England.

Yet Mary Queen of Scots was no lovelorn girl. With Darnley safely married to her, she moved to clip his wings before they could flutter. As the queen's partisan, Lord Herries, was later to report, '[Darnley] had done some things and signed papers without the knowledge of the Queen . . . she thought although she had made her husband a partner in the government, she had not given the power absolutely in his hands . . . [her] spirit would not quit [relinquish] any of her authority . . . And then, lest the King should be persuaded to pass gifts or any such thing privately, by himself, she appointed all things in that kind should be sealed with a seal.'[2]

Mary, it seems, had married a stud horse who would allow her to retain the Stuart name, and who might be usefully and publicly subordinated as a dynastic rival. She had not married, and nor did she want a superior partner in government. To Darnley's credit, he did manage to perform his primary function: his wife's pregnancy was apparent by the end of the year, with the baby born in Edinburgh Castle on 19 June 1566. A thin membrane about his head, supposedly, augured well; it was variously interpreted as offering protection from fairies, promising good luck, and indicating an ability to travel quickly. Soon enough, the English envoy, Henry Killigrew, was reporting that the child was 'well-proportioned and like to prove a goodly prince'.[3]

It is not clear when Darnley realised he had been had, and that he was unlikely either to be taken seriously as a monarch or granted that peculiarly Scottish prize, the Crown Matrimonial (which would enable him to rule in his own right). At first, all the signs that the callow and easily-led youth would be a king in more than name had been good: he had been given the title – albeit by his wife's proclamation rather than by the Scottish parliament – and his image and name had appeared on coinage. But realise he did, and that realisation provoked a simmering fury. Worse, it acted as an invitation to malcontents who resented their queen's reliance on foreign, Catholic servants – chiefly on the upstart Savoyard musician, David Riccio. The details of the horrific result are well known enough to hardly require rehearsal: Darnley involved himself with a group of plotters who intruded on the heavily pregnant queen's private apartments at the Palace of Holyroodhouse, dragged Riccio away from her, and stabbed him to death. Although Mary rallied and – to assure the world of her unborn child's legitimacy – embraced her treacherous husband back into the fold, the marriage was effectively over. What followed, and what resulted in Darnley sulking in his rooms at Stirling Castle during James's baptism, was a hollow pretence, characterised by mutual suspicion and endless scheming for possession of the infant. It was such scheming, indeed, that had led Mary in September 1566 to place their son first under the 'government' of the Countess of Moray, and the following March under the custodianship of John Erskine, Earl of Mar, in both cases behind Stirling's thick walls. Mar, for his trouble, had his keepership of the castle made hereditary – an act which would have consequences for James and his own wife's relationship.

If the marital breakdown of the royal couple was not enough to add an unpleasant undertone to the glitzy celebrations of the prince's baptism, the religious and wider political divisions were worse. Mary was, of course, a committed Catholic. But the Scotland to which she had returned in August 1561, following her time in France, had been effectively taken over by a Protestant cabal calling themselves the Lords of the Congregation: a group which included her illegitimate half-brother, James Stuart, later Earl of Moray. These men had risen in rebellion in the late 1550s, their pockets weighted – though not as much as they would have liked – with English gold, against Mary's mother and regent, Marie of Guise. Marie's subsequent mistake had been to assume that Scottish nationalism was simply antipathy towards the English, and that any moves to counter aggression from the southern kingdom would win Scottish hearts. In response to her English-funded rebels, she had therefore flooded Scotland with French soldiers and installed trusted Frenchmen in government – an act which certainly helped her anti-English and anti-Protestant narrative, but which indicated to a significant number of Scots that their country would become a French satellite (a prospect as alarming as English domination). A state of conflict ensued, fought between the rebels – who could claim to stand against Francophilia – and the regency government, which looked increasingly likely to sell Scotland's independence to the French Crown in return for armed support. Broken in health if not spirit, the Regent Marie had died in 1560, allowing the Lords of the Congregation to crown their coup with a parliament of dubious legality, with which they changed the course of Scottish history by outlawing the mass and making Scotland, like England, a Protestant nation. The country had become, like much of Europe, a battleground for competing faiths.

Mary, throughout her personal rule, had effectively balanced religious factions, delegitimating Protestant and Catholic zealots by insisting, for the most part, only on her private right to hear the mass and her intention not to interfere with the Protestant settlement passed in her absence.[4] At the baptismal feast, she was careful to ensure that she was seen seated between the Catholic French ambassador, the Count of Brienne, and the Protestant English Earl of Bedford. We would nowadays call this tolerance. However, tolerance was then a dirty word, especially in religious affairs; it was, from either side, a concession to heresy. It could not last, and it could certainly never be a long-standing policy. Sooner or later, any monarch would have to nail their colours to the mast.

17

The crunch came, ironically, in what ought to have been Mary's moment of dynastic triumph: James's baptismal ceremony. Beneath the glitter of feasting and festivities, tensions were apparent. The 4th Earl of Bothwell, a committed Protestant though high in the queen's favour, refused to enter the chapel. Likewise, Bedford could not countenance going inside for the religious ritual. The queen, it seemed, had been forced to show the hand she had held to her chest: as soon as the question of baptising the future King of Scots arose, the issue of which faith she would choose for him followed. The superintendent of Lothian, John Spottiswoode, was in no doubt about the Kirk's demands; he conveyed the General Assembly's request to the new mother that she baptise her son according to Protestant rites. Naturally, Mary could not, in conscience – or in the context of her European credentials – do otherwise than have her son inducted into the Catholic faith.

This flouting of the Kirk's wishes, of course, was unacceptable to the still powerful bloc of Protestants who stood near the throne. So too was it distasteful to the mercantile and urban classes who formed the backbone of the newly established Scottish faith. What their monarch had done was to announce her long-term plan for her country: Scotland should return to the spiritual jurisdiction of the papacy, if not in her lifetime then in her son's. Even before the ceremony, rumours were being circulated that she intended James be betrothed to a daughter of Philip II of Spain: then Europe's richest and most militant Catholic power. She had, therefore, to go, and go quickly – before the child who had been the cynosure of the celebrations at Stirling in December 1566 could grow into a faithful son of Rome.

Mary Queen of Scots' downfall has long excited debate. It is sufficient to say here that the two deepest problems in Scottish politics apparent in 1566 – the disintegrating royal marriage and the religious divide – collided in a grisly spectacle. The queen, possibly as an attempted sweetener to those horrified by the Catholic flavour of her son's baptism, pardoned some of those who had plotted with Darnley – and been denied by him – over the Riccio murder. Darnley, terrified that the fellow plotters he had thrown to the wolves were returning with vengeance on their minds, fled to his father's estates near Glasgow, falling ill on the way. Mary, fully expecting that his plotting would intensify in his father's ancestral lands, elected to entice him back to Edinburgh. There, his house was blown up in spectacular fashion, and he and his servant found smothered in the garden. This was shocking enough, but worse was to come. Mary then hastily wed the chief suspect, that Protestant 4th Earl of Bothwell who had refused to enter the chapel for the Catholic ceremony. Her reasons for doing so can only be speculated upon – a fact which has allowed romances and dastardly plots to be built around the pair. Mary's claim was that she had been ravished and thus compelled to marry him. Probably, the shock and stress of events led to a bout of her recurrent depression (at times throughout her life she was to veer between energetic high spirits and periods of seclusion, tears, and vocal desires to commit suicide), and the opportunistic Bothwell took advantage by forcing his attentions upon her. What is undeniable is that a quiver of magnates encouraged the match (admittedly under duress from Bothwell), and that the subsequent Protestant marriage ceremony certainly looked likely to defang some of the opposition from men of that faith, which had been catalysed by the Catholic baptism of Prince James.

The marriage was, however, a gift to those powerful Protestants who had been alarmed by the prospect of a Catholic prince and who distrusted their coreligionist Bothwell as much as their Catholic queen. Already the battle lines were being drawn. As early as May 1567, only a month after the Bothwell marriage, the English soldier Sir William Drury was claiming that 'at the Queen's last being at Stirling the Prince being brought unto her she offered to kiss him, but he would not but put her away and did to his strength scratch her. She offered him an apple, but it would not be received of [by] him, and to a greyhound bitch having whelps was thrown, who eat it and she and her whelps died presently. A sugar loaf also for the Prince was brought at the same time, it is judged to be very evil compounded.'[5]

This was nonsense – it was a deliberate attempt to associate the queen with the sinister, the witchlike, and the unnatural. Further, it played on existing early modern tropes which associated a tendency to administer poisons (and sundry other stereotypically evil acts) with carnal lusts, in effect making Mary appear to have been retrospectively guilty of adultery with Bothwell. Naturally, the obvious response to a supposedly killer queen was for those men – predominantly Protestant men – to rise in arms against the monarch they distrusted and the disreputable Bothwell, whom they had no intention of deferring to as king.

Thus began the protracted deposition of Mary Queen of Scots. She became pregnant to Bothwell and, in the fracas which followed her marriage, she refused to give him up. The pair's forces met the rebels at Carberry Hill in June 1567 and melted away under the oppressive heat. Bothwell fled to drum up support, leaving Mary to face disgrace and imprisonment (the claims of the rebels – that they intended only to dissociate her from her new husband – proving hollow). The queen was then placed in confinement at Lochleven, where her half-brother Moray helped compel her to sign a demission (that is, abdication) of her authority, notwithstanding the trauma of miscarriage which had laid her low. Under duress, she signed on 24 July 1567. When her ostensibly voluntary demission had been achieved, Moray was free to take up the reins of power. In preparation for just that, on the 29th, the infant prince was carried in his guardian Mar's arms to the parish church at Stirling. There, in a sparsely attended ceremony given respectability only by its dedication to following ceremonial precedents, he was crowned, the oath being delivered by James Douglas, 4th Earl of Morton (a formidable schemer who had been up to his neck in both the Riccio and Darnley murders), and the sermon delivered by Protestant firebrand John Knox. Thereafter, Moray was installed as regent, and the quondam queen regnant was left to fulminate and plot in her imprisonment.

Early in May 1568, she effected her escape, capitalising on the considerable party of supporters she had won throughout her period of personal rule. However, after making a stand at the battle of

Langside, her forces were routed, and she made the fateful decision to flee south, hoping to plead armed assistance from Elizabeth of England. That, of course, was not forthcoming; the English queen was quite willing to aid armed conflict in Scotland, but only if it was to England's benefit. What Mary gained was not restitution north of the border, but a show inquiry into Darnley's death, at which she was found neither guilty nor innocent, and a period of captivity with no end in sight.

Little of these celebrated events made their way into her young son's head, however – or, at least, not at first. Yet, as Mary Stuart vocally and emphatically argued her case from England, those in Scotland who had driven her out immediately began the long and ugly process of blackening her name. Engaged in this ignominious exercise was George Buchanan, who had been quite cured of his fondness for the queen (and monarchy as it then stood in general). An avowed Lennox man who had converted to Calvinism, he would pen his infamous *Ane Detectioun of the Duinges of Marie Quene of Scottes*: a scarcely plausible book of slanders and lurid aspersions which cast the departed queen as a wicked, murderous figure, embodying every negative stereotype about women which the extremist misogyny of the period could muster. She was, in its colourful language, a 'bludy woman and poysoning witch', who had cuckolded her late husband with the man who would become her final one.[6] The problem with – or the benefit of – these slanders, as with all slanders, was their plausibility, and the figure whose belief would be of paramount importance in the future was the little prince, who must be taught to detest and fear his mother and her religion. There was good reason for Buchanan to be assigned James's tutor; as a deeply learned and ardent reformer, and a Lennox man (and thus affiliated to the late king), he, at least, had the motive and the polemical power to light and keep burning a flame of hatred against Mary Queen of Scots and Roman Catholicism. As she had been overthrown and imprisoned, it was open season for those who saw in demonising her a means of shaping and developing the character of the son she had left behind. Indeed, to justify her deposition and feed Scotland's developing intellectual conversation about monarchy, it was necessary to paint Mary as a tyrannical criminal, deeply imbued with every perceived fault of her sex and every excess of wicked monarchs. The truth, from Buchanan's perspective, was of less importance than promoting what he viewed as sound and godly political theory.

Helpfully, for those who had seen Mary off – the new Regent Moray and his party – James can have had no real memory of his mother. This his custodians knew and were quite willing to take advantage of. In her absence, she could be whatever her son's guardians wished her to be, and what they wished her to be was something verging on the demonic. As he was to grow up in Stirling Castle, with Annabella, Countess of Mar, as the only high-ranking female figure, and the earl his male protector, he could not, in fact, recall either of his parents. This was not in itself unusual, of course; frequently, royal children of the period were fostered out to their own households under the care of appropriately aristocratic guardians. What was certainly unusual, however, was that he would be utterly discouraged from the biblical commandment of honouring his parents. Family – those in charge of him hoped – would be something James understood to be dangerous, something he would fear and distrust, something that would keep him in awe and terror. If he absorbed these lessons, his governors could fashion him as they saw fit. The only question was whether or not the process of education – or indoctrination – against his mother, Catholicism, and France would take root.

2

Coming of Age

The schoolroom at Stirling Castle, located in the Prince's Tower, reverberated each morning with the sonorous drone of Latin. The little king, who was alternately listener and speaker, was to remark in later life that his tutors had him speaking Latin before he could speak Scots. His days followed a pattern: Greek practised via the study of Isocrates and Plutarch in the morning; Latin after breakfast, studied through the reading of history; an afternoon dinner (his allowance for the day comprising two-and-a-half loaves of bread, three pints of ale, and two capons); and in the afternoon logic, rhetoric, writing, and perhaps a little arithmetic (with which the king struggled). During and following his mother's deposition, he remained at Stirling, where he was judged largely free of the political crises which shook Scotland in the late 1560s and early 1570s, and where he could be brought up as the model king his keepers hoped to craft.

And crises there were. Mary Queen of Scots did not sit quietly in England, and she was far from content to live the life of a disgraced private noblewoman, rusticated under guard in various country estates. Rather, she insisted that her voluntary demission of sovereignty had been signed only under duress, and that she remained Scotland's anointed monarch. Of course, this had little effect; in reality, she had left her supporters at home leaderless. The Regent Moray, meanwhile, had set himself the task of mopping up Marian resistance to his regime with his usual sangfroid, all in the name of the little boy who was then still in skirts. Yet not everyone was content to be ruled by the base-born uncle of the boy-king, not least the royal-blooded Hamilton family, whose leader, the Duke of Châtelherault, had once enjoyed the position of 'second person' in the realm, and who had thrown in his family's lot with Mary after her escape from Lochleven. Moray, a calculating man but one apparently plagued with hubris, ignored warnings that a plot was afoot, and was fatally shot by a Hamilton assassin in Linlithgow. In England, Mary exulted at the death of the half-brother who had become her bitterest opponent, but in the long run his departure from the Scottish political scene was to do her little good.

Her infant son can have had no memory of the man he would later castigate as 'that bastard who unnaturally rebelled'; James, ensconced in Stirling, had little contact with anyone save the Countess of Mar; his nurse, Helen Little (whom he would employ again for his own son, and yet, if his doctor is to be believed, would accuse of having been a drunkard); his group of 'rockers' (who attended his cradle); and the gentlemen of his household who ensured that the boy main-tained something approaching regal state as he lay on black-fringed pillows under a macabre, black damask canopy. His mother's exist-ence, even in his infancy, was conspicuous by its absence; only an image of his grandfather, James V, hung on his bedchamber wall. In his childhood illnesses – smallpox and measles – he was without parental care and, as he later claimed, he had been unable to walk unsupported until he was six; he would have been carried in the arms of first his nurses and then his gentlemen of the household.

Curiously, as Mary's own imprisonment in England was tight-ened (as a result of the 1569 Northern Rising, spearheaded by the Catholic Earls of Northumberland and Westmorland, which aimed to place her on Elizabeth's throne), so too was her son's custody. Moray's replacement as regent was Mary's former father-in-law, Darnley's father, the 4th Earl of Lennox. This was welcome news to Elizabeth, as the anglophile Lennox was quite prepared to govern Scotland in full compliance with English policy, possibly even to a greater extent than his servile predecessor.

One of his primary goals was to ensure the security of his grand-son, in whom his future as much as Scotland's now lay: '[A]nd to the end that all confluence and multitude of people [are to] be restrictit and halden furth of the said Castell, thairfoir my Lord Regentis Grace, with avise of the saidis Lordis of Secreit Counsale, findis gude and concludis as of befoir that our said soverane lordis maist nobill persoun sail be nuresit [nursed, nourished] and brocht up within the said Castell under the custodie, cair and governante of the said Earl of Mar, and that his Hienes sail na wayes be transportit furth of the said Castell of Striviling to ony uther rowme within the realme or outwit.'[1]

The old boss was to be much the same as the new boss, as far as James was concerned. What differed, however, was that the growing boy was, by the time of Lennox's accession to the regency, able to observe and form a relationship with Scotland's new powerbroker. For all his faults, the earl was at least a doting family man, who had genuinely lamented the murder of his son at Kirk o' Field. There is every reason to believe that his hopes and his somewhat misty-eyed affection descended on little James, who had the added attraction of a crown.

With the young king secure, the new regent set about finally bringing to an end the civil war which continued to be fought between the Queen's Party (loyal Marians who sought the exiled queen's restoration) and the King's Party (those dedicated to keeping her out, in her son's name). Here, Lennox had some success, in that he managed to oust the Hamiltons from their strategically useful base at Dumbarton on the River Clyde. This effectively cured the Hamiltons of their Marian support and allowed for their rehabilitation as loyal king's men.

It was also under Lennox's regency that the five-year-old James was allowed onto the public stage: the state opening of his first parliament, held on Tuesday 28 August 1571.[2] To perform his duty, he was given a shabby ceremonial entry to Stirling, whose Tolbooth was to host the meeting. As the Honours of Scotland (the Crown Jewels) were then locked safely in Edinburgh Castle, still in Marian hands, a sword and sceptre made of gilded wood were carried in the procession: a material symbol of how far the monarchy had fallen since the days of James IV, when Pope Julius II had ranked Scottish kings ninth out of twenty-six potentates (behind England at seventh) in the European order of precedence. Swathed in his robes and perched on his throne under its canopy of estate in the makeshift Parliament Hall, James gave a rehearsed speech: 'My lords, and ye, the true subjects who are convened here, as I understand, to minister justice; and because my age will not suffer me to exercise my charge myself, by reason of my youth, I have given power to my grandsire, as Regent and tutor [legal guardian] to me, and you to assist him therein, as you will answer to God and me thereafter.'[3]

Almost certainly, the words were written by Lennox himself, and designed to convey to the Scottish political nation the authority invested in him in right of his grandson. Famously, the king supposedly then looked up and, spotting a hole in the canopy over his head, asked where he was.[4] On being told that he was in the Parliament House, he quipped, 'Then there is a hole in this parliament.' Whether apocryphal or not, the exchange has long since taken on the complexion of prophecy, rather than an illustration (like the gold-painted wooden Honours) of the general air of disrepair into which the Scottish monarchy had fallen in the post-Marian era.

Lennox, veteran intriguer though he was, soon proved as unable as Moray had been to survive the prevailing tides of anarchy and jealousy which the deposition of Queen Mary had caused. On the night of 3 September, a raid was carried out on Stirling by disgruntled Hamilton followers, with the intent of kidnapping some of the King's Party. Though they were beaten back by the Earl of Mar, who had taken his orders to up security in the town and castle seriously, they managed to shoot Lennox in the back. The dying regent was carried up into the castle before his death, where the grandson who had so recently announced to the world his faith in the old man could glimpse his last moments. The memory of Lennox's death would remain very much in the boy's mind and serve as a reminder throughout his life of the risks of violent affray.

James had been fond of his grandfather, and the old man had been the only genuine close family left to him in Scotland. Although his keeper, the Earl of Mar, was swiftly instituted as regent – again, with Elizabeth of England's blessing, and useful in that it kept power visibly connected to the little king – James was, for the moment, left to the ministrations of the Erskines of Mar. In a more hands-on way, however, he was under the guidance of tutors who, now having him fully cut off from his family, could mould him as they saw fit.

*

The early modern period is not known for its leniency towards the concept of childhood. In addition to royal children often being packed off to their own households, noble children were frequently placed in the households of others (in order that they should learn how to serve graciously), whilst poor children were set to work as soon as they were capable. Even those of classes which benefitted from education faced extremely rigorous childhoods, with courses of academic study more akin to modern undergraduate courses.

Yet James's education was unusual even by the standards of the day. It was, essentially, an educational experiment, engineered by George Buchanan, with the goal of building the ideal Protestant monarch (a process begun in earnest from at least 1570). On paper, Buchanan was the ideal tutor. He had, in his younger years, lectured in Latin at the College of Guienne (where he had taught the brilliant essayist Michel de Montaigne) and the University of Coimbra, and he was a committed Calvinist and former principal of St Leonard's College, St Andrews. Accordingly, he was able to shape an unforgiving curriculum which not only gave James Latin but French, Greek, history, rhetoric, logic, and theology. The more experimental parts of his course were founded on religious instruction and theological study. Buchanan was, at heart, deeply suspicious of monarchy as it was then developing. Historically, Scotland had had a *primus inter pares* system, with the sovereign first amongst equals – or, at least, first amongst the heads of the great ruling families. The trend, as in many European countries, had – under James IV, James V, and Mary Queen of Scots – been to seek (with varying degrees of success) a more centralised authority founded on the primacy and divinity of the monarch. It had been the goal of all three previous monarchs, indeed, to raise the prestige and power of the Scottish Crown via visual splendour, ceremonial, and the forging of alliances, marital and otherwise, with the ruling powers of Europe.

This was all rather repellent to George Buchanan, who had travelled extensively on the continent and was thus a first-hand observer of both religious conflict and the caprices of foreign rulers and their governments. By the time he became James's tutor at Stirling, he was a thoroughly tetchy, sharp-tongued, short-tempered old man, who appears to have sought to batter his student into accepting his ideas under the weight of his rhetoric, his experience, his authority, and – when these failed to make an impression – his fists.

The ideas he was developing were, as was soon apparent, that James was just James. His kingship, which the child had known from as early as he could remember as inextricably bound up with his identity, was, to Buchanan, a title conferred on him by the people, and which could thus be taken from him by the people. This was not in any way democratic in the modern sense; rather, Buchanan was developing a classically inspired theory of resistance to sovereigns: if a king (or queen regnant) proved themselves ungodly or tyrannical, they might be removed with force, for their own good as well as for the good of the commonwealth.

The problem from the young king's perspective was two-fold. For one thing, Buchanan's terse, sometimes violent pedagogical strategy served rather to undermine the content of his teachings; if anything, James would come to see absolutism as a refuge and a bulwark against the possibility of being deposed by godly fanatics. For another, the division between his tutor's impassioned teachings and the reality of his kingship as it affected others around him was apparent. Annabella, the Countess of Mar, for example, once came upon a lesson during which Buchanan had been attempting – typically – to teach the king about the infamy of his family and the dangers of royal favourites, using the example of James III, whose minions had been hanged by rebellious subjects, in order to end their pernicious influence on sovereign and state. James, supposedly, had no taste for this particular historical example, and challenged his tutor, identifying himself with his long-dead namesake as one who would not stand being berated by a subject. Buchanan's response was to beat the king's backside, at which point the countess interjected, castigating the old man for assaulting the 'Lord's Anointed'. Buchanan, caustically, retorted, 'Madam, I have whipt his arse: you may kiss it if you please.' Evidently, the countess intended to keep James on a pedestal from which the tutor intended to knock him. It is little wonder that James came to prefer having his backside kissed by sycophants than whipped by formidable men, and even less that he came to associate his kingship with a right to divine protection than subject to resistance or even attack by those who had no respect for his title. Though he did write formal letters to Buchanan in Latin, addressing him as 'pater', or 'father', this was pure flannel – the stuff of convention.

The Countess of Mar has, historically, had a reputation as a redoubtable figure, thanks mainly to the remembrances of the courtier James Melville, who noted that she was 'wise and sharp and kept the King in great awe'.[5] The meaning of her keeping him in awe, however, is less clear than it might seem. Given James's later approval of her – and the evidence of her defence of his status – it seems likely that the hallmarks of her character were deference and respectfulness: attitudes that, throughout his life, King James would appreciate. Keeping him in awe, essentially, meant that she treated him with heightened respect. He did, in fact, write to her in tones of respectful appreciation, using her familial nickname:

Lady Minny,

This is to show you that I have received your fruit and thank you therefore, and is ready for more when ye please to send them, and shall give as few by me as I may. And I will not trouble you farther till meeting which shall be as shortly as I may, God willing. And so fare ye well as I do, thanks to God.

James R[6]

The historian Alan Stewart finds in this note the young king addressing a substitute maternal figure.[7] This she almost certainly could not be. The letter itself was an exercise in early penmanship and is somewhat stilted, as might be expected: it is what might later be termed a 'bread and butter letter'. The problem in accepting the Countess of Mar as 'mother figure' lies in her own attitude towards the king. An adjunct of her deference was a likely lack of warmth and genuine affection – the child, after all, was obscured by the Crown (it being surely noteworthy that she appears to have been unconcerned that James was being mistreated, but that the 'Lord's Anointed' was having rough hands laid on him). Whilst Mary Queen of Scots attempted to send gifts of clothes with a genuine maternal eye, the countess busied herself with providing amulets designed to guard against poison and ensuring that the Royal Wardrobe was kept in good order; rather than a substitute mother, the countess was an effective and deferential attendant who worked with the king's other servants in keeping his chambers well appointed, his pets housed and fed, and his household attendants paid. Under her watchful eye, James's private rooms were brightened, with green paint and green cloths purchased in the summer of 1574.

Sharing her attitude of respect were those whose jobs it was to keep the boy in his royal estate – his small team of household servants – and those noble boys who shared his schoolroom: Thomas Erskine of Gogar; William Murray of Abercairney, the countess's nephew; Walter Stewart, the son of Sir John Stewart of Minto; and the countess's own son, John, heir to the earldom of Mar. This last James nicknamed 'John Slates', and he went on to play a lasting, complex role in the king's life – but he would never, even at the height of his sovereign's favour, be viewed as more than a loyal servant, appropriately rewarded with titles, lands, a wife, and key governmental jobs but certainly never acknowledged as a surrogate brother. He was, further, elevated to the position of 2nd Earl of Mar when his father, the Regent Mar, died at the end of October 1572 (after dining, supposedly, with the devious 4th Earl of Morton, who went on to win the regency – and therefore control of its council – himself; exercise the office with a hitherto unseen sense of grandeur; prove another anglophile; and decisively end the civil wars in favour of the King's Party by driving the remaining champions, Kirkcaldy of Grange and the slippery Maitland of Lethington, out of the last remaining Marian stronghold, Edinburgh Castle).[8] Yet Mar's death had little impact on James. His guardianship was transferred not to the new Earl of Mar, who was too young for the role, but to the late Mar's brother, Sir Alexander Erskine of Gogar (with whose son, Thomas, James was being educated).

Anyone wishing to prove the moral rectitude of resisting monarchs – as George Buchanan was keen to do – needed no more evidence than the much-storied example of Mary Queen of Scots: a wicked, murderous adulteress who, it could be claimed, was rightly chased from her throne for the good of the commonwealth. As soon as James was able to understand, Buchanan thus filled his head with all the tales he had compiled – or invented – of the boy's evil mother's immorality, wickedness, and cruelty. A story has long circulated in which James and his fellow pupil, the ebullient John Slates, Master of Mar, fought over custody of the latter's tame pet sparrow. In the altercation, the sparrow was killed and, amidst the boys' tears, Buchanan – after a predictable swipe at the king's head – acidly commented that his charge was 'a true bird of the bludy nest of which he was come'.[9] In this one comment was summed up the tutor's distaste for the Stuart dynasty, his hatred for James's mother, and the bitterness and cruelty which he inflicted on the boy in the delivery of discipline.

Indeed, the success of the obloquy heaped on Mary Queen of Scots had risked being put to the test when an idea was floated between the late Regent Mar and Queen Elizabeth which would have seen the imprisoned Scottish queen returned home to suffer immediate execution – an idea which foundered on the reluctance of both parties to be seen to be to blame: Elizabeth was unwilling to be viewed as the murderer of a fellow sovereign, and Mar could not be sure that Buchanan's lessons would stick sufficiently to prevent James seeking revenge for his mother's death in the future. Nevertheless, the blackening of the king's family went on apace within Stirling's schoolroom. Following the St Bartholomew's Day Massacre, widely believed to have been the work of James's Guise relations, the Guises too would provide an example of how wicked the king's blood relations were. The lessons were clear enough: James's family was a source of shame, and he ought to work hard to eliminate its influence in the pursuit of Buchanan's ideal of kingship.

Tempering Buchanan's extreme pedagogy, however, was Peter Young – a younger, softer tutor (or preceptor, as he and the older man were known). Young was a graduate recently returned from studies at Geneva, the spiritual centre of Calvinist theology, where he had learnt directly from the esteemed scholar Theodore Beza. The keynote in the difference between the two tutors was, if Melville is to be believed, that Young was 'loath to offend the King at any time, and used himself warily as a man that had mind of his own weal, by keeping of his Majesty's favour'.[10] This strategy – of looking to the future – was to pay off; in time, Young was to find himself, like the 2nd Earl of Mar, treated as a useful and trusted royal servant. For the moment, he was content to encourage where Buchanan demanded, and to play his part in helping build an enviable royal library, which boasted amongst its 600 volumes Calvin's *The Institutes of the Christian Religion* (the foundational text of the faith); the *Icones*, by Theodore Beza (dedicated to James himself); *L'Institution des Princes*, by Tigurinis; Thomas Elyot's *The Book of the Governor*; several books of Ronsard's poetry (inherited from Mary Queen of Scots' library at Holyroodhouse); and Ascham's *Toxophilus* (the standard work on archery).

The fruits of the king's education were soon enough put on display. In 1574, Henry Killigrew, who had praised James's appearance as a baby, and had seen him again in the intervening years, produced a written description addressed to Sir Francis Walsingham in England, but certainly intended for Queen Elizabeth's eyes. It noted that the young king 'could use pretty speeches as to how much he was bound to her [Elizabeth], yea, more than to his own mother. He has well grown in body and spirit . . . He could speak the French tongue marvellously well and was able extempore to read a chapter out of the Bible into French and out of French into English . . . He likewise danced with a very good grace.'[11]

Evidently, from the first line quoted, James had been coached to dissemble well, and he had already won a reputation for eloquence. As time would prove, his love for his cousin Elizabeth was as much a thing of hot air and silent suspicion as was hers for him. Shared religion would force them into uneasy alliance, but the Scottish king no more loved Elizabeth than she could, famously, 'love her winding sheet'. Still, the educational attainments could not be denied, and it is refreshing to see that the image of the king as weak and bandy-legged in his childhood (variously ascribed to rickets and poor nursing) is less straightforward than is usually depicted – he would even have one William Hudson appointed as dancing master in 1579. The early struggles with walking he reported to his physician in adulthood – if James was not misremembering or exaggerating his infancy – appear to have represented no serious developmental problem (and, interestingly, his dance-loving future wife would report the same early-childhood debility).

Also sometimes exaggerated is the king's childhood being consumed by learning. In fact, two preceptors drawn from the Erskine family – Adam and David – were assigned the job of instructing James in the art of hunting with hounds and other sports, the former of which was to become one of his greatest passions. The desire that he might be presented as a martial figure, as well as a learned one, is supported by the earliest surviving royal portrait: the eight-year-old king stands with one hand on his hip, wearing velvet breeches of forest green, his sword dangling behind him, and a sparrowhawk perched on his gloved left hand. His eyes are wide-spaced, as his father's had been, though matched with the heavy lids of his mother; his complexion is incredibly pale; and his hair fair. The artist, the Flemish (or Dutch) Arnold Bronckorst was promoted to Scotland's first King's Painter, and he was followed in 1584 by Adrian Vanson. Whereas the only contemporary images of Mary Stuart date from her time in France, James and his Scottish court were officially recorded in oil and paint. And as with all paintings of noteworthy figures of the period, Bronckorst's makes a political statement, its message being that the King of Scots was coming of age. When he turned eleven, in 1577, the council acknowledged his development, though Morton ensured that no more honour was given him than some soft words and the confirmation of Alexander Erskine of Gogar as his keeper. What the regent missed was that those surrounding the king were beginning to chafe against the regency.

In his youth, James was a precocious child with nascent ideas about his own authority which, rather because of Buchanan's efforts than in despite of them, tended towards emphasising its special, divinely appointed status. Already, there was also developing a streak of nasty humour at the expense of others; when one Captain Ninian Cockburn told him a rambling story in French, James quipped, 'I have not understood a single word you have spoken, and it seems to me to be true what my lord Regent [Morton] says: that your French is worth nothing and your Scots scarcely more.'[12] As he grew older, this sense of humour was to sharpen, and throughout his life the king would delight in making sarcastic and boorish comments, secure in the knowledge that those on the butt end of his barbs were unable or unwilling to answer back.

Morton, in addition to making snide comments about people to the king, had been busying himself with the day-to-day running of Scotland in James's name. It was possibly because of the business of government that he neglected to develop much of a bond with his young sovereign, preferring instead to send him gifts (some jewels recovered from Edinburgh Castle when it fell, gold and silver buttons, and a football) and keep him in respectful obedience. Nor did he have a good relationship with the king's keeper, Gogar – indeed, Morton tried to oust him in 1575, without success. Gogar, however, had been warned and, from then on, he was alert to any chance to strike back at the regent.

For his part, Morton had done a creditable job of ruling Scotland, but he was far from universally popular. Although a staunch Protestant, he was wary of firebrands (such as the preacher Andrew

Melvill, spiritual successor to Mary Queen of Scots' *bête noire*, John Knox, who had died in 1572). His worry, which James would inherit, was that extremist reformers might strike as easily at the nobility and the monarchy as they did at the system of episcopacy. His solution, however, was inept, in that he simply deferred dealing with the matter (thus storing up the problem of Kirk infrastructure, left uncodified by the 1560 Reformation Parliament, for James to deal with). As dangerously, the regent made enemies amongst the nobility, extracting jewellery from the Countess of Argyll (Moray's widow, who had remarried but retained the valuable jewels which her late husband had expropriated from Mary Queen of Scots). The Earl of Argyll, as incensed as his wife, was joined in his enmity by the Earl of Atholl. The pair, who had been feuding themselves, were disciplined for their lawlessness by Morton, and, in their shared chagrin, they made common cause against him. Worrying, too – and ominous for the king's future attitudes – were the whispers of witchcraft that circulated in Stirling in September 1577, when the Countess of Mar and her brother became involved in the accusation and trial of one Violet Mar, who had allegedly attempted sorcery to bring about Morton's downfall.

Later in 1577, a comet streaked across the skies over Europe. It was reported in England early the following year that it had 'filled the Queen [Elizabeth] and her followers with great fear: for meantime she laboured with a very burdensome disease, so that from day to day she vomited blood in the greatest abundance'.[13] Comets, as everyone knew, presaged the deaths – or at least the downfalls – of important personages. Rightly might Elizabeth have worried; events north of the border were gathering pace. Atholl and Argyll put their plan into action, going directly to the young king. At Stirling, they requested that he go over the head of his regent by convening a meeting of the peers of the realm to judge their cause. This James eagerly did, and Morton waddled into the trap, immediately offering a token resignation in his indignation at being outmanoeuvred. To Morton's horror, James accepted this with alacrity, having been encouraged to do just that by Atholl, Argyll, and Gogar.

Morton, however, was unwilling to go without a fight. His response was to convince the new Earl of Mar, James's schoolroom fellow, that his uncle Gogar was obstructing him, Mar, from having the post of the king's keeper for himself. Only about sixteen, young Mar swallowed this, and willingly threw in his lot with the tottering regent. In April, a violent countercoup was thus staged, during which Gogar was seized by Mar's friends and ejected from the castle. James, who was evidently viewed as a source of power rather than a surrogate brother, despite their shared schoolroom experiences, was thus kept under the young earl's custody until parliament sat in July. With the king under Morton's new friend's supervision, the old earl was subsequently able to assume the role of First Lord of the Council, which, if not as great a prize as the regency, at least allowed him to keep a grip on power. But still he did not win James's affection – quite the opposite – and in truth there was little in the squat, porcine, elderly lord to excite the king's interest – for James, at twelve, was already on the brink of puberty. As hindsight soon enough proved, it would have been better for the former regent if he had gone quietly.

Though Atholl (who had been brokered as Second Lord of the Council by Robert Bowes, the wary English ambassador, who had been charged by Elizabeth with achieving stability) died suddenly – amidst rumours of poisoning by Morton, similar to those which had swirled around the former Earl of Mar's death – the new First Lord of the Council continued to make enemies, despite his weakened position. Morton, understandably, attempted to defend himself, calling in a team of physicians to perform a post-mortem on Atholl (with one reportedly licking the contents of the dead man's stomach, only to fall ill – unsurprisingly – afterwards), but he was on the backfoot. Even Buchanan disliked him (reputedly due to a falling out over a horse, with the old tutor never letting go of a grudge), and James cannot but have realised from recent events just how unpopular the former regent was. Happy to compound this general sense of disaffection was the thirty-four-year-old Captain James Stewart, the ambitious and adventurous second son of Lord Ochiltree. Stewart was a soldier-of-fortune and veteran of the Dutch campaign against the Spanish, who returned to Scotland in 1579 and quickly gained entry into James's service. This worldly and swashbuckling place-seeker, whose sister had been married to John Knox, became another of the growing anti-Morton community. But a still greater opponent was to come.

Central to Morton's period of rule had been his conflict with the Hamiltons, and he took the opportunity throughout 1578 to continue it. With the wholesale reduction of the once-mighty family, the position of 'second person of the realm' was open to the Lennox Stuarts – the family of James's father and grandfather, the late Regent Lennox – who had long and loudly claimed it for one of their own. As the Regent Lennox's line was a dead end, save James (Darnley having no other children and his other son, Charles, having died in England leaving a daughter, Arbella), the family's claim to a high place in the succession fell to the descendants of his youngest brother, John, 5th Lord of Aubigny, who had become a naturalised Frenchman and died there in 1567. His son, Esmé Stuart, 6th Lord of Aubigny, thus had good reason to consider a visit to his father's ancestral lands, the better to stake his claim. This was well known in Scotland, and it likely did not take much encouragement from Morton's enemies to induce James to write to France with an invitation. What was not known, however, was that Esmé, a man of inestimable ambition, had found support for the pursuit of his Scottish interests, and from none other than Mary Queen of Scots' quondam ambassador and loyalist, John Leslie, Bishop of Ross. Ross, who had ended up in Paris after visiting the Vatican, was even then concocting a scheme whereby James might be kidnapped and transported to France, where he could be converted to Catholicism. Esmé looked like being a useful tool in bringing this plot to fruition.[14]

Soon enough, Morton would have cause to lament his high-handedness against the Hamiltons. Soon enough, King James's developing sexuality would become of use to an opportunistic and acquisitive relative.

It is fair to say, however, that the coming of age of the king was an intense and curious one, surrounded as he was by mixed messages and competing forces, each inviting him to assume different identities. He was not a lonely child, in the sense of being deprived company – but the company which attended on him at all times was not his family, and nor did any of them aspire to be. Even those boys who had shared his schoolroom would be rewarded according to how well they served their master: Walter Stewart of Minto would become a Gentleman of the Chamber (the separate term 'Bedchamber' not coming into force in Scotland until 1603) and Keeper of the Privy Seal; Thomas Erskine of Gogar would become a 'server for life'; John Slates, the Earl of Mar, would have, as will be seen, a somewhat wilder relationship with the king. These were people James would come to distrust as turncoats, appreciate as loyal servants, and fear as malign detractors. He had no immediate family, and his mother was invariably referred to as an evil influence best kept as far away as possible.

Yet rather than becoming the subject of shame and the inspiration for moral improvement intended by George Buchanan, family was, to James, to become an object of profound fascination – a chimera which he would relentlessly pursue. It therefore should not surprise us that when passion came into his life, it should come in the form of a family member.

3

Man and Boy

History is littered with odd parallels. There remains one in the story of James VI and I that has, however, received little attention.

In 1547, long before the king was a glint in his mother's eye, their cousin Elizabeth found herself placed – happily, it seemed – with her stepmother, the dowager Queen Catherine Parr. As Henry VIII had died in January 1547, Catherine had been free to reignite her dormant passion for the true object of her affection, the outwardly charming and handsome Lord High Admiral, Thomas Seymour (brother to the Lord Protector, Edward, as well as to the late queen, Jane Seymour). The pair had wed, with what appeared to many to be indecent haste, in the spring, thereafter setting up house at Chelsea Manor. Fairly quickly, however, Seymour began exhibiting an interest in the thirteen-year-old Lady Elizabeth (the girl having lost the title of 'Princess' in infancy, when her father had his Archbishop of Canterbury, Cranmer, annul his marriage to Anne Boleyn). He would, it was reported, enter her bedchamber clad only in his nightshirt, falling upon her as she lay in bed and attempting to tickle her, kiss her, and slap her backside. His actions discomfited her governess, Mrs Ashley, who found them inappropriate enough to complain to his wife. Yet Catherine appears to have convinced herself that her new husband was engaging in horseplay, and her solution was to join in, perhaps hoping to disrupt the narrative that Seymour was pursuing the girl as a sexual object. Nevertheless, when the dowager found herself pregnant in March 1548 and thus unable to close her eyes to the admiral's misdeeds – and certainly in no position to thwart them – she sent Elizabeth to live with Sir Anthony Denny, where she might be free of the older man's advances. Catherine was freed too – to give birth in relative peace, which she did in August at her dower property of Sudeley Castle. Sadly, she succumbed to a fever shortly afterwards. Her attempts to quash the rumours, however, would prove to have been fruitless.

That the relationship between Seymour and the young Elizabeth was taken seriously is proven by its sequel. The admiral had never been happy about the governance of England as it had been constituted following Henry VIII's death – his brother, as Lord Protector, had essentially taken on the role of regent on behalf of their nephew, Edward VI, in the teeth of the late king's desire for a council to hold the reins of power. After launching various schemes to breed discontent, Seymour embarked on a plan to enter Edward's apartments at Hampton Court, with a view either to taking the king into his own custody or, more likely, persuading him directly to alter the existing polity (which Atholl and Argyll would later successfully do with the young James VI). However, the renegade was caught in the act, apocryphally drawing attention to himself when he shot one of the royal spaniels after it began barking. He was arrested and sent to the Tower, the investigation into his movements following.

Agents of the protector's council were quickly despatched to interrogate the Lady Elizabeth, and her servants were arrested. It became clear that the girl was under suspicion for having colluded with the doomed admiral in treason; it was even rumoured that she might have become pregnant to him. Evidently, despite the age disparity between them – she was just shy of fourteen and he in his late thirties when he began entering her bedroom – Elizabeth was considered to have been an active agent in what might have been a sexual entanglement. Thankfully, the teenage girl was already developing a talent for dealing with hostile interrogators, and she knew enough to say nothing incriminating. The council was forced to conclude that the impropriety had been entirely Seymour's, and that there was no evidence either of a sexual relationship or of her collusion in treason. The admiral went to the block without trial and alone.

Historians are now confident that the high-handed council – eventually – reached the correct conclusion. Recently, attention has turned away from whether or not Seymour had sex with Elizabeth (which he almost certainly did not) and placed instead on the motivations behind his behaviour. It has been noted, indeed, that 'Sir Thomas engaged in what would now be recognised as sexual grooming'.[1] This it was, even if the extent of the sexual element is open to debate – and it ought to be noted that men like Seymour were virtually expected to maximise any opportunities for self-advancement. His goals were probably partly based on attraction and, more prominently, on gaining the trust and future support of the boy-king's sister. Elizabeth's feelings are difficult to gauge – her famous comment, supposedly made on his execution, that 'this day died a man with much wit and very little judgment' is, like so much of Seymour's story, apocryphal – but it is possible she felt sympathy and affection for him, exactly as he had intended. Then, as now, young people might be easily taken in by older ones who affect to treat them as more mature and developed than they are.

Curiously, years later, a similar situation was to play out, when the thirteen-year-old James VI found himself the object of apparent affection and sexual interest to a charming, handsome, predatory man in his late thirties. So too did he find himself largely blamed as a prime mover and active agent in the affair. It is time, however, for the young king to be afforded the same sensitivity as his celebrated English cousin.

*

By anyone's measure, and certainly by French standards, the royal court of Scotland was a squalid affair. Following Mary Queen of Scots' deposition and captivity, the atmosphere of continental glamour had been lost: there were no longer widescale celebrations, no digging of artificial lakes, no firework displays or grand masques, and even the Palace of Holyroodhouse – a symbol of Stuart majesty – had been allowed to fall into disrepair.

In fairness, attempts were made to rectify this. In late September

1579, James was introduced to Holyrood, travelling despite high winds with his household from Stirling via Dunipace and Linlithgow. The king was moved – with all subjects between sixteen and sixty called to accompany the journey from Stirling – to his dynasty's great palace at the end of the Canongate (the burgh directly adjoining Edinburgh) and lodged there. The plan was for him to enjoy his palace and the homage of his nobility – an excursion would be made to Morton's fine house at Dalkeith – whilst preparations were undertaken for his ceremonial entry into the capital. These entries, popular throughout Europe, were opportunities not just for the populace to see their sovereign, but for citizens to voice their own expectations of the monarch in a festive, mutually appreciative way.

The population of Edinburgh and the Canongate swelled with the arrival of over 2,000 horses carrying a glittering array of barons, aristocrats, and gentry. On his arrival at Edinburgh, James was accompanied by Morton, Angus, Argyll, Montrose, Mar, Lords Lindsay and Ochiltree, and the Masters of Livingston and Seton, and soon joined by the powerful Home and Kerr families. The burgesses of the city, dressed in armour, gave a formal welcome, with the castle's guns blasting a welcome. All of this was, however, a prelude to the ceremonial festivities planned.

On 19 October, James took centre stage in the grand procession to mark him taking ownership of Edinburgh. Dressed in white-and-silver satin and riding under a canopy of purple velvet, he arrived at the West Port, where the magistrates provided a pageant recounting the 'Wisdom of Solomon': the biblical sovereign 'was representit with the twa women that contendit for the young child. This done, [the actors] presented unto the King, the sword for the one hand, and the sceptre for the other.'[2] This evidently made an impression on him, as identification with Solomon would become a key plank in the king's developing regal identity. It was, in a sense, conventional, as the wise biblical monarch was a popular figure whom sovereigns across the continent sought to emulate. But so too was it to prove useful in James's deliberate attempts to fashion a symbolic link between himself and the kings and queens of England, which he – as his mother still did – one day expected to rule. Both Henry VIII and Elizabeth I had been associated with Solomon and, whilst James could not claim blood descent from either famous Tudor monarch, he might still establish a sense of visual and thematic continuity.

The king rode onwards, pausing to listen to a Latin speech by the Calvinist preacher John Sharp. Doubtless this was not particularly welcome, smacking as it did of Buchanan's schoolroom lectures. Yet James was well cushioned from the fiery words: he was joined in his ride by the civic authorities and elites – the city provost, the baillies (or aldermen), and the guildsmen – dressed variously in velvets, satin, and silk gowns. As this gathering crowd, numbering some 300–500 people, passed under the city's overhanging galleries, from which music and cheers echoed, they reached their first grand spectacle. From the Strait Bow port, one of the numerous city ports (or gates), a painted globe descended, which was opened by mechanical means to reveal a young boy offering the solid silver keys to the city.

The colourful, noisy procession then worked its way down the High Street, which had been swept clean and littered with flowers, towards the Old Tolbooth. Here, Edinburgh's craftsmen had decorated the building and lain out the tools of their trade for inspection. 'Four virtuous ladies' – representing Peace, Justice, Plenty, and Policy (likely schoolboys drafted in to play the parts) – delivered orations on their respective themes before igniting a wheel of fireworks. Another female representation, Dame Religion, waited farther along the route, outside the forbidding heart of Scottish spiritual life, St Giles Cathedral. James accepted her invitation to enter and there listened to James Lawson's sermon on the importance of embracing the cardinal virtues. Psalm 20 was sung, which included the words:

> And grant thee according to thine heart, and fulfill all thy purpose:
>
> That we may rejoice in thy salvation and set up the banner in the Name of our God, when the Lord shall perform all thy petitions.

Now know I that the Lord will help His anointed, and will hear him from His Sanctuary, by the mighty help of His right hand.

Some trust in chariots, and some in horses: but we will remember the Name of the Lord our God.

They are brought down and fallen, but we are risen, and stand upright.

Let the King hear us in the day that we call.

This was no docile paean of flattery. Lawson's message was clear: the king was God's servant. The people, too, were a force to be reckoned with – and they had very clear ideas, or at least Lawson and his ilk did, of what their sovereign owed them. None of this was new to the student of Buchanan, but it is unlikely he liked the sound of it.

Escaping the cathedral, James passed down to the Mercat Cross, where he was treated to the sight of Bacchus, robed in a painted gown and garlanded with flowers, filling cups with the wine flowing from its fountain and passing them to all who walked by. The message was of the need for munificence. In time, James would learn it far too well – and would come to enjoy wine far too much.

Family and the importance of dynasty, for all Buchanan had scorned James's, were the next theme. The Salt Tron (where, historically, salt had been officially weighed, to ensure correct taxation on merchants and to stop corrupt ones cheating customers) had been decorated with visual displays of Stuart genealogy in the form of portraits. As James absorbed the scene, trumpets blasted and the assembled masses cried, 'Well fare to the King.' Here was something he had encountered in history books but had been discouraged from taking a source of pride in: his family and the place of successive Stuart kings in the history of the nation. Again, he would take this seriously and develop enormous pride in his descent. His illustrious, divinely appointed family was not a farrago of fools and murderers but what set him apart from all men and women, save his crowned peers. Indeed, amongst even royal houses his was remarkable: the

Tudors were mere parvenus when compared to the ancient lineage boasted by the Stuarts. Before long, he would allow this revelation of dynasty – and dynastic pride – to swell his head.

Furthering this theme, a planetary display had been set up at the Netherbow Port, where Edinburgh met the Canongate. Emerging from the gatehouse, a boy playing Ptolemy gestured to various gilded globes which marked out the alignment of the stars at the king's birth in 1566. Astronomy was something with which James was familiar, and so the verses read on the seven ages of man and the seven planets served simply as a public illustration of his educational attainments. Thereafter, he was free to pass on with his party to the Canongate, the fine, tall housefronts of which had been hung with brightly coloured tapestries and effigies of the nobles who kept city residences close to the centre of power.

With the entry deemed a success (despite injuries being sustained by those crushed in the crowds), further ceremonial could take place, not least of which was the opening of the 1579 parliament, held in a capital which could display and make use of the real Honours of Scotland. For James, however, this foray into Edinburgh was to be a brief sojourn, lasting only for the autumn and winter of 1579–80: a taste of the majesty which was bound up with his position before he was returned to the familiar surroundings of Stirling in February.

Throughout his debut, the young king had been both celebrated and lectured: he was welcomed as a sovereign, certainly, with all the visual and aural display the city (which had paid for everything) could muster; but so too was he given warnings bedecked in glitter. He must, as the entry festivities stated, be wise, godly, and virtuous – no less was expected of a sovereign of considerable monarchical descent who had been given an education commensurate with his station.

This was heady stuff for a thirteen-year-old, but James, by dint of his schoolroom experience, had been trained to understand it. He could not, however, be forced to accept everything presented to him in the manner it was intended. What he did learn was that kingship had a visual dimension. It required, both from the sovereign and his

45

subjects, a willingness to enter into the magic of majesty, with all the pomp and ceremony required to keep the monarchy alive.

Yet this was something he would struggle with. One thing that the schoolroom had evidently not taught the king was the importance of heightened manners and regal affectations, which led to an elevated sense of what we would probably now call 'theatricality' or 'showiness'. Indeed, this kind of pretentious hauteur was held in deep distrust by George Buchanan, and there is little evidence that Peter Young had the ability to instruct in it. Both men, essentially, had filled James's head with academic knowledge, whilst his instructors in leisure had introduced him to noble pastimes. There had been no one in Stirling willing or able to teach him how to project the imperious ceremonial expected of a monarch. In September, however, there had arrived in Scotland a fellow who boasted both the fascinating fact of a direct family connection and a knowledge of kingship as it was practised in the rarefied atmosphere of Henry III's French court. Entry into the political arena had been achieved; entry into adulthood and the world of sex would follow swiftly enough.

Born in about 1542, and thus around the same age as James's mother, Esmé Stuart is well known to those who have studied the history of James VI and I. Indeed, one might be forgiven for thinking that he had had no life prior to its intersection with the King of Scots. However, when Esmé and his small train clattered into the courtyard at Stirling Castle to launch their charm offensive on James, the Frenchman was already a seasoned courtier and politician with considerable experience under his belt. Having succeeded his father to the Aubigny title in 1567, he was engaged in 1576 on behalf of a French embassy to the Low Countries. In November of that year, he was entrusted with the job of formally thanking the Duke of Alençon on behalf of the Estates (the French parliament) and, by all accounts, he appears to have been a loyal and trustworthy agent of his nation's government. Rather than being, as has sometimes been suggested, a cat's paw of the powerful Guise family (of which James's maternal grandmother, Marie, had been a daughter), he combined national interests with personal ones: it was his goal to reignite a relationship between Scotland and France (the 'auld alliance' having been severed by the Scottish Reformation and its architects); to act in the interests of the captive Mary Queen of Scots, with backing by her man, the Bishop of Ross; to gain recognition of his Lennox Stuart claim to a place in the Scottish succession; and, in the pursuit of all, to climb as high as he could in Scottish affairs. All of this was, of course, in the power of King James, and soon enough the latter consideration would supersede the objectives it was intended to assist.

Familiar as he was with the French court, having been a Gentleman of the Royal Bedchamber there, Esmé cannot have escaped the knowledge of Henry III's infamous love of his mignons: those male favourites with whom the king allegedly had sex. Whether true or not (and historians remain divided), contemporary rumours depicted Henry's court as one of licentiousness and vice, ruled over by a sovereign who had extravagant affairs with men and women, and whose antipathy for war was thus rooted in an 'effeminate' nature. On meeting James, Esmé appears to have read in the boy's nature something of his as-yet latent sexual awakening. With an eye to his own advancement, the new arrival encouraged this, notwithstanding the fact that he had a wife, Catherine de Balsac (whom he repeatedly warned not to follow him to Scotland) and several children at home. Antonia Fraser, in a remarkably sensitive biography of King James, has noted that 'the first object which came his way was a man . . . had an equally attractive woman come his way at the same propitious moment, the homosexual inclinations of [the king] might never have been aroused'.[3] Though sympathetic, the reading is somewhat outdated. Esmé had a profound effect on the boy's tastes (not least in fostering a passion for the cultured and the polished), but he no more birthed James's interest in same sex partners than Thomas Seymour caused Elizabeth to be heterosexual. Rather, what almost certainly happened is that Esmé found that by encouraging the king's lust, and garnishing that encouragement with familial affection, he could win for himself the kind of favour that was otherwise difficult to secure. In other words, he recognised that James's emotional and physical needs included male relationships, and he accommodated himself: nowadays, we would say he took advantage.

Working in Esmé's favour was the retention of his looks, which greatly enhanced his personal carriage: he was 'of comely proportion, civil behaviour, red-bearded, [and] honest in conversation'.[4] Moreover, his genius lay in opening James's eyes to his own status, treating him as a divine object of reverence and wisdom rather than strictly as a student, and educating him not in dead languages but in the living delights of continental court culture and the colourful world of majesty to which he could aspire. His behaviour, as distasteful as the age-gap might make it seem to modern readers, was not, however, without precedent. In encouraging James's crush, Esmé was not only remodelling the Scottish court after the French but was viewed as drawing on a still extant – albeit often sharply criticised – tradition of pederasty, in which an older male figure would instruct a developing young male sexually as well as educationally. The king, for his part, threw himself eagerly into this exploitative relationship, doubtless thrilled that not only were his romantic feelings being encouraged, but that he was being showered with apparent love and affection from a member of his semi-mythical family.

The results were meteoric. Arriving only a few days before the king set out for Edinburgh, Esmé was immediately invited to join the cavalcade and take part in the ceremonial entry. James bestowed on his cousin the rich lands pertaining to the abbey of Arbroath and raised him to the earldom of Lennox (this in March 1580). The Lennox earldom was of especial importance, not only because it had been James's grandfather's title (albeit it had since been granted to the king's great-uncle, who was now induced to resign it in exchange for the earldom of March), but because it introduced Esmé to the Scottish peerage and, traditionally, Scottish aristocrats enjoyed certain perks of custom and access, due to the French influence that had governed the Stuart monarchy since before the Reformation. These ranged from the right of noblemen to keep their hats on in the presence of their sovereign to, more pointedly, the right of access to the royal bedchamber. Additionally came a slew of household and governmental positions: the new Earl of Lennox was appointed First Gentleman of the King's Chamber; Master of the Wardrobe; Chamberlain (a position which granted nominal authority over all royal departments); Master Household (a Scottish office); Governor of Dumbarton Castle; and he gained a seat on the Privy Council. This array of titles and roles emphasises not only James's immediate open-handedness, but the blurring of the period's line between private and public. The royal bedchamber itself was a site of political exchange and discussion, ceremonial, and social contact. It was not a private space (indeed, Mary Queen of Scots had held audiences with male ambassadors in her Holyroodhouse bedroom). The state bed, too, was a heavily curtained and thus walled-off pseudo room, from which James could hold court and into which he could invite special servants. Beyond this, some palaces – as at Stirling – boasted an even more intimate private bed, hidden from view, and in which the king might sleep alone or in company.[5]

How far exactly did the relationship go? The answer is very much open to interpretation. The biographer David Harris Willson admits – somewhat grudgingly – 'a sexual element', whereas Caroline Bingham's sparkling study of James's Scottish reign is noncommittal, acknowledging that the 'precise nature of their relationship remains a mystery'.[6] More recently, Alan Stewart has largely rejected the sexual interpretation by stating that James did not show any attraction to older men at any other point in his life. This is true enough. However, it does not follow that the king would seek to recreate the relationship with his cousin from the position of the manipulated youngster. Having fallen for an older man, James would rather seek to emulate the dynamic from the opposite side; he would, in all future relationships – with men and women – fashion himself as the wise elder. The opportunities for sexual congress (of any kind) were, further, made possible by the offices and positions Esmé was granted. He not only had access to James's most private spaces – he controlled who entered those spaces, as well as overseeing every aspect of the boy's dress, personal hygiene and toilette, and conversations. Given his unparalleled access to the king's person, it is possible that Esmé took the relationship he had initiated beyond the slaps, tickles, and dress-cutting that Elizabeth had endured at the hands of Thomas Seymour – although still this does not provide proof of exactly how far they went. Nevertheless, Esmé provided a pattern for the king which would govern James's understanding of love.

All of this was watched with jaundiced eyes by the English ambassador, Robert Bowes (whose sister had been, like Stewart's, a wife of John Knox). An invaluable observer of Scottish affairs, as well as an active proponent of England's interests, Bowes had every reason to fear French interests eclipsing those of his own nation at the Scottish court. He wrote acidly that 'the King is so much affected to him that he delights only in his company, and thereby [Esmé] carries the sway'.[7]

Nor was the sight of this swaggering Frenchman any more palatable to the Kirk and its clergymen; according to the chronicler David Moysie, they 'cried out continually'.[8] Another contemporary noted that 'the ministers in Scotland do daily preach in every burgh of that realm against [Esmé]', and one preacher specifically charged him with 'introducing prodigality and vanity in apparel, superfluity and banqueting and delicate cheer [drinking], deflowering of dames and virgins, and other fruits of the French Court'.[9] The fact that Esmé spoke no Scots and conversed with James only in French can only have exacerbated what they considered an immoral Frenchification of court and king, and in their rush to smear they engaged the usual assumption that one form of 'vice' naturally begat another. Moysie, employing coded language, wrote too of the 'great familiarity and purposes' which the king and his cousin had fallen into – a hint of contemporary public belief in the sexual nature of their relationship. More explicitly, David Calderwood condemned the French influence as fostering 'bawdy talk [which] provoked him [James] to the pleasures of the flesh, and all kind of licentiousness'.[10] An English agent summed up the attitude of the Scottish clergy on this point, noting their firm belief that Esmé 'goes about to draw the King to carnal lust', and the attack launched by the minister of St Giles, Walter Balcalquall, on 7 December 1580 said much in its warning that 'it shall be easier for Sodom and Gomorrah in the day of the Lord's judgements than it shall be for you'.[11] The worry, at least on the part of the religious-minded of James's subjects, was that their king had been seduced into all manner of vices with a flagrant disregard for the exhortations to virtue they had expounded. From the perspective of politicians and men of state, the problem was – as it was so often to be in the future – less that their king might have embarked on a sexual relationship with another man than that the relationship threatened their own influence. If Esmé Stuart held sway, as Bowes put it, they were likely to be left out in the cold. It was imperative that they act.

In the teeth of the Kirk's censure and the politicians' growing conspiracies to oust the upstart man who had so evidently put their boy-king in thrall, James continued to come out of the hard shell of learning and piety in which his tutors had sought to encase him. The summer of 1580 saw him embark on a royal progress through Fife and Angus, and he was even to be found wielding a crossbow and – in a vignette not usually associated with him – mounted and running 'right bravely' at the ring at Dundee.

Leisure of a more intellectual kind was fostered too. In his public rooms, the king began developing his passion for demonstrative and competitive poetry. This he did by patronising a band of writers (including the female poet Christian Lindsay), at the head of which stood Alexander Montgomerie, as master, with James himself serving as the inspirational Apollo.[12] This witty circle has been suggested – a little hyperbolically – as evidence of the king's attempts to fashion himself as a sovereign whose job it was 'to inspire and to command the activities of his national poets'.[13] More likely, it was a natural development of his own interests, which always were of a bookish bent. Together, these learned people formed a literary salon or workshop focused on discussing and translating foreign poetry, as well as experimenting with form in Scots. Poetry was rapidly developing as the primary means of storytelling and versifying, and it is clear that James – even if his own work, which would be published in *The Essays of a Prentice in the Divine Art of Poesy* (1584) and *His Majesty's Poetical Exercises at Vacant Hours* (1591), was conventional – believed himself to be at the forefront of Scottish literary development. Of comparatively less literary merit but providing a more immediate lesson was the sight in July of a drama staged at St Andrews, wherein a wild-man (played by one Skipper Lindsay) burst forth and, staring up at the window from which the royal party watched, warned Morton that his 'doom was in dressing'.

The king had learnt also of the benefits of courting foreign powers. No doubt hoping to remind him of English affection and thereby turn his mind from France, the southern queen's great favourite, Leicester, sent him a piebald horse as a gift. James was reported as offering 'to serve her Majesty [Elizabeth]' and bearing 'great love for her', even as he was being enticed to renew the Auld Alliance via joining England in its amity with France. Similarly, he was happy to claim a 'wish to marry in England' even as an 'embassy on the subject of his marriage, from Denmark' was spoken of, and the French Catherine of Navarre was a potential bride.[14] James tried, too, to ensure that he was seen continuing to promote domestic stability. In October 1580, he made a public show of attending Mar's wedding to Agnes, the sister of Lord Drummond, at Kincardine, alongside an array of his nobility.

All was not well, however. Part of the problem – and the invitation to criticism – stemmed from one thing James did not learn from Esmé or anyone: discretion. Later, in 1581, it was certainly noted that he was 'in such love with [Esmé] as in the open sight of the people, oftentimes he will clasp him about the neck with his arms and kiss him'.[15] From the moment he was seduced by Esmé until the end of his life, James would wear his heart on his sleeve, indulging in public displays of emotion which undermined any sense of majesty – a thing which monarchs such as Henry VIII (who publicly fondled Catherine Howard) and Elizabeth I (who tickled and romped with the Earl of Leicester) did more sparingly.

Esmé, far more than James, was sensitive to the rising tide of disaffection which greeted his elevation. Likely in order to stem it, and to better oppose the Protestant Morton, he publicly recanted his Catholicism and embraced Scotland's religion in June 1580. The following month, he sent a letter announcing his Damascene conversion (somewhat undermined by his secretly writing to the Guises that he remained Catholic) to the fortieth General Assembly of the Kirk. This was well received. So too was his insistence that one of his retinue, Henry Kerr, make a public acknowledgement that Scotland's faith was the only true religion. However, the sincerity of the earl's conversion is open to debate. Cynically, one might argue that rather than representing a sudden awakening to the ostensible truth of the reformed faith, it allowed him to kill two birds with one stone: he could ameliorate the censure of ministers over his corruption of their king, and he could please that king greatly by demonstrating that James, in all his youthful wisdom, had managed to convince him of the errors of Rome. The last seems in character, if one takes into account Esmé's history of manipulation of his younger cousin throughout his time in Scotland. For his part, James was reported by the visiting Jesuit Robert Abercrombie as being, in 1580, devoutly Calvinist, as confessionally he would remain – for lack, the priest claimed, of good instruction.

That Esmé's intention with this conversion was political is supported by what followed. Throughout the newcomer's rise, the former regent and current First Lord of the Council, Morton, had all but retired, largely contenting himself with laying out his gardens at Lochleven and attending to the marriages of his daughters. However, he had long been one of the nation's foremost reformist politicians and his bloody history indicated that an attempted return to power was possible – even likely. If such a rise came about, it would not bode well for the king's predatory lover.

Esmé's means of preventing Morton's comeback was twofold: the new earl built up a party around himself (rich in historically anti-Morton figures) and he decided to strike first. Central to his faction was Captain James Stewart, who had returned to Scotland at almost the same time as Esmé, and who likewise won James's favour through his supportive, deferential behaviour; he became a Gentleman of the Chamber in October 1580, instituting and leading a new bodyguard. The Earl of Argyll, too, saw a fresh opportunity to bring down his old enemy; he insinuated that the fallen counsellor had engineered a kidnapping plot, supposedly centred on seizing the king and carrying him to Dalkeith. This piece of scurrility immediately sent James into a panic and caused him to abandon a hunting trip and retreat to the safety of Stirling's familiar walls. Counter-rumours then emerged, concerning Esmé's alleged plans to kidnap the king and lock him up in Dumbarton. Thus, on an excursion to Doune with his beloved cousin, James took fright again – this time at the sight of weapons amongst his lover's attendants. When Mar, in an effort to protect the king, garrisoned Stirling, he found himself accused – unfairly – of confining him. Happily, James exonerated him.

This state of constant panic and swirling rumour encouraged the nervous king to confide in Bowes that he was learning the art of dissimulation, and that if any attempt were made to seize him, the perpetrators should find 'such inconstancy, perjury, and false-hood in him' that the plot would be worthless. This seems to have been intended as a warning to Elizabeth to cease her interference in Scottish affairs, given that Morton's supposed kidnapping plot was rumoured not to end with captivity in Dalkeith, but with James being sent to England. This was probably one of the most unsettled periods in the king's young life: it was a time of constant threat and the ever-looming fear of not only being separated from a man he loved (and whom he believed loved him) but deprived of his free-dom and treated with less than regal dignity.

The climax to this period of frenetic intrigue came at the end of December 1580, when Stewart made a dramatic entrance to a meet-ing of the Privy Council, falling on his knees and declaring to the king that the elderly Morton had been 'art and part' of the murder of Darnley. This was true enough – but, given the years that had passed, few suspected that the old man would ever pay for joining with the old Earl of Bothwell in regicide.

But pay he did. Morton was immediately arrested (one suspects that James, who was present at the council meeting, was primed as to what Esmé and Stewart intended) and imprisoned first in Edinburgh Castle and then at the fortress of Dumbarton. A litany of charges was written up, including the prisoner's alleged murder of the late Earl of Atholl and his having conspired repeatedly to kidnap the king and murder Esmé – although only his part in murdering Darnley would stick.

Morton's tottering and fall were watched with increasing panic by Queen Elizabeth, who had valued the former regent as a man who had largely acknowledged English interests in Scotland. Thomas Randolph, a veteran in Anglo-Scottish relations who had begun his career as an English spy before being granted ambassadorial status by Elizabeth, was sent north with instructions to effect Morton's release. This was, as seemed apparent, a direct battle between the settled state of Anglo-Scottish amity and the dangerous – from Elizabeth's perspective – influence of an upstart Frenchman. She voiced this through her representatives (having not yet established a direct epistolary relationship with her cousin), attempting to frighten James with spurious tales that his lover sought the Scottish Crown, that he was a seductive papist, and that through his malign influence, James had altered in his friendship towards her. This all fell on deaf ears. More ominously, she ordered a martial force to muster on the Borders and await orders to invade Scotland (though in the event it would be disbanded, and was thus more threat than danger), and activated her contacts in the northern kingdom, instructing those who opposed Esmé, including the 8th Earl of Angus, to agitate and plot against him. Wisely, the man who had probably actually smothered Darnley, Archibald Douglas, had already taken the opportunity to flee south, leaving Morton to be fought over by his accusers and would-be rescuers.

The king was not supine in the face of this assault from the south. In February, he issued a proclamation calling all fit men to arms, and thereafter a Convention of the Estates (a less formal, tax-raising assembly and one which did not require parliament's traditional forty-day summons) voted to raise a tax of £40,000 in the event of Anglo-Scottish war. In possibly one of the earliest displays of what would become a tremendous problem in Jacobean England and Scotland, the result was a profusion of libels – predominantly handwritten, railing notes attacking public personages – scattered about the court and city. Their chief target, naturally, was Esmé, who was derided as a debauchee and cuckold who had gleefully watched his wife being deflowered by another man – pure scurrility, but presumably believable enough for a man thought to be indulging in licentious sexual behaviour with the king.

Despite months of effort, both overt and clandestine, however, the English queen failed in her attempts to dictate Scottish policy. In response to her man Randolph's interference, a deeply offensive libel condemning his sovereign for her hypocrisy (she was then playing at negotiating a French marriage), and himself for his meddling, was posted to his gate. When Randolph complained to the king, James simply told him to locate the libeller himself, if he was so minded. Sourly, Randolph noted that despite his youth, James 'wants [lacks] neither words nor answers to anything said to him'. After a shot was fired through the ambassador's window, undoubtedly by Esmé's followers, he fled Scotland, leaving the doomed former regent to his fate. In June 1581, Morton – despite his mendacious denials of having conspired in the Darnley murder and his claim only to have had nebulous foreknowledge of the act, which he had not brought to Queen Mary because she was the deviser of the killing – lost his head.

James, on the morning of the execution, refused to read his former regent's last letter, and instead wandered his apartments in a fury of agitation. Elizabeth, on hearing the news that the king had addressed Morton as 'father' and promised him protection on the eve of his downfall, supposedly derided the king as 'that false Scotch urchin', demanding that her agents make him choose, once and for all, and apparently without a hint of irony, whether he was her friend or had thrown in his lot with Esmé and the disunited French – the Catholic militants of which were apt to cooperate with Spain. Likewise, without much self-awareness of her recent scheming, she rhetorically lamented, 'What can be expected of the double dealing of such an urchin as this?'[16]

Her answer came soon enough. As Morton's shaggy head mouldered on a spike above the Tolbooth, Angus was accused of treason and forced to flee south. In August, Esmé was elevated to the dukedom of Lennox as well as the lordships of Darnley, Tarbolton, Dalkeith, and Tantallon. In what appears to have been a pointed thumbing of the nose to Queen Elizabeth and her claims that Esmé aimed at the Scottish Crown, the new duke was also formally recognised as 'second person' in the realm – heir presumptive, should James fail to have issue. Material gifts fell on him too: in June, James lovingly handed over the remaining jewels from his mother's collection, including a pearl- and diamond-encrusted gold chain, and by October the new duke had received a gold cross, a diamond necklace with golden roses, and the famed Great Harry, all from the Royal Wardrobe.

Nor was he the only beneficiary of Morton's fall. Captain James Stewart had already received a position on the Privy Council in February 1581 and the earldom of Arran in April. More ominously, William Ruthven – a shapeshifting figure who had supported the ruination of Morton 'for his [own] office and to hold together what he haith gathered' – was granted the earldom of Gowrie and con-firmed as Lord Treasurer.[17] Ruthven's late father had been disgraced after having played a key role in the murder of David Riccio back in 1566; in time, both the new Earl of Gowrie and two of his sons would meet grisly fates.

For the moment, though, Scotland's future seemed assured – and assuredly pro-French. It rested, however, on something fragile: the young king's passionate relationship with the man who had groomed, seduced, and now sought to manipulate him. Soon enough, that relationship would be severed.

4

The End of the Affair

The ghost of James's father had finally been laid to rest, but the king's mother refused to give up her own. In her English captivity, the second-hand knowledge of her son's relationship with Esmé was music to her ears. Mary's dreams of restoration in Scotland had receded in likelihood with each passing year, but, sadly, she seems only to have thrown herself more deeply into them. Contact with her son had been tightly restricted. Early in her imprisonment, she had attempted to establish a long-distance relationship, sending him a gift of his first pony and saddle, with a note reading, 'Dear Son, I send three bearers to see you and bring me word how ye do, and to remember you that ye have in me a loving mother that wishes you to learn in time to love, know, and fear God.'[1] Elizabeth, however, would not let the present out of England. In the summer of that year, mooted plans for James to be sent south to be educated in England had also failed. Thereafter, the Scottish Privy Council had decided that all communication must pass through it. Mary's refusal to stand by her forced abdication – and therefore her refusal to address her son as anything but Scotland's heir – only ensured that her appeals got nowhere. Another attempt at sending a gift in 1579 – miniature golden guns, sent via the queen's French secretary, Claude Nau – were returned without James having seen them.

With the French seemingly gaining ascendance in Scotland, however, Mary saw the possibility of a change in her fortunes, reuniting with her son, and escaping her interminable and increasingly cruel captivity. To her delight, James had made the first move – probably at the instigation of Esmé, who saw in the deposed queen a means of strengthening Franco-Scottish relations, even if he had no intention of having her return to any sort of power which might threaten his own influence over the king. In tones of humility, James thus began sending humble letters to his 'good mother', assuring her that he was her 'obedient son'.

These were all the captive queen needed. In response, in early 1581, the idea flew back to her homeland of a potential 'Association': a Guise-backed plan by which she would, with Scottish and English support, be returned to Scotland to rule jointly with James. This was not entirely a new idea. Almost since her incarceration had begun, there had been talk of her returning to Scotland to operate as a titular sovereign (then with a regency governing in her name); and the Bishop of Ross had, since the mid-1570s, been working on her restoration (indeed, he had hoped Esmé would be a tool in his scheme), with James then being educated in France. What was new was the prospect of a peaceful restoration approved by both British kingdoms, which would see James remain where he was, with Mary at his side.

Ironically enough, though, Esmé – the man she had viewed as the answer to her prayers – was probably the one least inclined to help her. As soon as word spread of her putative return, the Calvinist political and religious community was in uproar. To Esmé, both his influence with James and his credentials as a Protestant convert were risked even by rumours of his attempting to help restore a Catholic queen. From James's perspective, the mother he had never really known was also more a political embarrassment than a victim. On 28 January, both men – first the king and then his lover – put their signatures to a document called the King's Confession (known more widely as the 'Negative Confession'): it swore that they abhorred 'all kinds of papistry in general and particular heads even as they are now damned and confuted by the word of God and Kirk of Scotland but in special we detest and refute the usurped authority of that Roman Antichrist'.[2] By March they were urging nationwide subscription and, in April, the General Assembly signalled its approval. The situation was not helped, however, by the arrival in the country of Guise and Spanish agents, the latter of which had Mary's endorsement to bring about the Association by force of arms.

Esmé thus remained in a vulnerable position. Ominous, too, was the inescapable truth that his faction included a number of former Marians – including John Maitland of Thirlestane (brother to the Machiavellian Maitland of Lethington, who figured so prominently in Mary Queen of Scots' personal reign), Lord Maxwell, and Lord Seton – who had been embraced back into the ruling faction after the civil wars, but nonetheless continued to be eyed with suspicion by those who had been on the side of the Kirk and the King's Party during James's minority. And Protestant suspicions were well enough founded. Trying to play both sides, the favourite was both mumming as a good Protestant convert and attempting to win continental Catholic support by appearing to encourage plots which would see a papal army (paid for by Spain) invading England from the north with the goal of liberating Mary Queen of Scots.

Yet affairs continued to simmer. For his part, the young sovereign took up his pen and wrote noncommittal letters to his distant mother, pointedly signing himself 'James R'. She remained a figure of some fascination to him, but, at root, he wished nothing to interfere with his personal rule in Scotland. Still, he kept his options open, hoping – quixotically – for a solution to the insoluble problem of how to keep Mary Queen of Scots alive, out of trouble, out of Scottish affairs, and all in a way which would keep his active conscience quiet. The Association would never have done this, as doubtless he knew, but something might yet be negotiated that would. In the event, the question of what to do about his mother simply rumbled on month after month and year after year without answer, but with wearying, rather sad hope on her side.

In the meantime, despite the general air of distrust and scheming which had settled over Scotland and England, and which had brought continental conspirators to both countries, James continued to enjoy what he evidently hoped would be a lasting affair with his cousin. Part of Esmé's appeal was, and continued to be, the way in which he could conjure up a world away from the backbiting of the political scene. His servant, one Montbirneau – a 'merry fellow, able in body and quick in spirit', according to one observer, and 'Lennox's right hand' to another – became a regular feature of court life, entrancing the king with displays of horsemanship and encouraging leisure and sporting pursuits.[3] Something of courtly festivity was gradually reintroduced to Scotland, albeit in a way which would have horrified the king's mother; early in 1581, when Morton was still languishing in imprisonment, the port town of Leith, near Edinburgh, bore witness to aquatic jousts fought out between rival boaters. A floating castle was also constructed, named 'the Pope's palace', and summarily fired upon and sunk (in an unsubtle attempt to silence those rumours of Esmé's lingering Catholic sympathies). In this atmosphere – masculine and martial as it was – James developed a taste for swearing and bawdy talk, for which he has often been criticised (frequently by those who compare him unfavourably to other monarchs, forgetting that the celebrated Queen Elizabeth had a mouth like a sailor).

Once again, as ever, the Kirk continued to look askance at the court and its people, castigating what it viewed as the irreligious use of the Sabbath for pleasure and pastimes, and, unfairly, complaining that James no longer listened as assiduously as he once had to hectoring preachers at dinnertimes. In fairness, of course, the king and his new friends were providing the censorious ministers with much ammunition. In July, the month after Morton's death, Captain James Stewart, raised to the earldom of Arran, married Atholl's daughter Elizabeth Stewart, the quondam Countess of March. The countess had been the wife of James's great-uncle, the aged Robert Stuart, Bishop of Caithness and now Earl of March – but the marriage had been unsuccessful and, apparently, unconsummated (despite having been arranged purely to provide more Lennox Stuarts). When she was found to be pregnant, the child was undeniably her lover Arran's, and hence a divorce on the grounds of March's impotence (his 'instrument', it was said, was 'no good') had been granted in May. The scandal of sex and infidelity in high places served merely to ratify what was being cried openly: that the influence of Esmé and his French train had corrupted king and court.

It is therefore unsurprising that, as time went on, those who detested Esmé's political power, abhorred his relationship with the king, or distrusted his shifting religious views, coalesced into an oppositional party. Unwisely, too, James began to enforce his genuinely held beliefs about the infrastructure of the Kirk – namely that it ought to be governed by a system of episcopacy (that is, rule by appointed bishops) in the teeth of vociferous Presbyterian ministers, who naturally favoured rule by presbytery (that is, by representative elders nominated from within). Possibly Esmé influenced the king's thinking on this matter, but it is more likely that James arrived at this view independently, probably as a result of his developing distaste for his schoolroom teachings and his desire to have a mechanism with which to supervise the Kirk.

At this time, if the court was earning the Kirk's enmity by its actions, the Kirk itself managed to stoke up every possible bit of princely distrust. It was in 1581 that it published its *Second Book of Discipline*, which sought to finally secure its status as an independent body capable of establishing its own systems of governance. This would have been unacceptable to any monarch of the age – indeed, from the perspective of ministers, it confirmed the Kirk as superior to what they viewed as the monarchy's secular rule. 'All godly princes and magistrates', it loftily announced, 'ought to hear and obey' the pronouncements of ministers.[4] Much more to James's taste was the attitude of moderate preachers like Patrick Adamson, Archbishop of St Andrews, who claimed that 'a Christian king should be the chief governor of the Kirk, and behoved to have Bishops under him, to hold all in order'.[5] To a precocious fifteen-year-old who had only just – on his birthday in June – formally begun his personal rule, this was very welcome. The king – who had, since his royal entry, begun to venerate his own exalted position – hardly needed the new men around him to poison him against the overbearing, theocratic, and anti-monarchical overtures of the state Church, but they were still quite willing to side with him and thus inflame the growing conflict.

James Stewart, the new Earl of Arran, was happy to tell James – accurately – that in Protestant kingdoms such as England spiritual affairs fell under the jurisdiction of the sovereign. He, at least, seemed willing to stand up to what he considered overmighty preachers, calling the articles they presented to the king 'treasonous'. Notwithstanding his conversion, Esmé, as always, was equally happy to take advantage, this time of the rift between king and Kirk: he cheerfully recommended one Robert Montgomerie, minister of Stirling, to the vacant archbishopric of Glasgow, and profited financially by the recommendation. This bit of sharp dealing appears to have been the proverbial straw that broke the camel's back, and those who had merely grumbled and sown rumours independently began to gather together to form concrete plans to separate their king from his lover.

This might not have represented such a danger – given James's obvious emotional dependence on Esmé – if the duke had retained a solid grouping of his own to counter it. However, the problem with faction, as always, was that it seldom survived the achievements of its short-term goals. Already, the party which had supported Esmé in ousting Morton and achieving political and personal supremacy over the king was beginning to fracture. Sir John Seton, a former Marian who had thrown in his lot with the duke, found himself on the receiving end of the petulant Arran's threats of violence when he refused to stand back from the king's horse at the earl's commandment. This sparked the indignation of Esmé, who took Seton's part and refused to ride with the king when James ordered the Seton men to remain at home the following day. The duke's siding with the Setons is explained by his own developing dislike of the quarrelsome Arran; the new earl had publicly complained about Esmé being given the job of carrying the crown to the parliament convened in October 1581 – a task to which he felt himself equal by virtue of having been allowed to usurp the powerful Arran earldom, which had pertained to the Hamiltons, who claimed precedence over Esmé's family in the line of succession. Thus, the parliamentary speech James gave, which invoked the possibility of an anti-papal league, was somewhat undermined by the infighting of his chief supporters. This 'variance' even resulted in two separate Privy Councils being held, one at Dalkeith under Esmé and the other at Holyrood under Arran. This was unedifying stuff, but it was all too typical of the kind of jealousies common when courts were governed by visible shows of precedence.

Arran, for his part, was quite aware of how unpopular his words and actions were making him, and his means of stemming the tide of disaffection was to make amends, first via an official reconciliation with Esmé in December, and then with the Kirk. This he did in conjunction with the king. In a piece of public theatre, on 14 March 1582, he made a formal apology for his seducing of the Countess of March – and their fly-by-night marriage designed to legitimise the child born to them – at Holyroodhouse, in James's presence. The following week, the king attended the baby's baptism, thereby giving – in what was an act of remarkable foreshadowing – royal approval to an unpopular noble marriage mired in adultery, divorce on the grounds of impotence, and public shaming.

It was not enough. Nor could the outspoken Arran maintain even a façade of approving the Kirk's more extreme views. By May, he was once again arguing vocally against its commissioners (who were again incensed at Catholic influences on the king when the Duke of Guise attempted to send a gift of horses) and their theocratic stance on Scotland's future. Esmé's appointee as Archbishop of Glasgow, Montgomerie, who had already faced student riots in the city, was then pelted with eggs when he tried to preach – an event the report of which sent the young James into gales of laughter. Yet, though seemingly silly, the attack was serious in that it signalled an emerging opposition to royal authority and those who were viewed as profiting from it. A storm was clearly coming. Nevertheless, the king hoped to maintain the *status quo* and the life of gradual empowerment, sporting, public ceremony, and private leisure that his cousin's arrival on the scene had brought. It was even reported that Esmé's man, Montbirneau, had been busy furnishing James with 'pictures of ladies to be commended to the King' – the implication being that a royal marriage might be engineered which was of advantage to the pro-French party.[6] There were powerful subjects enough, however, who were not content to let affairs continue as they were.

Most obviously, there remained kinsmen of the late but not particularly lamented Morton: the Earl of Angus (who had claimed asylum in England) and Douglas of Lochleven. To these were added the staunchly Protestant Lord Lindsay and the 7th Earl of Glencairn, the Masters of Glamis and Oliphant, as well as the powerful landowner John Cunningham of Drumquhassle, who had been James's Master Household and was an inveterate intriguer. The latter managed something of a coup for the emerging opposition party, securing by intimidation the support of the new Earl of Gowrie, William Ruthven, who had gained his title by helping Esmé and Arran bring down Morton in the first place. More worrying still was the inclusion in the plot to follow of James's old schoolroom companion, the Earl of Mar, and – significantly for the future – Francis Stewart, 5th Earl of Bothwell, nephew to the Bothwell who had married Mary Queen of Scots. Many of these men had, to combat Esmé's ascendancy, been earmarked by the English ambassador Bowes as worth cultivating. It was now time for them to be activated, especially as Anglo-Scottish relations had hit a low point – with James's refusal to even read a letter of advice coming from England.

The plan these men hatched was familiar enough and followed the time-honoured pattern of various schemes to seize control of kingdoms in both Scotland and England. It involved, quite simply, kidnapping the king.

In furthering it, James's new lifestyle left the plotters plenty of opportunity. Though he still resided largely at Stirling, he had, during Esmé's tenure as his mentor and lover, begun to spread his wings. His passion for hunting, which had been with him since childhood, had driven him beyond the rolling valleys of Stirlingshire, and in the late summer of 1582, he was enjoying his sport in Atholl, whilst Esmé was conducting his duties as Lord Chamberlain in Edinburgh. Little can have seemed amiss to the king; he had even, in June, written an apology to the English government and thereby taken the first steps in mending relations. Whilst he was enjoying himself – and the period of relative calm – however, a blow was falling in the city.

Without James's knowledge, a series of charges were being laid against Esmé and his alleged 'practices against religion, against the state, &c'. These were followed by 'articles' wherewith he was 'charged in his desire to overthrow the state and the established religion'.[7] These were, though, a mere sideshow. As the king rode south towards Perth, he was hailed by the Earl of Gowrie, whom Elizabeth had recommended in April 'for his courage and other good qualities as very fit to be about [James's] person and to do him service'.[8] At first, Gowrie made a show of those qualities, inviting his sovereign to enjoy his hospitality. James, oblivious, accepted. Gowrie took him to Ruthven Castle, where the king spent the night. In the morning, when he attempted to leave his chambers, he found himself denied, and the reality that he was a prisoner struck him. The sixteen-year-old king burst into tears, realising his predicament and what it meant for the life he had been leading and the man he had been leading it with.

James was no longer in control of his movements. The threat of kidnapping, so often rumoured, had become reality. Under guard, he was moved from Ruthven Castle to Perth, and stricter supervision. On 30 August, the men who had begun calling themselves the Lords Enterprisers extracted from him a proclamation, which declared that he remained at liberty (a transparent means of adding legality to the kidnapping and dissuading would-be rescuers) and ordering Esmé to depart Scotland.[9] At the same time, and with a display of disingenuousness which would put a cat next to an empty dish of cream to shame, Elizabeth ordered her household marshal, George Carey, north 'to make offer of her ready goodwill and care towards' her Scottish cousin, 'in consequence of some new troubles lately happened in that kingdom'.[10] These were troubles, naturally, which she had been stirring with a very long spoon for a very long time.

The duke had no intention of going quietly: he had a good thing going in Scotland and was not prepared to lose it. Instead, he set about trying to build up a party to counter what was effectively a countercoup. Transporting what he could carry from his house at Dalkeith to Edinburgh, he attempted to stir up civic and religious support, declaiming that he had never attempted anything against religion and exhorting the town council to summon the nobility and gentry of Lothian to rise up to free their king. This was obviously a lost cause, given the Kirk's attitude to him (it was at this point that the minister James Lawson made his attack on the vices Esmé had introduced to the court, centring on those 'French fruits' which had grown and soured).

James, for his part, showed himself to be his mother's son, and quickly began covertly getting out private messages which undermined the official statements he was forced to make (including a demand that the duke leave Scotland within fourteen days). In short, these were that Esmé must not leave him, and that he, James, was not acting freely. They were to have little effect, however. He was moved from Perth to Stirling (at the same time as the forced proclamation went out against the duke). This at first seemed welcome, as the surroundings were familiar; the king hoped, in fact, that he would be allowed the liberty to go hunting outside the castle walls, as had been his custom. It is likely at this point that he found the doorway of his chamber blocked again, this time by the Master of Glamis, who threw his leg across it (the early sources agree on the dramatic obstruction but disagree on the time and place). Rather than crying, this time he had the wit to hold his peace and listen as his captors laid out their demands. Chief amongst these were that he relinquish Esmé and, as was the common grievance of the nobility under the Stuarts and Tudors, that he re-establish the primacy of the ancient blood of the realm in his council, rather than promoting foreigners and new men.

The jig was up. Having gained no support worth mentioning, in September Esmé gave out that he was returning to Dalkeith; instead, he travelled westwards. Wise to him, the Lords Enterprisers ensured that a proclamation went to Glasgow forbidding any man to join up with him there. Thus foiled, the duke travelled on into Dunbartonshire, and to Dumbarton Castle, where he was forced to relinquish his governorship of the fortress and forbidden from forming a gathering of more men than the castle's captain could defeat in arms, if it came to it.

The Kirk fathers, meanwhile, were cock-a-hoop, publicly approving what has become known as the Ruthven Raid, and the Lords Enterprisers behind it, as 'good and godly'.[11] No less ecstatic was Queen Elizabeth. As Leicester reported, she 'thinks that the lords who have taken in hand this late reformation deal somewhat too slackly in that the Duke and others be not restrained, and that her Majesty advises them to deal substantially both for the weal of the King and the state lest this opportunity be lost'.[12] Evidently, she wanted no less than Esmé's head, to ensure that he could work no mischief to her disadvantage in the future. On 14 September, Bowes and Carey secured a meeting with James, and the former reported, with a degree of naïveté (given what the king had told him in the past about his propensity to lie through his teeth if he were ever imprisoned) 'his revived affection' towards the English queen. James could not, however, hide his 'anger' at his captors' accusations against Esmé. Cruelly, in an attempt to turn him against the man who was, in the king's mind, his first and greatest love, James's gaolers showed him letters from France which supposedly proved that the duke had been both an instrument of the French and that he had viewed his young lover as a pawn.

This appeared, at least, to strengthen the king against his favourite – though it is to be doubted how much he meant what he said when he subsequently assured the English embassy that, on reflection, his kidnapping was honestly meant and Esmé a man of little wisdom. Yet, again, he could not resist putting a sting in the tail. Although he agreed to the need for the duke's banishment, he cuttingly pointed out that the Ruthven Raid had been the product of three strands of thought: good intentions regarding the governance of the realm, ambition, and fear. His public actions, however, continued to follow his captors' instructions: he was induced to request an English passport for his disgraced lover, and to insist that the duke do as he had been bidden and leave the country, or risk being tried as a traitor. Nevertheless, Esmé – no doubt reluctant to be separated from his golden goose – spun out time and sought delays, hovering about the west and the Central Belt, hoping, probably, to be granted access to the king as he was moved from Stirling to Holyroodhouse. Autumn passed into winter, and still the fellow remained in Scotland. As Christmas approached, James was finally induced to write a firmer letter demanding that his lover depart immediately. This led a despairing duke to write to the king of his grief at the bad opinion supposedly developed of him, of the falsity of the charges laid against him, and of his lasting devotion. On 18 December, he wrote again:

> Sire,
>
> Whatever may befall, I shall always be your very faithful servant; and although there may befall this misfortune, that you may wish to banish me from your good graces, yet in spite of all you will always be my true master, and he alone in this world whom my heart is resolved to serve. And would to God my body could be cut open, so that there should be seen what is written upon my heart; for I am sure there would not be seen there those words 'disloyalty' and 'inconstancy' [the words James's letter had accused him of] – but rather these: 'fidelity' and 'obedience'.[13]

Was he speaking the truth? Probably not. It was, in fact, a political message in the guise of a love letter, designed to appeal to James's ego and to play on the romantic obsession Esmé had long used to gain and assert mastery over the boy. The hyperbolic language was as hollow as it was clichéd; the trope of cutting open the heart to inspect the engraved words had been old when Mary Tudor used it to express her regret at the loss of Calais. He went on, 'I desire to die rather than live, fearing that in your disdain you have found a cause for loving me no more. And should I thus fall from grace, then in truth it would be a greater punishment, and one more cruel to endure than death itself.'

Here, Esmé revealed his hand, using the conditional tense even as he employed the hackneyed trick of promising that he would rather die than lose his lover's passion. Evidently, by using 'should', he did not see his fall as either definite or final. Death, he claimed, was something 'which I long for, and shall long for, until the proofs you have of my obedience have freed you from all evil thoughts that you have formed of me . . . and to end my letter, I make you a very humble request – forgive me if I have offended you in anything, and remember your poor servant, who prays for you'. This was pure emotional manipulation, and, like a great deal of emotional black-mail, it worked. James, though he would remain a prisoner, would never forget Esmé Stuart, nor forgive the man – Gowrie – whom he blamed for parting the duke from him. Nor would he forget the Kirk's firebrand ministers who exulted in the separation, or that offi-cial endorsement of the Ruthven Raid.

For the moment, though, and with his last missive working on James, Esmé (along with his supporter Seton) left Dalkeith, left Scotland, and left behind the rich array of jewels he had been given. He travelled southwards through England, meeting in Yorkshire – by chance – Bertrand de Salignac Fenelon, Seigneur de la Mothe, the French ambassador to England. Fenelon confided in the duke that he was travelling to Scotland to work for his restitution and, indeed, when the ambassador reached James, he found the king much inclined to the French. With help from a subsequent French visitor, the Marquis de Mainville, assurance was won from the captive king that he 'had but one heart, and that was French'.[14] Most likely is that James was willing to enterprise anything, and to promise anything, that would deliver freedom and reunite him with the banished duke.

On reaching London, Esmé immediately sent word via his secre-tary to the resident Spanish ambassador, Bernardino de Mendoza, of the political situation in Scotland and the reasons which had compelled his departure. Thereafter, in January, he was granted an audience with Queen Elizabeth at Windsor Castle. As Mendoza reported to Philip II:

The Duke of Lennox and his people were closely guarded . . . until he saw the Queen, which he did four days after his arrival. She received him well and ordered him to be covered [to keep his hat on], as he was the first Duke [of Scotland] but he refused. She complained greatly of him in many respects, making seven principal accusations, including 'that he had generally endeavoured to weaken the new alliance between England and Scotland, and to renew the old relations with France'. The Duke replied to each point. The Queen thanked him . . . The next day Lennox returned to London, coming to lodge near the house of the French Ambassador . . . He was treated with less suspicion than before, being banqueted by the French Ambassador, and his people free to go about as they liked.[15]

True to form, Esmé was charming, convincing Elizabeth that he was not a Catholic agent. Less trusting was her spymaster, Walsingham, whose agent William Fowler (a poet and later, surprisingly, secretary to James's wife) tricked the duke into a conference and then reported Esmé's speeches against England, which were construed as part of an anti-English plot. Nevertheless, Elizabeth 'ordered for [Esmé] a ship with 50 arquebusiers [infantrymen carrying long guns, called arquebuses]' and he set sail across the Channel before moving on to Paris.

One thing the duke did not leave behind in Scotland was his new religion. This was not because of any genuine belief on his part – Esmé had always been a *politique* in religious affairs – but simply because he was hoping that he might return to James with his cover, including his Protestant credentials, intact. He had only to wait in France until circumstances in Scotland had shifted in his favour.

As it turned out, they never did. What intervened was illness and a death the duke could not have foreseen. It was reported in May 1583, indeed, that he was preparing his return to James in Scotland (via charming Queen Elizabeth and gaining her support for the journey); but on the 26th of that month, he died in Paris. With an eye to the future – particularly his children's future – he had kept up the charade to the end, not only dying an avowed Calvinist but, in one final emotional appeal, requesting before his death that his body be buried at Aubigny but his embalmed heart be sent to James.

71

Along with this gruesome memento went a letter, asking the king to 'be good to his bairns, and to take upon his Grace the defence of them'.[16] Despite his widow having him buried by Catholic rites, the heart, encased in a lead casket, and the letter went north in June, and both had the intended effect. In November 1583, Esmé's nine-year-old son Ludovic Stuart set out after his father's heart, and with his own train of Catholic retainers. Though he would never be the king's lover, as his father had been, he did become one of James's most trusted friends. On their first meeting, at Kinneil, the king acknowledged the French lad as the new second person in the realm.

Needless to say, James took the news of his first love's death hard – indeed, at first, he refused to believe it, clinging to hope by virtue of an earlier letter in which the duke had said he was recovering from illness. But the truth soon became clear, resulting in tears and a desire for revenge. Perhaps luckily, the king seemed never to realise that, whilst his passion for Esmé had been utterly genuine and intense, the duke had been using him from the beginning. For the moment, though, that lack of realisation ensured that first love equated to first heartbreak. This James had the ability to channel into his pen, writing as he did one of his most famous poems, which bore the ungainly title 'A Metaphorical Invention of a Tragedy Called Phoenix'. Prefacing the poem proper are two cryptic verses, the first of which is a 'form poem' in the shape of a vase or urn, and the second an acrostic with the first and last letters of each line spelling out 'ESME STEWART DUIKE [Duke]'. The narrative poem goes on to tell the tale of a rare and beautiful phoenix which is attacked by a jealous raven (an obvious play on 'Ruthven', which was pronounced 'Riven'). Frightened, the creature then hides between the speaker's legs (a sexual reference which leaves little doubt as to the nature of the real-life relationship on which the allegory hinges), which leads the raven and his fellow birds of prey to launch a combined assault on the phoenix and poet. The only solution is for the magical bird to flee to Arabia, where it immolates itself, only for a worm of ash to signify its coming rebirth. As Alan Stewart has noted, the casting of the phoenix as a female allows for a conventional love story to emerge. But so too does it hint towards what would be James's role in future relationships: in the affair Esmé had led him into, he, James, had played the woman. In its many rebirths – in the affairs he would go on to have with men and women – he would always be the male.

James, like Elizabeth, had been groomed by a manipulative and ambitious older man. As with the Seymour scandal, tragedy had ensued. The sequel to James's experiences, however, were more long-lasting. In future, the king would continue his obsession with family, and he would go on conducting affairs with men. Consequently, he would continue receiving censure on the grounds of morality and politics. Yet his tastes would not be binary. Nor would he or his subjects allow his preference for emotional relationships with men to imperil the Scottish succession. No matter his preferences in either sex or romance, the king needed a wife. But before that could happen, there remained one obstacle which might tarnish the idea of marriage to him in the minds of any prospective bride or in-laws. His mother, still publicly and continuously identifying herself as Scotland's true sovereign, remained alive and hopeful of her own fortunes. Whilst her son languished in captivity under Gowrie, her life, however, was about to enter its final, tragic act.

5

Madame and Mother

One of the remarkable things about the Lords Enterprisers, those masterminds of the Ruthven Raid, is their apparent lack of long-term thinking. Indeed, the great problem with the perennially popular tactic of seizing the sovereign's person – a problem which seems to have escaped would-be kidnappers of all monarchs – was that, eventually, some kind of accord would have to be reached whereby the liberated ruler did not instantly turn on those who had so ignobly treated them. The Enterprisers' behaviour gives a flavour of their wild thinking on their captive king's future: in May 1583, the regime sent a delegation to Queen Elizabeth begging for support, money, and, distastefully, proposing that the forty-nine-year-old English monarch should marry her sixteen-year-old cousin (or at least engineer a suitable match for him). It is extremely unlikely that James was consulted about this, and Elizabeth quite rightly brushed it aside.

Another danger was the eternal instability of faction. As Esmé's supporters had descended to infighting once the duke had ascended in the king's affections, so too did the Lords Enterprisers begin to bicker amongst themselves. This invited the new regime's opponents to take advantage – indeed, although Esmé had been unable to capitalise on them, disparate anti-Gowrie figures had begun to emerge even before the duke had fled Scotland.

Two of the chief men who began plotting James's freedom are of especial note. The first was the reportedly attractive Catholic 6th Earl of Huntly, who had been educated in France and been part of the anti-Morton faction in 1580–81. The second was Francis, 5th Earl of Bothwell, who abandoned his fellow Gowrie conspirators.

This was a man who epitomised what was a recurring problem for all sixteenth-century Scottish monarchs (as a result of successive royal minorities). Like many nobles and wealthy lairds, Bothwell had become a virtual mafia don, engaging his followers in turf wars fought in backstreets and lonely passes, making shady secret deals without recourse to the sovereign, and selling his influence and local power to factional and foreign leaders. On the credit side, he had all the superficial charm of his late uncle, the more famous 4th Earl. Like him, this Bothwell, too, fashioned himself – when it suited him – as a faithful son of the Kirk, and shared a seemingly contradictory desire for the acknowledgement of Mary Stuart's right to rule. Unlike his uncle, however, this Bothwell was quite prepared to take cash handouts from England, the government of which viewed him as a potentially useful mischief-maker north of the border. At any rate, Huntly and Bothwell went on to enjoy the king's favour and attendant political offices, notwithstanding their colourful exploits. Joining them were the more stolid Atholl, Montrose, and Seton, each of whom subscribed to a band, or bond – one of those documents, common to Scotland in the period, which added documentary weight to murky alliances.

According to the courtier James Melville, a veteran diplomat and memoirist (most famous for describing Queen Elizabeth's jealous demands as to whether she or her cousin Mary was the fairer, the taller, and the more able dancer), the king himself had an eye to the main chance when it came to his liberation. This is easy enough to believe. He had endured captivity, but it had terrified him. A story, indeed, circulated that he had etched on a wall within Holyroodhouse the words, 'A prisoner I am / And liberty would have.' To his horror, James later found that someone had added, 'A papist you are, and friend to a slave / A rope you deserve, and that you shall have.' Whether the tale was true or not, he had elected to keep his head down – and, as he had shown himself a model captive, conditions around him slackened. In June 1583, nearly a year after he had been taken, he was being housed in the royal hunting-lodge-cum-palace at Falkland. As Melville has it, James turned to him and requested his aid in effecting an escape: a thing which made the cautious old diplomat wary. Yet, courtier to his marrow, he could not refuse his sovereign's entreaties.

A plan was hatched whereby the sympathetic Earl of March would invite the king to St Andrews on the pretext of sharing with him 'wild meat and other fresh fleshes that would spoil in case his Majesty came not'. In reality, St Andrews would be a meeting place for the anti-Gowrie plotters. At the end of June, James was granted permission to ride out to this ostensible feast, and he took Melville. Waiting at Dairsie, a village on the way to the coastal town of St Andrews, were March and the town provost. These the king greeted 'with great joy and exclamation, like a bird flown out of a cage'.[1] James was, by his own estimation, a free man. Immediately, he issued a proclamation – much like those he had been forced to give out against the late Esmé – denying the Lords Enterprisers the right to approach his person.

Gowrie, for his part, knew that the game had been lost. His regime had lasted less than a year and, despite the proclamation, he was able to visit the king, albeit only with an air of abject penitence, submission, and supplication. James, realising that a show of magnanimity was required, curbed his instinct to rail against the earl who had imprisoned him and banished his lover to exile and death; instead, he issued a pardon, content – or forced by circumstance – to play the long game against a man he detested and feared. It was due to the whole affair, in fact, that James's infamous enmity towards the Ruthvens of Gowrie was seeded. Playing on the king's mind, too, was the fact that, during Gowrie's tenure, the earl had advanced monies to the Crown amounting to £48,000, which the king saw no means of repaying any time soon. As importantly, the lasting result of James's captivity would be a lifelong terror of confinement, conspiracy, the dangers of armed bands, and – as an antidote – an unshakeable belief in the sacred, untouchable nature of his person.

The king's position was suddenly one of renewed strength – or, at least, that is how he wished it to be perceived. He was now seventeen and determined to rule not as a fragile child at the mercy of others but as a sole sovereign; in July, he loftily announced his intention to rule as 'a universal King', impartial to and above all. A new, Catholic-flavoured Privy Council was appointed, on which sat young Huntly (who had won royal favour by virtue of his part in the ousting of Gowrie, and who was worth cultivating due to his power in the Highlands), Montrose, Crawford, and Argyll. Significantly for the future, John Maitland of Thirlestane, former Marian and Esmé supporter, took a seat alongside another seasoned politician and quondam Marian, Robert Melville of Murdocairnie. All of this was quite alarming to the English government, who had no idea how affairs might play out, particularly in relation to their royal house-guest, Mary.

Aside from James, the main figure to profit by the crushing of the Gowrie regime was Esmé's sometime ally, the Earl of Arran. Arran, whose vainglory (and that, apparently, of his ambitious wife) apparently knew no bounds, was less inclined to make a show of reconciliation to the failed Lords Enterprisers. When the hapless John Slates – Mar – came to James with his tail between his legs in August, Arran judged his submission to be lacking in true redemp-tion – and, more probably, lacking in what Arran considered the respect the younger man owed him. He high-handedly ordered Mar from Scotland. Like Esmé, the earl departed – in fact, he jumped before he was pushed, fleeing before the official banishment was pronounced. Unlike Esmé, Mar managed to make a return, reap-pearing in March 1584 with fresh plans to seize his king. For all James exulted in his newfound freedom, he seemed unable to take advantage of it – or, at least, this is the interpretation he was willing to let observers construe.

Instead, what appeared to the outside world to have happened was that Arran had simply stepped into the shoes of the deceased Esmé. Though there is no suggestion that he was possessed of those 'French fruits' which had drawn such scandal – the relationship never drew accusations of sexual impropriety – he was nevertheless 'a scorner of religion' who was quite prepared to press his boot on the neck of anyone who opposed the new regime.[2] He carried himself, it was reported in 1584, 'with a princely presence and gait' – but there lay the problem: he was not a prince and yet his pride and ambition were overweening, and he was quite prepared to govern Scotland as though he were its sovereign lord. James, however, was not quite a crowned puppet. He was aware that Arran was a useful political tool – and lightning rod – in the thorny business of governance. There thus was born a curious Scottish government, with, at its head, a young king deeply smarting from his recent humiliating captivity, energetic, and eager to rule – and, at his side, an apparently all-powerful counsellor who, for all his faults, was possessed of the kind of ruthless political ability necessary to rule a kingdom seething with rising and falling factions.

What was unclear, at first, was what that regime would intend in terms of international relations – particularly with England, France, and the captive Queen of Scots.

*

Sometime in the early 1580s, Elizabeth of England went through the menopause. This marked an end to her long policy – which she had operated with consummate skill – of playing the international marriage market, and it marked her rebirth (largely against her will) as a warrior queen. So too did it refresh the succession question, which had known its last great flap in the 1560s.

Since the days of Thomas Seymour, when she had been only the Lady Elizabeth, an illegitimate royal daughter and sister, she had only grown more attractive as a bride. After the successive deaths of Edward VI and Mary I, and her own accession to the English throne, she had, indeed, become possessed of one of the most desirable hands in Europe. Although, in 1559, she had announced to the House of Commons that 'in the end, this shall be for me sufficient, that a marble stone shall declare that a Queen, having reigned such a time, lived and died a virgin', no one had listened.[3] Elizabeth shrewdly took advantage of this collective male deafness and used the elusive prize of her bridal bed to extract maximum political capital for England.

For years, the English queen had fostered good relations with the Valois of France (the matriarch of which, Catherine de Medici, had never ceased hoping Elizabeth would accept one of her sons as a husband). She had entertained suits from Philip II, her former brother-in-law; from Scotland; from Sweden; from Austria; and from amongst her own English nobility. What set her apart from her father, in terms of foreign policy, was that she was never acquisitive of other kingdoms; she preferred, wherever possible, to focus her military exploits on enforcing English governance on territories she believed legally or rightly pertained to England's Crown (Ireland – which Henry VIII had raised from an English-ruled lordship to a kingdom – and Calais being two obvious examples). Her job, as she saw it, was to protect English interests. From that perspective, it was always better the Scots should fight amongst themselves than they should collectively seek allies on the continent. It was her good fortune that the Scottish Crown was, throughout much of her reign, weak, and the political community divided and open to bargain-basement foreign bribery.

This meant both that she could save money and that she sought to influence Scottish affairs with soft words, threats, promises, or an ill-advised schoolmarmish attitude of seniority (where Henry VIII had insisted on putting Edinburgh and its environs to the flame and sword). What allowed her such power over the northern kingdom was not, as Henry VIII had insisted, a shaky, supposedly ancient legal right to suzerainty, but the fact that she had in her gift the right to declare her successor. This had led Mary Queen of Scots to enter into a policy of Anglo-Scottish amity in the 1560s, with the carrot being recognition of the Stuart claim to the English succession. So too had it led successive Protestant, pro-English Scottish governments to give England's queen almost treacherous levels of access to domestic policy. Only when the Stuart sovereigns acted against what she considered English interests, or when extra-British influences (such as the irruption of Esmé Stuart) were brought to bear on relations did this general drift towards Scottish servitude really halt – and, when it did, Elizabeth was driven to abandon the carrot and bring out the stick.

One of the chief wielders of the English government's stick was the inflexibly Protestant, fiercely intelligent Sir Francis Walsingham: the queen's long-standing secretary and unofficial spymaster. He was despatched – very much against his will – to Scotland in September 1583, with a delegation of eighty Englishmen. However, both Elizabeth and the dyspeptic Walsingham were badly misguided in their approach. The English queen had apparently instructed her man to act in as hectoring and imperious a manner as possible, likely as a means of re-establishing English authority over Scottish affairs. Not helping matters was the fact that Walsingham was perennially ill and in almost constant pain, neither of which can have been helped by the long journey north.

As ordered, the spymaster absolutely refused any private dealings with Arran. On gaining an audience with James, he proceeded to berate the king for daring to change his counsellors without having received his English cousin's blessing. Quite why he or Elizabeth thought that this show of power would do anything to win any monarch to their way of thinking is difficult to explain – it can only be imagined that the queen assumed that flexing her muscle would cow the Scottish king into remembering who was the senior partner – and who held those precious English succession rights – in their relationship.

James, with all of the confidence won from his escape from captivity, was in no mood for condescension. In a display of royal hauteur equal to that of his cousin, he, 'with a kind of jollity said he was an absolute King, and therefore prayed [Elizabeth] that he might take such order with his subjects as should best like himself, and that [she] would be no more curious to examine the affection of his counsellors' than he was of hers.[4] In this he was quite right, and it is difficult not to admire his dishing out of some home truths.

The reality was, however, that Elizabeth, by dint of her history of interfering in Scottish politics (with cash handouts, where needed), and with a number of powerful Scots in her pocket, was a bear not to be poked. She had long demonstrated how capable she was of causing trouble for the Stuart sovereigns, and this public slap in the face was something she was unwilling to let pass.

Her method of retaliation was characteristically mischievous. She threw her support behind the disgraced Lords Enterprisers, chiefly Mar and the Master of Glamis (he of the leg thrown across the doorway to prevent the king's escape during the Ruthven Raid). Angus (who had chosen exile in England first after failing to prevent Morton's execution, and again after James was liberated from his Gowrie captivity), also remained in the English armoury. Added to this cabal of malcontents were the almost-forgotten Lords John and Claud Hamilton, who had been implicated in the deaths of James's first two regents, and who had been forced to flee Scotland in 1579, when Morton had come after them. Both had sought a return to power, and both had fetched up in England, where they were considered useful tools by its wrathful queen, who allowed them to travel to France.

In April 1584, the plan took shape. Mar, who had been haunting Edinburgh since sneaking illegally back into Scotland, organised his ragtag faction and marched on Stirling Castle, to which he had some claim as hereditary keeper. Arran's military experience, however, proved of use to the king; together, he and James amassed a 12,000-strong force and advanced on the castle, which quickly surrendered. Although the captain of its garrison was hanged, Mar and his fellows had already fled. Ironically enough, despite having been foremost amongst the original Lords Enterprisers, Gowrie had taken no part in Mar's English-sponsored, hare-brained scheme. Nevertheless, he was taken up before Stirling capitulated, and James was able to get his revenge for the Ruthven Raid when the man he had made an earl went to the block in May. Reportedly, Arran helped achieve the conviction, promising Gowrie mercy if he confessed to having supported the latest tumult – and then reneging on that promise. If true, this piece of chicanery would not have been out of character. Nor was Gowrie's evil genius forgotten; Cunningham of Drumquhassle, who had persuaded the earl into leading the Ruthven Raid, lost his head in 1585.

For the moment, with victory against the rebels came the sharing out of honours, the better to impress upon the world – and England – the security of the Scottish government and the fact that the King of Scots was no schoolboy to be lectured by his fellow monarchs. Arran became chancellor, Montrose the treasurer, and Maitland of Thirlestane gained the secretaryship. Lest this turn of events should give the perpetually disapproving Kirk ammunition, James summoned the preacher Andrew Melvill (who was rapidly becoming the Knox to James's Mary) to explain a vitriolic sermon he had delivered. Refusing to acknowledge secular authority over his tongue, the minister and his like-minded peers were forced to flee, as the Mar plotters had done, into English exile (the act of which indicates that their indignation was as much political as strictly religious, given the English Church was also riddled with what they perceived as the structural errors infecting their Kirk).

To further stake its authority in spiritual affairs, the king's new, muscular government granted James supremacy over the Kirk, with the right to appoint bishops. Here it is difficult not to see James seeking an English style of religious polity. It has become something of an historical cliché to point out that the two countries' Reformations differed in that England's came from the top down, driven by the monarch and sweeping over willing (and washing away unwilling) clerics and laymen. But Scotland's Reformation had certainly not come from the bottom up. Rather, it had been driven by evangelical clerics, who had won over swaths of the civic middle classes before preaching downwards and reaching upwards. By these means, the Kirk had gained sufficient mercantile, popular, and noble support to try to push aside the Crown. This was naturally intolerable to the Erastian-minded James – and in declaring Crown supremacy, he was attempting to claim royal authority over all estates, temporal and spiritual. To not do so would be to allow a dangerous rival power to the Crown to divide the loyalties of his subjects.

Along with this newfound spiritual authority, the infrastructure of the Kirk, which had never been formally ratified, was declared: episcopacy was in, 'pretended [false] presbyteries' were out, and

General Assemblies (those national meetings of Kirk elders, which had been deciding ecclesiastical policy since the Reformation) were illegal unless specifically called by the sovereign. Unsurprisingly, this legislation soon earned the sobriquet 'the Black Acts' amongst the Presbyterian elite, who saw themselves being castrated and tyrannised by an upstart earthly authority and his irreligious chancellor.

It was from around this time – in August 1584 – that one of the most famous and illustrative pen portraits of the king dates. Henry III's ambassador, Monsieur de Fontenay, arrived, likely with the secret mission of ensuring that James's heart remained French, notwithstanding the death of Esmé. Outwardly, Fontenay's goal was to gauge the king's attitude to the cobweb-covered Association with his mother. In a letter to Mary's secretary, Fontenay's brother-in-law, Claude Nau, he wrote that James

> is for his age the premier prince who has ever lived. He has three qualities of soul in perfection. He apprehends and understands everything. He judges reasonably. He carries much in his memory and for a long time. In his questions, he is lively and perceptive, and sound in his answers. In any matter which is being debated, be it religion or any other thing, he believes and always maintains what seems to him to be true and just, so that in several disputes on religion I have seen him take the cause for Monsieur de Fentray [a Catholic] . . . He is learned in many tongues, sciences, and affairs of state, more so, I dare say, than any others of his realm. In brief, he has a marvellous mind, filled with virtuous grandeur and a good opinion of himself.[5]

Part of this was pure flattery. Yet we can glimpse in the description some of the successes of Buchanan's – and Peter Young's – efforts in educating the younger king. The prodigiousness of memory, the languages and scientific knowledge: all of these were the products of the Stirling schoolroom. The certainty in his own beliefs and arguments, too, stemmed from his lessons in dialectics and rhetorical debate; in time, this would graduate to insistence on the veracity of his convictions and an utter inability to accept viewpoints and arguments which ran counter to what he had worked out to be truthful and correct.

In terms of faults, Fontenay was as assiduous in his description. James, he wrote, 'hates the dance and music in general, like all fopperies of the Court, be they amorous talk or curiosities of dress' and evinced a particular abhorrence of earrings. This is problematic, and one can only assume that the young king had decided to present himself as a model of anti-courtly virtue; either his previous efforts on the dancefloor and his employment of musicians were shows, or the attitude he displayed before Fontenay was. Given that, in future, the king would show a marked fascination with 'fopperies of the Court' (attending masques and plays; indulging mawkishly in amorous talk; and favouring men – though not women – who knew how to deck themselves out in the elaborate finery of the period), we can assume the latter. The possibility exists, of course, that James was undergoing a godly fit – or hoping the world would think he was. In 1573, the General Assembly had shorn Scotland of all holidays save the Sabbath, which led to women in Aberdeen being rebuked for 'playing, dancing, and singing filthy carols on Yule Day'.[6] In 1583, five men were publicly shamed in Glasgow for celebrating Christmas Day. A general air of cheerlessness, it seems, was very much in vogue. As James had once been commanded to be a faithful son of the Kirk, now he was striving to be taken seriously as its master.

More infamously, Fontenay wrote that 'his manners are aggressive and very uncivil, both in speaking, eating, clothes, games and conversation in the company of women. He never stays still in one place, taking a singular pleasure in walking up and down, but his carriage is ungainly, his steps erratic and vagabond, even in his own chamber. He loves the chase above all the pleasures of this world, living in the saddle for six hours on end . . . he has a feeble body even if he is not delicate. In sum, to put it in a word, he is an old young man.'

The lack of manners is understandable, given that he had never been provided or taught a gracious, princely model of decorum (although it remains a failing in Esmé and his French retinue that no effort – or no progress – had been made in improving the king's manners). His lack of grace in the company of women is more understandable; even at the height of the duke's supremacy, the Scottish court had for too long been what we would now call 'laddish', full of bawdy jests and muck-splattered hunting boots. Fontenay's comment on James's graceless gait, however, has become the focus of much (largely unwarranted) attention, being inflated into a splay-footed, grotesque parody of a walk. However, the description gives away little and serves only to suggest a restive teenager – still in the process of developing physically – who loped around the room in high dudgeon. It does not suggest a limping, lurching, comic figure. Indeed, given James's 'six hours' at a stretch bouncing around the Scottish countryside in the saddle, it is a wonder he could walk at all.

Chief amongst the ambassador's political assessment of the king were three chief defects: 'The first is his ignorance and failure to appreciate his poverty and lack of strength, overrating himself and despising other princes. The second is that he loves indiscreetly and obstinately, despite the disapprobation of his subjects. The third is that he is too idle and too little concerned about business, too addicted to his pleasure, principally that of the chase, leaving the conduct of business to the Earl of Arran, Montrose, and the Secretary [Maitland].'

The first was real enough and indeed well spotted; it became King James's defining fault, in that his lack of financial acumen was a hallmark of his reigns. Even at this stage, however, it was evidently manifest: he had been warned as early as May 1580 that he was £40,000 Scots in debt, and yet he had gone on to hand over state jewels to his lover. Throughout his life, he continued in that vein, exulting – rather pathetically – in lavishing cash he did not have and gifts he could not afford on people whose joy in them delighted him. But not every penny went on gifts given for pleasure. To maintain and project his princely state, the king had to keep a sprawling royal household. The accounts for 1582 indicate that this had grown to include two Masters Household; clerks and accountants; twenty-four gentlemen-in-ordinary; six gentlemen-in-extraordinary (i.e., specially placed over and above those required); servers, cupbearers, carvers, and valets (who attended the king's publicly taken meals); pages and grooms (who lit the fires); wardrobe masters, valets, and a tailor; a surgeon and a physician; musicians; preceptors and ministers; seamstresses and laundresses; door porters and their guards; staff of the great halls (charged with seeing to the glittering array of utensils and drinking vessels); an enormous kitchen staff (comprising cooks, pastry chefs, cellarers, larder keepers, and pantrymen); and a stable staff (with masters, horse-keepers, lackeys, furriers, and saddlers). The expense was prodigious. So too was the cost of distributing gifts and patronage to keep this army of servants loyal.

That he had an overblown sense of his own importance, too, was unsurprising. It was the natural reaction against those teachings which had sought to stress his relative unimportance in comparison with religious authorities. It was also inflated, reportedly, by Arran, who had supposedly 'put the opinion of absolute power in his Majesty's head'.[7] For the dislike of other princes, we can probably thank his recent brush with Elizabeth and Walsingham, which had merely represented the latest and most overt attempt to subordinate his authority. Certainly, the king would later be willing to claim – inaccurately – that he could live securely amongst his people whilst Elizabeth hid away in fear; and in 1585 he felt bold enough to tell the minister James Gibson that he did 'not give a turd for thy preaching!'

That James was addicted to the chase – he could never resist hunting with hounds, prizing it above all other forms of hunting, and certainly above hawking – is another aspect of his character that has become legendary. Yet the hours, days, and weeks spent on horseback did not discernibly hamper state operations – a fact which, even at the time, James was keen to point out, claiming that he 'could do as much business in one hour as others would in a day'.[8] Further, when he chose, the king could be remarkably business-like; he once complained at the lack of attendance of his Exchequer officials with an exasperated, 'I have been Friday, Saturday, and this day waiting upon the direction of my affairs, and never man coming!'[9]

Nevertheless, the inescapable fact is that his contemporaries, from Fontenay onwards, viewed his dedication to leisure pursuits as a problem, and the criticisms would grow to such weight that it ought to be conceded as a fault.

Of the second criticism – the king's indiscreet and obstinate love affairs, and the condemnation they drew – more must be said. As has been seen, the dependence on Esmé Stuart had indeed brought the censure of Kirk and statesmen. However, the duke had been dead for over a year at this point. Who, then, was the king loving indiscreetly?

By this time, a new face had arrived on the scene: Patrick, Master of Gray. Gray was the son of Patrick, 5th Lord Gray, and had been married briefly in 1575 to Elizabeth Lyon, a daughter of the 8th Lord Glamis. However, this marriage failed – for unspecified reasons – and Gray had moved to France, where he converted to Catholicism, inveigled himself into the service of Marian exile Archbishop James Beaton, and announced himself in favour of Mary Queen of Scots' cause, earning her trust – and her money – as an agent working towards the Association. Beaton and Mary, sadly, had misplaced their trust.

Gray returned to Scotland in 1583 (in the company of Esmé's son, Ludovic, 2nd Duke of Lennox) and immediately won James's affection – likely because he was, apparently, physically attractive, being 'pre-eminently beautiful' if 'too feminine to please some tastes'.[10] Indeed, Fontenay openly warned of Gray's influence in his August report; in October, the young master was appointed a Gentleman of the Chamber, Master of the Wardrobe, and a Privy Councillor. This allowed him a high degree of access to the king. Needless to say, Gray's religious and political affinities – lightly as he wore both – assured him the 'disapprobation' of plenty of James's subjects, and eyes were trained on this potential successor to Esmé in the king's affections. Luckily for James, there existed a time-honoured model by which he could indulge those affections: the court favourite. This position outwardly meant no more than friendship or special confidence. In reality, it was malleable enough to suit the inclinations of individual sovereigns. However, as James knew from his history lessons, Scottish favourites were seldom popular: James III's had been hanged by rebellious nobles, and James V's failure at Solway Moss had been derided as the fault of his hated favourite, Oliver Sinclair. Favourites were also invariably described, in our James's case, as 'minions' or 'bedfellows'. The latter was not an unusual description, as bed-sharing was endemic even in royal households. However, given the weight of evidence of the king's tastes, it would be naïve (or wilfully blind) to imagine a man as effusive and uninhibited in his affections as James was content to cuddle.

On the subject of Mary herself, Fontenay hedged. In an addendum to his lengthy letter describing the King, he added, 'At one thing I am astonished: that he has never made any inquiry regarding the Queen, neither of her health, nor of her treatments, nor of her servants, nor of her living and eating, nor of her recreation, nor any like thing; nevertheless, I know that he honours her much in his heart.'

The final clause was almost certainly more a politic addition than a true belief. In the conference with Walsingham, too, was apparently forgotten – or at least diplomatically unmentioned – the sad figure of Mary Queen of Scots. Both James and Elizabeth would certainly have liked her to fade away without comment. But Walsingham, the proactive and outspoken wing of the Protestant political nation in England, Marian supporters on the continent, and Mary herself were hardly about to let that happen. Walsingham and his fellow Puritans, indeed, wanted the captive queen publicly condemned as an example of papist harlotry, with a bloody execution to follow.

In the same month that Fontenay wrote his description, Queen Elizabeth despatched another delegation northwards, this time led by Henry Carey, Lord Hunsdon, one of her Boleyn cousins. Clearly, she had decided that, the stick having failed, it was time to redeploy the carrot. Unlike Walsingham, Hunsdon was empowered to treat with Arran, which he did at Berwick. The wind suddenly began to blow favourably again in the direction of Anglo-Scottish amity. Reading this, the Master of Gray abandoned his supposed

Catholic-inspired partiality for the Queen of Scots and encouraged James to consider her a lost cause. Gray had, by this time, realised that his position made him a man worth paying off, and he was quite willing to sell his influence to every and any bidder. This was good news for the English, whose goal now was to end any idea of the Association, establish an unbreakable alliance with the Scots which left the hapless Mary out in the cold, and therefore – from Walsingham's perspective – lay the groundwork for finally ridding the world of the unwanted queen. Coldly, James did as the forces around him were encouraging, and abandoned his mother to her fate, ending the correspondence with her, which had begun under Esmé, in the autumn of 1584.

The diplomatic bags which passed up and down Britain were not, however, short of letters for long. In early 1585, Elizabeth despatched Edward Wotton north. She knew as well as anyone the state of her cousin's finances, and, niggardly though she could be, she had decided that offering him a pension was worth assuring herself of his friendship – or at least his neutrality in her looming war with Spain. The irregularity of both the sum – it fluctuated, but averaged out at £3,000 a year – and its arrival was a particularly neat move in keeping James relatively inclined to good behaviour in the hopes of more.

As importantly, she and he began to correspond directly. James was, at this time, developing a taste for the finer things in life – in May, on escaping plague in Edinburgh, he enjoyed a banquet and play at Dirleton Castle – and was keen to continue living lavishly. This required money and, so he believed, the English treasury was full of it. By August, he was addressing Elizabeth as 'madame and mother'.[11] This was hardly to her taste, as she much preferred to use the diplomatic conceit of siblinghood in her correspondence with fellow monarchs. Still, the nineteen-year-old James appeared to revel – in tones of wide-eyed innocence – in language which drew attention to his childless, fifty-one-year-old cousin's advancing age. More pleasing to the English queen was the king's announcement, in March, that the Association, which had caused so much intrigue in Britain and beyond, was 'neither [to] be granted nor spoken of hereafter'.[12] Mary Stuart's dreams had been shattered. Rather sadly, she blamed not 'my child' but Gray, whom she claimed had made James write the hateful letter she received informing her of her abandonment. She probably could not imagine that things were about to get worse.

6

The Serpent Slain

James, for the moment, could smile to himself. Already, he could hear the jingle of coins dropping into his purse. Soon enough, dark satins and silks would be out and pastels with gold and silver threads would be in. Yet, officially, the purpose of what the English called the 'gratuity' (or, as he termed it, the 'annuity') that the King of Scots was to receive from southern coffers was the establishment of an official league of Protestant British nations. In mid-August, he wrote of his desire that 'the conclusion of the amity and league go forward, whereunto I do already fully assent'.[1] In July, the newfound harmony between the kingdoms was threatened by the killing of Lord Francis Russell, son of the Earl of Bedford, by Scottish warden of the Middle Marches, Sir Thomas Kerr of Ferniehirst. From tragedy, however, came opportunity. Kerr had been appointed to his post under Arran and, by inflating what was one of any number of Borders skirmishes into a threat to the amity, Elizabeth's man Wotton was able to achieve another English goal: pushing out the chancellor.

Amidst floods of tears – for public consumption – James ordered Arran's arrest and a week-long imprisonment at St Andrews Castle. Gray, who saw an opportunity to further his own influence with his royal lover, immediately set about securing the high-riding chancellor's more lasting disgrace. This was especially important because the handsome young Gray had recently remarried – this time to one of James's cousins, Lady Mary Stewart. However far he had gone with James and whatever the precise nature of his own preferences, homosexual activity was not considered a lifestyle choice; men were largely expected to marry. Yet Gray could not know that his sovereign would later prove himself entirely amenable to – even encouraging of – his favourites taking wives, so long as it did not keep them from dancing attendance on himself. There thus still existed in Gray's mind the possibility that James might turn away from his embraces knowing he now shared them with a wife. Consolidating his position was critical, and ousting Arran would prove useful. Early efforts to arrange the chancellor's assassination (which only came to light later) proved unsuccessful. There was, however, a woman south of the border who was happy to help Gray if it meant increasing her own influence in Scotland.

As always, Elizabeth was absolutely attuned to events. News of Arran's tottering state was brought south by Gray, who spent some months in England spilling his guts about Mary's continental intrigues and working to further destabilise the all-powerful chancellor. Consequently, the English queen encouraged him to return to Scotland to ensure that Arran's parlous state was tipped into outright downfall; additionally, she released those lords who had been forced into English exile, ostensibly so that they might travel into Germany. Needless to say, Mar, Angus, the Master of Glamis, and the Hamilton brothers eschewed a jaunt to the continent and beat a path straight to Stirling Castle, their religious differences set aside, there to confront the man whose rise to power had kept them out of it. They arrived in early November, having built up an army along the way. Surprised, Stirling was unprepared to mount resistance – indeed, James and his chief minister had barely had time to reconcile following the latter's loose house arrest. The canny Arran knew at once that he had been had and, after attempting to kill the young man he viewed – rightly – as a double-dealing turncoat, he attempted to tell the king something of the nature of his new lover. Gray, however, had far more power over James's mind than did the self-aggrandising earl. Outflanked, Arran beat a hasty retreat, fleeing Stirling. Gray locked the gates behind him lest James should have a change of heart and follow.

It is unlikely that James was sorry to see his chancellor go. Arran had been useful, but there had never existed the kind of emotional bond between king and minister as had existed with Esmé Stuart. Moreover, no king, especially one with James's sense of self-importance, appreciated a subject displaying such hauteur as Arran had shown. Nevertheless, the king was not minded to be converged upon by a gang of exiled rebels. Grudgingly, he went to the negotiating table, receiving the apparently repentant exiles in a conference in Stirling's frosty Great Hall. Despite the usual protestations of loyalty, the men who had chased away Arran had demands, not least of which was the chancellor's permanent exclusion from the Scottish body politic. This James agreed with equanimity, stripping the once mighty counsellor of the chancellorship and his earldom (and, thus deprived, Arran retired from the scene and lived in obscurity as Sir James Stewart, only to be ignominiously murdered in the course of a private feud ten years later).

The king was asked also to allow those ministers who had fled to England to return and resume preaching, as well as to agree not to enforce the Black Acts of the previous year. On both counts James acquiesced, although he insisted Andrew Melvill be given the thankless job of scouring the north for Jesuits rather than being allowed to fire off insults and recriminations from St Andrews' pulpits, and that the Act which had granted him supremacy remain on the books as a legal fiction. He would also be recognised as having a role in convening General Assemblies, though these were established as annual meetings, whether he liked it or not.

Determined to make the best of an unasked-for upheaval, James had demands of his own. He wanted his apologetic rebels to put their money where their mouths were, re-embracing them into the political fold on the proviso of future good behaviour. The rebels agreed, and it was time for good faith all round. Glamis's doorway-blocking abilities gained their reward, as he received a seat on the Privy Council and captaincy of the King's Guard. Lord Claud Hamilton, with Guise backing, continued to agitate without success for the Catholic cause, but he nevertheless went on to receive the lordship of Paisley with its semi-ruinous abbey and thriving burgh-in-barony. In December, Lord John Hamilton was restored to his former lands, given a place on the Privy Council and the captaincy of Dumbarton Castle. Although he would quarrel over precedence at court with his former ally Angus over the course of the next two years, he would remain a loyal king's man, receiving the marquessate of Hamilton, earldom of Arran, and lordship of Aven in 1599. Mar, who had enjoyed such a chequered relationship with the king, beginning in the schoolroom at Stirling, would take his reconciliation with James seriously and become one of the Crown's most devoted servants.

A settlement had been achieved and the decks were thus cleared for the formalisation of the Anglo-Scottish Treaty of Berwick. Although James attempted to insert some recognition of his succession claims, Elizabeth – who was an old hand at evading just that – demurred. Her counteroffer was the inclusion of the words 'nothing shall be done to the prejudice of any title [James] may pretend unto this crown, unless by the said King's unkind usage towards her Majesty which, God forbid, he shall justly deserve the contrary'.[2] Neatly, easily, she had used James's impatience and greed for her throne to buy his good behaviour. She knew, and he knew, that his succession was apt to be supported by Protestant courtiers on both sides of the border, but she was as keen to downplay that fact as he was to capitalise on it. Not surprisingly, she wrote north of her glee at James's 'gladsome acceptance of my offered amity together with the desire you seem to have engraven in your mind to make merits correspondent [i.e., to return the friendship]'.[3] As ever, the English and Scottish sovereigns were locked in their curious embrace: one based on shared religion and the overweening threat of Catholic Spain, but soured by fragile trust on both sides. As the English government had desired, so had James behaved. The truth was, though, that securing the King of Scots on the payroll was only a prelude to its – or at least its intelligence services' – true intentions.

By anyone's measure, Mary Queen of Scots had been sold out. James had excited her hopes only to dash them, and in the cruellest way: for money (which, admittedly, he badly needed) and via dealings with the woman and state who had imprisoned her under shaky legality for nearly two decades. In her despair, Mary raged at her son's lack of loyalty and spoke darkly of willing her succession rights not to him but to the King of Spain's daughter, who could claim descent from England's John of Gaunt. Rather than doing anything concrete, however, she lapsed into fantasies of escape and fell ever deeper into religion (having truly awoken to it in a way she never had during her personal rule).

Those fantasies of escape were what really interested her enemies. Spiderlike, Walsingham set about building a web in which to decisively entrap her. His mission, as he saw it, was to lure the Scottish serpent into a plot against Elizabeth's life, which could be discovered and condemned – and Mary with it – before it met its goal. Thus began the activation of a slippery agent, Gilbert Gifford, who was sent to Mary's prison at Chartley, where he posed as a friend. Having been deprived of outside news, the queen naïvely accepted him and welcomed the 'secret' channel of communication he proposed, whereby letters would be smuggled in and out of the manor house via beer barrels. With this means of communication opened, all the spymaster had to do was wait – and he did not have to do so for long.

Alerted to the fact that Mary could now be spoken with again, the Jesuit John Ballard enlisted a group of disaffected Catholic gentlemen (Anthony Babington chief amongst them) and convinced them of the moral and religious rectitude of assassinating Elizabeth and replacing her with the Scottish queen. This crew – not overfurnished with a sense of reality – quickly put their plans in writing and submitted them to Mary via the Gifford channel. In principle, she agreed to them, happily unaware that every letter in and out of Chartley was being decoded and pored over by Walsingham and his men. In her acquiescence, the government agents had everything they needed to condemn her, and they had only to forge postscripts in an attempt to get written documentation of the names of the men involved in the plot.

Mary Stuart, veteran prisoner, thorn in the side to Elizabeth and her government and political embarrassment to her Protestant son, was doomed. Yet, for all his delight – a rare pleasure in a life increasingly racked by pain – in her downfall, Walsingham could not rest on his laurels. He had demonstrated, to his own satisfaction, that the Scottish queen had plotted against his own sovereign's life. But he could neither force Elizabeth to execute Mary nor be sure whether the Anglo-Scottish amity would survive such a step. Eyes turned northwards.

On hearing that his mother had been accused of complicity in another scheme to assassinate Elizabeth, James was more annoyed than anything. According to the new French ambassador – who was naturally sympathetic to a former queen consort of France – in September 1586 the king tutted that 'his mother might drink the ale and beere which her selfe had brewed'.[4] In other words, she was to be left to face the consequences of her own actions. At this stage, it was unclear exactly what those consequences would be – James, undoubtedly, did not think Elizabeth would go as far as execution; his solution was that Mary be kept even more strictly, so that she might 'meddle with nothing but prayer and the serving of God'.[5]

It became clear by October that a full-scale trial was intended for the Queen of Scots, but Gray still apparently thought his king 'content [that] the law should go forward, her life being safe, and would gladly wish all foreign princes should know how evil she had used herself towards [Elizabeth], and that she received favour through her clemency'.[6] James clearly hoped that some good would come of this: Mary might be tried, spared, but subsequently tainted in the eyes of those foreign powers who had backed her – whilst Elizabeth would win golden opinions for her forbearance. He was in an unpleasant position himself. He had no personal feelings towards his mother beyond the fascination she had held for him in his younger years. Now, on the one hand, she stood in the way of his security as sole king and was better gone, and, on the other, failure to attempt to save her would win him universal condemnation and humiliation, it being both ungodly for a son to abandon his mother and a slap in the face of his nation to allow its quondam queen to be slain like a criminal subject of another kingdom. Scottish opinion was, indeed, already turning against England. Though Mary had faded from many minds and her name had been blackened by popular preachers, national pride chafed at the indignity being done her.

Nevertheless, the trial began at Fotheringhay (where Mary had been moved in September) in October 1586. The Scottish queen denied every charge and made a quite correct technical argument that she was not subject to the laws of England and certainly could not, as though she were a subject, have legally committed treason against a woman who was not her sovereign but her peer. But the time for legal niceties was past. The commissioners who had tried her met again in the Star Chamber at Westminster and declared her guilty of seeking Elizabeth's 'death and destruction'.

Obviously, James was required to send some form of representation south. His choice speaks volumes: he picked Archibald Douglas, the man who had suffocated Darnley (though James probably did not know it, given he allowed the fellow to be given a show trial in early 1586 and exonerated) and gone on to a career as a spy for Walsingham. Amongst Douglas's secret instructions, bizarrely, was a request to make a proposal of marriage between James and Elizabeth: a revival of the Lords Enterprisers' wildcard offer back in 1583. Such a marriage – between a twenty-year-old king hoping for heirs and his post-menopausal, fifty-two-year-old cousin – would have brought no benefit to either nation. Elizabeth and her council, after presumably lifting their jaws from the floor, politely demurred. Likely they realised the proposal was a crude attempt by the Scottish king to throw in a last-minute diplomatic distraction and thereby halt proceedings against his mother (who would, if such a *mésalliance* had come to pass, have become Elizabeth's mother-in-law, despite being younger and a prisoner awaiting condemnation). Elizabeth's final – and often ignored – offer of marriage thus came from a conniving King James; her long history of courtships and proposals ended not with a bang but a whimper.

At any rate, Douglas wisely did not press the issue, because James undoubtedly did not wish him to. Instead, he reawakened his relationship with Walsingham. The spymaster greeted his old agent warmly and instructed him that it would be better for both countries if Mary was executed without fuss or fanfare. Douglas relayed this message north, where James's panic rose about the runaway speed of affairs. Better heads and stouter hearts were needed if he wished to match wits with Walsingham and find some acceptable, bloodless solution.

Unfortunately, the most able men in Scotland were reluctant to become involved. The obvious choice was Maitland of Thirlestane, who had once been a Marian and whose brother had had such intimate knowledge of the accused queen. Maitland was, like most effective politicians, intelligent, cunning, and devious (and, like most politicians, effective or otherwise, widely disliked). Yet he refused to go south, probably aware that entangling himself in Mary's business had led to his brother's death, his own disgrace, and trouble for just about everyone who made the effort. Nor would the self-interested Gray go – probably because he knew he risked losing the king's affections if he tried and failed to secure the miracle of a peaceful outcome. Hurriedly, one William Keith of Delny, a former valet and minor official who had begun collecting the king's English annuity, was chosen. In his dispatch bag on the journey south was a strongly worded letter from a harried King James, which instructed Douglas to 'reserve up yourself [dilly dally] no longer in the earnest dealing for my mother for you have done it too long, and think not that any dealing will do good if her life be lost, for then adieu with [to] my dealing with that estate [England]'.[7]

This, really, was his worry – if Mary was to lose her head, he would be forced by political pressure to cut off Anglo-Scottish relations (and the England-to-Scotland flow of cash) in retaliation. His fear was not for his mother, but for the potential political fireworks which might erupt in Scotland if she was seen to be a victim of English hostility.

Keith met with Douglas, and on 5 November they had an audience with Elizabeth, in which they attempted to play for time, requesting a delay in proceedings against Mary until Scotland could send Privy Councillors south. The English queen played for time herself, promising an answer in five days. Before that time was up, she provided her parliament – most members of which were baying for Mary's blood – with her famous 'answer answerless'. In truth, Elizabeth was as much in a quandary about what to do as James. In her agony of indecision, she even recalled Leicester from the Low Countries for counsel. Undoubtedly, she wanted the Queen of Scots dead – the woman had given her a recurring headache for decades and had turned it into a permanent migraine when she had entered England – but she did not want the blood of an anointed sovereign on her hands. Nevertheless, she could not deny the outcome of the trial, and had to inform the Queen of Scots that she had been judged guilty and must prepare her soul for death.

This news also reached her son. Gray wrote south to Douglas, noting that 'the King nor no man ever believed the matter would have gone so far'. He included instructions on what was to be done: a warning was to be delivered to Elizabeth that James 'can no longer remain on good terms with the Queen or estate of that realm' in the event of Mary's execution – if he attempted to, 'he will find it hard to keep peace with the realm'.[8] Privately, however, Douglas was busily assuring the Earl of Leicester that the Scottish king was merely putting on a show – and that if Mary lost her head, James would do nothing.

Near the end of November, James took up his own pen, writing a powerful but ill-advised letter explicitly intended to reach Elizabeth's eyes. It blamed the English parliament for the miserable state of affairs, but did not spare its mistress: 'A strange example indeed, and so very rare, as for my part, I never read nor heard of the like practice in such a case. I am sorry that . . . [Elizabeth] has suffered this to proceed to my dishonour, and so contrary to her good fame, as by subjects' mouths to condemn a sovereign prince descended of all hands of the best blood in Europe. King Henry VIII's reputation was never prejudged in anything but in the beheading of his bedfellow [Anne Boleyn: Elizabeth's mother], but yet that tragedy was far inferior to this, if it should proceed as seems to be intended.'[9]

This was meant as both a warning and a reminder of the perceived cruelty of Elizabeth's actions and the danger it posed both immediately (to Anglo-Scottish relations) and in the long-term, when her name would be as inextricably linked with tyrannical murder as her father's had been. It was also incredibly provocative, no doubt due to desperation. Elizabeth, publicly at least, had always venerated her father and avoided the subject of her mother. The insecurity of her sovereignty, which had in part led to so many attempts against her life, stemmed not just from Henry VIII's execution of Anne Boleyn, but from the annulment her father had pushed through via his reformist Archbishop of Canterbury, Thomas Cranmer. Elizabeth's resultant illegitimacy had never been legally overturned, with the queen preferring to let sleeping dogs lie. Her Protestant subjects were largely willing to forget the legal fact of her illegitimacy, putting their faith in parliament's acknowledgement of her queenship and her anointment; yet some Catholics at home and plenty abroad were quite willing to shake the Tudor closet for skeletons left over from her father's time. To have her upstart Scottish cousin drag them out, especially when she was in the throes of agonised self-doubt, was intolerable.

Nevertheless, James directed Keith to show Elizabeth the letter, that she might 'see the inward parts of my heart where she should see a great jewel of honesty towards her locked up in a coffer of perplexity, she only having the key which by her good behaviour in this case may open the same'.[10] This elaborate construction merely built insult upon injury. On hearing James's words, the English queen fell into a passionate Tudor rage. When it subsided, she sought to regain the advantage, sensing as she did a means of deflecting blame from her own part in the unfolding tragedy. She coolly sent Keith a note informing him that if his king had not sent 'so strange and unseasonable a message as did directly touch her noble father and herself, she would have delayed proceedings' against his mother.[11] This was a lie, but it would be a useful, politic one. It was now, according to Elizabeth, James's fault that Mary was facing imminent execution. The opportunity for the Scottish king to send noblemen south to plead for his mother had passed; England's queen announced that she would accept only commoners to argue the doomed woman's case.

Gray could no longer avoid implication. James despatched him south, on the basis that his father, the 5th Lord Gray, and not he, was the nobleman. Accompanying him was Sir Robert Melville of Murdocairnie, that veteran Marian who had enjoyed pre-eminence under the Arran government; George Young, a diplomat and clerk of the Privy Council whom James had made Archdeacon of St Andrews in 1584; and Sir Alexander Stewart.

Gray's mission was genuine. It involved pleading for some non-violent means of proceeding against Mary whilst issuing surety for her future good behaviour. Wisely, James's instructions ceased calling Elizabeth 'mother' and instead adopted her favoured address as his 'dearest sister'. It laid the flattery on with a trowel, praising the English queen as 'a generous and pitiful [merciful] Princess', whilst emphasising the uncouthness and repugnance of regicide. Mary was, throughout, his 'dearest mother', whose restraint (closer confinement) he again proposed as the solution to her plotting. Suggested also was the eminently sensible idea of shipping Mary out of England (the destination was unspecified, but presumably France or Scotland) where she could be held under the surety of trusted kinfolk. Accurate also was the king's judgement that Mary's execution might provoke more dangers than her continued life. Yet, if the unfortunate Queen of Scots continued to plot, he argued, she might then face any punishment Elizabeth could devise. Somewhat pathetically, James went on to tell Gray that if none of these suggestions met with approval, he might turn the matter over to the English council and invite them to suggest whatever conditions or security they wished to ensure Mary behaved – if only she could be allowed to live. In a further attempt to achieve this goal, the king wrote also to the Earl of Leicester, denying that he had been in any kind of illicit contact with his mother since Gray's last sojourn in England, especially on the subject of pressing her English succession claims, and adding, 'My religion ever moved me to hate her course, although my honour constrains me to insist for her life.'[12]

Gray and his little embassy reached London in the midst of the Christmas Revels. There they found an unreceptive Elizabeth, who scornfully – and falsely – told them that she had no idea if Mary was alive or dead. They were in an impossible situation, officially charged with reversing a verdict which had already been passed, even if the death warrant was unsigned. Both Walsingham and William Cecil, Lord Burghley – Elizabeth's oldest and most powerful minister – were, however, focusing their energies on ensuring that their mistress put her signature to the fateful document. Nevertheless, as the grip of winter tightened, the English queen listened to Gray's party, giving away nothing, either to them or to her own bloodthirsty counsellors. Nor were the Scottish delegation fooled. False rumours reached them that Mary had been executed already, prompting George Young to write, laconically and prophetically, 'We deal for a dead lady.'

Gray, especially, was keen to put as good a spin on the farce as possible. He wrote to James that he had advanced every argument with which he had been empowered, but Elizabeth had merely told him to 'tell your King what good I have done for him in holding the crown on his head since he was born; and that I mind to keep the league that stands now between us, and if he break, it shall be a double fault'.[13] Again, she was proving adept at shifting blame for what might happen when – not if – Mary's blood was spilled. Supposedly, he had then requested a reprieve of fifteen days, which was refused; on chancing a request for eight days' grace, his fellow envoy, George Young, received from the English queen the devasting retort, 'Not for an hour!'

An anxious Gray was forced to conclude that 'all is for nothing' and to beg James, with an eye very much on his own future, to 'consider my upright dealing in your service, and not the effect'.[14] Not helping matters was the wildcard envoy Sir Alexander Stewart, whom the king heard had been secretly assuring the English, as Douglas had done, that the execution would not result in a breaking of the amity, and that Elizabeth might apologise for killing James's mother by sending him gifts of dogs and deer. According to de Courcelles in Scotland, James threatened to hang Stewart as soon as he returned north of the border – 'before he put off his boots' – and that he, James, should 'follow [hunt and chase] somewhat else than dogs and deer'.[15]

For all her haughty bravado, in truth Elizabeth continued in her paroxysm of indecision. Her solution was to go to the gutter. She attempted, unsuccessfully, to induce Mary's gaoler, the severe but morally upright Sir Amyas Paulet, to murder his charge; when that failed, she bowed to the inevitable and signed the death warrant on 1 February, handing it to her secretary, William Davison, who took it to the council – which gleefully and immediately despatched it to Fotheringhay. Shabbily, the queen then attempted to deny that she had meant Davison to actually do anything with the deadly document (thus, allowing her to blame him for despatching it and herself to feign ignorance and innocence of the execution). That it had been her decision is not in doubt. Elizabeth was far too good a politician to allow a decision in favour of an execution – one which might result in full-scale war – to be left to an overzealous secretary or an administrative error.

Defeated, Gray's embassy was subject to rumours that its leader had been plotting against Elizabeth. However, this tale derives from a French source and is less reliable as an account of the debacle of their failure and more useful in assessing the febrile atmosphere that had fallen, in the eyes of observers, upon the British kingdoms during that dark winter. At any rate, the Scots were packed off, and found themselves receiving official thanks from James's council for their efforts in early February (without Alexander Stewart dying with his boots on at the end of a rope).

On the 8th of that month, the inevitable blow fell. Mary had lain awake on her bed the previous night, only to be roused and dressed early in the morning. Her legendary beauty had long since dissolved into dropsical middle age. Her dignity, charm, and poise remained. Though she required support, she made her way into the dank Great Hall of Fotheringhay. A woman who throughout her tumultuous life had been more schemed against than scheming, Mary's final tragedy was being subjected to a gruesome, botched execution which required two blows of the axe and, chillingly, some sawing to sever

the remaining sinews. Amongst her possessions was found a miniature of the son she had not seen since his babyhood.

Davison, the assigned scapegoat, was sent to the Tower, where
he lived in some comfort with his salary intact (he was eventually
given an exorbitant fine that no one expected him to pay). Elizabeth
fell into a panic. It was her custom when, having made a decision
of any import, to immediately regret and seek to undo it, and her
wrath and fear swept over Burghley and Walsingham. But it was
done. By Valentine's Day, she felt able to pen a pathetic letter to
James (who had lapsed into silence), addressing him as 'my dear
brother', calling the execution 'that miserable accident which far
contrary to my meaning hath been befallen', and begging him to
believe 'how innocent' she was in the matter.[16] Adopting a loftier
tone, she invoked as proof her princely lineage and, without irony,
her forthright nature, which would have led her to admit culpability
had she been responsible.

The letter was borne north by Robert Carey, a son of Lord
Hunsdon and a man James esteemed. However, Carey found himself stopped at the border, to which George Young was sent to tell
him that he might only come forward if Mary still lived – otherwise,
he might return to his blood-stained mistress.

The suspense lasted for some weeks. The news of the execution
could not be shut out or ignored, though. Douglas, in London,
received an account of it, and Young returned to the king with
official confirmation (though without Elizabeth's letter, which
Carey would not hand over to anyone but its intended recipient).
Verifiable accounts of James's immediate reaction are contradictory.
The chronicler David Calderwood claimed Maitland (who had risen
to the positions of vice-chancellor then chancellor in the wake of
Arran's fall) had to clear the private royal rooms of spectators for
shame's sake, because the king 'could not conceal his inward joy,
howbeit outwardly he seemed to be sorrowful' and that he admitted
that night to his inner circle 'I am now sole King'.[17] This smacks of
being an accurate assessment of the king's character and situation,
although it is probably more born of hindsight. David Moysie,

another invaluable source of anecdotes of the era who had the benefit of being employed by the Scottish Privy Council, noted James's 'great displeasure' and that he 'went to bed without supper' when the news reached him. At the time, Ogilvie of Powrie reported that he showed no reaction at all but fled for the hunting field, whilst the English claimed he took the news 'very grievously' and delivered politic speeches about revenge.[18] Some amalgamation of all, by which the king showed various reactions over the days, seems more in keeping with a young man who had no idea how to deal with overwhelming news which might have any number of fearful repercussions. Definitely, he retired with a small party to Dalkeith, where he refused to entertain Carey or any representation from England. This was relayed to Carey, who continued to insist that his letter was for the king's eyes only. When English pressure was brought to bear, James caved, sending Sir Robert Melville to Foulden, in the Borders, to officially accept the month-old missive.

When Elizabeth's somewhat grubby letter reached him, James was forced to be more demonstrative: 'Madam and dearest sister, whereas by your letter and bearer Robert Carey, your servant and ambassador, you purge yourself of yon unhappy fact . . . I dare not wrong you so far as not to judge honourably of your unspotted part therein, so I wish your honourable behaviour in all times hereafter may fully persuade the whole world of the same.'[19]

He went on to consider the future: 'I look that you will give me at this time such full satisfaction in all respects, as shall be a mean to strengthen and unite this isle, establish and maintain the true religion, and oblige me to be, as before I was, your most loving.' He had not been fooled by her protestations of innocence, but he was willing to publicly accept them. In a move worthy of his letter's addressee, though, he was careful to make clear that his acceptance and future goodwill hinged on Elizabeth's recognition of his succession rights – that 'satisfaction in all respects'.

If James was willing to turn a blind eye to the execution of a Scottish monarch, however, plenty of his people were not. Walsingham was soon receiving word that Edinburgh's streets were being littered with placards against England and its queen. Sent to him was an illustrative example: a piece of hemp rope bearing a slip of parchment with a railing verse:

> To Jezebel, that English whore
> Receive this Scottish chain
> A presage of her great malheur
> For murdering our Queen.[20]

To help alleviate the rising tide of discontent, James decked himself out in mourning. In one possibly apocryphal anecdote, however, his attempts were undermined by the arrival of the vainglorious Bothwell at court, clanking about in full armour and announcing that it was the only fit mourning for a murdered Queen of Scots.

Despite the brief uproar, the dust began to settle. Even if he had not really confided it to anyone, the truth was that James finally was sole king. One loser in his increased prestige, though, was his pretty young lover, Gray. As the scheming fellow had predicted, implication in the failed attempts to save Mary's life had lowered his stock. Their affair petered out, and Gray's enemies struck. Sir William Stewart accused him of having been involved in the Stirling affair (which had ousted Arran) and he was immediately imprisoned in Edinburgh Castle. In May 1587, formal arraignment came for a catalogue of infamy, not least of which was Catholic intriguing, plotting to murder Chancellor Maitland, letting Mary's execution go forward, and, significantly, making illegal use of a counterfeit stamp to prevent James marrying (Gray presumably not wishing a royal bride to interfere with his own personal relationship with his sovereign). The king intervened – as he often would when he could – to ensure his lover did not face the axe; instead, Gray was quietly pushed from the political stage and allowed to enjoy semi-retirement on the profits of his estates. He would, in the future, become – curiously enough – a friend to the queen whom he was accused of trying to deny a crown, and ultimately be awarded £20,000 of back pay in 1606.[21] His more immediate future involved extended periods on the continent where he could and did continue to engage in religious politics.

The romantic entanglement with the handsome young man had been brief and, from the king's perspective, emotionally unsatisfying. To Gray, it had also brought more trouble than it did material rewards. It had, simply, not been serious. Rather, the good-looking favourite was the first in what would become a succession of short-term amours: people who profited – if they could – by their royal master's affection and attentions.

What James needed was not an empty romance – in whatever form it took – with a pretty male face, but marriage and issue with a female one, ideally possessed of a large dowry and the ability to win over his heart. It was time for the sole king to find a suitable wife.

7

The Marriage Game

Human sexuality is an endlessly interesting and notoriously complex field of study. Emotional attachments, romantic feelings, and sexual arousal are not always perfectly aligned. In modern terms, one might recognise in the early modern period a range of overlapping sensations: heterosexual relations (based on sexual attraction between the different sexes); homosexual relations (defined as sexual activities between members of the same sex); homosocial relations (comprising emotional and even romantic bonds between members of the same sex); and heterosocial relations (that is, emotional or romantic bonds formed between people of different sexes). King James exhibited, to differing extents, all of them, with the last being the one at which he was least adept (his relations with women being adequate sexually but stunted emotionally). Complicating – or embellishing – each of these types of relationship was, further, a host of social rituals, performances, and conventions, including courtly love (as a means of conducting heterosexual and heterosocial relationships) and numerous codes and practices of male friendship and bonding (which might well encompass or cloak sexual contact).

Throughout his youth, James had exhibited homosexual and homosocial proclivities – but his heterosexual tastes were latent. His attitude towards females had, however, been negatively conditioned during his days under the lifelong bachelor and misogynist Buchanan (who had died in September 1582). In his youth, indeed, the king had written verses on the subject, which make for painful reading:

Just so are women all by nature vain;
They cannot keep a secret unrevealed;
And where they once detect or spy disdain,
They are unable to be reconciled;
They are fulfilled by gossip without worth;
They let the smallest crime consume their earth.

Ambitious all, without regard or shame,
All born to lust for every gilded thing,
Each desiring to win a noble name
By false affection and by flattering,
Great craft they have indeed, yet are all fools;
They lie to stir; their fancies are their schools.

Convince me, then, you dames of worthy fame,
Since for your honor I employed my care,
How women's faults are hereby less to blame
Because they follow nature everywhere,
And you shall win my praise, despite this scorn,
And nature through your sex shall be reborn.[1]

The poem was, in fairness, playful: an invitation for the speaker to be proven wrong. The notion that women were greedy, ambitious, loquacious, wily, and full of misguided confidence was, though, common enough. Ironically, the accusation that they had a propensity to harbour grievances and deal dishonestly was one which applied to James as much as anyone. Of course, neither his prejudices nor his visible preferences mattered one bit in international marriage negotiations, which were geared solely towards securing the Scottish succession.

At this stage in his life, if portraits – such as that kept at Falkland Palace – are accurate, the king was an attractive prospect. In the image, as in others of his youth, he retains a little baby-faced puppy fat which serves to highlight a clear complexion. He is clean-shaven, has golden brown hair, and his heavily lidded eyes glare out with a hint of suspicion. Otherwise, his features are neat and regular, carrying more than a hint of his father, who had been noted for his pleasing appearance (though James would never achieve either his father's or his mother's height). But his chief attraction, in the eyes of prospective brides, was that he wore a crown – and now no one else was claiming it.

The question of the king's marriage had been discussed and debated since his babyhood. In the 1580s, it took on a more serious tone, with a Spanish Habsburg match briefly and implausibly floated in 1584. However, Frederick II of Denmark was the first to make a serious proposal. Accordingly, he sent out Danish ambassadors, who had arrived in 1585 and who were brought to Dunfermline Palace, where they were invited by the king to make their bid. However, discussions had fallen into farce. Before they were allowed to engage in serious negotiations, James informed them that plague was nearby, and that they might get down to business in St Andrews; he would provide an escort. The Danes, however, found no team of horses and guards awaiting them and so set out – unhappily – on foot.

Likely, the timing was to blame. An alternative possibility, however, is that the king was irritated by the ambassadors' opening demands: Denmark wanted no less for the Oldenburg dynasty's eldest daughter, Elizabeth, than the restitution of the Orkney and Shetland islands – that strategic archipelago which Denmark had pawned to Scotland on the marriage of Margaret of Denmark to James III, and which the Danes had never bought back. The question of the islands, Frederick made clear, was the sticking point when it came to a Danish-Scottish match – and thus the negotiations ground onwards, tediously, never reaching anything like agreement.

In 1586, James had tried a little harder, sending his old tutor Peter Young to Denmark to exchange portraits: one of himself for one of Princess Elizabeth. The following year, Frederick, growing impatient, forwarded a rather threatening ultimatum: either the King of Scots should marry his daughter or immediately hand back the islands. James, playing for time (partly due to Queen Elizabeth's disapproval of the match), brushed this off with a bluff show of mock regret for his 'slackness' in playing the swain, and sent Young abroad again – this time with Sir Patrick Vaus of Barnbarroch. Unfortunately, the pair were unable to achieve much, due primarily to Danish cavilling over the dowry, though they did return with further commendations of Princess Elizabeth's beauty. Unfortunately, in exasperation at the lack of progress, Frederick pledged his eldest daughter elsewhere – to Henry Julius, Duke of Brunswick-Lüneburg. Thereafter, if a Danish match was still sought, it would have to be with Frederick's second daughter, Anna, of whom Young provided a favourable report.

In June 1587, another prospective bride entirely was thrust forward, when the Huguenot poet Guillaume de Salluste du Bartas, whose poetry James had translated for his 1584 *Essays*, arrived. His largely self-appointed mission was to float the idea of marriage between the king and Catherine de Bourbon, the sister of the Protestant Henry of Navarre (soon enough to change his coat and become the Catholic Henry IV of France). Catherine, at least, appeared to have Elizabeth's approval (for the moment). James's response was to entertain the poet, whom he much admired, to a theology lecture delivered by Andrew Melvill at St Andrews. Du Bartas sang the praises of Catherine (who was seven years James's senior), but James, like Henry VIII during the pursuit of his political match with Anne of Cleves, wanted honest opinions. In September, he sent William Melville of Tongland (brother to the courtier James Melville) abroad, and the fellow returned with a portrait and a laconic report of the Frenchwoman's 'rare qualities'. Her putative charms were somewhat deflated, however, by contradictory and uncharitable claims out of France that she was 'old, crooked, and something worse if all were known'.[2]

Nevertheless, two potential roads to the altar had become clear. The French match, though it would have brought considerable prestige (France being one of Europe's superpowers) risked involving Scotland in that nation's constant religious wars – an outcome the Scottish Crown could not afford. The Danish match looked set to risk losing the Orkney and Shetland islands, which was also impossible to countenance. At the forefront of James's mind, though, was the potential dowry his bride – wherever she came from – might bring, and here the Danes looked to be the more open-handed. Naturally, both brides were also good Protestants, which would keep the Kirk happy; but Catherine was Calvinist, as were the Scots, whereas the Danes subscribed to the softer Lutheranism.

Complicating the marriage question was, naturally, Queen Elizabeth. Just as she had with Mary Queen of Scots' marriage, the English queen thought it her privilege to advise on James's match. This she did via hints and threats about the English succession. Her method would be to promote first one match and then the other, committing her support to one whenever its competitor looked likelier to succeed. This policy of interference, demurral, and delay only betrayed the truth about her position: Elizabeth did not wish James, as she had not wished his mother, to marry at all. Complications in the various periods of Anglo-Scottish amity, which a new consort and concomitant alliance might bring, were something she neither needed or wanted, and if that meant that the Scottish monarch, like herself, would be unable to produce heirs, that was too bad. Future political stability was for God to ensure. Yet she could hardly come out and say this – and reality dictated that James would marry. Her concession, so as not to lose her advantage, was to pull back from firm commitment to any match: in any future contingency, she might then rebuke her cousin for not having heeded her sagacity – only wait, never commit.

With the execution of Mary Queen of Scots, however, Elizabeth's overbearing attitude towards Scotland had suffered something of a blow. In the aftermath, James felt himself able to stretch his wings politically. Anxiety on the part of the English council followed. Burghley and Walsingham, the architects of Mary's death, who were themselves temporarily on the outs with their queen, frantically attempted to use every sympathetic (or bought) Scot at their disposal to impress upon the king the necessity of turning away from 'passionate pleasing men' who would fill his head with anti-English sentiment.[3] Elizabeth herself sent north Lord Hunsdon, this time with instructions to repair the amity. In July 1587, James was confident enough to list his demands: formal recognition, in writing, of his succession rights, the right to be consulted regarding the marriage of Lady Arbella Stuart (his first cousin – the daughter of Darnley's deceased brother), and lands in northern England (this last to frustrate any attempts to prevent his succession on the grounds that he was an alien who lacked English property). Menacingly, he had Archibald Douglas intimate that only by the granting of these requests could he be prevented from seeking some form of revenge for his mother's execution.

Adding some muscle to this threat was the voice of the Scottish parliament. Although James was able to steer business through it – notably the Act of Annexation, which gave the Crown inalienable control of 'temporalities' (former Catholic Church lands' revenue) and thereby allowed him to finance new peerages for loyal men – the members were not happy (and nor would the king be when it became apparent that this short-term measure would sever bishoprics from their dioceses and have to be undone). At its close, Chancellor Maitland gave an impassioned speech, which the nobility present threw their weight behind. Plenty of men present spoke of revenge and promised that they would be ready to take up arms for the late Queen of Scots at the first word from their sovereign.

Of even greater worry to the English were rumours that both France and Spain stood ready to land forces in Scotland to back any such revenge scheme. James, no doubt delighted at being catapulted onto the European political stage, was eager to make the most of it – at least financially. Despite the fact that he was, confessionally, a devoted Calvinist, he began to communicate with the great Catholic powers, and so began a long and worrisome – to the English – career of double-speak, in which he would attempt to present himself as all things to all men, if those men would give him what he wanted. His attentions fell, understandably, given his heritage and history, on Henry III and the powerful Guise family. This served only to irritate the Spanish, whose sovereign, Philip II, decided to make good on his daughter's English descent by exaggerating the late Mary's supposed bequest of the Stuart succession claim. By accident or design, James had managed at once to encourage Catholics at home to believe he was softening to them, and to stir up the greatest foreign Catholic power to condemn him as a heretical Protestant.

Hunsdon, nonplussed, accurately ascertained that the young king's schemes were predominantly focused on improving his finances. Thus, he suggested to Elizabeth that she increase his pension. Although the payment would continue to be calculated and disbursed idiosyncratically (sometimes a little more, sometimes a little less, depending on the king's behaviour), James had managed at least to turn the tables on his English cousin and make her, for once, wary of him.

At home, as his marriage negotiations gathered pace, James still needed companionship, his lover Gray having fallen. His choice this time fell, dangerously, upon a Catholic well known to him: George Gordon, 6th Earl of Huntly, who received Gray's property of Dunfermline Abbey as a gift. In his youth, Huntly had spent time in France, where he had gained that country's manners and an education at the University of Paris. On his return to Scotland in 1581, he had sought to ingratiate himself with the young king; he would 'wholly bend and apply himself' to James's humour, and he had the honour of having been involved with the king's liberation from the Lords Enterprisers after the Ruthven Raid. Thereafter, the northern earl had sought to emulate Esmé Stuart's mastery of James, attempting to fashion himself as a tutor and wise elder. But was the relationship sexual, in any degree?

The answer is probably not, though it is apparent that James had feelings for the earl. In September 1584, Huntly had fallen in love with a woman: a daughter of Sir Thomas Kerr of Ferniehirst. In a display of jealousy quite unusual with the male objects of his affection, James absolutely forbade the match – yet he would, later, happily allow Huntly to marry one of Esmé's daughters. Harry Potter, in his study of the feud between Huntly and his great rival, the Earl of Moray, has suggested that the earl was 'a reincarnation of [James's] first love'.[4] What is equally arguable, however, is that the king had developed a crush on Huntly in 1583 – likely as a substitute Esmé – and possibly even pursued him romantically. It does not follow, however, that Huntly gave his sovereign what he wanted, despite somewhat prurient gossip – such as that expressed by Justice Clerk Bellenden, who acidly noted, 'The Earl of Huntly's lying in his Majesty's chamber and preaching papistry, truth it is I think he be a papist, but not precise as he had not rather lie in a fair gentlewoman's chamber than either in the King's, or yet where he might have an hundred masses'.[5]

The slight was probably intended to have bawdy overtones – but Huntly simply used the bedchamber as a means of trying to influence the king religiously and politically. Moreover, James was never an inveterate sex pest who forced himself on anyone who caught his fancy. He was, however, willing to shower favours and affection on those who found themselves the object of his desires, whether they chose to reciprocate or not. Huntly might be better thought of as having strung the king along throughout a career, and homosocial relationship, which was characterised not by sexual passion but by a kind of long-suffering affection on James's part, as the lovestruck king fitfully attempted to win over a man who by turns seemed to encourage his love only to dash his hopes. Certainly, we find in James's letters to the earl a foretaste of what would become a hallmark of his later notes to his more famous inamoratos; despite Huntly being four years older, the king habitually signed off, 'Your Dad, James R.'

This is necessarily speculative, of course, but Huntly's refusal to engage sexually would also explain both the brief recovery in Gray's fortunes (he having been more willing to indulge his monarch, in whatever form James expected), and the fact that, in the evident absence of Huntly, the fresh-faced young Alexander 'Sandy' Lindsay, a brother of the Catholic Crawford, was soon being noted as the king's 'only minion . . . [and] nightly bedfellow'.[6] He was, according to the spy Thomas Fowler, 'a proper man, and Huntly's wholly'.[7] It seems that, from James's perspective, if he could not have Huntly, Sandy was the next best thing. At any rate, the condemnations against the earl's ascent were less about any vice or moral failing into which he led the king, but about his devout Catholicism and violent courses.

Indeed, Huntly's blood-feud with Moray over property in the north had become legendary in its own time. But, in July 1586, before the drama of Mary's execution had overwhelmed events, James had called a meeting at Holyroodhouse at which he demanded a general end to all noble disputes. At this convention, political theatre was the order of the day. Huntly and Moray were invited to shake hands and share a drink, before the king took them each by the hand and publicly walked them to the Mercat Cross of Edinburgh, where the city had laid on an outdoor banquet (essentially a drinks party). Thereafter, Huntly's star had risen, probably helped by his Catholicism as much as the king's romantic attachment, as this was a useful tool in his renewed Franco-friendly policy. At the opening of the 1587 parliament, which had closed with howls for revenge against England, the earl, elevated to the Privy Council, had carried the sword of state and been sworn in as one of the Lords of the Articles (those statesmen who framed the legislation to be put before parliament).

Yet all was not perfect in the new relationship. As Alan Stewart has noted, 'Scotland's state papers of the period are littered with conflicting accounts of James's favour towards the earl, and Huntly's irritation with James's insistence on maintaining positive relations with England'. This was to be the pattern, and it further indicates that Huntly had not slipped into the position of lover-cum-political ally departed first by Esmé and then by Gray. Rather, his challenge was to play the role of guide and adviser to the king without giving James the lead either romantically or politically – a task made difficult by the fact that Huntly sought to take James in an unambiguously pro-Catholic direction, which was entirely against the slippery king's will. In the doing of it, the earl carefully built up a party comprising a number of Catholics, such as the Earl of Erroll, Ludovic, the 2nd Duke of Lennox, and Lords Seton and Maxwell (the latter of whom was officially banished in April for his plotting). Joining in were the Protestants Atholl and Montrose, not out of religious sympathy, but because they opposed the primacy of Maitland as chancellor. From James's perspective, a politico-religious balance did have to be struck domestically, and throughout the winter of 1587–88, he set about countering his promotion of Huntly by 'the setting out of sermons [published under the title *A Fruitful Meditation*] thereupon against the papists and Spaniards'. On 5 February, he engaged Huntly's uncle, the Jesuit James Gordon, in a theological debate (with the king obviously arguing the Protestant position). According to the Spanish ambassador, James won the day.

Nevertheless, in early 1588, James was alerted to just how dangerous his friend might be. Rumours reached court that Huntly, along with Crawford and Montrose, intended to engage in a pincer movement, riding from the north with a Spanish army whilst Lord Claud Hamilton and the outlawed Lord Maxwell rode from the south. There were no Spanish soldiers, in fact – but the threat of militant Scottish Catholicism was real enough, and Maxwell had indeed returned in April, despite his banishment. The king was induced to raise a force against him and ride to the south-west, where he watched as Langholm, Caerlaverock, and Threave Castles each surrendered before the royal show of force, culminating in a siege at Lochmaben and the errant lord's capture.

James had learnt to be wary of Huntly – but he nevertheless retained a soft spot for him. Indeed, it was in the summer of that same year that the Privy Council voted in 5,000 marks for Lady Henrietta Stuart, Esmé's daughter and Ludovic's sister, to be brought over from France as a bride for the earl. James, as noted, not only condoned but encouraged the marriage – probably, if his later attitudes are anything to go by, because it had been made for policy and not love, and therefore did not appear to threaten his own ongoing affection for the groom. Further, it embraced Huntly into the extended royal family, given that the Lennox Stuarts were James's kin. In a fit of marriage fever, he wrote poetry for the nuptials, watched the festivities – featuring the god Mercury cavorting with nymphs, as well as a pastoral comedy – and publicly rejoiced when the bride and groom made a politic renunciation of their Catholicism in favour of

Scotland's faith. Not everyone was convinced. To many, it looked as though the king had reduced one Catholic in Maxwell only to very publicly renew his fondness for another in Huntly.

That summer of 1588, however, is not famous for what was going on in the north of Great Britain, but the threat posed to its southern shores. England's long cold war with Spain had ignited into open conflict in 1585, which helps account for the English government's anxieties about James's reaction to his mother's death (it always being possible that he might reach an accord with Philip II and allow Scotland to be a backdoor for Spanish troops). It also explains why James felt himself in a position to toy with Catholic support and make demands of Elizabeth: Scotland was strategically important, and the favour shown to Huntly might have been useful in mitigating against potential Spanish-backed Catholic attacks on its Protestant king. Further, James's seeming softness towards those associated with the Roman faith might well induce Elizabeth to make him a better offer. The truth was, however, that he no more wished for the Spanish to conquer England than its queen did, for fear that his kingdom would be next and his own claim to the English throne imperilled. And the idea of that conquest was alive and well.

Philip II's Great Armada had been known about for some time; indeed, Sir Francis Drake had even been employed to delay its sailing the previous year. In July 1588, it set sail.

*

At 4 p.m. on the 19th, a lit taper was set to a pitch-soaked rope that formed one of the English coast's warning beacons, and the whole thing burst into flames. The fellow who had lit it and his partner – both trustworthy householders over thirty – moved to light the other two ropes that formed the trio of lights. Those three lines of beacons acted as a signal to the next set along the coast, and then the next, and so on; inland, pairs of similarly manned ropes were lit, until the chain of warnings licked up into the sky, around and within southern England. The Spanish fleet had been spotted off the Lizard in Cornwall; the ships were sailing up the English Channel in a crescent formation. Seeing them, the post horses galloped for London, from whence the defence forces began their march to the appointed place at Tilbury.

So began the almost legendary saga of the first Spanish Armada. In hindsight, it is easy to be taken in by the mythical status the English victory achieved in the years afterwards, and to thus overstate the Armada's prospects of success. It was, in truth, a weak scheme, predicated on seizing control of the Channel so that a poorly coordinated troop transport from the Spanish Netherlands could then be organised, culminating in an invasion. Expert English seamanship and appalling weather conditions combined to scatter Philip's great fleet amidst wind-blasted confusion and fiery destruction.

At the time, however, no one could have predicted this. As the sea battle was fought (a sea battle assuredly not being what Philip or his poorly chosen general, Medina Sidonia, had wanted or expected), Elizabeth and James worked themselves into a panic about the potential outcomes of a Spanish invasion. At the end of July, in Scotland, the new English ambassador, William Ashby, boldly and precipitately promised the king that his pension would be increased to £5,000 a year and that he would receive an English dukedom – if only he would firmly commit to helping repulse the invaders if the crisis came. Ashby, clearly, had no idea that the Armada had already failed, and its surviving ships were even then desperately dragging themselves on a circuitous journey up the east coast with the intention of circumnavigating Great Britain to return home. In response to the stunning offer, James wrote to Elizabeth, accepting gladly, promising to put his kingdom, his subjects, and himself at her pleasure 'for the defence of your country', and hinting at the succession by promising to conduct himself as 'your natural son'.[8] Ashby, too, wrote to Walsingham of the promises he had made to secure Scottish support. And then, for the reckless ambassador, relief turned to fear.

In August, the undeniable failure of the Armada became known. It also became clear that Ashby, in his panicked efforts to get James to agree to oppose Spain, had exceeded his commission, making promises his queen had not sanctioned. He wrote southwards, apologising for what he had done. However, given the general relief and concomitant sense of exultation felt in England over its apparently divine escape from the Spanish threat, he did not suffer.

King James, of course, was less thrilled about having been duped. It became clear to him that Elizabeth was not going to name him as her successor or, indeed, give him anything he asked for. He decided to treat those Spanish sailors who were wrecked off his coast with grace and mercy. Around nineteen ships foundered, and throughout the autumn, as bedraggled mariners found themselves on Scottish soil, he ensured that Scotland and its king were magnanimous hosts. In October, forty-six Spaniards stranded in Edinburgh were granted safe conducts, fed, and given passage on Scottish merchant ships heading to the continent. In December, no less than Medina Sidonia's nephew proved to be a survivor – James entertained him lavishly, and the fellow was ultimately just one of several hundred of Elizabeth's enemies who received Scottish aid, all from a smiling king who maintained that he was doing no more than Christian charity.

Additionally, James resolved to continue courting Catholics in Scotland, England, and abroad, with the aim of widening his appeal as the southern kingdom's heir. This was necessary, not only because Elizabeth refused to name him or publicly announce his acceptability as her heir, but because the king had gained a reputation in her country for being 'unacceptable', the committer of 'many horrible, detestable, and cruel facts . . . which hath so far alienated men's hearts in England from him'.[9] Though this was unfair, it was clear that without the Queen of England's explicit support, which he seemed unable to get, he would have to make himself as attractive to as many people as possible. To prove to the world his sense of duty to his dynasty and state, he would, no matter how many obstacles Elizabeth might throw in his way, marry.

8

The Second-best Bedfellow

It was a truth universally acknowledged in the early modern period that a princess in possession of a dowry must be in want of a husband. Husbands of suitably lofty title and rank were, naturally, preferable. Historically, the princesses of Denmark had provided proof of the maxim, with one – Margaret – having, as has been noted, matched with a King of Scots.

Frederick II of Denmark-Norway was a colourful character – by reputation, a boisterous, outgoing, hard-drinking man who nevertheless brought his country to the brink of a greatness it would go on to achieve under his son. After a wayward youth, Frederick had married at the age of thirty-eight – to the fourteen-year-old Sophie of Mecklenburg-Güstrow, who was, by the standards of the day, a flaxen-haired, blue-eyed beauty. The couple presided over a peripatetic court that travelled about the king's dominions and his seven royal castles – but, even as it moved, it provided a hub for the developing Danish Renaissance, in which Sophie, no less than her husband, promoted cultural and scientific endeavours. Amongst the queen's clients were the playwright Hieronymus Justesen Ranch, historians Arild Huitfeldt and Anders Sørensen Vedel, and her Chief Court Mistress's foster son, the renowned astronomer Tycho Brahe.

Together, the pair had produced a quiver of children: Elizabeth (born in August 1573), Anna in December 1574, Christian in April 1577, Ulrik in December 1578, Augusta in April 1580, Hedwig in August 1581, and John in July 1583. The signs were, therefore, that marriage to one of the Oldenburgs was a safe bet in terms of their procreative potential.

They were, too, by all accounts, a loving family, although in their earliest years, the children had been fostered out to Sophie's grand-parents, Duke Ulrich III of Mecklenburg-Güstrow and his wife Elizabeth. It was at their imposing Wendish castle at Güstrow that the girl who would become Queen of Scots had received her earliest education. This was not, admittedly, a prodigious one. The golden age of educating royal women, which had benefitted figures such as Mary and Elizabeth Tudor and Mary Stuart, had largely given way to post-Reformation educational goals for females based on religious instruction, languages, and – in Denmark – Lutheran ideals of obe-dience and appropriate conduct. At the latter, the Oldenburg girls excelled, being raised to be well-mannered and decorous, if – at least in Anna's case – a trifle imperious. These, along with an ability to speak Danish and Low German, would be Anna's legacy from her grandparents.

Rustication at Güstrow had come to an end when Christian was two. At this point, the Danish government grew worried about its probable heir being raised in a German dukedom. The royal children were thus returned to their parents, where they could bear witness not only to their father's methods of governance, but to their industrious mother's cultural patronage. This, given Anna's later career, proved to be as much of an education as her schoolroom at Güstrow had provided. Sophie was, according to one of Burghley's spies, who felt compelled to borrow from *Proverbs*, 'a right virtuous and godly Princess which with motherly care and great wisdom ruleth her children'.[1]

In 1580, Frederick decided it was time to nominate Christian as his successor (the anticipation of which had moved the Rigsråd to repatriate the royal youngsters). The voters in what was essentially a mock election were drawn from across the kingdom – but in reality, nomination, voting, and results were ceremonial, as there were no alternative candidates for the position of future sovereign. Duly, Christian was elected at the Diet of Odense in 1580, 'on which occasion there were English musicians and a French dancing master with the Court'.[2] Yet it was not until 1584 that the kingdom's estates gathered to pay him official homage.

The entire royal family joined in this grand ceremonial event, assembling at Viborg in Jutland on Sunday 14 June 1584. The next day, Frederick and his son appeared on a 'richly decorated tribunal' in the town square, holding hands as the chancellor, Niels Kaas, opened proceedings with an oration on the solemnity of Christian's nomination. Sophie then led her daughters in paying their own ceremonial obeisance, followed by the counsellors of the Rigsråd, the nobility, the clergy, and the commons. Remarkably, the seven-year-old Christian reportedly conducted himself well during the hours of hand-shaking, cap-doffing, and exaggerated bowing. Anna, who was nine – the earliest age at which, according to her later physician, who presumably had it from her, she could walk unaided – was thus first-hand witness to the pageantry and ceremony which marked out the great occasions of royal life. At this point, she was a spectator. In the future, she would be the recipient of similarly elaborate professions of loyalty.

At her brother's investiture, Princess Anna was likewise introduced to the glamorous world of cultural spectacle, festival, and revelry which was later to play so large a role in her life. A play titled the *Acclamation of Solomon* lauded Christian as the wise son of the biblical King David, and the party rolled on for three days, following which King Frederick took his family on an extended tour of his realms which lasted until July, taking in the cities of Odense, Ringsted, and Lund. Thereafter, the two eldest boys were sent away to begin their formal studies at Sorø Academy, whilst the girls were left under their mother's wing, to learn how a woman might find alternative routes to exercising power than the occupation of a directly political role.

By this time, young Anna was developing into a willowy girl, taller even than her older sister, and possessed of golden hair and fine, if strong, features. Both Sophie and Frederick saw in her, as they did in all their daughters, an opportunity to increase Danish prestige by finding a husband equal to her charms.

*

Scotland's interest in matching its king with a daughter of Denmark was largely based on economics: the Danish king was a wealthy man, who counted Norway amongst his dominions, collected the revenue of seven bishoprics, enjoyed 'an annual revenue of 200,000 dollars . . . from the duties on Hamburg and Rostock beer, and controlled trade passing through the Øresund, or "the Sound"'.[3]

Yet Frederick had steadfastly refused to countenance any marriage between any of his daughters and the King of Scots unless the question of the Orkney and Shetland islands – which had taken on the complexion of a personal obsession – was settled in his favour. This stumbling block, which had caused such a delay in negotiations that it had removed the Princess Elizabeth from candidacy as Scotland's consort, looked insoluble. Indeed, the only thing that could advance the Danish match was Frederick's death. He complied, falling ill suddenly and dying at the age of fifty-three at Antvorskov in April 1588, conveniently at the same time the Scottish estates voted James an unprecedented special tax of £100,000 Scots, to be gathered over three years and used in making the country ready to receive a queen. Suddenly, the blockage was gone and, though the Princess Elizabeth was now out of reach, the kingdom's second daughter remained in play.

By this time, Queen Sophie, who had been excluded from politics by her husband and his Rigsråd, was chafing to enter the fray. Her son – and Denmark's newly elected sovereign – was in his minority, and she was eager to rule as regent on his behalf. This, unfortunately, the Rigsråd – particularly Chancellor Niels Kaas and minister Jørgen Rosenkrantz – were unwilling to countenance. The politicians' expectation was that the young dowager would retire to Nykøbing Castle, where she had met her husband.

Sophie, however, was unwilling to be relegated to the political wilderness. Immediately, she demonstrated her resistance by taking charge of her husband's funeral arrangements, assuring herself a visible place in the cortege as it wound its way to Roskilde Cathedral. Forced to capitulate, the Rigsråd grudgingly agreed that its dowager might remain in Copenhagen with her daughters, acting as guardian to the new king. She was thus in an ideal position to engage in what had become a very personal interest: matching Anna with the Scottish king.

Thankfully, Sophie did not share her late husband's preoccupation with the islands; her overriding motivation was that her daughter be matched with a man of suitably high rank. The other competitors for Anna's hand – Maurice of Nassau chief amongst them – did not offer the same prestige as marriage with a crowned and reigning sovereign. The dowager's first move was to send to Scotland a portrait of her second daughter, hoping that it would prove as attractive to the king as the miniature of her eldest had done, and thereby dissuade him from any thought of Catherine of Navarre. This was hardly an unrealistic hope: Anna was, by anyone's measure, very pretty.

In unwitting support of the Danish dowager, but probably of more immediate interest to James, was the attitude of his subjects, who would accept nothing but a Protestant queen and wanted an end to their king taking – often Catholic, always unpopular – men into either his bedchamber or his heart.

James's displays of sympathy to the Catholics – mainly to Huntly, but right down to the Spanish mariners – had not been ameliorated by his writing Protestant tracts or his thrashing of Catholics in debate. In early 1589, the Kirk petitioned him to purge his household and government of papists and, in February, the king was handed letters by Ashby, written by Huntly and his fellow Catholic Erroll, to the Spanish king. These letters invited the recently humiliated Philip II to invade, and damned not just the two earls but the ever-troublesome Maxwell, the Catholic-to-his-bones Lord Claud Hamilton, Crawford, and – oddly enough, given his religion – the Protestant Bothwell. The plotting was shown to have been going on for years – and Ashby included in his packet a note from Elizabeth (who had been shown everything before James), who smugly told him that she had warned him about his surrounding himself with men like Huntly. He must, she said, and her ambassador echoed, take action.

This James did, but it hardly constituted punishment. The seemingly untouchable Huntly was warded in Edinburgh Castle (his own choice of prison) and both James and Chancellor Maitland went to dine with him – the former cheerfully and the latter grudgingly. The king, indeed, could not resist kissing his favourite, 'to the amazement of many' – still, Huntly retained an ineluctable hold over him. James went further, claiming he knew the earl was innocent, refusing to go hunting until the fellow was released and, when that happened in March, inviting him to sleep in the royal bedchamber.

What Maitland made of all this is difficult to guess. His position was unenviable. The men who had been accused of the Spanish plot were all his enemies, and quickly they set about spreading rumours that he had framed them in order to ingratiate himself with the English. Probably the wary chancellor had joined James in dining with Huntly in Edinburgh Castle to keep an eye on things and prevent the favourite influencing James against him. When the earl was freed, Maitland began encouraging the king not to let him too far back into favour – a move which James accepted by sending Huntly away from court in the late spring. Seething, the favourite had no choice but to agree. Yet, before he went, he, Bothwell, and Erroll invited the king to a hunting party and jointly tried to convince him that his chancellor was, in fact, the evil plotter. Eternally fearful of seizure, James realised the danger these men posed in having got him alone. However, he maintained his courage and did not bend to their will. Defeated, Huntly departed for the north. As had become customary, James fell into a depression at losing the dashing earl's company and began sending him frequent letters.

Nevertheless, domestic religious and political tensions continued to run high. The exiled earl was reported to be gathering his followers (noble and otherwise) with the intent of marching upon Edinburgh. James, on hearing this, returned to his capital and showed his faith in Maitland (who had James's mind, if Huntly had his heart) by lodging with him. He issued a summons for a royal army, such as he had led against Maxwell the previous year. The unreliable Bothwell came north – ominously, with a troop of Borderers – but rather than attacking the king, he chose instead to try to divide him from Maitland, promising that he would answer any charges so long as the hated chancellor had no part in condemning him.

126

Meanwhile, Huntly, Erroll, and Crawford had combined and were on the march southwards through eastern Scotland, capturing the loyalist Master of Glamis as they went. The rebels were intent, however, on framing their actions not as a rebellion, but – as was the familiar war-cry of the period – as a means of re-establishing the correct form of government, which prized the primacy of the nobility over new men. It was a weak argument – a fig leaf, designed to cover up what were a slew of separate self-interests – rather than a genuine showdown between Crown and nobility; and James was in no mood to listen to the man whose affection he had chased like a lovesick schoolboy. 'What further trust,' he asked, 'can I have in your promises? What confidence in your constancy, or estimation in your honest meaning? Are these the fruits of your well conversion?'[4] This remarkable letter – a lover's lament, familiar through the ages – indicates that Huntly had pushed the king too far and given too little of himself in return. James was beginning to tire of the elusive fellow who had captured his heart but appeared intent on using his love only to his own advantage. For his part, the earl had presumed too much. He was commanded by his sovereign 'never to trust hereafter but such as I trust. And finally to repent you of all your faults.' Rapidly adding to the king's desire to take a wife was the falling of scales from his eyes when it came to Huntly.

Still, the country was in arms. In April, James had raised an army and sent to Edinburgh to enlarge it still further. His goal now was to ride on Perth, where Huntly, Erroll, Montrose, Crawford, and Bothwell had holed up. When he reached it, he found that the birds had flown north, to Aberdeen. Accordingly, the king took his troops – which had by then grown to around 2,000 men – up through Dundee. He had become, quite remarkably, a commander-in-chief: 'His Majesty,' it was reported, 'would not so much as lie down on his bed that night but went about like a good captain encouraging us.'[5] This was a new James, and one which is still scarcely recognised by those more familiar with his earliest and final years – the soldier-king who 'must visit [his] watches nightly . . . comfort them, be pleasant with them'.[6]

Eventually, the confrontation came at Brig o' Dee. By this time, men had melted away, notwithstanding their sovereign's encouragement. It did not matter. In a standoff reminiscent of Mary Queen of Scots' battle at Carberry Hill, no battle was fought. Brig o' Dee had a far happier outcome from the royal perspective. Despite Erroll's encouragement, Huntly was reluctant to engage in open fighting, and the rebel army began to desert when they realised that the king had come in person to face them down. The favourite did not surrender, but he also failed to provide opposition. James entered Aberdeen without weapons being raised, and from there he first issued an order for Huntly's castles – chiefly the enormous stronghold of Strathbogie and Erroll's Slains Castle – to be reduced, alongside a predictable secret message that the earl's life would be spared if he sought royal mercy. Knowing he was beaten, Huntly did just that, committing himself again to imprisonment – in Borthwick Castle – and this time being denied James's presence. Crawford, his tail between his legs, followed suit, blaming the whole messy affair on its leader.

With military achievement under his belt, the king was free to return to Edinburgh. There, another of the rebels, Bothwell, was keen to make his own peace. He managed to gain a royal audience, during which he flung himself at James's feet and assured him that he had joined with the fallen favourite only as a means of ridding the realm of Maitland's apparently malign influence. This cut little ice. Bothwell and Crawford were declared traitors, the former locked up in Tantallon and the latter in St Andrews Castle. Unfortunately, the king's punishment proved all too light, and soon the rebels were freed and restored to favour, which only exacerbated whispers in the capital – which Bothwell and his men had rampaged through when the king had been in the north – that James was soft on Catholic-heavy intrigues. A devout Protestant bride would help solve that problem and might also allow James's battered heart more faithful companionship than Huntly had provided.

On 28 May 1589, Edinburgh was further convulsed by riots. Ostensibly, these were predicated on a groundswell of public opinion against a French match and in favour of the Danish one. The king, so the rioters claimed, must ally with Denmark and thereby improve trading conditions; he must not match with France and risk dragging Scotland into that nation's endless wars of religion. All signs pointed to marriage with Anna being far more popular than matching with Catherine of Navarre – this despite Chancellor Maitland being strongly in favour of Catherine.

Although he was never a slave to public opinion – nor even particularly heedful of it – James was as leery as any ruler of rioting mobs. Though he had hoped to keep the French proposal in play, the rioting encouraged him to jump. On 2 June, he appointed the wealthy George Keith, who was Earl Marischal, as envoy to Denmark, along with Lord Dingwall and the lawyer John Skene. Their express mission was to finally sign off on the marriage. Rather than admitting that he was bowing to public pressure, of course, the king claimed divine inspiration. He had, he said, locked himself away with his portraits of Catherine and Anna and prayed for guidance, and God had answered: as a result, he had 'resolvit to marry the Danish Princess'.[7]

However, he had no intention of selling himself cheaply. His opening demand for a dowry was 'ten hundred thousand pounds Scots': an astronomical sum.[8] It was unlikely that he expected to get quite so much but, as he doubtless was aware of Queen Sophie's enthusiasm, he decided to ask big, as gaining even a fraction of his demand would mean a considerable cash injection into Scotland's coffers. Nor was getting as much money as possible the only thing on his mind. He wanted no less than Danish recognition of Scotland's legal possession of the Orkney and Shetland islands, a mutual alliance against Catholic threats, free trade between the nations, military support if Scotland were ever threatened, and similar support should he be required to forcefully assert his rights to foreign titles. This last, obviously, was a pained – and a dangerous – admission that Elizabeth might never recognise him as her heir, and he might one day be required to invade England to press his claim to its throne.

As he expected, these demands were subject to negotiation. In the end, he accepted a more reasonable offer of a £150,000 Scots dowry and promises that the islands might remain under Scottish sovereignty until such a time as the boy-king Christian IV reached his majority and developed his own policy regarding them. This was deemed adequate, and the Danish match, which had for the better part of a decade bobbed and sunk, changing its bride as it did so, began to harden into reality.

Queen Sophie rejoiced. Where her late husband had succeeded only in matching their eldest child with a duke, she had netted a king – and not only a King of Scots but, she knew as well as anyone, a potential, even likely, King of England. Whether Denmark would have to help James militarily in gaining the English throne was an unknown – but it would certainly be in the country's interests to do so, given one of its daughters would now share the dishonour if Scottish succession rights were inhibited or denied. It was thus with the active willingness of both parties that the marriage treaty was signed in late July, and the dowager set about organising the wedding.

The Danish government was keen for a low-key, inexpensive affair. This was not, however, to Queen Sophie's taste. She was determined that Anna, in being matched with a monarch, should be given a wedding commensurate with the grandness of the match. She did not expect the groom to be present, of course – the ceremony would be by proxy, and was intended mainly to ensure that when Anna left her home country, she would enter her new one as its queen. The proxy nature of it, however, in no way lessened what the dowager wished to be a splendid display of Oldenburg – mostly her own – achievement.

The soon-to-be Queen of Scots, too, appears to have been of a mind with her mother. On 28 July, the fourteen-year-old Anna was said to be 'so far in love with the King's Majesty as it were death to her to have it broken off, and [she] has made good proof divers ways of her affection, which his Majesty is apt enough to requite'.[9] A fairy tale was being spun, with James as the handsome prince and Anna the princess bride. Even Queen Elizabeth accepted the situation, appreciated that it was at least a Protestant match, and put on her diplomatic face: she wrote that she had the 'gracious mind to yield the King all honour at his marriage'.

Sophie got her way despite the Rigsråd, and no expense was spared. Some 300 tailors set to work on the wedding dress, and servants were despatched out of Copenhagen and into the fashion capitals of Europe with instructions to return with the latest trends, as elaborate and fussy as they were: one gown, as Anna's biographer Ethel Carleton Williams notes, was 'of peach and parrot coloured damask with fish-boned skirts lined with wreaths of pillows round the hips'.[10] Although it is easy to laugh at mother and daughter feverishly launching into wedding preparations, this was not purely a matter of pride. Rather, it was a political display. Women – and men – were what they wore, and outfits were taking on elaborate, allegorical meanings. In outfitting Anna in expensive new fashions, the nation of Denmark was engaging in a visual display to proclaim its wealth, its splendour, and its premier place on the European chessboard. Equally important was signalling to the Scots that their new consort intended to add to the majesty of their king and Crown. To reinforce this message, new liveries were sewn for Anna's servants and, more splendidly, a solid silver coach was built, which was to travel with her and allow her to show herself off in the various ceremonial events marking out the major stages of her new life.

In the midst of all this activity, the bride was engaged in two important occupations of her own: sewing shirts for her new husband (this being symbolic as well as practical, in that it demonstrated her position as an obedient and loving wife) and learning French – a language that remained a *lingua franca* of royal courts and in which James was known to be expert. Scots she would not gain until she arrived in her new kingdom; but then, given her obvious intelligence, she would master it swiftly.

Across the North Sea, James was keen to show that he was as enthusiastic about marriage as the bride. The English spy Thomas Fowler reported on 5 August, with some asperity, that 'this King desired so much the lady as he regarded not any other matter nor would stand upon it . . . whereupon they [the Danes] made a public provision for her transporting hither and marriage without doubt, which [being] so known in most parts of Europe it were, they think, the greater disgrace both to the lady and all that Council if it should not go on'.[11]

But how much did the king desire his new wife? He certainly gave every appearance of having been overcome by passion – although this might merely have been politically motivated. Interestingly, however, he promised his then bedfellow, the shallow Sandy Lindsay, the title of Lord Spynie, to be confirmed legally the following year. This was, basically, an amicable brush-off, as well as being a pay-off for the thousand crowns the favourite had loaned his sovereign. The king was clearing out his bed – just as he had tried, by distancing himself from Huntly, to clear out his heart. This usefully demonstrates James's bisexuality. He evidently envisaged that his new wife would, in one person, fulfil both his sexual and his emotional needs, and thus he would have no need for a pretty male to cater to just one of them. This was to prove, in time, a chimerical expectation.

On James's mind also were money matters and, still, public opinion. On 10 August, he summoned a Convention of the Estates and requested that they 'contribute more bountifully towards this marriage': a request he expected to be met 'because of their interest in the league with Denmark'.[12] It had been noted, cattily, that 'he has neither plate nor stuff to furnish one of his little half-built houses, which are in great decay and ruin. His plate is not worth £100, he has only two or three rich jewels, his saddles are of plain cloth.'[13] This was an exaggeration, but it was not the kind of reputation James wanted. Orders thus went out to begin refurbishing the royal palaces whose queen's apartments had fallen into disrepair through disuse, and those properties which were to form part of the new consort's jointure. Nevertheless, the king was astute enough, whatever the nature of his feelings, to give every impression of passion for the girl he had not yet met; and in this, his rich education in history provided ample models of chivalric romance and courtship on which he could – and soon enough would – draw.

As 20 August – the date for the proxy wedding – drew near, the Oldenburgs gathered at the magnificent, spired Kronborg Castle – immortalised as Shakespeare's Elsinore – overlooking the Sound. The Scottish Earl Marischal crossed the North Sea again, this time to stand as his sovereign's proxy in a marriage ceremony conducted by Lutheran rites. The nuptials over, he escorted Anna to the west wing of the castle and – briefly – lay beside her on the richly decorated bridal bed to seal the marriage beyond doubt.

On the completion of the proxy marriage, Anna of Denmark became the legally recognised queen consort of a foreign kingdom she had never seen and a king she had not yet met. Across the water, James – who had given up his bedfellow and was eager for a new one – professed his desire that she join him as quickly as possible. This Anna was prepared to do, and plans were immediately set in train to convey the new queen – and her silver coach, and her retinue of servants, and her magnificent new wardrobe – to Scotland. What neither King nor Queen of Scots reckoned with, however, was the freak weather that determined to keep them apart.

9

'Tis Thou Maun Bring Her Hame

The early modern period coincided with what has been hyperbolically termed 'the Little Ice Age': a time of rapid global cooling which resulted in far colder weather conditions than we experience today. Even by its standards, the autumn and winter of 1589–90 were extreme. Wild storms pummelled the coasts of Scotland and Scandinavia, ripping off sails and tearing holes in the wooden hulls of even the finest sailing ships.

Anna, the new Queen of Scots, set out into the heart of these roiling seas just as they began their furious rise in September. Her escort constituted eighteen warships, led by the Danish admiral, Peder Munk, aboard the flagship *Gideon*. Onboard was not only the young queen, but a raft of Danish elites, including scholars Niels Krag and Dr Paul Knibbe, diplomat Breide Rantzau, and Scotland's own Earl Marischal, making his return journey. The seas, it was hoped, would bow before this superior display of naval power and elite society. Yet in Scotland, William Ashby, watching for Anna on England's behalf, reported to Walsingham – who was on his last legs and would die some months later – that her 'arrival is uncertain, depending upon wind and weather'.[1] Watching from Scotland also was King James, who had made 'great preparations at Leith to receive' his bride, and who spent two weeks at Seton Palace, which afforded a good view over the water.

As the days wore on, however, the gunmetal horizon beyond Scotland failed to conjure up sails. Amid the tempests, the Danish cohort was unable to maintain its formation and, though it had set out boldly, found itself forced onto the coast of Norway. The *Samson*

and the *Joshua* collided; the *Gideon*, on which Anna sailed, sprang
a leak, leading the admiral to have to crawl to her to tell her – as
though she needed told – that the prayers he had instructed the
divines onboard to send heavenward were not working. Nor, across
the water, did James's orders for prayers and fasting do much to calm
the seas; indeed, frighteningly, a cannon even broke free of its moor-
ings and nearly crushed the new queen to death.

Anger and impatience grew as a consequence of James's anxiety. He demanded that the recently rehabilitated Bothwell, in his
position as hereditary Lord High Admiral, sail out and personally
retrieve the bride. However, the king was thwarted by his council,
which demurred at approving what might be a suicide mission.
Their hesitancy was understandable. Gales and rainstorms had been
sweeping across Scotland, too, and in September a ferry carrying Jane
Kennedy, an old favourite of Mary Queen of Scots who had been
earmarked for a plum position as First Lady of the Chamber in the
new queen's household, collided with another vessel and sank in the
Firth of Forth, taking Jane and around sixty others to watery graves.

It was thus not until October that the king had firm news of
what was happening across the North Sea, via letters brought by the
Privy Councillor Andrew Sinclair, who had managed the crossing.
Anna, thankfully, was said to be 'in good health, and her company,
but sorely beaten with the seas. She put out twice for this coast
[Scotland], but both times [was] driven back by contrary winds.'[2]
Nor had two attempts been enough. Sinclair, indeed, reported that
'the Queen and all the fleet has been in great pain and danger, having
at five several [separate] times been driven back by storms and contrary winds, sundry of the ships having leaks, especially that wherein
the Queen was'.[3] Her Danish advisors were, understandably, keen
to return – probably overland – to Denmark, but Anna was already
beginning to show the mettle which would characterise her later life.
'She is,' claimed Sinclair, 'most forward hitherwards' – determined
to come.

Anna herself wrote a business-like letter in French, dated 3
October: 'We have already put out to sea four or five times but

have always been driven back to the harbours from which we sailed, thanks to contrary winds and other problems that arose at sea, which is the cause why, now winter is hastening down on us, and fearing greater danger, all this company is forced to our regret, and to the regret and high displeasure of your men, to make no further attempt at present, but to defer the voyage until the spring.'[4]

For a fourteen-year-old, young Anna had a head on her shoulders. Her regretful acceptance of the inclement weather, however, was not good news to her husband. Having entered into marriage, he was now keen to show the world how committed he was to it. Already he had written to Elizabeth asking her to send north a company of actors to provide entertainments, and he had requested of Lord Derby in the Borders 'a brace of fat stags baked after the English fashion . . . and other provisions . . . in readiness against her landing'.[5] Mungo Graham, a Master Household, had even spent hundreds of pounds on spices for a feast of welcome. James's attempts to send out Bothwell having failed, he set about despatching Colonel William Stewart – 'who has often shown alacrity in this affair and is devoted to the service of both of us' – with the task of collecting the queen.[6] This was deemed more acceptable (Stewart having safely made the passage across the North Sea and back before), preparations were begun, and on 8 October, he wrote to Anna, wishing her 'a safe, speedy, and happy arrival in these parts'; he was, he claimed, 'one who to you alone' he had 'vowed his entire life'.

But something much grander was already developing in the king's mind, and at this stage, he took probably the most adventurous decision of his life thus far. He decided that he would hazard his own person on the wild seas and fetch his bride home in person.

This was not the decision of a coward. Fresh from his military adventures up the east coast, the king was keen to display himself at his best and bravest. Though he would remain physically cautious of proximity to other people, especially strangers, his decision gives the lie to the pusillanimous King James of legend. Further, he knew his history and was anxious to be seen entering into the chivalric conceit of the ardent wooer pressed by passion into endangering his own life in pursuit of love. He would be doing no more than living up to the legacy of his grandfather, James V, who had set out boldly to claim a French bride.

At first, he kept his intentions to himself – which was part of the courtly ideal (the lover being required, ostensibly, to travel incognito). On hearing rumours about his departure, Bothwell and the young Duke of Lennox (Ludovic, who had just turned fifteen) made formal protestations – which James likely welcomed so that he could demonstrably overcome them. This he did by ordering the provisioning of five ships at Leith, on which were to sail the Lord Chancellor (Maitland); the Justice Clerk (Bellenden); the Provost of Lincluden (Robert Douglas, Collector General); John Carmichael (Warden of the West March); Sir William Keith of Delny (the Master of the Wardrobe, who had been part of the attempts to save Mary Queen of Scots' life); the lawyer John Skene; the ever-useful Peter Young, serving as Almoner; and Sir Patrick Vaus, who had joined Young in the previous Danish excursion. Altogether, these men and their fellows amounted to a party 300-strong. Pointedly, it appears that Sandy Lindsay, who advanced considerable monies towards the trip, was excluded from at least the bulk of it – this despite the spy Fowler claiming that 'every minion of the King's stable and bedchamber were sent onboard'.[7] Fowler had, in 1581, really led the charge that James was 'too much carried [influenced] by young men that lie in his chamber and are his minions'; by this time, though, commentators were drawing distinctions between what they believed to be hopeful minions and genuine sexual partners, or bedfellows.

To be left in control of Scotland was a regency council, with Lennox at its head and, remarkably, Bothwell as deputy. James no doubt hoped that active occupation in government alongside a Duke would satisfy the man's desire for noble primacy and thus keep him out of trouble. Unfortunately, Bothwell would see the inferior position of deputy as another slight.

Of course, not everyone was happy about the prospect of the king leaving the country. With an uncharacteristic awareness of public opinion, James took a strange step, and one which was to become a signal feature of his kingship in both Scotland and England. He took up his pen and decided to blurt out his feelings – and justify his actions – on paper, so that the literate amongst his subjects could see his mind and the illiterate could hear it read out to them. On his decision to marry, he announced, 'As to the causes, I doubt not it is manifestly known to all how far I was generally found fault with by all men for the delaying so long . . . I was alone, without father or mother, brother or sister, King of this realm and heir apparent of England. This my nakedness made me to be weak and my enemies stark. One man was as no man, and the want of hope of succession bred disdain. Yea, my long delay bred in the breasts of many a great jealousy of my inability, as if I were a barren stock.'[8]

James's opening of his heart – or as much of it as he wanted seen – has been interpreted by Michael B. Young as proof of the king's awareness that his subjects suspected and disapproved of his same-sex activities, and that he thus sought to counter the 'disdain' murmured against him by taking a wife. But the letter is probably better read as an acknowledgement of necessity and, interestingly, a surreptitious attack on Elizabeth. The king's reference to his lack of family, which might have provided him with counsel and advice, is worthy of note. This was true enough, and it is evident that the twenty-three-year-old James genuinely still felt a sense of lingering deficiency – produced by an upbringing which had been filled with the notion that his family was a thing to be ashamed of. Part of his reason for marrying, and this was likely honest, was his lack of close family members, which a wife might, he hoped, rectify.

Secondly, there are two references to England which should not be ignored. His claim to be 'heir apparent' to Elizabeth signalled his willingness to promote himself as heir to the English throne even without its current queen's acknowledgement. By suggesting that his marriage might prove he is not 'barren stock', he played on Elizabeth's supposed claim, reported by his courtier, James Melville, upon hearing news of his own birth in 1566: 'The Queen of Scots,' she had allegedly lamented, 'is lighter of a fair son, and I am but a barren stock.'[9] His letter was thus a public, if indirect, slap in the face to England's queen, advertising to his people that he would do what she had not: marry and provide heirs via a family of his own making.

Exhorting his Scottish subjects to live in 'peace and quietness till his returning', he made the short journey to Leith, intent on going to Norway to prove his love and fetch his wife. Frustratingly, though, the weather refused to provide smooth sailing. James's ship was damaged as it rode at anchor, forcing a delay to the planned departure on Sunday 22 October, and it had to be hastily repaired. That done, and the vessel being outfitted with sails of red taffeta, he was finally able to set sail. Thus began a four-day crossing which remained remarkably clear and calm, before the sea rose again and washed his fleet onto Flekkefjord on the frigid Norwegian coast.

For the first time in his life, James was free of the day-to-day worries which were part and parcel of governing Scotland, and he was determined to make the most of it. From Flekkefjord, where he showily insisted on lodging 'in the same place as [Anna] had slept earlier', he and his party rode to Tønsberg, where the king spent six days lodging in the home of one Jorgen Lauritsen (and where he listened, on 16 November, to a sermon preached in the Marien Kirke by the Scottish minister David Lindsay).

Thereafter began the sixty-three-mile ride across increasingly frozen land to Oslo, where Anna was living as she awaited better weather. In the city, James was provided with accommodation by the Shoemaker's Guild. There, he might well have smartened himself up in preparation for first meeting his bride, as his red velvet coat, spangled with gold stars, and sable cloak were well dirtied. This he was disinclined to do. Rather, his mind was still on the conscious self-fashioning which the fantasy of chivalry demanded; the ideal ardent lover would not pause to beautify himself but rather could not wait a minute before thrusting himself, mud-splattered boots and all, into his fair lady's presence. Accordingly, as the memoirs of David Moysie record, on arriving in Oslo, James made for Anna's lodging in the Old Bishop's Palace and 'passed quietly with boots and all to her highness'. It was more gesture than anything; a similar scheme would later be intended by Elizabeth I's favourite, the Earl of Essex, as he sought to caparison himself as the ardent, chivalrous knight eager to see his lady upon his unwarranted return from Ireland. Happily, in the King of Scots' case, it was successful.

What did the newlyweds make of each other? For James, his hopes were certainly met in physical terms. The girl before him, despite her late experiences dodging cannons and being thrown about a ship's decks, retained all the beauty and freshness of youth (to which the king was always attracted). A miniature of Anna in her youth indicates that she was comely rather than beautiful but possessed of all the requirements of Renaissance good looks: long fair hair (and elsewhere James would reveal his penchant for women's long locks), pale skin, and good physical proportions. From her perspective, notwithstanding her new husband's state of muckiness – more a sign of his passion than slovenliness – James was likely also pleasing. He was no golden Apollo, as his father had once been, but was 'tall, slim, and thin under the eyes': a winsome rather than a ruggedly handsome man, who nonetheless had inherited Darnley's blue eyes rather than his mother's hazel ones. The pair made an exceedingly good-looking couple – certainly a more attractive pair than, for example, the forty-something Elizabeth I and the stunted, pockmarked twenty-something Duke of Anjou would have made, had their on-again-off-again courtship come to anything. In their natures, too, there might have been a meeting of the minds; she was reportedly 'both godly and beautiful', which boded well for his theological interests.[10]

The pair did more than stare at one another. James, still playing his role of the courtly swain, attempted to steal a kiss 'after the Scottish fashion', which she 'refused as not being the form of her country'.[11] Students of the period will likely recall Henry VIII attempting the same thing – and being met with the same refusal – during his first meeting with his own political match, Anne of Cleves. The result for James and Anna was far more rewarding: 'After a few words privily spoken between his Majesty and her, there past [passed] familiarity and kisses.' We do not know what those words – spoken in French

– were, but evidently both young people knew well enough that they were being watched and thus agreed to put on a show of mutual affection. That accomplished, the king departed after half an hour.

The following day, he returned to the Old Bishop's Palace, *sans* his muddy riding boots and clad this time in blue velvet; he went in state, with six heralds preceding him. At this meeting, formal agreement was reached for an in-person wedding ceremony – to take place the following day, also in the palace.[12]

On the day appointed, David Lindsay presided. The hall in the Old Bishop's Palace was hung with fine tapestries and decked out with red damask chairs and carpets. The local bishop presented his own Latin blessing after the ceremony, and the couple were then free to enjoy 'a reasonable banquet being on such an accident' [i.e., sudden organisation]. Thereafter, they would have been bedded – although whether they consummated the marriage immediately or decided to wait is unknown. Whatever they achieved physically, we do know that they conversed somewhat on the wedding night. Later, sinisterly, it would be alleged that a witch had gained demonic access to the chamber and listened in on every word.

For the moment, though, a general air of happiness between the couple prevailed, as they hunted together and accepted gifts from Nordic dignitaries. Unfortunately, the sense of jollity was not shared by the king's retinue. No doubt embarrassing James greatly, his party seemed determined to descend into unseemly internecine warfare. Chancellor Maitland, as always, was at the root of it. He had accompanied the king across the sea not because he wanted to, but because James valued his counsel and wished to publicly show the fellow's acceptance of the match (Maitland having argued in favour of Catherine of Navarre). Further, the king sought to protect his unpopular chancellor from what would likely be a dagger in his guts the moment the royal back was turned at home.

On the wedding day itself, the Earl Marischal (who had remained with Anna in Oslo since the original sailing from Denmark had failed) began to quarrel with the chancellor over precedence. Having been James's envoy in Denmark, he naturally felt himself owed a higher position in proceedings than Maitland. The chancellor, however, wittily and rightly pointed out that since the king had come in person to collect his bride, the position of envoy had been abrogated. Although James managed to shut them up – at least for the day itself – they were soon at it again; why, the chancellor suddenly wondered, was the Earl Marischal attempting to get away with drawing upon the new queen's dowry to pay his own expenses? Maitland had not been to blame for the developing feud – but he showed no sign of letting it lie.

A change of scene was in order, which would at least keep the men too active with preparations to stain the Norwegian snow with one another's blood. Sir William Keith was thus sent to Denmark, to the court of Anna's brother, Christian IV, to discuss a meeting of the sovereigns. Whilst waiting for these plans to solidify, James took the opportunity to give his new wife the first of her 'morrowing gifts' – the charming Scottish name for her jointure portion. First to be promised Anna were the lands of Dunfermline Abbey. Over the course of his time abroad, the king would also bestow upon her the palaces of Linlithgow and Falkland. He could not know it at the time, but in doing so, he was sowing the seeds of future conflict between his wife and chancellor and sparking in the queen what would be a lifelong fascination with acquiring property.

For the moment, James and Anna were determined to avoid conflict. They were focused instead on family. The king's ships – amongst them the small *Falcon of Leith*, hired from John Gibson, and the 126-ton *James Royal*, hired from Robert Jameson – were sent home without the couple. As soon as the dowager Queen Sophie heard that her new son-in-law had arrived in her son's dominions, she saw to it that both he and her daughter were invited to the twelve-year-old Christian's court. This was immediately accepted. King James was not only eager to meet his new, extended family, but to firm up relations between their realms. In time, his decision to visit Denmark would be validated: Christian IV would repeatedly visit his sister and brother-in-law, the two having built up a friendly relationship that would embrace Scotland, England, and Denmark-Norway in amity.

Nor, at this time, was James eager to return to factious, fractious Scotland – which was in any case still not ready to receive its queen (the Master of Works, or royal architect, William Schaw, having come to Norway with the king).

As winter tightened its grip, travel plans were organised. The king and queen spent most of December in Oslo, awaiting sledges sent up from Denmark. When these arrived, they sledded down the coast, lodging at the Båhus Fortress near the Swedish border before continuing 'across the frozen-over Gotha-Elf, and the Swedish Landflig, which at that time alone separated Norway and Denmark, through Varbjerg, Halmstadt, and Helsingør [Elsinore]'. In doing so, they passed through Swedish-controlled lands – but any danger from the King of Sweden was avoided by the despatch of William Murray; he not only gained safe conduct from John III but received an armed escort of 300 to guide the newlyweds through his dominions. As a result, they were even able to spend New Year's Day (at the time celebrated by gift-giving) in considerable style in the company of John's brother Karl – beginning a mutual relationship with Sweden and Swedish affairs which would endure. Unfortunately, the weather again voiced its displeasure, and they were prevented from crossing to Kronborg Castle for three days.

When they finally arrived, Queen Anna was in her element. In addition to property (and prestige, decorum, dancing, and English literature), her family would remain one of the things closest to her heart in future years. Nor was James averse to such a welcome – seemingly with genuine pleasure and great deference – into the embrace of a loving family. With alacrity, he agreed to the pleas of Lutheran ministers that he marry Anna – for the third time – according to their rites. These nuptials were celebrated on 21 January 1590 and, following them, the groom distributed 2,000 thalers to the castle's servants. In the days that followed, the king betrayed his joy – and the flavour of the ongoing festivities – in a letter addressed to the bedfellow he had ejected to make room for Anna: Alexander Lindsay, rewarded for services rendered with the promise of the lordship of Spynie. He wrote 'from the Castle of Kronborg, where we are drinking and driving o'er [passing our time] in the auld manner'. It is possibly during this visit, indeed, that the king first developed a taste for strong liquor which would only grow as he aged; James Melville was quick to record that James 'made good cheer and drank stoutly'.[13]

For all this festivity, one thing the journey had not succeeded in doing was healing the divisions with the Scottish ranks. In fact, the general air of spirituous festivity had only served to exacerbate arguments. Chancellor Maitland had now developed a following, the heads of which butted with those who adhered to the Earl Marischal. Keen to get in on the action, Dingwall was at war with the Constable of Dundee, and Maitland's protégé, Sir George Home, advanced his goal of pushing Sir William Keith out of his mastery of the Wardrobe (with Keith, a kinsman of Marischal, being accused of dressing more finely than the king). It was clear that the honeymoon would have to have an end-date.

Once again, the weather dictated when this would be. It was agreed that James and Anna should remain, for safety's sake, in Denmark until the spring thaw – in April – and thus that they might depart only after the wedding of Princess Elizabeth (whom James had once sought to marry) and her fiancé, Henry Julius (who was by this time the ruler of Brunswick-Wolfenbüttel).

The months leading up to departure, however, were not tainted by the petty arguments of the Scots. On the contrary, King James enjoyed his first trip out of Scotland immensely, over and above the Danish drinking bouts. Here was a country in which a princely student could really exercise his mind. In addition to the more familiar entertainments – dramatic interludes, hunting, and the ubiquitous mediaeval chivalric tournaments – there were opportunities for enlightened intellectual pursuits. On 7 March, James travelled into Copenhagen, visiting the Royal Academy, and listening to lectures by Dr Hans Olufsen Slangerup and Dr Anders Christensen. In the middle of the month, he went over to Roskilde, at the cathedral of which he listened to Latin speeches delivered by Mathias, debating the doctrine of predestination afterwards, 'with acute perception', with the extremist theologian Niels Hemmingsen.[14] Further speeches were given at the University of Copenhagen, where Dr Paul Madsen spoke before the king; in return, James took to the lectern and read a three-hour Latin oration of his own. In thanks – one assumes genuine – the university awarded the scholar-king a silver goblet and cover.

Another excursion saw the king take his wife out via Frederiksborg and Horsholm to the island of Hven in the Sound. Here, the famed astronomer Tycho Brahe held court. On the island were housed an underground laboratory, the Stjerneborg ('castle of the stars') and, above, a newer, more opulent observatory, Uraniborg. The facility sat amid fragrant orchards – doubtless less pleasant during that terrible winter – and fishponds. Later drawings of the place show a pretty, walled Renaissance palace, rich in domes and cupolas. Uraniborg's interior was no less splendid: it was filled with sextants and quadrants; equatorial armillary spheres; a library; Copernicus's own triquetrum; and even a printing press on the southern range of the complex which would in time publish Brahe's own text on astronomy. In this setting, Brahe had become famous for his observations and his willingness to receive students from across the globe. Less salubriously, he was notorious for the disdain with which he treated his intellectual and social inferiors; he must, too, have made quite a sight, having a scar across his forehead and a brass nose held in place by paste or glue (he had lost his actual nose in duels in the 1560s). His snobbery, of course, made him particularly receptive to the favour of a king and queen. James appears to have been charmed – obsequious intellectuals scored double points with him – and he was happy to gift Brahe two of his English mastiffs and a Latin inscription:

Est nobilis ira Leonis
Parcere subjectis et debellare superbos.
Jacobus Rex

[The lion's wrath is noble
Spare the conquered and overthrow the proud]

As Alan Stewart notes, the lines were on James's mind at the time. He also wrote them in the hymn book belonging to Henrik Ramel (King Christian's tutor) and later made them into the motto on his twenty-pound coins. They thus formed a fitting commemoration of what had been a stimulating experience. Indeed, the only downside might have come in the form of an unpleasant reminder of James's past: amongst the wonders of Uraniborg was a prominently displayed portrait of George Buchanan (probably given to the scholar by Peter Young). On seeing it, James professed himself pleased. His real thoughts (given he had banned Buchanan's writings – with unclear results – in 1584) can only be guessed at.

But what did the queen make of the excursion to Uraniborg? This is difficult to answer, as she left no written account and seems to have been content to appear as a smiling, gracious appurtenance to her new husband. On the one hand, it is difficult to imagine that a fifteen-year-old with no classical education can have had much interest in the obscure scientific objects, or the scientific thinking, which were the treasures of Renaissance intellectualism. On the other, both James and Brahe were devoted lovers of poetry as a means of intellectual inquiry. James's love of the poetic arts was still very much in play (he had been busily writing verses on the vagaries of the weather prior to leaving Scotland, and whilst in Copenhagen claimed he was 'addicted to the literary arts'), and Brahe had published a 234-line elegy to Urania in his *de nova Stella* (1573). Further, in 1602 he would publish his *Astronomiae Instauratae Progymnasmata*, to which James contributed commendatory verses.[15] Anna herself would never be a poet, but she certainly became a passionate devotee of the art and patron to some of the most talented writers of her era; she would, indeed, attempt to instil a love of poetry in her children, providing her eldest son with an edition of Guy du Faur's witty quatrains. Whether she enjoyed her time at Uraniborg or not, it is at least worth considering that there lay in the trip the seeds of shared interests between herself and her husband, which ought to have boded well for their life together.

Although scholarly pursuits were the hallmark of the Danish visit,

James was still mindful of Scotland. In February, he had written home that his people should make ready to receive him. In March, ahead of the inevitable return, he despatched William Schaw – who had been busily bearing witness to Danish architectural developments and practices – back home to ensure Holyroodhouse, Stirling, and Linlithgow were in readiness. He also ordered the ships required to carry himself and Anna home to set sail. But so too did he take care of Scots abroad, paying a visit to the lately arrived Scottish tapestry-weaver, Thomas Kingo, who had settled in Helsingør.

As proof of the onward march of time, Colonel William Stewart, who had once again been sailing back and forth between the kingdoms, arrived to make his plea for the king's return, alongside assurances that all was in readiness for his arrival. In response, James ordered red velvet to make up new hangings, as well as new saddles (one in black velvet trimmed with gold and one in silver lamé). Clearly, the King of Scots had developed a taste whilst abroad for the material splendour which enhanced royal prestige; and he was keen to ensure that his Scottish court did not disappoint its new queen.

The prospect of Anna's life in Scotland was also much in her mother's mind. Sophie, who apparently hoped to ensure the new Queen of Scots enjoyed an appropriate level of dignity, chose – unwisely, as it would happen – Chancellor Maitland as her instrument, asking him to take control of the setting up of the queen's household.

As the preparations for the wedding of Elizabeth of Denmark and Henry Julius were underway, yet another bevy of Scotsmen arrived. These had been sent over by Lennox, acting as First Lord of the Council, to add weight to Colonel Stewart's request for a swift return of the royal couple. At the head of the delegation was the minister Patrick Galloway – a man who shared James's support for episcopacy and so who was well placed to make a favourable impression as he sought to draw the king from his pleasurable holiday. Somewhat undermining Galloway's mission was the fact that, in the king's absence, Scotland had been largely peaceful, suffering only minor skirmishes and civic disorders in the capital. Nevertheless, it was clear that James needed to stick to the plan of returning following the wedding – if for no other reason than, as Maitland knew all too well, the cost of the whole affair was mounting with each day that passed (and, from the chancellor's perspective, rising too was the number of schemes which might be forming against him at home).

The royal wedding marked a final family affair. Even Anna's grandfather, Duke Ulrich, travelled from Güstrow (his wife, Anna's grandmother, having died in 1586). On the wedding day, the youngest brothers of the house of Oldenburg led the procession to the chapel at Kronborg, with Princess Elizabeth being led behind them by little King Christian. As the senior royal ladies, Anna and her mother, the dowager, followed. With the nuptials having been celebrated, the usual feasting, banqueting, and drinking ensued.

Now it really was time to face reality. Two days after the wedding – the time in between presumably needed to nurse hangovers – James and Anna boarded Admiral Peder Munk's patched-up *Gideon*, which would sail at the head of a fleet of thirteen ships, some Scottish and some Danish. This was bittersweet for the new queen, who would be leaving her family – almost certainly for the last time, in some cases – but who, on the credit side, could look forward to a new life as a crowned consort. For James, it was probably just bitter. The trip abroad had constituted one of the happiest periods of his life. He had been surrounded by a loving family (even if not his own); he had been treated with absolute deference and respect; and no one had been trying to kidnap or contain him. Most importantly, of course, he had claimed a bride whom he found attractive sexually, and who might come to meet his considerable emotional needs. What exactly he required of a woman emotionally, however, was not altogether clear.

10

His Will Revealed

If James thought that marriage with a prominent and powerful Protestant dynasty would either silence the conniptions of his Kirk or cow his nobility into behaving, he had another thing coming. Both clergymen and aristocrats had been anticipating the arrival of their king and his queen: the first to ensure that she behaved in accordance with Scottish doctrine, and the second because a new consort offered fresh opportunities to gain powerful positions – and excuses to make trouble if they failed to secure them.

The fleet out of Denmark arrived at Leith at 2 p.m. on 1 May 1590. Alongside the returning Scots was Anna's train, numbering around 200, including a preacher, Johannes Serin (who would convert from Lutheranism to hard Calvinism but remain with the queen for life); a jeweller, Jacob Kroger (who would prove to be something of a villain); a secretary (Calixtus Schein); and her favourite waiting women, Anna Sophia Kaas (sometimes known as Kroas or Roos) and Cathrina Schinkel. James, undoubtedly, was keen that his young bride have some home comforts, and as eager that Scotland – rich as it was in ancient sovereignty – should impress the Danes.

Leith, which had been repeatedly razed and rebuilt during the tumultuous sixteenth century, was suitably decorated for a reception. A force of 200 caparisoned soldiers was present – when they saw the arriving ships, they fired off cannon, sparking a gun salute around the port. Lennox, Bothwell, and Lord John Hamilton then boarded the docked *Gideon* to welcome the sovereigns, and James and Anna, after receiving their obeisance, followed the lords ashore,

149

to a carpeted wooden platform on which they listened to French verses delivered by James Elphinstone of Innernochtie.

Although the king had issued an advance warning that the new queen was not to be pressed by a noble concourse of position-seeking ladies, few had heeded it. The competition for place was too great. Thus, a gaggle of aristocrats had decked themselves out in their finery and assailed the platform, forcing Anna to accept the greetings of her new noble subjects. The men of the now disbanded Regency Council came first – the peers of the realm followed. Amongst this colourful display were, however, men and women who would come to earn the queen's enmity. The Earl of Mar was chief amongst them. It is true that the young John Slates had had a youth steeped in factional intrigue, but, given the weakness of the Crown and the rival power blocs surrounding the king, he could hardly have had anything else. Since his rehabilitation, he had become a truly reformed character and regained his sovereign's trust. Nevertheless, he would, years later and due to his following James's orders, become Anna's bitterest foe (much to the king's exasperation). With him was his mother, the dowager Countess Annabella, who had once criticised Buchanan for striking the Lord's Anointed. She would share in the hatred her son earned from the new queen. Chancellor Maitland introduced his wife, Jean Fleming – both would also fall into her disfavour. Lest it appear that Anna simply came to hate everyone in Scotland, it is of course worth pointing out that these were just a few of the faces welcoming her at Leith.

For his part, James was bursting with pride – in himself as much as in his new wife. He had silenced the doubters and proven that he was quite capable of sexual congress with a woman (Anna having turned fifteen during his time abroad, it is likely that their marriage had been fully consummated). He allowed his bride to retire to the adjacent King's Wark – an upmarket lodging and sometimes Customs House – whilst he remained on the decorated scaffold to take 'the chief of the dames by the hand, every one after another [before departing] to the South Leith Kirk in the Kirkgate to praise God'.[1]

Thereafter, the royal couple was forced to remain in Leith for five days, due to Holyroodhouse still not being fully furnished and dressed. There was thus time to arrange a suitably grand ride out of the town and through Edinburgh and the Canongate. This took place on 6 May, when the silver coach had been unloaded and brought to a high shine. Pulled by eight white horses and flanked by James, Bothwell, Lennox, and Lord John Hamilton, Anna and her ladies rode in it through a thronged capital. Edinburgh, despite its own chequered history of being fired upon, invaded, and burnt, was as well decorated as Leith. It was small, composed mainly of a High Street surrounded by a maze-like network of wynds and side streets, and it had been built upwards rather than outwards. As a consequence, the wealthier townsfolk could take advantage of their upper galleries and windows to look down on the procession.

Holyroodhouse, when it was gained, presented a fine aspect. The former abbey guesthouse, which had been improved beyond recognition, would not have presented a fairy tale palace (as it does to modern eyes), but rather a model of continental civility. Its royal apartments had finally been fitted out with rich red velvet, and Anna's own rooms were decorated in cloth-of-gold and cloth-of-silver. The palace had been steadily improved by successive Stuart monarchs (chiefly James IV and V) until it had become the premier living quarters of the monarchy. It would never be Anna's favourite residence, but it was unquestionably an important one in signifying the message James sought to project: that the latest Stuart sovereign had taken full possession of Scotland, and that he, by virtue of his new wife, would not be the last.

Some days of comfort and revelry were allowed as the king and queen got to know each other better. On both their minds was the coronation and accompanying royal entry into the city (the ride through it having been a prelude). The date was set for 17 May – a Sunday – but the entry was vetoed by the Kirk from taking place on the same day (their objection being to any form of drunken revelry infecting the Sabbath). Nor was the date the only cause of disagreements. The king, irritable due to a painfully swollen hand, insisted on the coronation involving anointment by holy oil – a ritual which Kirk ministers declared 'a superstitious rite amongst Christians, borrowed from the Jews'. Yet James was immovable. Anointment had a long history in Scotland and, importantly, in the southern kingdom on which he had his eye. His defence rested on the biblical basis of the ritual and, when that failed to convince, he simply insisted on the docile Robert Bruce conducting affairs. In this he won. Anna would get her anointment.

Of concern also was the expense. James had spent prodigiously on his Scandinavian tour, but the perennial problem of the Scottish monarchy at the time was its finances – or lack of them. As though his pockets were bottomless, the king ordered lengths of purple velvet and Spanish taffeta for Anna's coronation robe; crimson velvet to dress the footmen; and red broadcloth to line the furniture of his Danish guests. Concerned at how those guests might view proceedings, he also rented rooms in Edinburgh (each stocked with bed, coal, and candle) for visiting dignitaries, as well as renting fifteen extra featherbeds (then a luxury) at two shillings a night, outfitting trumpeters in French hats, and – curiously – having golden banners made up bearing his own arms and those of his 'bedfellows' (presumably meant in the sense of his bedchamber attendants).[2]

Yet, oddly enough, James was also quick to cut corners wherever he could. Indeed, he asked if he might borrow from Mar a pair of stockings, half-joking that 'you would not that your King should look like a scrub on such an occasion'.[3] To the modern eye, King James presents a curious blend of having been penny-wise and pound-foolish. When he thought he had money, he would spend extravagantly and give generously – almost blindly. When minor savings could be made, he would strive to prove himself a niggard. At any cost, he was loath to be thought penurious, though he would frequently and politically plead poverty if it meant chiselling money out of his compatriots. Yet his gestures of economy were never sufficient, and, throughout his life, the king had a grasp of finances that would cause an accountant to swoon. The problem, which would grow worse, was that his understanding of the gift-giving economy that underpinned courtly – and thus government – life invariably involved giving large cash gifts to friends and supporters (whereas the cannier Elizabeth of England favoured more material – cheaper – ones). His antipathy towards accounts and finance is well evidenced; it was not that he had no conception of them, but that he disdained even considering them. Frequently, he would resort to rhetoric which scorned commercialists; he had, during the wrangling over Anna's dowry, claimed he would be 'no merchant' for his bride, and he later told one English parliament that where a contract began, affection ended; another he thanked for their 'no-merchantlike dealing'.[4] His weak grasp of finances was one of the less agreeable things he would soon find he had in common with Anna (if he did not instil it in her himself).

On the day of the coronation, splendour having won out over economy, two processions departed Holyroodhouse for the nearby abbey. James led the first, clad in purple velvet and ermine and followed by first his household, then the nobility, the clergy, and those knights who attended. Anna's procession followed, this led by the Danish aristocrats who had come with her to Scotland (wearing diamond-and-gold chains), followed by a band of lairds (Scottish landowners of the gentle class, known by the style 'surname of location'), burgesses, the Lyon Herald, Sir David Lindsay of Rathillet, and Chancellor Maitland, who bore the queen's crown (and who was, the following day, formally granted the lordship of Thirlestane as part of the celebrations).

Anna herself followed, supported – significantly, as the queen's eyes were as much trained on asserting their rights as her husband's – on her right by Robert Bowes, who remained the resident English ambassador. On her left walked Admiral Peder Munk, along with Stene Brahe and Breide Rantzau, the two Danish ambassadors. Following this glittering array were the dowager Countess of Mar, Lady Seton, Lady Thirlestane (Maitland's wife), Anna Sophia Kaas, and Cathrina Schinkel. Inside the abbey, the latter pair escorted Anna to the sanctuary, whereupon the preacher Patrick Galloway (who had visited the royal couple in Denmark) took the pulpit, led the opening prayers, and read Psalm 45 which, unsurprisingly, was so much to James's taste it might have been pre-arranged:

> You love righteousness and hate wickedness;
>   therefore God has set you above your companions
>   by anointing you with the oil of joy.

Following this, Lennox, Hamilton, Bruce, and Lindsay begged the king that they might conduct their office. On the request being granted, Bruce declared his right to crown the new queen, before beginning the ritual of anointment. This involved the dowager Lady Mar undoing the royal gown to reveal Anna's breast, before standing back so that Bruce could pour upon the flesh 'a bonny quantity of oil'. When she was redressed, Lennox, Hamilton, and 'the virgins of Denmark' (the young Danish ladies) then took the anointed queen to a curtained attiring chamber, where she donned her coronation robes and took up her new place at the king's side.

James then called for the crown, which was handed to him. He passed it to Lennox – who was the premier noble in the realm – and the duke and Maitland shared the duty of placing it on Anna's bare blonde head. The tableau was completed when Bruce received the sceptre from Hamilton and passed it to her, and William Douglas, 9th Earl of Angus, handed her the sword of state.

Anna of Denmark was thus transformed into Anna, Queen of Scots. This was a moment of triumph, but only of a fleeting sort. Having achieved the position, she was now expected to fulfil its requirements. Chief amongst these was the provision of male heirs – but she might also have hoped that she could make her husband happy and offer emotional and political support. The nature of his emotional needs was soon enough to be illustrated.

Not only the selection of psalm hinted at the king's demands; the whole ceremony was rich in symbolic display of them. They were crystallised in Bruce's next speech: 'We, by the authority of the King's Majesty, with the consent of his states, representing the whole body of his country, place the crown on your Majesty's head;

and we deliver this sceptre to your Highness, acknowledging you to be our sovereign Queen and lady, to whom we promise all points of office and obedience, dutiful in those things that concern the glory of God, the comfort of the Kirk, and the preservation of his Majesty; and we crave from your Majesty the profession of the faith and religion we profess.'[5]

Lindsay translated the request into Danish, and Anna voiced her agreement: 'I, Anna, Queen of Scotland, profess, and before God and His angels wholly promise, that during the whole course of my life, as far as I can, I shall sincerely worship the same eternal God according to His will revealed in the Holy Scriptures. That I withstand and despise all papistical superstitions, and ceremonies, and rites, contrary to the word of God, and I will procure peace to the Kirk of God within this kingdom. So God, the Father of all Mercies, have mercy upon me.'[6]

Her vow almost certainly derived from James's pen. Like the elaborate requests made to the king throughout the proceedings, and the gracious permissions he gave, it was heavy on promoting the centrality of his role in his wife's queenship. In her avowal, Anna was simply parroting the Jacobean line: she would follow her sovereign in religion and serve God according to the scriptures (a favourite method by which James stood up to the Kirk was by explicating his own scriptural interpretations). In short, the coronation had served not simply to elevate and glorify Anna, but to present her husband as her lord and master. This was standard enough, but, in his emotional attitude to women, James was to show himself deeply conservative. If the newly crowned queen was to win his heart in any meaningful way, she would need to become his servant and pupil.

With the ritualistic aspects completed and the king's demand for primacy over his wife made clear, the Lyon King of Arms began a thundering cry of 'God save the Queen!' which was taken up by all present and joined by the blast of trumpets. The day, however, was still young. Over the course of several more hours (the ceremony lasted seven), and in a nod to the hotter voices in the Kirk, the preacher Andrew Melvill delivered 200 Latin verses. To balance out his brand of Calvinism, Bruce was then allowed to give his own speech on the benefits which would accrue to the nation as a result of it gaining a consort. After this, the entire congregation was exhorted to sink to its knees and raise its hands in obeisance, before each member in turn swore oaths of fealty. When these were concluded, Patrick Galloway finally drew the long day to a close, pronouncing a valedictory blessing. Anna, still crowned and robed, was led by Maitland back to the palace, for an evening of festivities. For all she had read her lines well, what she thought of the demands made on her would become clear soon enough. And soon enough, too, further requirements would follow.

*

Two days later, the wheels of Anna's silver coach were in motion again. This time, mounted noblemen bore a pall of purple velvet above it. The occasion was the state entry, which was designed so that the civic authorities could, in a convivial and mutually respectful – and drink-fuelled – atmosphere, lay out their own expectations of the queen. Leading the procession was 'an absolutely real and native blackamoor' bearing a sword. Behind him came fifty Edinburgh men with blackened faces:

> For some were clad in silver pure,
> And some in taffeta white like snow:
> Ay two [by] two in order stands,
> With batons blank into [held in] their hands.
> Each and in order kept his place,
> As well the foremost and the last,
> These Moors did march before her Grace,
> While she into her palace passed.[7]

The inclusion of a black man and men dressed up in blackface was not novel; the royal entry had been modelled on that arranged for Mary Queen of Scots' similar entry into Edinburgh.[8] The poet John Burel equated these counterfeit 'Moors' with the 'Inds', or Native

Americans. He described them as 'Leaving their land and dwelling place, / For to do honour to her Grace'.[9] The single real black man was certainly not from the New World. However, it is clear that the English fascination with American 'savages', which was then current, was something with which the King and Queen of Scots were keen to associate themselves, probably as a means of further linking themselves with tastes and cultural developments south of the border. The fact that Anna adopted a seal featuring 'a savage, wreathed about the middle, holding in his left hand a club erect' would certainly bear this out.[10]

The queen and her train were welcomed by magistrates at the tapestry-lined West Port, where a globe – likely the same one used in earlier entries, including James's – was lowered from a music-filled gallery. When it opened, out stepped a boy dressed in red velvet and a white taffeta cloak: he was playing Edina, the physical embodiment of the capital. As her husband had been previously, Anna was handed the city's keys, as well as a jewel and a gilded Bible – the demand being that she would prove herself a protectress of religion.

With her gifts in hand, the queen was then driven from the Grassmarket up the West Bow, where the sight of a plethora of mathematical instruments greeted her. Another boy – playing Astronomia this time – appeared to deliver Latin verses written by the schoolmaster Hercules Rollock, these predicting her fecundity. The expectation here hardly requires explanation; there had been speculation about the queen's pregnancy – obviously tittle-tattle – as early as March 1590, when the royal couple were in Denmark. But he also predicted rain – upon which townsfolk stationed in the galleries above began throwing down sugary treats. Escaping this saccharine assault, the party rode on. Nine maidens, singing as they played organ music, awaited at the Butter Tron. Their demand was not just – again – that the queen should provide Scotland with heirs, but that she should become an artistic patron.

At the next stop (and at each station, a new team of men – mostly local craftsmen – took up the poles of the royal canopy) the queen encountered the forbidding hulk of St Giles Cathedral. Outside the building a stage had been constructed, on which stood Virtue and her four daughters: Prudence, Justice, Temperance, and Fortitude, each swathed in black silk and wearing garlands of flowers around their necks. Virtue handed Anna a crown, whilst the daughters sang their own requirements: their new sovereign lady must not be lazy; she should love justice; she should retain her humility; and she must be temperate. To better illustrate their points (a necessity, given the speeches were given in Scots and Anna did not yet speak it), the four figures held up their symbols: an astrolabe, a sword and scales, a club and shield, and an hourglass and bridle.

At this stage, the procession halted. As Psalm 120 was sung, the queen debarked from her coach and was taken into the cathedral by Lord John Hamilton and Peder Munk. Robert Bruce had once again been drafted in, and his choice of text this time was Psalm 107, which thanked God for calming storms and leading His people into safe havens. Whether or not Scotland would prove a safe haven was, as yet, an unknown.

When the religious duty was done, Anna left, only to find that the conduits were flowing with claret and a pageant had been set up. This showed the lineage of the Danish monarchy and displayed the arms of previous Scottish queens consort. At the Salt Tron, in furtherance of the theme, an artificial tree had been built, which illustrated James and Anna's common descent from Christian I of Denmark (whose daughter had married James III and thus begat the ongoing Stuart dynasty), and a supine actor sprang up, revived by the queen's presence, to deliver a Latin speech. Nearby, boys dressed as Bacchus and Ceres stood by a table weighted down with sweetmeats and rich foods. The delicacies were intended to represent Anna's Scottish jointure properties, and when the boys began sharing them amongst the crowd, the lesson was that the new queen should be a gregarious and open-handed mistress.

The final spectacle took place at the Netherbow, which marked the city's border with the Canongate. Not to be forgotten, James appeared – not in person but represented by a boy playing Solomon, who received balsam from another actor garbed as the Queen of

Sheba. If the message was not clear, a schoolboy stood ready to make it so: Anna, he sang, was Sheba and James Solomon. Everything she had seen, every honour she had been given, everything she had received – including her crown – was in his gift, and she was in his debt. This included a rich jewel, commissioned by the burgess William Fairlie and carved by jeweller David Goldsmith, called the 'A', which was lowered by a silk rope from the gatehouse.[11] Thus laden, the procession made its way back to Holyroodhouse, where the dancing, feasting, and banqueting could begin.

The general air of frivolity could not last. On the 23rd, the city gave the Danish ambassadors a tour of the royal Coin House, and the next day James went to St Giles to thank Edinburgh for the honour done his wife. Still expressing his generosity, he joined Anna at Leith on the 26th, where the pair watched a large part of the Danish party sail off with presents of solid gold chains carved with the king's image. With the show over, it was now truly time for the king and queen to see how well they matched as people – or rather whether Anna was willing to behave as her husband wished and needed.

*

Scotland had not seen a royal couple performing a grand romance since the earliest days of the king's parents' marriage. From the new couple's first days together, the signs were good. Both James and Anna appeared content in one another's company and were, in fact, to go together on their first joint – if small – tour of Scotland. Their goal was to visit the queen's new jointure properties, with which James hoped to impress her, and over which she hoped to cast a judicious eye.

Already, even before the coronation, she had exhibited an interest in her lands. On 12 May, the Danish ambassadors Stene Brahe and Breide Rantzau had, along with Peder Munk, inspected the palace at Falkland. The palace's keeper, James Beaton of Creich, gave them a tour of what was a small but remarkably opulent building (it having been built up from a hunting lodge to an architectural feast under James V and Marie of Guise). The lawyer John Skene had then issued the charter which officially endowed the new queen with her properties, and, in a symbolic gesture, a fistful of soil had been handed over to Peder Munk. On 13 and 14 May, ownership of Dunfermline and Linlithgow followed. Anna had probably been gratified by the reports of Falkland, but she was keen to see it and her other new acquisitions. To quieten tensions in Edinburgh, James made a solemn promise to the Kirk to 'amend his former negligence and to execute justice without feed or favour' (which he would follow up in late summer with the ingratiating claim that the Scottish Kirk was the sincerest in the world and superior to the masses in English preached south of the border – an easy assertion for a man who had no first-hand experience of Anglican services). That done, he was free to escort his wife out of the city.[12]

Their journey first took them to Linlithgow. Like Falkland, this palace had been greatly enhanced by James V; built of mellow sandstone and styled after the châteaux of the Loire valley, it rose in graceful symmetry beside a picturesque freshwater loch. Today it lies in majestic ruins, but the evidence of its once opulent galleries and magnificent central fountain remains as testament to its former splendour.

Still, as lavish as her surroundings were, Anna found herself less impressed by her husband's way of life. From the start, she found his courtiers to be overly familiar with their sovereign – as had long been the custom amongst the entitled Scottish elite. Worse, this laddishness had resulted in a general air of bad manners and ribaldry. On visiting her husband's suite of rooms (the king's and queen's apartments were stacked one atop the other), she was grossly insulted by one gentleman (whose name and the nature of whose insult were, unfortunately, unrecorded). This was intolerable to the young queen, who was used to Danish courtesy. From then on, she determined to reform the lax Scottish court along more deferential lines.

As a result of her distaste for Scotland's tradition of high levels of access to the royal family, she insisted on keeping those Danish ladies who remained to her by her side (a retinue of sixteen Danes having stayed). These were to form a barrier against the pushy Scottish ladies who felt it their right to roles in her household. The courtier William Dundas sourly noted in June that 'contrary to the humour of our people, [she] hath banned all our ladies clean from her'.[13] Anna was starting as she meant to go on, by exercising the traditional right of the consort to assign places in her own household. It was, however, both impolitic and, from her husband's perspective, an unwelcome display of independence.

James, however, was not entirely at odds with her way of thinking; indeed, he had appreciated greatly the ways of the Danes. Soon enough, it was reported that 'things are beginning to be strangely altered . . . the pattern of the Court of Denmark is greatly before the eyes of our King . . . the royal household is diminished of the best of his servants'.[14] Things were changing, even if it disturbed the cosy system long enjoyed by the Scots.

In July, this more decorous court moved on, this time to Anna's jointure lands at Dunfermline, crossing the Forth by ferry to get there. Here was a less impressive sight. Though attempts at refurbishment had been made (in May, the King's Precept had granted William Schaw £400 Scots for 'the reparation of our house at Dunfermline before the Queen's Majesty's passing there'), the building had not been given an external makeover since the time of James IV.[15] Although its interior had been tidied up (and the queen's own bed shipped in), it proved a disappointment. What must have been apparent was that the Scottish Crown, for all its antiquity, was living on past glories. To her credit, however, Anna did not view matters negatively. Rather, she saw an opportunity to institute her own construction programme. The visit thus took on the complexion of an architectural survey, which prompted the idea of building a new palace downhill, connected to the old one via a gallery (although, in the event, it took a decade to see completion). What could not be converted into positivity, though, was the fact that when he had granted her the lands of Dunfermline Abbey and its palace, James had neglected to include the associated lands of Musselburgh and Inveresk, which, though they lay across the Forth, had long pertained to the regality of Dunfermline. These had been snapped up in

1587 by Maitland, who had an interest in landholding and building of his own (indeed, on his elevation to the lordship of Thirlestane, he had begun constructing there a fine tower house). Thus was born a feud between queen and chancellor which had already been brewing since she learned of his early opposition to her marriage. The fact that her mother had asked Maitland to organise her household – a right which Anna knew to be her own – had, ironically, only added insult to injury.

Thus somewhat soured, the tour next took in Falkland Palace, which boasted a real (or royal) tennis court and all the French architectural features remaining from James V's period of upgrading. By now, however attractive (or promising) her new properties had proven, the role her husband intended for her must have become obvious to the new queen. All three buildings were designed for pleasure: pretty stages on which she might enact a thoroughly submissive, decorative role. A politically active wife seems to have been the furthest thing from James's mind.

Whatever her thoughts on this, the question remained of how to staff her household in the long term. Whether she was to be a political or an ornamental queen, she needed a body of servants and attendants able to project a sense of majesty (requiring payment of '£4541 Scots in money' annually for her living expenses, 'plus substantial amounts of wheat, barley, oats, capons, hens and geese'). What she sought – with James's endorsement – was a bevy of staff (from Masters Household down to coalmen) equal to that of the army surrounding the king. To fill this array of positions, though, required both tact and an intimate knowledge of Scotland's corpus of elites.

James, in an effort to be helpful, thus gave that seasoned courtier Sir James Melville (who had been knighted at her coronation) the position of First Gentleman of her Household, with the intention that this expert on court ritual and fount of knowledge of Scottish society might provide a helpmeet.[16] For all his experience, however, Melville was by this time something of a curmudgeon, who had little in common with a fifteen-year-old girl. Worse, from Anna's

162

perspective, she immediately sensed that her right to assign her own positions was under threat. So began the first royal spat. When Melville arrived to begin issuing advice, the queen – who suspected, probably rightly, that he was to keep tabs on her – asked, 'whether he was ordained to be her keeper'. He answered that he knew her to be descended of 'so noble and princely parents . . . that she needed no keeper, albeit her dignity required to be served by honourable men and women, both old and young, in sundry occupations'.[17] Put out by his smooth words, Anna murmured darkly that she was being 'evilly dealt with'. Fortunately, however, she resolved to tolerate his presence and to appreciate his advice in building up an appropriate queen's court. James and Anna were thus able to create dual establishments commensurate with their rank. At joint dinners, tables were set up separating his household from hers, and even then distinctions were made between rank and nationalities. To the top table went wine, meats (capon, beef, dove, geese, and fish), and the finest bread; to the bottom went coarse bread and ale.[18] James and Anna, as was the Scottish custom, dined publicly in the presence chamber – a style they would later import southwards as a contrast to Queen Elizabeth's preference for taking meals privately.[19]

What they were never able to do, however, was to live within their means. Year on year, their expenses – inflated by the necessity of maintaining their royal state and buying the loyalty of staff and aristocrats with gifts – would grow: a problem not helped by the reality of economic inflation. Nevertheless, at this early stage, all seemed illusively idyllic, with the seeds of conflict buried under fairly fragrant soil. Whether Anna would choose to water them remained to be seen.

It had become clear, though, that James's emotional needs no longer demanded a wise role model – he had burnt his fingers with Huntly on that score and was unwilling or unmindful to seek a replacement for Esmé to replicate the full-blown affair (from his perspective) of his youth. What his heart craved now was an obedient, dutiful, compliant inferior in age and wit: in other words, the ideal (or idealised) submissive wife. Now that he had won a willing bride from across the seas, he hoped that she would prove tractable enough to win his love.

But something would soon cross the ocean in the royal couple's wake. Indeed, as he had taken his sad farewell of Denmark and the honeymoon period it had been, the king cannot seriously – even as his ship had rocked in those strangely stormy seas – have envisaged the horrific legacy it would inflict on both his psyche and his subjects.

11

Toil and Trouble

Anna's tenure as Scottish consort began not with a bang but with a witch hunt. This did not, however, stem from Scottish attitudes and beliefs but from Danish ones. Indeed, it had all started in Denmark.

In the months following James and Anna's departure, Copenhagen, that hub of stimulating, intellectual thinking, had fallen under a pall of terror. Admiral Peder Munk, casting about for a reason as to why his original mission to carry Anna from Denmark had failed, blamed Christoffer Valkendorff, the treasurer, of not adequately provisioning the navy. The inquiry into what had gone wrong went all the way to the Herredag, the Danish High Court, which supported Valkendorff by blaming the foul weather. However, the treasurer pointed out that there might well be a link between ongoing witchcraft trials and precisely those freak storms.

There then unfolded a terrifying tale of black magic and devilry. A woman named Karen Weffuers (or Weaver) was named as the principal agent. Her supposed sorcery had involved sending storm-raising demons to sea in empty barrels. Under torture, she confessed to this unlikely act, naming Anna Koldings as her partner in crime. Koldings, too, confessed, and she was soon joined by Maren Matts Bryggers, Maren Mogensis, and Margrethe Jakob Skrivers. Although the word was not yet in use in connection to witch gatherings, a supposed coven had been discovered.

The news was not slow in reaching Scotland, where witchcraft had been a crime punishable by death since 1563. There had been no wide-scale hunts, however, until the Scottish authorities got wind of what was going on in Denmark. When they did, they assumed that the Danish witches could not have acted alone, but rather that they must have kept demonic company with like-minded creatures at home.

These suspicions appeared to be confirmed when a maidservant, Geillis Duncan, confessed – at the compulsion of her employer, one David Seton, who distrusted her folk healing – that she had attended a demonic meeting at the church of North Berwick. This had comprised, it seemed, hundreds of witches, and was attended by the Devil himself. 'In a hollow voice', this terrifying, Satanic apparition had invited the hellish parishioners to 'kiss his arse' (which was, apparently, 'cold, like ice').[1]

At first, James was – understandably – sceptical, less of the existence of witchcraft than the veracity of wild confessions and accusations. However, his mind changed as those accusations began to land on more and more names: Barbara Napier (who would plead for mercy owing to pregnancy and eventually be acquitted, to the king's fury), a middle-class Edinburgh kinswoman-by-marriage to the Douglases; Dr Fian, also known as John Cunningham, who was a respectable Lothian schoolmaster; Robert Grierson, a ship's captain; and Euphemia MacCalzean (who was, like many others, burned at the stake), the daughter of the late Lord Cliftonhall, former Provost of Edinburgh. The accused were rounded up and conveyed to Holyrood, where, according to the pamphlet *Newes from Scotland*, the king conscientiously set about proving or disproving their guilt, employing his detective skills in the process. According to this account, his scepticism was quashed during the course of the investigation; interrogation records, however, paint a blacker picture of James and his fellows assuming guilt throughout. Sceptical though James could be, he was always credulous when accusations of witchcraft touched his own person.

It is always interesting to trace the birth of a mania, and it seems that this bizarre chapter in Scottish history sparked James's interest in the occult. It further marked what would be a lifelong fascination with the operation of the law and his own role in it (he seldom liked to miss an opportunity to interrogate accused malefactors personally). The accused witches were indeed brought to Holyrood, where the king could question them. It was in the royal presence that Dr Fian signed his confession, before managing to escape. On his recapture, he favoured discretion and, ultimately, he recanted and went to his death without making any further admissions.

Agnes Sampson, a midwife of good character, was amongst those accused. The unfortunate woman was subjected to having her head shaved and her naked body inspected for the marks with which Satan supposedly stamped his slaves. These, according to the inspectors, were apparent on her. What was considered – and reported to be – more damning, however, was her own open and chilling confession.

Expanding on the original tales of the North Berwick church, which she had obviously heard all about, Agnes confirmed the presence of upwards of a hundred celebrants. They came, supposedly, by sea, travelling in sieves. Geillis, the original accuser, would play a Jew's harp to entertain the congregation of the damned, whilst the Devil preached. According to *Newes from Scotland*, whose job it was to justify the witch-hunt, what made Agnes's confession different from Geillis's, however, was that the old woman apparently admitted that she had spied on James during his wedding night in Oslo – a claim which she supposedly proved by reciting the words spoken between the king and queen. The alleged words are unrecorded, but given the motives of the newsletter, the veracity of the tale is questionable.

James, however, was ready to believe anything; and the witches of North Berwick were ready to say anything. Toad venom, it emerged, had been gathered with the intention that his clothes should be poisoned. A corpse had been dug up, disarticulated, and its rotting limbs strung to the legs of a cat, which was christened Margaret and then hurled into the sea (this supposedly achieving those persistent wild storms). But the most worrying admission of all was yet to come. A wax effigy of the king himself had been fashioned and handed over to the Devil who, appearing at Prestonpans 'clad in a black gown, with a black hat upon his head', had then passed it around the coven.[2] Each witch had held it, saying, 'This is King James the sext, ordained to be consumed at the instance of the nobleman, Francis, Earl of Bothwell.'[3]

Having been emptied of her wicked knowledge, Agnes Sampson was garrotted and burned at the end of January 1591. Geillis Duncan went to her execution at Castlehill the following December, crying out that she had lied about Euphemia (who had already been burnt) being involved, and that Barbara Napier too was innocent – all, she said, had been confessed at the instigation of her cruel master, Seton, and his son. Probably she was telling the truth, and this pair were the only devils who had ever been at work.

To the king, these unfortunate men and women hardly mattered – as confirmed witches, they were better off in hell. That Bothwell, however, might have been a prime mover in the coven was genuinely horrifying; the fellow had been lately entrusted with a key role in the governance of the Regency Council. The earl was summarily called in by the Privy Council and warded in Edinburgh Castle, where it was hoped he would be separated from devils, witches, and corpse-strung cats. The charge against him became more plausible when it was apparently confirmed by another accused witch, Ritchie Graham, who testified that Bothwell had sought to discover how long the king would live.

Bothwell, naturally, denied everything and immediately saw the hand of his enemy, Maitland, at work. In this he was probably right; certainly, the idea that he was really consorting with witches in North Berwick or anywhere is a nonsense. Yet his career – especially his having involved himself with Huntly's foolish rebellion in 1589 – left him vulnerable. So too did his reputation as a stirrer and potential leader of factious nobles. As Ashby noted, 'Bothwell is able to offend more than any subject in Scotland, for his place and birth and the offices he bears, beside an able and undertaking man . . . without him the malcontents dare nothing, so as the winning of him will be the bridle of the rest.'[4]

Unfortunately for James, the earl showed no taste for being bridled himself. On 21 June, he imitated the daring of his infamous uncle, the 4th Earl, by escaping from Edinburgh Castle. The news reached the king at Tullibardine, where he had been performing in a masque held for the wedding of Lilias Murray and John Grant of Freuchie (a celebration in which Anna had joined him). Bothwell was immediately proclaimed to have 'had consultation with necromancers [raisers of the dead], witches, and other wicked and ungodly persons' with the goal of taking James's life.[5]

The king was in a panic. Yet, troublingly, Bothwell found an unlikely partisan – and one whose support was a source of both outrage and embarrassment to James: Queen Anna. As Bowes reported, 'It is said that her Majesty has been moved by Bothwell's friends to show favour towards him.' She therefore 'made suit to the King in Bothwell's favour, [but she] found him so moved, chiefly against such as had entreated her to deal therein, as she let it fall, with his good contentment'. Her reasons were complex. Since the allegations of witchcraft had surfaced, the new queen's feelings can only be imagined. She had left an idyllic life in Denmark only to find herself wed to an increasingly neurotic and fearful husband, who governed a realm full not only of witches – which were no new thing to a Dane – but dangerous nobles and their followers. Nevertheless, she stuck by James at first and did something she did well: she engaged in another ceremonial entry, this time into Perth, to help illustrate the strength of the Crown.

Where she could not please her husband, though, was in failing to reach an accord with Bothwell's chief enemy, Maitland. Despite the secretaryship going to Richard Cockburn of Clerkington in April 1591, Maitland retained the chancellorship and James's high favour (indeed, as a token of friendship, the king had attended the wedding of a Maitland niece at Thirlestane in February). During that same year, Anna's simmering anger over the lands of Musselburgh and Inveresk boiled over. Dr Paul Knibbe, who had been of her party during her first attempt to reach Scotland, was shipped over from Denmark in July to calm matters. Enjoying the backing of the Danish government, his goal was to secure the chancellor's agreement to relinquish those lands he held which rightly pertained to the queen's jointure property. Maitland, however, was caught in a bind: he had been selling the lands off, evidently hoping that he might receive hard cash for them and leave their new owners to face the queen's wrath.

Bothwell, meanwhile, had begun something of a guerrilla existence. From hiding in the Borders, he had appeared at Dalkeith, Crichton, Leith, and even the Canongate, where he openly challenged Maitland. This he could do because, despite the accusations against him and the national sense of fear being whipped up by the king, there were plenty who believed that he stood falsely accused, probably thanks to the chancellor's machinations. A refutation to Ritchie Graham's claims was even circulated, which held that Bothwell was a 'noble personage' conspired against by 'an infamous person [Graham] moved by the disposition and humour of his devilish nature' at the behest of courtiers who 'obscure the great majesty' of the king.[6] Amongst these anti-Maitland sympathisers was the queen. After an attempt to reconcile with the chancellor – undoubtedly at James's insistence – was met only with what she perceived as another insult, she appears to have, probably unwisely, decided to let the principle of her enemy's enemy being her friend guide her.

The lack of wisdom in her actions can be read in the evident glee with which the English ambassador was thus able to inflate the idea that there was trouble brewing in Scotland: 'There be of the nobility, gentlemen, boroughs and common people generally, grown to that disliking of the King for his careless guiding and government as [much as for his] uncredible writings. These open exclamations of the King [are] general amongst all sorts of his subjects, and daily such murders and havoc [take place] amongst his subjects who should be preserved under his protection, and [there is] a muttering amongst them for that the King doth nothing to it; in times past both in England and Scotland kings have been deposed for far less occasions than now are given them.'[7]

James was growing unpopular. His long absence had allowed quarrels to multiply. The rumours of deposition were likewise worrying. Long periods of royal minorities and regencies had devalued the monarchy, allowing the idea of republicanism, whether classical or theocratic, to flourish. The king's 'uncredible writings' – his open letters and tendency to try to persuade his people publicly – had done little more than make them roll their eyes. James had, or so Bowes claimed, simply gained a reputation for being ineffectual: a speaker rather than a doer. And whilst he could hector, lecture, and write, it was well known that the king would rather surround himself with a select band of boon companions in the countryside than be anywhere near the *hoi polloi*. This in itself was not unusual. Few early modern monarchs loved their people; their default position was to hold the masses in suspicion. Canny sovereigns, however, made effective play of their affection for the general public – James V of Scotland and Mary I of England (before the smoke of Smithfield had clouded her reputation) passed into legend for going out amongst ordinary folk and righting wrongs. Queen Elizabeth once confided that she distrusted her subjects as ever misliking their present government, but her genius was to hide this and in public use her considerable charm to court people with smiles and badinage. James, by contrast, preferred to try to persuade from a position of intellectual and hierarchical superiority, and ultimately to distance himself from his subjects. It showed.

Queen Anna was not immune to this supposed sense of disaffection either. An English observer in Berwick noted, 'Also their [the people's] great disliking of their Queen, for that she proves not with child, so that in the Parliament in November next it cannot be but that great mischief will be ruffling amongst them through their many feuds, as they will not let to [refrain from] saying openly that so long as this King reigns over them never any luck or grace will be in Scotland.'[8]

Through no fault of her own, Anna had not met the primary demand which had been foregrounded at her ceremonial entry into Edinburgh. But more sinister – and equally unfair – things were being said. Due to her anti-Maitland attempt at intercession on Bothwell's behalf, the gossip ran that 'the Earl and the Queen had some unlawful manner atwixt [between] them, so that none in

Scotland dare name the Earl to the King'. The hearsay was that the sixteen-year-old queen was not just trying to intercede on Bothwell's behalf; she was having an affair with him. Needless to say, this was bunkum. It would, however, set a pattern for the means by which courtiers would attempt to drive a wedge between the royal couple. Stirring up trouble between royal spouses for personal political gain had, admittedly, become something of a national pastime amongst the Scottish political elite – but whether it would succeed in causing a definitive break between James and Anna remained to be seen.

*

Bothwell's wanderings forced the king and queen to live in a state of suspense. The tension saw its first frightening break at the end of December 1591. They were in residence at Holyroodhouse when, on the 27th, the earl appeared in the company of a band of fifty supporters. The intruders entered via the stables and thundered through the palace, tearing keys from porters' hands and, when they reached James's apartments, attempting to burn down the door. When this failed, Bothwell turned his attention to the real focus of his anger – Maitland – whose rooms he tried to breach next. At the same time, his men set to work with hammers on Anna's door, presumably hoping to gain access to the king through her apartments. Thankfully, Edinburgh's citizens, ever alert to goings on in the palace, appeared in multitude, forcing the attackers to retreat before they could reach anyone. In their departure, however, they left the Master of the Stables and his twin brother dead (inspiring a heartbroken James to pen a commendatory sonnet). So too did they leave behind a number of their own men – eight captured Borderers who were summarily hanged. Bothwell, of course, slipped the net. Just as bad, the attack wreaked havoc on the king's fragile ego, and suddenly even his friends – notably young Lennox, who had already been in trouble for a clandestine marriage to a daughter of the executed Gowrie – became suspect.

If the king and queen expected this assault to turn public opinion in their favour, they were to be disappointed. The following day, gloating Kirk ministers – including his own chaplain, John Craig – condemned James for the troubles. This was their revenge against his having spoken so fairly on his return from Denmark, and at the General Assembly in August 1590, only to have 'forgot his promises'.[9] Further, ministers were outraged at the lax treatment still being afforded Catholic noblemen. In some ways, of course, the king had made a rod for his own back. His consistent lack of ruthlessness and his obvious softness towards any man who could charm him had encouraged Bothwell's renegade ways, and his double-tongued attitude towards the Kirk – standing up to it then backing down with fair promises – ensured that its ministers, too, felt they could say what they liked.

Not even his great Stuart palace was left to him. As a result of the Bothwell raid, he was forced to take Anna to Nicol Uddart's Edinburgh townhouse in Niddry's Close, whilst issuing a proclamation (on 10 January 1592) belatedly and lamely condemning the earl for his part in the Brig o' Dee rebellion – this to prove that he was not soft on rebels. Further humiliation awaited. When the king rode after Bothwell – perhaps hoping to regain the military reputation he had briefly enjoyed, and thereby proving that he was a man of action – he and his horse fell 'into the water of Tyne near Haddington, where he was speedily rescued, and yet not before he was sore wet'.[10]

Seeing all this indignity – always anathema – Anna attempted to improve matters via a peaceable conclusion. On 5 February, she pleaded for the life of the eminent surgeon John Naysmyth, who had been of Bothwell's party. So too did she continue to try to press for Bothwell's rehabilitation, only being dissuaded by the English agent, Roger Aston, whose wife was one of her ladies. Again, Anna's interference was largely James's own fault; he had promised Bothwell his life – as was his custom – and the queen, who lived by the motto 'honour goes before life' could not accept his breaking that promise. Nevertheless, it was clear that the new queen viewed herself as having some degree of political agency. This only served, however, to make her a more obvious target for troublemakers.

Soon enough, one of Scotland's chief miscreants – James's former love interest, and Bothwell's one-time ally – burst onto the political scene once again: Huntly was back and at the root of fresh mischief. In late February, news circulated that he had finally murdered his perennial enemy, James Stewart, 2nd Earl of Moray. This had been a long time coming; the reconciliation the king had forced between them had barely lasted the length of time they had all held hands. Huntly had, moreover, been energised by the political ructions Bothwell had been causing – mainly because he too foresaw a means of ridding Scotland of Maitland. As a result, when James had called for a final arbitration, the two rivals had begun travelling south in February, only for Huntly to corner Moray at his mother's castle of Donibristle, burn the unfortunate earl out, and fatally stab his reputedly rather lovely face. Although James had been within sight of the smoke from the fire, he had allegedly done nothing.

Once again, James's previous softness came back to bite him, as rumours spread that he had had foreknowledge of Moray's murder. He did nothing to silence disgruntled gossip about his selective sense of justice, instead only issuing a proclamation declaring his own innocence in the matter (which obviously had the opposite effect amongst scandalmongers). Old feelings evidently died hard, with the one who got away this time getting away with murder and receiving no royal condemnation. Anna, however, was also to be caught up in the tide of slander and sedition. False romances were soon being spun that she had been the dead earl's lover, and that James had condoned Moray's slaying out of jealousy. In these tales, she was cast as the vengeful sexual incontinent. The queen, on hearing of these rumours, immediately suspected Chancellor Maitland and his wife of fanning them, and she was probably right. It stretches credulity to believe that so many false tales touching the chancellor's enemies (the queen herself chief amongst them) did not at least have the approval of the Maitlands.

Outraged at being labelled a murderer and cuckold, the king bowed to his wife's pressure and relieved the chancellor of his office in March 1592. Maitland would all but retire from court until April the following year, but, almost immediately, James's inherently pacific nature kicked in. He attempted to broker a peace between his wife and the man who, however devious and hated he might be, had a first-class political mind. Sensing the chance to involve herself in Scottish affairs, Queen Elizabeth (who was secretly funding Bothwell's exploits in an attempt to force James to abandon his Catholic friends) also wrote north, this time to Anna, asking her to make peace with Maitland. It was to no avail. For now, the King and Queen of Scots were on their own.

In another climbdown – this one to try to win the favour of the Kirk – James finally allowed his parliament to override the 1584 Black Acts; the 1592 Golden Acts, passed in May, handed over power to the Presbyterian system and General Assembly, leaving episcopacy trampled in the mud. Cannily, though, the king did retain nominal spiritual supremacy, which he attempted to demonstrate by assiduously attending the Assemblies. More immediately, the Kirk was handed a snooper's charter: ecclesiastical courts were empowered to fund poor relief out of fines for subjects' sexual indiscretions. As importantly, no new bishops would be appointed until 1600, with James's supporter, Patrick Adamson, not being replaced as Archbishop of St Andrews on his death in 1592.

As if to remind James of his existence after the drama of the Huntly affair, Bothwell decided to strike again in late June – a final roll of the dice before his English funding ran dry. This time, his target was the indefensible Falkland, which a company of his Borderers fired upon in the middle of the night. As the palace was awoken by the tumult, the earl led another small force through a postern gate which gave access to the royal apartments. However, the palace guard was ready, and it drove him off – though he fled with the royal horses so as to prevent pursuit. In despair now, the king and queen were forced to Dalkeith for their protection. James, his paranoia at fever pitch, began 'lamenting his estate', having now decided that there were traitors in his inner circle. His worries were only fuelled by claims, promoted by his former lover, Gray, that the Kirk minister Robert Bruce had encouraged Bothwell in his endeavours; another old flame, Sandy Lindsay, likewise found himself accused of having sought to protect rather than help hunt down the errant earl. Nor was James gratified when libels (thought to be the work of Bothwell's men) singled him out as a 'bougerer' [buggerer] who did not touch his wife – rumours that carried the whiff both of truth and of the involvement of someone with knowledge of what had once gone on in his bedchambers.

His suspicions were not without foundation. In August, one of Anna's Danish ladies – Margaret Vinster, who had been left in Scotland in exchange for Anna Sophia Kaas and Cathrina Schinkel, both of whom had left when Dr Paul Knibbe and his Danish embassy left after appealing to Maitland in 1591 – fell in love. Her choice was John Wemyss of Logie – a Bothwell-supporting laird who had been imprisoned in Dalkeith for having helped plot the Falkland raid. She decided that, as his life seemed in danger, she should help him escape, and so she sweet-talked the guards into releasing him, pretending that she came from the king, who wished to interrogate their prisoner.

Margaret was thus able to bring her lover directly to the royal apartments and, on entering, the pair used a rope to lower Wemyss out and down to safety. Presumably they worked quietly; James and Anna were both asleep in the curtained bed either in the same room or in a private chamber nearby. When all was revealed in the morning, the royal pair quarrelled, he suspecting her of having known all about the lovers' plans, until both were in tears. However, publicly the king made a show of laughing off the whole affair.

Not all was doom, gloom, rumour, and suspicion, however. In December 1592, the royal couple attended the wedding of James's friend Mar to Marie Stuart (a sister of Lennox). On occasions like these, James and Anna could relax and enjoy one another's company, and the queen, too, could give gifts in the pursuit of building her own band of friends. This she did with the new Countess of Mar – a noted Catholic (who would, in fairness, convert to Protestantism not long after). It was in these early years, in fact, that Anna began to develop strong sympathies for the Roman religion, which James, when he accepted that she was a political animal, would show himself willing to use to his advantage.

The wedding, however, was rudely interrupted by religion in a far less welcome way. News reached the king that one George Kerr had been arrested and was found to have been smuggling papers which, apart from the signatures of several major Catholic nobles, were entirely blank. Quickly uncovered was a conspiracy which has become known as the affair of the Spanish Blanks, whereby Scotland's Catholic lords were engaged in a Jesuit-organised mission sponsored by Spain. The papers were intended to be taken to Philip II, who might fill them in as he saw fit; the Scottish Catholics had given him a blank cheque by which they might support invasion or any other means the Spaniards could devise of restoring the Roman religion. Philip and the Jesuits had needed no encouragement: Father William Crichton, the Scottish leader of the militant missionaries, was already planning a combined invasion of 30,000 Spaniards to join 15,000 Scots. If Queen Anna was flirting with the Catholics, she was potentially dipping her toe in dangerous waters. But so too – significantly for the future – was James, who was rumoured to have been personally soft on the plan, judging that it might be useful to know of Spanish invasion plans if the Spanish might be of use to him in pressing his English succession claims.

As a result of this discovery and the furore it caused, James renewed his attempts to broker peace between his wife and the banished chancellor, whom he knew would prove invaluable in managing the outcome of the conspiracy's discovery. Anna, however, was not to be drawn, and stoutly opposed her husband, insisting again that both Maitland and his wife had been poisonous slanderers of her own person.

Thus, without decent counsel, the king attempted once again to don military garb and ride north, in the hope of confronting some familiar, rebellious faces: Huntly, Erroll, and William Douglas, 10th Earl of Angus (a new convert to Catholicism). When he arrived, however, the men had already fled, and he was forced to return south having accomplished nothing. The result, naturally, was a renewal of howls from his Protestant subjects that he had been, as he always was, soft on a man he had incontinently loved for too long. This was the final straw, and the king determined once and for all that his wife – who had by now proven herself to be far too independently minded – would mend fences with his most useful politician.

Accordingly, in the summer of 1593, James appointed a council to oversee the queen's estates. Faced with such a body fighting his royal enemy's corner, Maitland capitulated. After James honoured him with a personal visit – the conversation during which might be imagined – the chancellor wrote Anna a letter of apology, feigning a lack of understanding over the causes of their feud and offering his services in making things right. In June, parliament thus approved her lordship over the disputed lands, and the following month Maitland was voted a return of the £20 Scots he had paid for them. He almost certainly was not happy, but he was back in power.

Over the moon, of course, was Queen Anna. Throughout, she had displayed a tenacity over what she viewed as her absolute rights which never waned. Rather than proving herself compliant and subservient she was, despite her youth, a prize fighter when it came to standing up for what she viewed as her own. Her conduct throughout 1593 – buoyed as it was by victory – was thus somewhat preening. She embarked upon a friendship with another of Lennox's sisters – the flamboyant Henrietta, Countess of Huntly, who had wed the troublesome earl in 1588; in May, the three women – Marie, Countess of Mar; the nominal Calvinist convert and crypto-Catholic Henrietta, Countess of Huntly; and the Lutheran queen – showed themselves off by handing out gold coins to the mariners who had brought Danish ambassadors Niels Krag and Steen Bille to Scotland (their mission being to ensure the Scottish parliament did as it had promised with regard to the queen's new lands).

That parliament, of course, had more pressing business. As it gave Anna what she wanted, it officially deprived Bothwell of his lands (though against Huntly it did nothing). The wild earl, however, was still at large and was not about to accept this state of affairs. He began courting the Kirk, knowing it to be hostile to the king and court, presenting himself as its loyal son (in contrast to James's slipperiness). So too did he publicly win his way into Queen Elizabeth's good graces – probably an easier feat, given that she was always keen to sow division north of the border.

Suitably girded with a new reputation as an honest Protestant with the best of intentions, Bothwell returned, with all the unpleasant predictability of a summer outbreak of plague. During his absence, he had crossed into England, to replenish his coffers and receive further instructions from Elizabeth on how best to provoke his own sovereign. Duly, on 24 July, he made another assault upon the royal household, again at Holyroodhouse. This time, he arrived early in the morning, wearing a disguise, and was admitted by Marie, Countess of Atholl, a daughter of that Earl of Gowrie who had imprisoned James in 1582 and been executed two years later. With his friend, the English-paid John Colville, the outlawed earl went directly to James's chambers and managed to gain entry without the need of a hammer or flaming torch. The king rushed half-dressed from his bedroom to his outer chamber, only to find Bothwell on his knees, his sword on the floor beside him. Crying 'treason', James bolted for the door which provided access to his wife's chambers, but found it locked from the other side.

Near hysteria, James was forced to return to Bothwell, to whom he delivered an impassioned speech regarding his royal state. He would rather, he declared, be slain than go captive with a man who could not, in any case, take his immortal soul. Bothwell, however, was all smiles. Pushing his sword towards the king, he bid James take his life if he would; he had not come as a regicide but as a penitent. Dramatically, he even reportedly laid out his long hair, inviting his sovereign lord to put his foot upon it to show how the balance of power stood.

Somewhat calmed – but probably still terrified – the king accepted this apparent submission, and an agreement was reached whereby Bothwell would face a show trial, be pardoned, and then retire in a state of grace from the political arena. The earl agreed – probably intending to honour the agreement about as much as James did.

The tumult at the palace had not gone unnoticed. Indeed, word of it – and the potential threat to Anna – had reached those Danish ambassadors still in the city after having seen to the transfer of the queen's new lands. They had despatched the trustworthy Sir James Melville to see that she was safe and, hearing the cries aimed at the palace from outside, the king himself left Bothwell, gained entry to his wife's rooms, and took her to a window where both could be seen. 'Things,' he called down, in an echo of his father calling down from the same room on the night Riccio had been murdered, 'are fully agreed.'[11]

The immediate threat dealt with, James set about resetting his shaken political chessboard. With Maitland back as chancellor, this was doubtless an easier task, and the king had soon stocked his government with men whom he deemed better off in his circle than outside it: these included the now-rehabilitated former rebel Maxwell. When he felt himself secure enough, he began intimating that he was watching Bothwell's behaviour and waiting for an opportunity to get his revenge. He was not, however, willing to strike against those Catholic men implicated in the Spanish Blanks affair. Indeed, in November, he gave tacit approval to an Act of Oblivion, which would see them all forgiven if they submitted to the Kirk – a prospect which had Queen Elizabeth cattily railing at him on paper for having been 'seduced'. Nor was the Kirk convinced; it promptly excommunicated them, despite James's legal chicanery.

In December, the king evidently felt enough time had passed that he might rescind his pardon of Bothwell. Nor was this unjustifiable. Despite his pardon, the earl had continued arguing against Maitland, brawling, and generally making a nuisance of himself. James thus had every reason to ruin him. Only the previous month, the king had prepared the ground, employing the loyalist Sir George Home to provide protection, whilst Bothwell had spent his time duelling (inconclusively) with Sir Robert Kerr of Cessford. The earl was declared a traitor once more, and put, as the Scottish terminology ran, to the horn. Unsurprisingly, this only emboldened him to begin fresh outrages. When, in April 1594, Bothwell appeared at

Leith with a small following, the king rather pathetically rode into Edinburgh, crying out at St Giles that if the people would help him capture his rebel, he would – he promised – proceed against Huntly and his friends. Bothwell, realising that he might be outnumbered, fled north.

Unfortunately for James, his rash words soon came back to haunt him. Not only was another Catholic conspiracy immediately unearthed, but the runaway Bothwell had immediately gone to Huntly for aid and support. Given his promises, the king had to act. He sent north the inexperienced, seventeen-year-old Earl of Argyll, who led the royal forces in the battle of Glenlivet. Argyll's troops were swiftly routed, but when James himself rode forward, the man who had once been the object of his desire, and who had since become so toxic, surrendered. What Huntly did not do, however, was hand over Bothwell, and the rakehell managed to flee once again. This would be his last escape. Though he fetched up in England and continued to be a source of worry for the next year or so, southern financial support dried up and he retired to the continent (where he lived on, in increasingly reduced circumstances, until 1612).

Huntly would have a happier fate. The following year, he and his partner in conspiracy Erroll were allowed to leave Scotland, returning quietly – and without the king's censure – sometime later. It was clear that James could not rid himself of his lasting affection for the man, whose Catholic sympathies might prove useful. Nor, as time would prove, was he ever much good at learning lessons of the heart.

Although the terrible drama and suspense of Bothwell and the witches was over, the king's relationship with his new wife had also been tested. And it had been found lacking. The beautiful, submissive queen of his imagination had proven illusory. In her place was a determined young woman who was happy to engage in high-level politics, especially if doing so might safeguard her rights. Love would be difficult for him with such a wife. This was not Anna's fault. James's chances of being happy with any woman – body and soul, as it were – were slim, given his outrageous demands of the female sex and his comparative willingness to fall in love with unsuitable men.

But we should not assume that this led to unhappiness or embarrassment on either side of the marriage bed. On the contrary, both parties remained affectionate and were on the brink of achieving all that the marriage required. Despite the stresses on the king and queen, Anna, finally, was pregnant.

12

Disillusion

Queens consort were in terminally unstable positions until they performed their primary duty. Daily, their bedsheets were inspected, and their diets and minor maladies made the subject of ambassadorial despatches: conditions of stress which, one would assume, would rather inhibit than encourage pregnancy. Anna was no different. In summer 1590, the Earl of Worcester – sent north by Elizabeth to give the new Queen of Scots England's welcome – had suggested that a slight toothache presaged the breeding of children. This had obviously proved untrue.

On 8 October 1593, however, Bowes casually noted that 'it is now generally thought that the Queen is with child'.[1] Surrounding her, to his chagrin, was a bevy of Catholic ladies, including Henrietta Stuart, Countess of Huntly, who remained one of her best friends. Still, Anna was determined that she should do as she pleased. When the king attempted – probably at the insistence of his council – to discourage the queen from keeping company with Catholic women, she stood her ground, and she put her foot in the stirrup and galloped off when James asked her to refrain from riding.

Despite outward shows of amity, all was not well in the royal marriage – at least from a modern perspective. Anna herself 'complained to the King that sundry near about him have used over-large liberty in their speeches of her'.[2] In other words, she felt herself still under constant attack from his friends and advisers – and she was certainly subject to disapproving words from the clergy who, unsurprisingly, had condemned her 'lack and want of godly and virtuous exercise among her maids' and her 'night walking and balling'.[3] It is no surprise that the young queen much preferred the company of her Catholic friends, who had none of the dour attachment to cheerless austerity which characterised men like Andrew Melvill.

However, in her natural preference for gaiety, she handed her enemies a cocked weapon. Before she had been slandered as an unfaithful wife; now she was 'stung with the venom and deceit of Papists'.[4] However, as mother of Scotland's heir, she might look forward to enjoying a position of power. It was thus with her own certainty of her state that she allowed her old enemy Maitland to kiss her hand in November, and in December – when the child within her had quickened – the news was confirmed.

If Anna was pleased, James was ecstatic. Given the years of instability and the endless attacks on his person and kingship, he now had proof that he was a success as both king and husband. That he had developed no passionate love for his wife – if anything, she appeared to be a frustrating disappointment to him, wilful as she was – that hardly mattered. God had given the match divine sanction. In what was very likely his first physical relationship with a woman, he had proven himself not just capable but effective (it being popularly believed that to become pregnant, a woman must experience climax). More importantly, he had ensured the succession and thus might offer himself to England not as another childless monarch but as the soon-to-be patriarch of a viable dynastic line.

Though her private feelings are open to debate, Queen Elizabeth wrote to Anna from Hampton Court professing herself delighted: 'We . . . deliver you our most affectionate salutations as one whom we very highly esteem for your virtue, and for your sincere and constant desire to preserve the amity between the two realms, the interruption of which is sought by the subtle workings and malicious practices of the common adversaries.'[5]

The 'common adversaries' were the Catholics and, cleverly, the English queen was joining in with those voices on James's council attempting to nudge Anna out of her friendship with Henrietta and her ilk. Elizabeth was to have no more luck. The Countess of Huntly was part of the birthing preparations and was noted as receiving 'the plurality' of the queen's kisses.

The site chosen for the royal birth – after some debate, to which the queen claimed indifference – was Stirling Castle. Its royal apartments were swiftly brought up to scratch and, at the end of December, James escorted his wife there and left her in what would become her confinement. Medical opinion held that, to ensure safe delivery, the expectant mother ought to be kept warm; as a consequence, the queen's apartments would have been festooned with rich tapestries, with all windows but one blocked. In this hothouse atmosphere, she would enjoy a world of female attendance.

The conditions, unpleasant as they must have been, did not preclude a successful birth. On 19 February, news broke out into the much colder world beyond the queen's apartments that she had achieved her mission on three counts: the child was born, the mother was well, and, most importantly, it was a boy.

Scotland erupted in a display of fiery thanksgiving at the arrival of its new prince, who was immediately awarded with the dukedom of Rothesay, earldom of Carrick, barony of Renfrew, and lordship of the Isles. He was named Frederick Henry – thereafter known, according to custom, as Henry. The choice was obvious in its intentions – Frederick came from Anna's father and, ostensibly, Henry derived from James's. As Darnley had been named Henry in his mother's hopes that he might one day inherit the English Crown as Henry IX, so too was the new baby.

Although Anna had come through the ordeal well, political and domestic matters still intruded on her happiness and relief. At this stage, Huntly, who had been asked to voluntarily ward himself, decided to abscond (no doubt in the certain knowledge that James would do nothing). In April, Henrietta joined him. In the same month, the queen's household was rocked by a greater scandal, as Jacob Kroger, the jeweller who had come with Anna from Denmark, joined forces with the king's servant Guillaume Martyn in robbing their royal mistress. The pair fled with their purses full of stolen jewels, entering England with cock-and-bull stories about having

been granted permission to leave Scotland. In the southern kingdom, they augmented their crime by meeting up with Bothwell. The
whole trio was arrested by the Governor of Tynemouth Castle, but
only the two thieves were conveyed back to Scotland, where they
were hanged in Edinburgh.

It was probably due to this turmoil that Anna at first displayed
a hands-off approach to organising the baby's living arrangements
and christening festivities. It was James, after all, who had the duty
of sending out ambassadorial despatches to guests and Henry's prospective godparents. His first choice for godmother was his own:
Elizabeth. In April, he wrote south: 'Since God has blessed us in the
birth of a young son, which we doubt not was advertised to her good
liking and contentment, we could not omit, having due respect to
the blood, amity and friendship betwixt us, heartily to invite her
among the first by these presents to direct witnesses to assist the
baptism appointed to be on 15th July next to come.'[6]

The fact that the invitation did not go out until April was due
to some 'jealousies' (suspicions) between the Scottish and English
monarchs (arising largely due to Bothwell having been allowed to
roam England). Confident in his fatherhood, James went further,
requesting his ambassadors to 'call to the Queen's remembrance how
oft in her letters to us not only was their [his rebels] receipt within
her dominions disavowed, but also sundry advices interposed, mixed
with sharp and vehement admonitions not to suffer such indignities
most unseemly for a prince'.[7] The king, clearly, now thought he had
one-upped his haughty cousin, and he had every intention of making hay whilst the sun shone.

He ought to have been less sure of himself. Despite the birth of
Prince Henry, the state of the royal marriage was still being used as
a political football. The prolific letter writer (and former Bothwell
adherent) John Colville was soon noting that 'it is certain that the
King has conceived a great jealousy [suspicion] of the Queen, which
burns the more, the more he covers it. The Duke [Lennox] is the
principal suspected [of stirring up trouble]. The Chancellor casts
in materials to this fire. The Queen is forewarned, but with the

like cunning will not excuse till she be accused. *Hæc sunt incendia malorum* [these rumours set dangerous fires], and the end can be no less tragical than was betwixt his parents [Mary Queen of Scots and Darnley].'[8]

Not helping matters was the fact that, partly due to poor communications between Scotland and England, and partly due to the king's desire that a new chapel be constructed in the courtyard at Stirling, the christening date was pushed back. This only fanned the flames of gossip about the state of the marriage, and, ridiculously, Colville went on to report that James 'repents that he has made such convocation to the baptism, for, upon the jealousy mentioned in my last, he begins to doubt of the child. I think he had not been baptized at this time if so many princes had not been invited.' Even with a new prince mewling in his cradle, attempts were being made to drive the king and queen apart, and again on the flimsiest and most salacious of pretexts.

This kind of dangerous nonsense added importance to the baptism which, as James's own had been, was an attempt to show the world that Scotland and its monarchy were stable and the realm's future secure. In addition to Elizabeth (whom it was expected would send a proxy), dignitaries across Europe were invited, as well as the cream of Scotland's political nation. To pay for the show, Anna's dowry was drawn upon, and the king had parliament levy a tax of £100,000 Scots.[9] In another display of his ineffectual economy, however, James begged Sir Walter Dundas to provide his own silver spoons for the expected days of feasting.

On 30 August, all was ready. Queen Elizabeth had sent up the Earl of Sussex, and joining him were ambassadors from Denmark, the States of Holland, and the dukedoms of both Henry Julius (James and Anna's brother-in-law) and Ulrich (the queen's grandfather).

On the day itself, Henry was carried to Anna's outer chamber from his nursery (where he was attended by James's former nurse, Helen Little) by Marie, Countess of Mar and the queen's ladies. He was then handed in turn to Lennox and Sussex, whilst a procession of Scottish noblemen (Hume, Livingstone, Seton, and Semple) formed, bearing amongst them the ducal coronet, towel, basin, and laver. Under a pall of velvet, this august group conveyed the infant into the new chapel, the interior of which was draped in velvet, where the proud father waited (the mother not traditionally being present in the chapel, in a holdover of medieval Catholic practices). The Bishop of Aberdeen conducted the ritual, which included the use of chrism (at James's insistence and, predictably, despite the Kirk's displeasure), and thereafter the return journey was made to Anna's rooms.

Back in the royal apartments, the queen took part in the ritual of receiving gifts from the ambassadors, which she passed to Sir James Melville to display on a carpeted table. It groaned somewhat under the display of English bounty – silver plate and gold cups. Yet, as on James's birth, Elizabeth masked whatever her true feelings were and put on a graceful show of delighted magnanimity. By this stage, James and Elizabeth had become embroiled in a tedious game of verbal tennis, each attempting to place responsibility for continuing amity between their kingdoms on the behaviour of the other. Anna was quite willing to take to the court herself, however. In thanks, she wrote,

Madame and dearest sister,

Having understood by both your letters and the report of your ambassador . . . together with your liberal present and gift, the tokens of your kindness, how lovingly and worthily you have conceived of our son, in whom God has blessed us. We are moved by the greatness of such courteous affection to discover our thankful acknowledging thereof, not only by mouth to your ambassador, but by writ unto yourself, that as you have had hitherto the causes of such favourable disposition towards us, flowing from the merits and amity of the King of Denmark, our unwhile [late] dearest father, so we doubt not hereafter, by our deserts and behaviour to enlarge the same and to procure a longer continuance thereunto, and rather the more seeing it has pleased God to bless us in our son, so near in blood belonging to yourself, in whose birth we perceive you to be so well contented that in the universal gladness of other nations, your joy not only has more appeared but surpassed theirs.[10]

Anna had joined the intra-British political fray, and it is clear that she shared James's desire to use their son as leverage to encourage the English queen – or, rather, the English people – that the benefit of a royal family with an heir was as much theirs as the parents'.

There followed the revelries, which took place in Stirling's magnificent Great Hall. There, James and Anna sat at the top table whilst the foreign guests sat along the eastern wall and the Scottish elites opposite. Into this company came the Queen's Moor (who stood in for the initial idea of the king's pet lion), pulling behind him a chariot which carried ladies playing Ceres, Fecundity, Concord, Liberality, and Perseverance. The women played out a silent comedy, or dumb show, before the chariot was dragged away. In its place sailed in 'a most sumptuous, artificial and well-proportioned ship' on artificial waves 'lively counterfeit with all colours'.[11] Its taffeta sails were embroidered with arms and emblems, and on its decks cavorted Thetis, Neptune, and Triton, each of whom helped toss out sugared confections formed to look like shellfish.

The mood was festive and joyous, but the event was primarily a piece of political theatre for the guests. When the week of revelry – featuring mock battles between Christians and Moors – was over, they departed, laden with gifts. Only when the party atmosphere had dissipated did the question of how the new prince would be raised – and by whom – seriously arise. Its answer would cause the greatest emotional break yet seen between king and queen.

*

Traditionally, Scottish monarchs had been raised within Stirling Castle's walls. This was of particular relevance to James – who had been one of them – and it had become doubly important that the new royal baby be protected due to the unpredictable Bothwell and the general aristocratic unrest that had long infected Scottish politics. The king feared – with good reason – that the prince might be seized and used as a pawn to oust James himself. That, after all, was how he had gained his crown.

As a consequence, he argued stoutly that the Earl of Mar, whose family had been hereditary keepers of Stirling Castle since 1566, must have sole custody of Prince Henry. Mar had, too, consistently proven his loyalty since his rehabilitation.

Anna, keen observer of property rights as she was, was outraged. Had not the previous consorts of Scotland been given Stirling as jointure properties? Had not Margaret Tudor, wife to James IV? Had not Marie of Guise, wife to James V? Certainly, royal infants had been raised at Stirling – but Stirling ought to have been hers. The hereditary keepership had, indeed, only been bestowed on the Mars when James was an infant in need of protection from the then consort Darnley and his allies. Was she, like Darnley, to be publicly denounced as being at odds with her sovereign? This she would not countenance. And it was no simple maternal or postpartum rage – Anna was aware of the political perceptions of being denied the right to raise her son. Accepting that the Mars would do so was tantamount to allowing herself to be cut out of the political scene and left toothless if James should – as he was always worrying about – be seized or slain, or even if he should fall from his horse and break his neck. Battle lines were drawn. Anna knew that she could not afford to oppose her husband directly; instead, she focused her fury on the unfortunate Mar and his family, beginning a feud that would last for years.

Unfortunately for her, James considered his son and the appearance of a stable dynasty his trump cards. For two years, a manuscript titled *A Conference About the Next Succession to the Crown of England* (written by Jesuit Robert Persons under the pseudonym R. Doleman) had been circulating, and now it was moving to publication in Antwerp. This text forensically analysed the candidates for the English throne and disputed the importance of hereditary right.

James's claim was dismissed in favour of that of the Spanish Isabella Clara. Means were needed to counter this, and chief amongst them was that the Scottish king appear the common-sense choice as England's next monarch: a strong male ruler who kept his wife in check. Anna had been altogether too politically active, and he now intended to stand firm against her.

The queen, however, would prove his equal. Immediately, she launched her offensive against the Mars (who were blameless in the affair and only doing as their sovereign dictated). In March 1595, she came up with the idea of abandoning the quest for Stirling; instead, she requested that James hand over both the prince and Edinburgh Castle. When this failed, she took the more perilous tack of indulging in courtly intrigue. In doing so, she realised something James had always known: that Chancellor Maitland (for all her previous troubles with him) was a useful man to have on side. Maitland had, after all, the boon of being disliked by Mar; and the chancellor's sense of grievance and willingness to play dirty against his enemies might actually be helpful to the queen now that they shared an enemy in the hapless earl.

James foresaw this possibility and attempted to outmanoeuvre her, forcing a reconciliation between the prince's keeper and the chancellor. Yet Maitland was not going to become a pawn of the queen any more than he had been of the king. In April, he had 'a long conference' with Anna (who was now fluent in Scots) during which he encouraged her machinations. His goal was almost certainly to widen the breach in the royal marriage at the same time as reducing Mar. Yet it was also probably Maitland who cautioned the queen to deal carefully – and, in Stirling that month she, having, it was said, broken from her scheming with the chancellor, visited Stirling and spent an apparently agreeable time in the company of her son and the dowager Lady Mar.

This was mere show. By May, the queen was again intent on causing trouble. Her means of doing so was to use illness as an excuse to remain at Linlithgow and thereby avoid Lord Glamis's marriage to Anne Murray at Stirling. This she did for a couple of interesting reasons. For one thing, the marriage was supported by the Mars, due to old Annabella, the dowager, being a great aunt to the bride. For another, it was around this time that James developed a sexual interest in Mistress Murray.

*

Having proven himself capable – presumably even fond – of heterosexual relations, it seems James was keen to widen his horizons. It was, further, common practice to refrain from carnal activity when the female partner was pregnant (sex being thought to endanger the child's life). It is not known for certain when the king first found himself attracted to the teenage Anne Murray, but it seems likely that it was during his wife's first pregnancy. Likewise unclear is how long it lasted, although the endorsement of her marriage might have represented the king breaking it off (which would certainly mean it was short-lived). Around the time of the wedding, on 10 May 1595, a letter from Sir John Carey to Burghley declared the bride 'fair Mistress Anne Murray, the King's mistress', and the next month he repeated the claim.

James, helpfully, left his own evidence of what he had been up to – this time not by public embraces but in writing. In 'A Dream on his Mistress, my Lady Glammis', the god Morpheus transports the lady to his bed as he lies sleeping. It is a somewhat overwrought poem ('ports of horne' being metrically required to describe the windows through which Morpheus enters), but the erotic overtones of the bedroom are difficult to ignore, and certainly indicate a sexual element to James's relationship with Mistress Murray. Nor does he stop at the bed, describing her 'silken hands' about his neck, the ravishment of his dreams and mind, the 'piercing' of Cupid's bow, and his 'earthly parts' consumed with flames of love. In some ways it was a poetical exercise, but it certainly represents the king's willingness to use poetry to help fashion physical lust into romantic love. In reality, Mistress Murray was simply, like the Master of Gray, Sandy Lord Spynie, and – though she was obviously of far higher rank and importance – Queen Anna, a sexual object rather than someone who had aroused James's romantic feelings. This is certainly indicated by his other poem on her: 'A Complaint on his Mistressis Absence from Court', which likens the lady to, in turn, a flower, a precious stone, a light, a rose, and a bird. Even in 'A Dream . . .', it is noteworthy that the apparition-mistress presents him with objects – an amethyst (a symbol of courage) and writing tablet – which suggests less a deep love affair than a man who expects the object of sexual attraction to prove a useful tool in making him a more courageous man and a better versifier.

All of this was intolerable to Anna. Nor was she alone. The Master of Glamis (the bridegroom's uncle) was opposed, on the grounds that he had wished his young nephew to marry a sister of Sir Robert Kerr of Cessford (reportedly, the master had also been pocketing the young lord's lands and foresaw trouble ahead on that score). Naturally, Cessford too was an opponent, bringing with him Scott of Buccleuch. Finally, Maitland opposed the match on the grounds of his own antipathy towards Mar and his family; as Aston reported, 'The Chancellor seems not to deal, and yet is in as deep as the rest.'[12] All of these men had, not surprisingly, become the queen's new best friends. She even stomached making amends with Maitland's hated wife, Jean, whom she believed to be a particularly venomous slanderer. Widening her horizons, she also indicated to the English agents at court she desired a portrait of Queen Elizabeth – one can assume with the intention of gaining support from that quarter in achieving her ultimate goal: custody of the prince.

Nevertheless, the marriage went ahead. Indeed, poor Mistress Murray, the cause of passion and enmity, was reported as intending 'to handle the matter so that her marriage shall rather make peace than any troubles, and that for this cause she is a dealer with the queen, Mar, the Master of Glamis and others for making well of all things'.[13] At the same time, the illness Anna had used as an excuse to avoid the Glamis-Murray wedding proved to have a real enough foundation; she was reported 'well furtherly with child' in May.

In response to the evident plotting afoot, James despatched Anna to Stirling (much against her will; though she could visit with her son, she did not intend to visibly condone Mar's custody again). What she did not know was that he had written to the earl, instructing him not to deliver Prince Henry up to anyone, 'and in case God call me at any time, see that neither for the Queen nor Estates, their pleasure, you deliver him till he be eighteen years of age, and that he command you himself'.[14] Sadly, the queen's ongoing sickness proved to be symptomatic of coming tragedy; her reported pregnancy ended in miscarriage in July. She thus conceded – at least publicly – Mar's custodianship of Henry. In truth she was simply playing the long game.

Further tragedy awaited in that Maitland, who had been ailing, died on 3 October. As much as he had been an inveterate game player, the chancellor's loss was keenly felt by the royal couple, not least because it marked the departure of a shrewd political mind. Indeed, the chancellor – who had always tried to keep an eye on Crown finances – was not replaced by one man: a group of eight, known as the Octavians, would eventually be required to attempt to bring some form of regulation to the king's spending. Despite their good efforts, the group – denounced in Presbyterian circles as anti-English and pro-Catholic – would face sustained political attacks, due to their immediate assault on Crown pensions, unnecessary retainers, and untaxed imports.

In the absence of Maitland, Anna required another supporter, and here her choice was both wise and unwise. She knew as well as anyone how her husband had been consistently willing to lend an ear to Huntly, and with that in mind she turned to his wife, Henrietta (whose sister Marie, as Countess of Mar, had become *persona non grata*). The idea behind this was that the queen might gain the support of Scotland's Catholic community in the pursuit of her son, at the same time she was attempting to win Protestant support from abroad. In addition to trying to win Elizabeth's goodwill, in December she asked for portraits of the English queen's great favourite, the Earl of Essex and his sister Penelope, Lady Rich – both of whom were in high favour with James (despite Essex's ham-fisted early attempts at contact, when the young earl had written northwards begging for the king's intercession on behalf of Davison, the secretary who had despatched Mary Queen of Scots' death warrant to Fotheringhay). Essentially, Anna was doing exactly what her husband was doing, though at this stage they had separate goals. Both were engaged in attempting to win as wide a support base as possible, at home and abroad, both Catholic and Protestant: she in order to gain custody of her son, and he to gain acceptance of his right to the English throne. The tragedy was that two married people, so alike in their scheming, were at loggerheads over the matter of their child.

Nevertheless, this breach precluded any future chance of the king passionately loving his queen. As he had long suspected, and in spite of her doing her primary duty, she was less a subservient doormat than a fiery, intelligent woman who would fight for what she wanted with an unnerving tenacity. If it seems odd that James was unsatisfied by having achieved a family of his own, the reason lies in his nature: the king was, throughout his life, a man of ideals, if not a hopeless idealist. Born of both his academic studies and his exalted position, he had romanticised notions of family, of government, of women, and of himself. Reality could never compete.

However, all was far from lost. Though the war over Henry would rage on, there were – in addition to the obvious fact of their marriage – two things which held the royal couple together: sex and succession. Anna would go on firing out children with the regularity of a ceremonial gun salute, and she would add her shrewd mind – and the network of Catholic friends and acquaintances she was building up – to James's attempts to win universal support for his claim to England's throne. For all that divided them, and for all that romantic love was banished from their relationship, the promise of another crown would keep them united.

13

All Things to All Men

There is a charge often levelled at Mary Queen of Scots: that she ruled from her heart rather than her head. In truth, this is a condemnatory accusation which contemporaries, at least in the 1580s and early 1590s, more often hurled at her son. In the latter part of the 1590s, however, as Prince Henry was being reared by Mar at Stirling (to his mother's ongoing chagrin), the king began to flex his political muscles. Queen Elizabeth, in her sixties, could hardly go on forever. If James and Anna wanted a smooth succession, it was time for the Scottish king to put his house in order.

The first sign that a corner had been turned came, appropriately enough, early in 1596, when the queen was able to boast of the £1,000 Scots saved by the council tasked with managing her estates. From this council the Octavian group of financial advisers was born. In the summer, further good news emerged in the form of another royal pregnancy, and Anna was delivered of a daughter, Elizabeth, on 19 August. The choice of name was, yet again, a ploy to encourage association with England, which had come under strain when the English had imprisoned the famous 'Kinmont Willie' Armstrong, causing the Scottish Warden of the West March, Scott of Buccleuch, to raid England to free him. Elizabeth had raged and, by means of sharp letters and the threatened suspension of James's annuity, she pressed the king to side with her and send Buccleuch south to be disciplined. Yet religious matters made it doubly important that the English queen be mollified. At the start of the year, she had written to Anna with a request: 'Sister, I beseech you let a few of your own lines satisfy me in some one point that is boasted of against you, which this bearer will tell you.'[1] What Elizabeth had heard boasted against the Scottish queen was, quite simply, that Anna had become a Catholic convert.

But had she? It has become the norm for historians to declare that Anna of Denmark officially joined the Roman faith, but the evidence supporting a conversion is thin. The date of the supposed switch of faith, firstly, is variously given as the early 1590s, the mid- to late 1590s, or the turn of the century. Numerous Jesuits, notably Robert Abercrombie, even claimed to have performed the conversion (he dated it to 1600). More convincingly, the queen herself wrote to the Vatican on 31 July 1601, asking the courier 'to publicly confess the Catholic faith from our name towards the Holy Apostolic See', and begging Clement VIII's forgiveness for 'attending the rites of heretics'.[2] Unfortunately, this grand announcement of her faith appears less of a smoking gun when one considers that, in 1599, her husband – who most certainly had not converted, and who remained confessionally a Calvinist – had also been addressing the Pope in 1599 as 'beatissime Pater' and signing himself 'obedientissimus Filius'.[3] Further, the later Pontiff Paul V would write, in the next century, 'considering the inconstancy of that Queen and the many changes she had made in religious matters, and . . . even if it might be true that she might be a Catholic, one should not take on oneself any judgement'.[4] If Anna had truly converted, it seems odd that even the Vatican had no proof of it and entertained doubts about her. What therefore seems both a safer and likelier assumption is that Anna was a *politique* rather than a doctrinaire; she was quite willing, in these years especially, to join with her husband in making use of her (genuine) Catholic sympathies and friendships, blowing them into plausible rumours of conversion in order to stave off papal opposition to their English succession.

That James was in on this chicanery would seem proven by his own political manoeuvres throughout the year. The long-time Catholic schemer Erroll was welcomed back to Scotland in the summer. In response, the Kirk sent a delegation, led by the ubiquitous Andrew Melvill, to Falkland. It was at this febrile meeting that the minister took the king by his coat sleeve and, famously, called him 'God's sillie vassal' [meaning simply God's instrument or tool] and told him that there were two kings and two kingdoms in Scotland: 'There is King James, the head of the commonwealth; and there is Christ Jesus, the King of the Church, whose subject James the Sixth is, and of whose kingdom he is not a King, not a Lord, not a Head, but a member.'[5]

Ironically enough, this was not new thinking, but rather a variation on mediaeval Catholic politico-theology. In the earlier period, Church and Crown had largely been (sometimes uneasy) bedfellows, bartering jurisdictional powers according to circumstance. Gregorian views of Church supremacy over temporal affairs had increasingly been tempered by the *realpolitik* of kings and emperors ruling in partnership with (and sending money to) distant pontiffs. What was new was that the reformists sought a polity in which Church and Crown were no longer erstwhile allies, with one secular body and one spiritual body both under God, and questions of superiority rarely pressed too hard. Rather, the Presbyterians held that the Crown was to be acknowledged as operating a separate jurisdiction from the Kirk, and that, obviously, there was no place for the Vatican or any Roman-style hierarchy in ecclesiastical polity. A king might have rightful temporal jurisdiction, but the Presbyterians wished him to acknowledge his religious position as a Kirk member, and subject in matters spiritual to Kirk authorities.

In their attempts to re-energise Protestant zeal in the face of what they saw as creeping Catholicism, the Kirk's foremost men launched an attack on both king and queen. Another firebrand, David Black, of St Andrews, declared that he and his fellows ought not to bother praying for Anna, 'for she will never do us any good'.[6] To Black, no one was Protestant enough; he launched attacks too on Queen Elizabeth and James himself – all royals were 'Devil's bairns'. This latest outbreak of conflict between Crown and Kirk was, however, not to blow over. Rather, it would climax in a showdown which haunted the king for the rest of his life.

*

Above. A posthumous image of James's parents, Mary Queen of Scots and Lord Darnley.

(The Picture Art Collection / Alamy Stock Photo)

Left. James in 1574, by court painter Arnold Bronckorst. The image was intended to show a martial young monarch in hunting garb.

(Fine Art Images/Heritage Images / Alamy Stock Photo)

Stirling Castle, where James spent his childhood under the care of the Erskines of Mar and the tutelage of George Buchanan and Peter Young. (John Carroll Photography / Alamy Stock Photo)

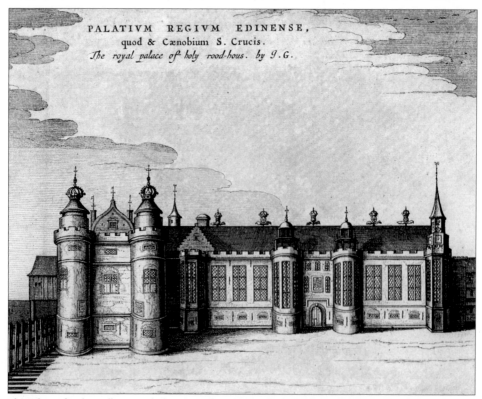

The Palace of Holyroodhouse, Edinburgh, as it would have looked in James's lifetime. This palace had become the architectural heart of the Stuart dynasty. (Niday Picture Library / Alamy Stock Photo)

Esmé Stuart, 1st Duke of Lennox – James's French cousin, whose irruption into Scottish politics marked the young king's emergence into adulthood. (Classic Image / Alamy Stock Photo)

Anna of Denmark, daughter of Frederick II and James's queen consort. Her sharp political machinations would exasperate her husband, though they would not cost her his affection.

(The Print Collector/Heritage Images / Alamy Stock Photo)

Elizabeth of England. The English queen was allied to James thanks to their shared religious affinity and sovereignty, and yet resentful of his emerging status as her heir apparent. (incamerastock / Alamy Stock Photo)

Above. The North Berwick witches being preached to by the devil, after a woodcut in 1591's 'Newes from Scotland'.

(Charles Walker Collection / Alamy Stock Photo)

Right. James around the time of his marriage. In his youth, he bore a strong resemblance to his late father, Darnley.

(Balfore Archive / Alamy Stock Photo)

James in his middle years. The king developed a fondness for elaborate jewels and materials, quadrupling royal wardrobe spending in his first years in England. (Chronicle / Alamy Stock Photo)

Above. Robert Cecil, 1st Earl of Salisbury – one of the architects behind the Stuart succession and James's ablest English minister. (Ian Dagnall Computing / Alamy Stock Photo)

CONCILIVM. SEPTEM NOBILIVM ANGLORVM CONIVRANTIVM IN NECEM IACOBI · I ·
MAGNÆ · BRITANNIÆ · REGIS · TOTIVSQ · ANGLICI · CONVOCATI · PARLEMENTI ·

Robert Winter · Christopher Wright · John Wright · Bates · Thomas Percy · Guido Fawkes · Robert Catesby · Thomas Winter

Above. A seventeenth-century engraving of the Gunpowder Plotters conspiring, by Crispin van de Passe.

(Lebrecht / Alamy Stock Photo)

Left. Robert Carr, 1st Earl of Somerset, with whom James fell in love in 1607.

(The Print Collector/Heritage Images / Alamy Stock Photo)

The Lyte Jewel: a locket given to the king by Thomas Lyte. It promotes James as King of Great Britain, a title he claimed for himself but which did not unite his kingdoms legally. (Granger, NYC. / Alamy Stock Photo)

A miniature of Anna of Denmark from c.1612. Recurrent illness would plague her from this period until her death. (Granger, NYC. / Alamy Stock Photo)

George Villiers, 1st Duke of Buckingham – the man whom the king began to address as both his 'wife' and 'son', and who supplanted the recalcitrant Somerset in his affections. (Ian Dagnall Computing /Alamy Stock Photo)

Henry, Prince of Wales: an aspiring militant Protestant hero whose death in 1612 shocked Europe.
(Peter Horree / Alamy Stock Photo)

Princess Elizabeth, later Queen of Bohemia. Her marriage to Frederick V, Elector Palatine, eventually forced a reluctant James into the Thirty Years War.
(ICP / Alamy Stock Photo)

James in his final years, by Daniel Mytens. The king was by this time suffering recurrent illness, and his plumed hat is pointedly shown off, indicating his desire for an end to conflict.

A woodcut depicting Prince Charles being welcomed home from Spain by his loving father. Unfortunately, the affair of the failed Spanish Match had pushed father and son apart politically. (Photo12/Ann Ronan Picture Library / Alamy Stock Photo)

Charles Turner's 1816 painting The Family of King James: it is an imaginary dynastic image, showing the king as he wished to be viewed – as a patriarch. (The Print Collector/Heritage Images / Alamy Stock Photo)

Icy air penetrated the Tolbooth, nipping at James and his council, including the newly formed group of Octavian financial advisers. The king was soon to be further chilled, however, when cries from the High Street broke in upon him: 'The sword of Gideon!'; 'Bring out Haman!'; 'Armour! Armour!' A coup was in the offing, and it had manifested in the sudden appearance of an armed and dangerous mob.[7]

James was terrified, and with good reason. A considerable number of his subjects were on the move both politically and religiously. For some time, rumours had swirled about the second Spanish Armada; in October it had been repelled by bad weather, but that would not deter the Spaniards from trying again – and perhaps attacking Scotland as well as England. Presbyterian preachers had found willing listeners across the nation: men and women who might be encouraged to fear the Catholic threat. Now, clergymen had combined with militant laymen – nobles and landowners – who had grievances of their own: their places as the king's natural counsellors were, after all, being usurped by the charmed circle of Octavians. It was these agitators, whose goals were to forestall the return to influence of Huntly, remove the Octavians, and surround James with godly counsel, who had, without long-laid plans, summoned a mob.

The king and his ministers barricaded themselves in the Tolbooth. For hours fear reigned within. Whilst Edinburgh's civic authorities tried to subdue the crowd, James issued promises of negotiation. When arms were laid down – temporarily – the king slipped out. Through crowds of men – and city wives, worked into a terror by the perceived Catholic threat – he went to Holyroodhouse, from where, the following day – 18 December – he fled to Linlithgow on the pretext of going hunting at Dalkeith.

Yet the coup was still in train. By chance, James met Argyll on the road. The earl was on the way to join the rebels, but on meeting the king he was inclined to think again. Back in Edinburgh, the rebels were not inactive; they immediately set about galvanising what was a national movement confined to the capital only by circumstance. Luckily for James, their efforts were as extempore as the royalist countercoup, and their attempts to win widespread support failed to bear fruit. The king, though far from secure, reacted with care: in reasserting his position, he courted the nobility to his side, allowing the blame for the 'tumult' to be cast upon the hapless city. In winning over Lord Hamilton, whom the rebels were also wooing, he robbed the uprising of a potential leader. From Linlithgow, the council declared the disorder treasonous and bound over the city to keep the peace at the price of 20,000 marks. The coup failed, and the cause of Presbyterianism was dealt a blow from which it would take years to recover. Yet the day lived on in James's mind as a dark and dangerous one, and his distrust of 'rascal multitudes' would increase. But he had won. In addition to having proven himself a family man – or at least a man with a family – he was now intent on showing the world (particularly England) that he was an effective, competent, and forceful sovereign over whom subjects could not run roughshod.

Nor was his growing family, and all that it said about his dynasty, forgotten. Princess Elizabeth was baptised in a comparatively low-key ceremony on 28 November at Holyroodhouse. The English ambassador Bowes carried the infant, and, as it would turn out ominously, Anna's lady, Beatrix Ruthven, was provided with a black velvet gown for the event. The baby was then delivered up to Lord and Lady Livingstone (the latter a Catholic) to be raised at what would become the *de facto* royal nursery at Linlithgow.

But the central tension in the realm remained between the royal family and the Kirk – and both were intent on displaying their strength. Competition to do just that arose in a fresh outbreak of witchcraft trials, these stemming from an accusation made in 1596 against one Christian Stewart. In the spring of 1597, the Kirk was attentive in hunting and rounding up as many witches as possible – but James, who by now considered himself an expert on the subject, was keen to demonstrate his expertise. He had published his own book *Dæmonologie* – a text in the form of a classical dialogue, which sought to answer sceptics such as the confusingly named Englishman Reginald Scot (whose own *The Discoverie of Witchcraft*, published in 1584, had sown doubts about the reality of the phenomenon).

Though heavy on convention, James's book remains interesting (his claims that necromancers could reanimate corpses which could then creep through the windows of unsuspecting folk without making 'anie dinne' being particularly chilling). Its real value, however, lies in that it indicates that the king was not only a witch-hunting enthusiast, but that he was seeking to both outflank the Kirk and present himself as a deeply pious and learned monarch: the equal in learning and piety, in fact, to previous sovereigns of England.

A more direct use of his newfound political nous came in his handling of the General Assembly. James exercised his right to pick the location of this most important Synod of Kirk elders, and he chose Perth (thereby denying Andrew Melvill the opportunity to host it somewhere that he, Melvill, could be sure of an army of zealous supporters). The meeting thus proved more amenable to the king's wishes – helped in part by James's bribes – and Melvill, in an unintentional compliment, complained that 'where Christ guided before, the Court began then to govern all'.[8] He was right, though the key word was 'began'. The Assembly agreed to rein in overt criticisms of the king and his counsellors, and the king – in apparently commensurate capitulation – agreed to accept a commission that would guide him on ecclesiastical matters. What resulted was a recumbent body of commissioners who agreed with James that the Kirk should indeed have representation in parliament (a right which had fallen away after the Reformation). This was no win for the Kirk, however. In practice, it allowed the king to handpick men for appointment to vacant bishoprics: men who would represent the Kirk in parliament but in reality owe their position and loyalty to the Crown. Royalist bishops did not yet form a majority of the clerical estate (this would take until 1606) and he did not even appoint the first until 1600, but James's intended direction of travel was clear. On realising this, all the likes of Andrew Melvill could do was refuse to recognise the men as bishops and treat them as ministers equal to themselves. Furious, the preacher condemned the king's actions, his writings, and the presence of ministers in religious conferences. James, cheerfully, saw him off to attend to his long-held post of Principal of St Mary's

College at St Andrews University, and thereafter quietly banned him from the General Assembly which met in 1600.

With an unprecedented sense of mastery over the Kirk, the king and queen were able to continue their tentative pro-Catholic agenda. In January 1598, the Earls of Huntly, Erroll, and Angus were all formally restored to their forfeited estates by Act of Parliament. With glee, Anna joined her friend Henrietta, Countess of Huntly, in attending the session's opening (or 'Riding'), cheering even as the Kirk's ministers shook their fists. James would be emboldened too, reviving enough of his old affections to raise Huntly to a marquessate the following year, despite the fellow's submission to the Kirk having been, as usual, a sham. The Crown was coming into its own.

Adding a further layer of fresh polish to it was the arrival of the queen's younger brother, the ebullient Duke Ulrik, who reached Scotland – having travelled through England incognito – in the middle of March. Such visits always served as a shot in the arm of the monarchy, playing up as they did its international links. Naturally, revelry and the politics of display played a large part in this. A company of English actors arrived in April to perform satirical interludes (drawing the attention of the civic authorities); feasts and banquets were held (one hosted by the Duke of Lennox and another at Baillie MacMorran's opulent townhouse at Riddle's Court); and plans were discussed for the canvassing of continental support for the Stuarts' English claims. The duke was eventually packed off not just with plans but with gold, jewels, and horses – a poor reflection on the meagre christening afforded Princess Elizabeth. All of this the king could ill afford. It was small wonder that, in the same year, the treasury had to default on its loans from the banker Thomas Foulis (who would only see partial repayment between 1606 and 1620). As ever, James could not fund his lavish lifestyle, but he had neither the means nor the intention of curbing it.

European agitation for recognition of the Stuart claims to England went on apace. James's old tutor, Peter Young, was put into yoke again, this time travelling with David Cunningham, Bishop of Aberdeen, to Denmark to persuade King Christian to lend his support. The pair won golden opinions from the dowager, Sophie, but the Danish king was only willing to offer sending an ambassador to England; he would give no firmer support until Queen Elizabeth was dead. When the little embassy returned in November, James put a brave face on their meagre achievements, but in truth he was disappointed that his dynasty was not winning outright recognition as England's future rulers. As though all this were not enough, a further display of royal stability was waiting in the wings: Anna was pregnant again, this time being delivered of another daughter, Margaret, at Dalkeith on Christmas Eve.

Yet this was not merely a time of waiting but of consolidating. Scotland, divided roughly between the south-west/north-east Highland Line, had long been as divided in terms of culture and ethnicity. Whilst the royal court held sway in the largely Scots-speaking lowlands – to the east of the mountainous dividing line – beyond it lay Gaelic-speaking peoples (in James's eyes, a barbarous and uncivilised lot) who lived under a clan system and answered to their chieftains (who might or might not enjoy working relationships with the Crown). Hitherto, James was able to engage only in sporadic episodes of interference in this world of rivalries and power struggles, and otherwise had to rely on occasionally loyal Highland chiefs as intermediaries. Now, he was intent on securing Crown interests across the Highlands and Islands as well as abroad – securing the country's outer borders (for example, via James Spens' attempted plantation of Lewis), as well as taking advantage of the country's Scandinavian alliance and concomitant continental prestige. It was thus from a position of growing strength that the king and queen continued courting influential English Protestants. Through no fault of their own, however, their primary contact, Essex, soon turned out to be an unsafe bet.

Throughout the 1590s, after the high watermark of the first Armada in 1588, England had experienced a gradual decline in its fortunes, mostly due to an increase in military expenditure, but also caused by an increasingly archaic system of government and repeated bad harvests. Queen Elizabeth, for all the glitter of her gowns and the poetical rhetoric poured out by flatterers, was beset by the expensive problems of subduing Ireland and warring with Spain. In January 1599, Niels Krag (who had attempted that initial crossing with Anna from Denmark to Scotland) visited Elizabeth's court. There, he found not a haggard old woman in her sixties, but a vigorous one. Pointedly, she danced with Essex and said, 'You might congratulate me because many years have passed, and though asked to renounce my kingdom, though someone [is] not yet so infirm that can still dance like this, and do other things, despite my wasted body.'[9] This was no doubt intended to reach both James's and Anna's ears – and certainly, the English queen's acid comment that 'I would have you reprove the Scots envoys' (those tasked with winning continental support for the Scottish succession) was an overt thumbing of her long nose at her cousin and his wife.

Though the elderly Elizabeth outlived Krag by a year, her dancing partner did not. For years, Essex had been the queen's favourite – as stepson to the love of her life, Leicester, he was well trained. However, he was also hopelessly romantic and absolutely in thrall to the chivalric ideals so popular amongst his class, and he overrated his own military and political competence. Later in the year, his dreams of glory led him to embrace what was at first an enforced mission to Ireland, where the seeds of his ultimate tragedy were sown. James and Anna, meanwhile, were left sending their secret correspondence to his spymaster, the invalid Anthony Bacon (the clever brother of the fiendishly intelligent Francis). But even this did not last. Essex failed to bring the Irish to heel, returned without warrant to England in September, and burst in on the queen when she was in a state of undress. This marked the beginning of his end. There followed house arrest, during which he schemed and plotted a coup against his enemy, the queen's Principal Secretary, Sir Robert Cecil. In a skewed mirror of the attempt against James and the Octavians in 1596, the earl attempted to drum up popular support; but Londoners seemed less easily worked up against imagined Spanish Catholic conspiracies than had the Edinburghers, and the Essex coup found itself with a clear leader but no mob of armed insurgents. He was arrested, tried, and sent to the block in February 1601 (with Bacon dying a natural death shortly afterwards). Luckily for James – for Essex had implicated him in his schemes – the earl had burnt his correspondence. Cecil himself then slipped into the Scottish royal couple's good graces and became, with help from the fawning Henry Howard, the chief architect of the future succession, counselling patience whenever James looked like importuning Elizabeth with demands. The reliable Mar and Edward Bruce (soon rewarded with the lordship of Kinloss) acted as further go-betweens in what would become a smoothing of the path to the English throne.

Writing southwards, however, was not the only exercise for James's pen. In 1598, he had set out his opinions – idealistic, as always – on the paternalistic virtues of absolute monarchy in *The Trew Law of Free Monarchies*. In 1599, he expanded on the theme in a different way in *Basilikon Doron* ('royal gift'), subtitled *His Maiesties Instrvctions to his Dearest Sonne, Henry the prince*: a how-to manual on kingship (of Scotland, in particular) intended initially for his son and a select circle of readers. James, evidently, had learned something else from Buchanan, for the long-dead scholar had written that he intended, fruitlessly as it turned out, that his own works should continue as tutors to the king. In providing Henry with a book in lieu of direct parenting, James was not showing himself indifferent to fatherhood but rather demonstrating a long and deeply held faith in the power of the written word.

This text has – understandably, given it is one of the few guides to kingship penned by a king – been of considerable interest to scholars. On first glance, it appears an exercise in hypocrisy. On the subject of wives, for example, James writes,

> Treat her as your own flesh, command her as her lord, cherish her as your helper, rule her as your pupil, and please her in all things reasonable; but teach her not to be curious in things that belong to her not. Ye are the head, she is your body. It is your office to command, and hers to obey, but yet with such a sweet harmony as she should be as ready

to obey, as ye to command; as willing to follow, as ye to
go before; your love being wholly knit unto her, and all
her affections lovingly bent to follow your will . . . And to
conclude, keep specially three rules with your wife: first,
suffer her never to meddle with the politick government of
the commonweal, but hold her at the oeconomicke rule of
the house; and yet all to be subject to your direction; keep
carefully good and chaste company about her, for women
are the frailest sex; and be never both angry at once but
when ye see her in passion, ye should with reason dampen
yours.[10]

On several of these counts, James tacitly judged himself a failure;
he had certainly not taught Anna to stay out of politics, nor had he
managed to make her obey him (at least not in terms of agreeing
to Mar's custody of Henry). It had not helped that the queen had
shown no inclination to be schooled, of course, and thus we can
infer that James was warning his son not to marry a thinking woman
such as he himself had wed – or, if he did, not to let her have too
much licence.

Further hypocrisy has been detected in the inclusion in the book
of one misdeed casually placed amongst other wicked acts: '[T]here
are some horrible crimes that you are bound in conscience never to
forgive: such as witchcraft, wilful murder, incest (especially within
the degrees of consanguinity), sodomy, poisoning, and false coin.'

By including 'sodomy' on the list of unconscionable deeds, James
has long enjoyed a reputation as a shameless hypocrite (which in
many respects he was). However, there are other interpretations of
his condemnation. It has been argued that by damning sodomy –
and remaining committed to legal penalties for it – the king thereby
revealed that throughout his various same-sex exploits, he had never
gone as far as full intercourse (there being innumerable other things
men and men, and men and women, can do in bed). Yet it is also
worth remembering that the king was writing a book of advice for
his son, not himself. It is therefore possible that his goal was to ensure

that Henry did not succumb to what James viewed as regrettable vices of his own. It is certainly true that the king had an anxiety about heredity: he wrote that 'virtue or vice will often, with the heritage, be transferred from the parents to the posterity' – and it is unsurprising that he sought hereditary excuses for vices he perceived in himself (as when he accused his wet nurse of tippling). It should be noted, too, that at this stage in his life, James was engaging in regular sexual activity with his wife. He might therefore have viewed sodomy – if he ever engaged in that particular act – as belonging to his past. The new king – the master of the Kirk, conscientious father, and sovereign-in-waiting of England – was not the 'bougerer' or slave to 'bedfellows' of the years prior to his marriage.

Unfortunately, the family man was about to suffer a blow. In March 1600, the infant Princess Margaret died at fifteen months old at Linlithgow. This would only be the first of several domestic tragedies. It was, however, comparatively small news in comparison to the bloody scandal that was about to overwhelm the bereaved parents.

*

No one knew quite what to make of the story when they heard it. When it reached the queen, she burst into tears. How – quite literally, *how* – had such a thing happened? How could it be that two young men had been brutally stabbed to death on the upper floor of their own tower house on a fine summer's day? One of them was no less than the Earl of Gowrie, who had travelled on the continent, met with Queen Elizabeth, and, recently, opposed James's desire to raise money for an army to press his English succession claims. What exactly had gone on? Similar questions were on everyone's lips, and James was not slow to answer them – or, at least, to give them his version of events.

It all started with the discovery of a pot of gold. On hearing that the king was hunting at nearby Falkland, the sometime courtier Alexander, Master of Ruthven, brother to the 3rd Earl of Gowrie, had gone to tell James that treasure had been discovered locally, but that the earl was oblivious. Ruthven's ostensible intention had been that the king should come to Gowrie House (since demolished and now the site of Perth's County Buildings) to inspect the treasure. On being hailed by the familiar man, James digested this news, finished his hunting, and then decided to do as invited; he dismissed his companions, Lennox and Mar, and took horse. His party, however, fortuitously elected to follow in his footsteps and managed to overtake him.

On being greeted by Gowrie himself, the king was given a simple meal by the apparently disgruntled earl, whilst his party received a hasty dinner. During it, though, Ruthven prevailed upon James to leave the table and go upstairs. This the king did, going through a series of chambers and up into the tower, apparently uncaring that each door was locked behind him. In the upper tower room waited a mysterious man. Before James could do or say anything, he was seized by Ruthven from behind; the young man, dagger in hand, swore vengeance for the killing of his father (that Earl of Gowrie who had been the architect of the Ruthven Raid back in 1582). James, for his part, threw out promises and curses, not least of which was the mortal danger into which Ruthven's soul would fall if he killed a king. This availed him nothing, and a life-or-death struggle ensued, during which the mystery man stood back. James, gaining the upper hand, managed to get to the window and cry, 'Treason!' Those of his hunting party who had not joined the dinner heard and raced upstairs, breaking down doors and demanding hammers to aid entry to the tower room. Luckily, one of the party, the thirteen-year-old page John Ramsay, found another entrance; when he burst in, James cried to him, 'I am murdered!' Needing no more encouragement, Ramsay slew Ruthven on the spot. Meanwhile, the diners had been assured by Gowrie that the king had left the property after he departed the table. When they went to see the truth of this, the wicked earl took a party of eight armed men up to the tower. These were met by the fighters upstairs, and Ramsay's sword was again put to good use. When the fracas subsided, Gowrie, too, lay on the floor dead. The mystery man had vanished.

The problems with the story are legion. The timings, the passages of men from room to room, the motivations behind James's willingness to go wherever he was bid, the stranger in the tower – the whole thing is a mass of unlikelihoods. Nevertheless, it was the king's story and he was sticking to it. Chief amongst its doubters were some – though not all – of the Kirk's ministers, who were as alert as anyone to the inconsistencies. Yet, given James had, in his own mind at least, subdued his clergymen, he was adamant that they must proclaim his miraculous delivery from danger. The king's interest in numerology kicked in: five was now a magical number (joining James's fascination with nineteen: 19 June being his birthday and 19 February Prince Henry's), and 5 August was to become a national holiday.

The more sceptical ministers met in the East Kirk and, despite their reservations, decided that they might go so far as to admit that the king had survived a dangerous situation. They said as much to the new chancellor, John Graham, 3rd Earl of Montrose (who had gained the position the previous year), whose job it was to peddle the king's story. He was supported by the minister David Lindsay and so, however grudgingly, it was repeated at the Mercat Cross, to a general rejoicing. But still questions and doubts lingered – indeed, they were only amplified by repetition of the tale.

What really happened? This remains one of the most puzzling questions of James's reign. The mystery man, at least, was identified – dubiously – as one Andrew Henderson, who was mysteriously pardoned after confirming the king's story. Of course, it is possible that the story was substantively true – although if Gowrie and Ruthven had plotted to kill James out of vengeance, they were remarkably – almost farcically – inept about dispatching someone effectively.

One suggestion has been that the pot-of-gold tale was a red herring, and that James had tried to solicit sex from the reputedly attractive Ruthven (whom he knew well enough as a courtier) and, on being rebuffed, he panicked at the prospect of scandal and had the master and earl silenced. This is wholly unlikely. The king was not, and never had been, a sexual predator, still less one who stooped to murder to quieten rumours about his sexuality.

There remains the possibility that James had – in the style of a modern mob hit – engineered the whole slaying from the beginning, in the hopes of being rid of men – indeed, a whole family – for whom he had borne a deep hatred since 1582 (and to whom, into the bargain, he was in debt, with the executed 1st Earl of Gowrie's £48,000 spent on behalf of the Crown not having been repaid). In this reading, a murder plot there was, but it was James's, not Gowrie's or Ruthven's. This, too, is unconvincing. The king had, if anything, always been too soft rather than too bloodthirsty. A ruthless and calculating mafia don he was not.

More likely is the possibility that Gowrie and Ruthven, rather than discovering secret treasure, had been involved in the ongoing traffic between England and Scotland and one – Ruthven, most likely, as Gowrie seemed rather bemused and unprepared – had engineered James's arrival at Gowrie House with the intention of convincing him to provide them official posts. What might then have panicked the king was the probably unintentional intimation, on Ruthven's part, that he was to be held captive. This was still, and would remain, one of James's deepest fears. Whatever Ruthven really said, if it were threatening or lacking in deference it might have alarmed the king and led Ruthven to try to quiet him. The entire thing was probably not a murder plot on anyone's part, and the day should not have ended in anyone's blood being spilt. A hare-brained scheme of Ruthven's had simply gone wildly, confusingly, tragically awry. What mattered, of course, was that James – terrified and horrified in equal measure – believed wholeheartedly that the men had meant to kill him, and God had delivered him from danger.

Whilst the official story was being trumpeted to a curious – and suspicious – public, however, holes were being poked in it closer to home. Queen Anna did not believe a word of it.

Why, she wondered, when her tears had subsided, had her husband told her on the morning of the deaths 'that he wished to be astir betimes, as he expected to kill a prime buck before noon'?[11] The queen was at this time about five months pregnant, and she had long held Ruthven and his sisters, Beatrix and Barbara, in deep affection.

For two days she confined herself to her chambers, refusing to be dressed.

James, understandably, was worried at this latest display of his wife's troubling capacity to think for herself. Worse, his queen's incredulity threatened the veracity of the story he was even then having spread through Scotland and beyond. Deciding to take the bull by the horns, he went to her directly, but found her intractable: she claimed that 'Nothing he said could make her believe that her young friends had been disloyal' and 'she hoped Heaven would not visit her family with its vengeance for the sufferings of the Ruthvens'.[12]

His response was illustrative of his concerns at the time. Rather than fight, he took his own advice in *Basilikon Doron*: 'Be never both angry at once but when ye see her in passion . . . with reason dampen yours.' In an attempt to simultaneously cool his wife's passion and keep up appearances, he treated her to the sight of 'a funambulous [tightrope walking] acrobat . . . [hired] to play strenge and incredible practicks' before the whole court at Falkland.[13] If there was disharmony between the royal couple, the wider world – and England especially – was not to be made too aware of it. James intended people to think he was a loving husband, a devoted father, and a divinely protected king – not a man who had been involved in a suspicious and bloody affray in which even his wife suspected his guilt.

The Ruthven girls fared less well. James, in a display of malicious vengeance so different from his usual bluffness, wished to reduce the entire family. The earldom was abolished, and the name 'Ruthven' banned. The hapless Beatrix and Barbara, along with one Christian Ruthven, were sent from court, despite the queen's pleas. Anna, though, remained unwilling to sit back whilst her friends were suffering; she wrote south to Sir Robert Cecil (who at this stage considered her a loquacious and untrustworthy woman) and managed to arrange for Barbara to travel to England, where no doubt the queen hoped to reconnect with her when the time came.

Following this unpleasantness, Anna's health declined – a dangerous thing, given her pregnancy. She chose to go to her own palace at

Dunfermline, which was finally close to achieving the vision she had had for its reconstruction back in 1590. On 19 November 1600, she was delivered of her second son, Charles. The infant, unfortunately, appeared sickly, and so was conveyed by litter to Holyroodhouse, to be baptised, as his sisters had been, by David Lindsay. Thereafter, the baby was returned to Dunfermline, and Alexander Seton, Lord Fyvie (a polymath lawyer and jurist with a deeply Catholic background) was appointed his keeper. Anna, who had been too sick to attend the baptism, was still in the process of being wooed into good behaviour by her husband.

By this time, James appears to have accepted his wife's proactive nature. It drove him to distraction, certainly, that she failed to be biddable, but – one hopes – the shared experience of bed-sharing, children, and the loss of a child had bred between them a sense of mutual affection. To James, his wife was family, and of the kind which granted him prestige and honour. For all she had failed to be the emotional support he craved, she had earned love of a different – and a more lasting – sort. Accordingly, on the occasion of Prince Charles's baptism and her own illness, he showered her servants with gifts and had largesse thrown to the people. In the new year, he turned to the Edinburgh jeweller George Heriot, from whom he purchased his wife a jewel worth £1,333 Scots. Gifts were always a sure means of regaining the queen's affections. James's safety among the rest of his subjects and on the world stage, however, was less easily assured.

What looked like more potentially bloody trouble arrived in the autumn of 1601, when an Italian calling himself Ottavio Baldi strode into Edinburgh, intent on securing a royal audience. For some months Baldi bided his time, but eventually he gained his meeting. Ottavio Baldi, it turned out, was actually Henry Wotton, half-brother of the Edward Wotton whom Elizabeth had used in Scottish affairs in the past. Henry had recently been in Tuscany, the duke of which had sent him to warn the king of rumours about a foreign assassination attempt, with poison the probable means. This shook James – but he thanked the mock-Italian, who donned his disguise once more and set off for Florence. For his troubles, Wotton would be jokingly greeted by James as 'Ottavio' in the future, as well as being knighted and retained as a diplomat. For the moment, security in Scotland was tightened and the king once more grew suspicious of those around him.

Thankfully, this latest scare did not affect the royal marriage. Almost as soon as Anna had recovered from Charles's birth, she was back in her husband's bed, and pregnancy soon followed. Robert, Duke of Kintyre and Lorne, was born on 18 January 1602. In celebration, Edinburgh Castle fired a salute, and the king joined his wife at Dunfermline, presenting her with another gift: a diamond – a symbol of constancy. Preparations were immediately put in train for a baptism at Dunfermline Abbey in May, which – given the sex of the child – was to be somewhat more lavish than those afforded his sisters.

Souring the planned festivities, however, were the bizarre actions of a visiting merchant, Humphrey Dethick. In a sudden frenzy, Dethick drew his rapier and set upon the courtier John Chambers, who was then being barbered. Chambers was slain and the barber wounded; Dethick was quickly restrained. The killer was then examined by the surgeons who had attended the new prince's birth, Naysmyth and Schöner (the former that same man who had once been of Bothwell's faction and was protected from James's wrath by the queen). Remarkably, the medical men declared Dethick sane, notwithstanding he had had a breakdown of some kind the day before the murder, and, on being interrogated, claimed that he was acting out a Spanish prophecy which had instructed him to kill. He was swiftly imprisoned, and his mental state continued to deteriorate, though his ultimate fate is unrecorded. Nevertheless, the baptism and its festivities – including a chivalric tournament – went ahead. Prince Robert, however, did not thrive. On being moved to Linlithgow, he weakened further and died on 27 May.

Infant mortality was, of course, always high. Anna, for all she had been somewhat depressed during the prince's short life (not helped by more attacks by the Kirk on her friend Henrietta), was able to rally. Touchingly, it was recorded that she had the emotional strength to tell James, 'If it please God to take one of our children,

He will send us another, for I feel myself with child.'[14] In fact, she was not again pregnant – but clearly she and her husband were still cohabiting enough to make it a possibility. Sex and succession thus kept the king and queen together even as domestic political concerns divided them. Anna's perennial grievance over Mar's custody of her son remained at the forefront of her mind. In September, a face from the past joined her in her efforts. This was Patrick, Master of Gray, former lover of the king during the last drama of Mary Queen of Scots. Gray had long retired, with apparent good grace, from active involvement in Scottish public life. However, he now saw a chance to flex his atrophied political muscles, helping the queen to argue against Mar. In a curious tableau, this duo – James's wife and former lover – even entertained Anne de Gondi, wife of the visiting French ambassador, whilst the ambassador hunted with the king at Falkland. Anna was not an idiot and knew of her husband's reputed tastes. However, she was presumably confident that Gray (who was by this time married with eight children) was far from a threat, and Gray himself was courtly and polished enough to treat her with the deference and respect she demanded of those who sought her favour. In his youth he had been an unsuccessful and untrustworthy politician; now, he was a more reliable prospect, mostly because his ambition had been tempered.

The queen, essentially, was biding her time in the quest for control of her son, and still she was intent on being her own mistress, at least in affairs which touched her closely. Towards the end of 1602, Beatrix Ruthven was brought secretly to her apartments by Ladies Paisley and Angus. Anna, who loved Beatrix, spoke privately with the young woman in spite of James's unilateral proscription of the whole family. James's loyalist spy, Sir Thomas Erskine, lost no time in telling his sovereign all about this bit of spousal disobedience, and understandably Anna thereafter marked Erskine as an enemy. Happily, the fellow's meddling had no dramatic sequel; the queen convinced her husband that no treasonous matter had been discussed, and thereafter she won a victory in convincing him to grant Beatrix a pension and to cease harassing her. From James's perspective, this was worth doing for the sake of keeping up a show of Stuart familial harmony. Appearances still mattered in terms of his English ambitions.

Rumours out of London in the late winter and early spring of 1603 did not bode well for the life of the English queen. Dark news, indeed, was in the air. In the middle of March, word arrived that Anna's grandfather, Duke Ulrich, had died. Death, however, had a busy month. Queen Elizabeth, who had for so long been James's frustrating 'madame and mother', and behind whose back he had recently been busy – with his wife – courting Catholic powers and engaging in secret correspondence with England's secretary, fell ill at Richmond Palace. This was to prove her final illness, and each day news was awaited out of the southern kingdom.

It came after darkness had fallen. A begrimed messenger, the familiar Sir Robert Carey, appeared at the gates of Holyroodhouse near the end of the month. The enterprising fellow, in hopes of advancement, had stolen a march on his fellow countrymen and England's council. With dried blood still on his face from a fall during his wild ride north, he was admitted to James's bedchamber. There, he acknowledged the King of Scots as King of England, France, and Ireland, falling to his knees in homage. James, cautious now the moment had come, begged proof. In response, Carey, who had escaped Richmond before its gates could be locked, produced a ring: a token that his mistress had died in the early hours of the morning on 24 March. Her long, infuriating refusal to name her successor had, in the end, proved no match for death or the machinations of Sir Robert Cecil (who had quickly endorsed spurious rumours that on her deathbed she had gestured in approbation on hearing James's name). Soon enough, the official proclamation of Elizabeth's Privy Council – which had been hastily renamed the 'Great Council' of England – arrived, carried by Sir Charles Percy and Thomas Somerset (son of the Earl of Worcester).

The master of what he had once described as a 'wild, unruly colt' was now possessed of a 'towardly riding horse'. James VI of Scotland was now also James I of England.

14

Succession

In early April 1603, James stood with Anna in Edinburgh's High Street. In full view of the citizens, many of whom had seen either the queen's royal entry, or the king's, or both, he embraced her. This was one final public spectacle of joy and royal harmony. Two days previously, on a Sunday, he and Anna had attended a farewell sermon at St Giles, following which James had stood up and, true to form, delivered his own speech, in which he laid out his intentions for his personal union between the kingdoms to be followed by a political one (along with a promise to return to Scotland at least every three years). Now he was bidding his wife what was intended to be only a brief goodbye – she was to follow him on his journey southwards in twenty days. Already, £6,660 had been borrowed to ensure all would pass with suitable glitter.

The reason the king travelled ahead of his family was said to be that Anna's new English ladies could not receive her until an appropriate period of mourning for the late Elizabeth had passed. This was only an excuse. In reality, James and his Scottish council knew that, despite his proclamation as England's king having been despatched to the localities, there might be armed resistance to the new regime on the road; Thomas Lake, whom Cecil sent north, had already arrived with George Carew to apprise him of the state of play. News did not always travel fast, and in the weeks prior to Elizabeth's death, rumours had agitated northern England about the Scottish king supposedly being in the Borders with an army, ready to invade. As he prepared to leave his capital and begin his journey to his new one, there were thus multiple conflicting aims foremost in James's

216

mind: he must present himself as a family man travelling without his family, and he must take possession of London as quickly as possible, despite the dangers of travelling through England when there might still be sections of society who would think him worthy of resistance rather than welcome.

Although he did not visit his heir, he did pause to write a letter to the nine-year-old Henry (accompanied by a copy of *Basilikon Doron*). He wrote,

> Let not this news make you proud or insolent, for a King's son ye were, and no more are you yet; the augmentation that is hereby like to fall to you is but in cares and heavy burdens. Be merry, but not insolent; keep a greatness, but *sine fastu* [without pride]; be resolute but not wilful; be kind, but in honourable sort. Choose none to be your playfellows but of honourable birth; and, above all things, never give countenance to any, but as ye are informed they are in estimation with me. Look upon all Englishmen that shall come to visit you as your loving subjects, not with ceremoniousness as towards strangers, but with that heartiness which at this time they deserve.[1]

This was well-intentioned advice, and it appears that, at this early stage, the king was intent on crafting his son not as a miniature version of himself, but as a dutiful paragon. With Scotland – so he thought – settled, he and his retinue of 500 could ride to Dunglass and thereafter out of the country.

Heartiness James was feeling in full measure. On setting foot on English soil, he was welcomed at Berwick by Sir John Carey (brother to Robert, who had first carried the news of the succession north). England's outpost was, at least, safe; its new monarch had sent an advance messenger to alert the castle's governor and town mayor of his coming. Carey ordered the soldiers stationed at the garrison to fire off their muskets and set off the cannon, as a general signal to the townsfolk to begin rejoicing. Ceremonially, James was handed the keys to the castle (by a gentleman porter whom the king swiftly knighted) – which he handed back, assuring the dignitaries of the town's liberties and charters. In the market square, he was met by the mayor, who presented a purse of gold, whilst the recorder read out welcoming speeches. In the church, he was welcomed by Toby Matthews, Bishop of Durham, who delivered a sermon, and thereafter he passed on through the rising smoke of celebratory bonfires and more cannon shot to lodge in the palatial quarters appointed for him.

The following day, James was greeted by arriving English nobles (the rush northwards on the part of the English aristocracy having begun), who joined him on a tour of Berwick's fortifications. In a display of his own military prowess, such as it was, the king then lit and fired a cannon himself. When news arrived of trouble in the West Marches, he was able to show a more practical generalship, ordering the newly knighted porter, Sir William Selby, to lead a force to quell the routs.

James's welcome at Berwick was an encouraging sign, with even the ensuing rainstorm declared a presage of sunshine. It also indicated the shape of things to come. On entering Northumberland, he was entertained lavishly by the county's sheriff, Sir Nicholas Forrester. At Widdrington, Sir Robert Carey (who earned a place in the royal bedchamber, which he would lose at the insistence of the council soon enough) hosted the king. In mid-April, James reached the capital of northern England, York, where he lodged in the King's Manor and met Cecil's half-brother, Thomas, Lord Burghley, President of the Council of the North. Here, he showed a rare awareness of public feeling, likely born of the novelty of the reception he had received throughout his journey: on being offered the use of a coach to York Minster (where a sermon was to be preached), he said, 'I will have no coach, for the people are desirous to see a King, and so they shall, for they shall see as well his body as his face.'[2] Accordingly, he strode to the church – further evidence that, even in his middle years, he had not gained a physical disability such as might draw comment.

It was on the following Monday that the king was finally to come face to face with the man who had not only helped him to the throne, but with whom he had plotted since Essex's downfall. Sir Robert Cecil was possessed of England's ablest political mind. Though he was hunchbacked (a fact which drew people to borrow Sir Thomas More and Shakespeare's uncharitable slur on the crook-backed Richard III, by scrawling 'toad' on the secretary's gate) and unpopular, he had raced through the heart of England to meet his sovereign at York.

James had, he knew, become – eventually – the master of his own house in Scotland. However, he was not overblown in confidence; he appreciated the debt he owed Cecil in securing his succession and, moreover, knew that though he was an experienced monarch, he knew very little about his new country. Cecil, by contrast, was experienced in managing England's affairs as well as its international relations, and he was eager to hold on to power. If anything, indeed, the little secretary was too cautious and too resistant to any sort of innovation; the machinery of the late queen's government was antiquated, yet he would prove unwilling to seriously reform it.

Nevertheless, James did not think twice about confirming the secretary in his position and solidifying a partnership which hitherto had been a cloak-and-dagger affair. Cecil, who had learnt the efficacy of courtly flannel at Elizabeth's feet, was soon writing of his new sovereign, 'His virtues are so eminent . . . I have made so sufficient a discovery of his royal perfection as I contemplate greater felicity to this isle than ever it enjoyed.'[3] There was genuine hope beneath the fawning. According to Bishop Godfrey Goodman, the English people had grown 'generally weary of an old woman's government'.[4] In James, a man of family and apparent stability – and possessed of a proven fine mind and high ideals – much hope was placed.

Swelling as it went, James's party continued in what was rapidly becoming the early modern equivalent of a Roman triumph. The people, relieved at the smoothness of the succession, formed cheering multitudes and displayed 'sparkles' (one of James's favourite words) of affection. From York, the royal train and its hangers-on rode to Doncaster (where the king lodged at the Bear Inn); to Newark (where he ordered the summary hanging of a pickpocket who had chanced his luck amongst the great crowd – a fact which did not draw much criticism at the time, despite being later inflated into an act of tyranny); to Burghley House (with Burghley thereafter travelling up to Berwick to meet the queen); to Burley-Harington in Rutland; to Hinchingbrooke (the home of Sir Oliver Cromwell, uncle of his famous namesake, reached only after the king had suffered a fall from his horse which put his arm in a sling). At each stop, the size of the train and the volume of lyrical adulation grew. All of this was very much to James's taste: lavish welcomes suited his penchant for deference and fed his love of poetry – especially that which was heavy in classical allusion and obsequiousness.

Yet something of greater import was rapidly being born in the king. Throughout his journey, his joy at the welcomes he received spurred him on to begin conferring knighthoods and elevations with abandon. Although old servants had to be rewarded – Peter Young was given the deanery of Lichfield, before it was pointed out that James had no power to do this – new faces were also showered with honours. This was not entirely the result of generosity, nor was it new. As early as 1591, James had sheepishly admitted, 'I have offended the whole country . . . for prodigal giving from me.'[5] Rather than reining in his extravagance, however, it was about to be unleashed and to soar beyond anything seen in Scotland.

James, naturally, justified it to himself. Queen Elizabeth had been decidedly stingy in handing out honours, and the new king was determined to right that wrong; if her favour had been bestowed too frugally, his generosity would redress matters. Unfortunately, public discontent at Elizabeth's perceived meanness (in terms of honours, patronage, and financial handouts) was a nut to which James decided, on his journey, to apply a sledgehammer. If she had been miserly, he would be the soul of bounty. Yet, despite his illusions, the king was hardly the seventeenth-century equivalent of a modern lottery winner. Rather, it was as though he had been handed a fistful of credit cards (each with eye-wateringly high interest rates).

What would turn out to be a lasting – indeed, an uncontrollable – generosity was also encouraged by the sight of his new subjects' palatial living conditions. In Scotland, even the upper nobility tended to live in a style comparative to English upper gentry (Scottish noble houses tended to be fortified strongholds, with their splendour deriving either from scale or from interior fixtures and furnishings). The English nobility, on the other hand, were living as princes, and in palaces no less splendid than Linlithgow or Holyroodhouse, designed to display wealth and power rather than act as defendable buildings. To the new king, if these were the lodgings of subjects – albeit mighty subjects – then it was incumbent upon him as their sovereign lord to outspend and outstrip them. For a man who was already careless about money, and who had just inherited the English Exchequer's debt of some £430,000, this was to bode ill for the future.

After journeying through Royston (which he would earmark as a future favourite hunting lodge), on 3 May James reached what was then one of the grandest of all non-royal residences in his new realm: Theobalds (often pronounced 'Tibbalds'). This awe-inspiring, red-brick palace had been constructed by Elizabeth's late minister, Lord Burghley, and passed into the ownership of his second son, Cecil. Reached by a road flanked by cedars, it stood three storeys high and boasted towers surmounted by gilt lions bearing vanes and pennants. Cecil himself led the king inside, there to amaze him with sights certainly never seen in any Scottish home: an indoor garden, for example, had been constructed within a large hall, with the ceiling featuring a moving planetarium (with a mechanical sun crossing during the day and stars twinkling at night); natural light poured in through numerous windows and landed on artificial trees adorned with fruit and birds' nests. It was in this pleasure palace that the king presided over the first meeting of his English Privy Council and began organising the composition of his government and household.

Cecil, swiftly nicknamed James's 'beagle', would be at James's right hand, acting as Principal Secretary; Sir Thomas Egerton, Lord

Ellesmere, would be Lord Chancellor and Keeper of the Great Seal; the following January, Lord Henry Howard (who would become the 1st Earl of Northampton in March 1604) joined the council; Edward Somerset, 4th Earl of Worcester, landed a key role as an adviser; and Lord Thomas Howard (created 1st Earl of Suffolk in July 1603) became Lord Chamberlain. Awarded places on the Privy Council too were the Scots Mar, Lennox, James Elphinstone, Edward Bruce, and Sir George Home. James would live henceforth as both a Scottish and an English monarch; in his new palaces, the public rooms (including waiting chambers, guard rooms, and presence chambers) would be staffed by a mix of Scotsmen and Englishmen; the privy chamber would likewise be mixed in its composition, with its staff having access also to the 'secret' or privy lodgings hidden behind it; but, at the heart of these most private apartments, the bedchamber would be staffed almost exclusively by Scots (as, in his capacity as King of Scots, James was required to allow access to his bedchamber to men of certain ranks and privileges). In a show of openness to all his high-ranking subjects, he would eat in public beneath an ornate baldachin, inviting favoured Scots and Englishmen to converse with him at mealtimes. Post horses would henceforth beat up clods of earth on the Great North Road, carrying messages, seals, news, and Scottish governmental matters back and forward. Until 1611, the king would rely on Sir George Home (later Earl of Dunbar), a crypto-Catholic whom he had once employed to spy on Anna and who had proven himself a workhorse, for his yeoman's work in helping to manage Scotland. James would, in time, boast, 'Here I sit, and govern Scotland by the pen. I write and it is done, and by a clerk of the Council I govern Scotland now, which others could not do by the sword.' At this early stage, and in the full glow of adulation, he could congratulate himself on having brought his home nation sufficiently to heel for it to bear his absence without descending into internecine conflict. Whilst at Theobalds, arrangements were also made for his first visit to the capital.

During Elizabeth's reign, the population of London had risen from under 100,000 to around 160,000, with upwards of 10,000 immigrants. The number was increased still further by well-wishers and place-seekers descending on the capital in advance of the new sovereign's arrival – around 100,000 more people are estimated to have sought lodgings, with the letter-writer and courtier John Chamberlain complaining that 'many run thither . . . as if it were first come, first served, or that preferment were a goal to be got by footmanship'.[6]

The press of people meant that many of those inhabiting the metropolis lived cheek by jowl, and outbreaks of disease were not only common but tore through the population with horrifying speed. During the summer of 1603, the plague paid one of its intermittent visits, which accounts for James being met at Stamford Hill (four miles outside the city) by the Lord Mayor; it also explains the king's distaste for the enormous crowd which swarmed out to meet his arriving party. It was small wonder that he would come to dislike London and that the initial delight he found in the welcoming crowds would return to his usual contempt: indeed, Sir John Oglander later recounted that James, on being told that a great concourse of people had flocked to see his face, delighted in embarrassing those present by joking, 'God's wounds! I will put down my breeches and they shall also see my arse!'[7] The king unwisely viewed his English accession as a break from consistent demonstrative engagement with his people; no longer would he have to live in close proximity to lesser mortals. Whilst a King of Scots was first amongst equals and expected to have regular contact with his subjects, a King of England might distance himself, delegate, and allow access only to the favoured few. From now on, he would engage with the *hoi polloi* only on organised progresses and at state events. The inevitable result was irritation on the part of those left outside and a frenetic army of place-seekers creeping in backdoors and through privy entrances, where their boldness was inevitably rewarded.

Shaken by reports of climbing mortality rates and potentially plague-ridden subjects, James was induced to halt his open-handedness and remain outside the city proper, first staying at Lord Thomas Howard's Charterhouse. After a brief visit to the Tower, he embarked on a tour of his new palaces: from Greenwich, downstream from London, he stemmed the flow of honours (no doubt hoping to also stem the flow of arriving courtiers), proclaiming that no further men would be knighted until his coronation. He did, however, manage to elevate Cecil to the title of Baron Cecil of Essendon.

Delighted as he was at the thought of exploring the hunting grounds of his new properties (amongst them Richmond, Greenwich, St James's Palace, and Hampton Court), James was unable to avoid the business of kingship. From the moment of his arrival, he and Cecil were being importuned by men who felt that the beginning of the new reign should mean the righting of perceived wrongs. One fellow wrote that he had 'served Robert Bowes, deceased, former ambassador of the late Queen Elizabeth in Scotland, for nine years in that country.[8] He was promised promotion but Bowes's death destroyed his hopes and left him in poor circumstances. He asks that he be granted the next soldier's pay of 8d a day that shall become available in the garrison at Berwick.'[9]

From another: 'In November two years ago the late Queen Elizabeth ordered Alderman Holmeden and Alderman Anderson ... to find accommodation for 24 Turks and Moors at 6d a day until shipping could be found to convey them to their own country ... But the owner of the house where they were accommodated has lately arrested him for the sum of £23 2s, which he claims to be due to him, and which was not paid, as promised by the late Queen. He is held responsible for the debt simply for having brought the Turks and Moors to that house, and he asks Cecil to arrange for its payment without delay.'[10]

But the problems requiring to be dealt with were not all in England. For a man who had coveted his new throne for so long, James had been remarkably short-sighted about the aftermath of his departure in Scotland.

*

A small but well-armed party beat hooves through the great valley which led to Stirling. Banners flew, trumpets blew, and, around the august travellers, steel clanked against steel. At the centre were Queen Anna and her women. Ringing them were mounted supporters. The queen's moment of victory had come at last – and it spelled trouble in the leaderless kingdom.

King James, on balance, had been an effective ruler in Scotland. Recent historians have been far more favourable towards him than those of previous generations, recognising, for example, his re-establishment of authority in the localities following the ructions of the Reformation, his attempts to repair a Crown tarnished by successive minorities (and the deposition of the previous monarch), and his remarkable ability to survive frequent attacks. What he did not do, however, was safeguard Scotland's standing as an independent political player – due partly to a lack of financial nous and more so because he had no intention of keeping Scotland independent. One eye throughout his reign had been trained on England's throne, which ensured that much of his policy was filtered through the lens of how an overbearing English government might respond; his dream, moreover, was of subsuming Scotland's sovereignty along with England's into a unitary Great Britain ruled in perpetuity by his dynasty. His efforts to strengthen the Crown certainly grew more skilful but tended towards ultimately setting forth ideological positions of absolutism and union. Probably, it is because he genuinely (if erroneously) believed that Scotland and England had automatically merged into one kingdom via the Union of the Crowns that he abandoned the former without much thought as to the immediate aftermath of his departure. After all, if there was now only one kingdom and one king, he had simply left the northern part for the southern part of his realm. All that was needed was for the governmental institutions to catch up with political reality.

Queen Anna, however, was not so careless. Almost before the dust had settled in her husband's wake, she began to put into action her longstanding desire to gain custody of Prince Henry. This was not born of maternal longing; if she were to ride into England as its queen consort, it would be demeaning to do so whilst publicly separated from the heir to both thrones.

Henry, now aged nine, encouraged her via a letter which included the words, 'Seeing, by his Majesty's departing, I will lose that benefit which I had by his frequent visitation, I must humbly request your Majesty to supply that lack by your presence (which I have more just cause to crave, since I have wanted [lacked] it so long, to my great grief and displeasure).'[11] This was all Anna needed. Coupled with the fact that James had taken the Earl of Mar south (he having been long involved in the cross-border negotiations ahead of the English succession), her proverbial ducks were all in a row.

The queen and her party (which she had been building for years) rode from Edinburgh to Stirling via Linlithgow. At the gates of the castle, she was met by Lennox and Henrietta's sister Marie, the Countess of Mar. Marie, no doubt alarmed by the sight of the armed men, refused access to all but Anna and her women. The queen, however, was not put off by the forced separation from her supporters. She, Lady Argyll, Lady Paisley and her daughter, and the queen's favourite, the young Jean Drummond, entered. Inside Stirling's walls, they were entertained to dinner, during the course of which Lady Mar – who was put in a wretchedly awkward position – raised the issue of the king's written command that Henry be kept in Mar custody. Anna's response was violent. She threw herself into a passionate argument, notwithstanding the fact that she was pregnant, and the dinner descended into argument, with her ladies taking her part. As the dispute intensified, the queen fainted and was carried to her apartments in the palace.

Marie, who had stood her ground, realised the gravity of the scene and the necessity of getting her version of events to those in power. Hastily, she sent messengers to those Scottish Privy Council members still resident in Edinburgh, along with fast riders with instructions to travel south and inform the king. When she had recovered from her faint, Anna did the same.

Obviously, the council was easier to reach than the king. Its members despatched a party of men to Stirling with their decision: they commanded that Marie and the Mars' claims over Henry be upheld until James decided otherwise. Thwarted, Anna fell again into illness, this time with tragic results: she lost the son she had been carrying. Dangerously, rumours immediately began emanating that she had 'taken some balm water that had hastened her abort'.[12] These would inflate later into even more ludicrous tales that she had beaten her own belly in rage, bringing on the miscarriage, and even that she had never been pregnant at all, and had merely been acting out to gain public sympathy.

All involved in Scottish affairs were soon dragged into an unedifying 'blame game'. The new chancellor, the 3rd Earl of Montrose, wrote south denying all culpability in the tragic turn of events north of the border, even as Mar was on his way up with orders that Anna begin her descent through England without Henry. James received a letter from Lord Fyvie, Prince Charles's guardian, which advised him that 'physic and medicine requireth a greater place with her Majesty at present than lectures on economics and politics. Her Majesty's passions could not be sa well mitgat and moderat as by seconding and obeying all her directions, quhilk [which] always is subject to zour [your] sacred Majesty's answers and resolves as oracles.'[13]

It was clear that no good solution could be found to the impasse in Scotland without the king's intervention. For his part, James, charmed as he was by his new residences and their well-stocked hunting parks, was in a quandary. He was well aware that the smoothness of his succession owed as much to his reputation as a stable family man as it did to Cecil's machinations, and he was loath to let his new subjects know of any marital strife.

This time, the king sent Lennox, with instructions to meet Mar and accompany him to Stirling. With the duke went letters: one for the earl, which told him to release the prince secretly into his mother's care, and another for Anna, full of reproofs couched in loving words. Lennox reached Mar at York, and the latter, with new instructions in hand, rode on to Stirling. The Scotland through which he passed, alarmingly, was not peaceful; the troubles over the queen and prince had excited a nervous and potentially violent panic about the realm being abandoned by its ruler and about to be robbed of its heir. This James might have foreseen and taken steps to assuage, had he not been so eager to leave and so blinded by his idealistic view that his kingdoms were now one.

On arriving at Stirling, Mar found the queen in a fury, unwilling even to receive him into her presence. Anna was utterly unwilling, too, to be formally handed custody of her son by Mar (whom she blamed for her miscarriage, in addition to the years of perceived public humiliation she had endured at his and his family's hands) at Stirling or anywhere. Her overriding concern was that gaining custody of her son should not be publicly construed being in Mar's gift.

This, naturally, put the unfortunate earl in a predicament. He refused to hand over his letters from the king until Anna would see him. The queen wrote south, accusing Mar of slandering her and criticising James directly for favouring the earl. James, still desperate to repair relations, wrote,

My heart,

Immediately before the receipt of your letter, I was purposed to have written you and that without any great occasion excepting for to free myself from the imputation of severeness, but now your letter has given me more matter to write, though I take small delight to meddle in so unpleasant a process, I wonder that neither your long knowledge of my nature, nor my late earnest purgation to you can cure you of that rooted error that anyone living dare speak or inform me in any ways to your prejudice and yet you can think them your unfriends, that are true friends to me.

I can say no more but protest upon peril of my salvation and damnation that neither the Earl of Mar nor any flesh living ever informed me that ye was upon any papist or Spanish course or that ye had any other thought but a wrong conceived opinion that he had more interest in your son and would not deliver him unto you.

God is my witness that I ever preferred you to all my bairns, much more than to any subject; but if you will ever give place to the reports of every flattering sycophant that will persuade you that when I account well of an honest and wise servant for his true and faithful service to me, that is to compare or prefer him to you, then will neither you nor I be ever at rest or at peace. Praying God, my heart, to preserve you and all the bairns send me a blithe meeting with you and a couple of them.

Your own,

JAMES R[14]

It is an interesting letter, as full of attempts at what would now be called 'soft soap' as it is of warnings and implicit criticisms. Perhaps most interesting, however, is his warning that 'when I account well of an honest and wise servant for his true and faithful service to me, that is to compare or prefer him to you, then will neither you nor I be ever at rest or at peace'. He was writing of Mar, but there was a larger import to his words. In the years since his marriage, his relationships with men had either ceased or been remarkably well hidden. By warning his wife that their relationship would never be happy as long as she harboured jealousy, he was intimating that in the future his passions might lead him to stray. Now that he had all but secured the English throne, he might indulge himself as he wished – as numerous English kings had done before him. Moreover, as swiftly became evident, his head had been turned in his new kingdom: his homosexual desires were rapidly to be rekindled by the bevy of attractive young men, splendidly and fashionably clad and coiffed, and eager to be of service.

On receiving his letter, Anna's response was to demand an apology from Mar, which he refused to give. This forced James to again intervene and to again excite his wife's anger by playing up the earl's good work in helping pave the road to the succession. Angrily, Anna wrote that she 'would rather never set foot in England' than wear its crown as a result of her enemy's favour.

Defeated, James wrote from Greenwich in May that the prince

might be given into the custody of a more acceptable member of the Scottish council, 'to be given to her [Anna] and disposed of as she pleaseth'.[15] The most suitable man for this job was the realm's only duke, and so Lennox rode for Stirling with an escort of noblemen, arriving on the 19th. The intention was that he bring Henry out of Stirling as his ward, riding with him in a procession which pointedly excluded Mar, and ceremonially conferring the boy's custody on his mother. Anna, at last, had won.

On the 23rd, the queen rode in triumph towards Edinburgh.[16] The castle's cannon blasted a welcome, and orders were issued for a new coach, as well as taffeta, velvets, and satins to clothe the royal family (and the queen's fool, Thomas Derry). At Holyroodhouse, preparations were made for the exodus southwards, and ready to instruct Anna on her new kingdom's customs were Lucy Russell, Countess of Bedford, and Frances Howard, Countess of Kildare, who had already crossed the border to ingratiate themselves with their new sovereign lady. At the end of the month, the queen rode in her new carriage to St Giles, Prince Henry accompanying her in order to advertise her authority and soothe the turbulence which had risen on the king's leave-taking.

Although a bout of illness called Princess Elizabeth's departure into question, in the end she recovered, and so Anna, Henry, and the princess were able to begin their journey out of Scotland together (only Prince Charles was to remain behind until the following year, owing to his underdevelopment). King James, in distant London, thus had his wish: a picture of family unity was provided as his wife and two eldest children joined Lennox in travelling to Berwick, where they met Cecil's older brother, Thomas, Lord Burghley, who pronounced Anna 'a magnificent Prince, a kind wife, and a constant mistress'.[17] The queen was treated to a less martial welcome than her husband. Awaiting her was a cluster of other Englishwomen (including the Ladies Scrope, Rich, and Walsingham) who were jostling for positions. With the acceptance of the ravishing Lady Rich (formerly Penelope Devereux, sister to the late Earl of Essex and a woman who had sent the Scottish royal couple her portrait during Essex's period of cross-border intrigue), Anna was loath to accept these women into her household. She had spent her time in Scotland building up networks of people she trusted and worked well with, and, as ever, she was not prepared to let her choice of people be made for her. Thus, despite James having sent up a quantity of the late Queen Elizabeth's clothes and jewels (which had provoked an argument with his new council) along with the old queen's tirewoman-in-ordinary, Blanche Swansted (charged with dressing Anna's hair in the style of Elizabeth), the new queen was immovable. She was determined to be Queen Consort of England on her own terms.

The reliable Lennox was once again pressed into service as the king's instrument. The first battle was over the choice of her Lord Chamberlain – a post James wished an Englishman to fill, and which Anna was adamant should remain filled by her existing Chamberlain, the gentleman John Kennedy (not to be confused with John Kennedy, 5th Earl of Cassillis). Duly, James despatched lists of appointees he insisted his wife give place to; and Anna sent – via Lennox – her own list, with his names scrubbed out in favour of her own people. This was not sheer wilfulness on the queen's part but rather her exercising her rights in the teeth of her hypocritical husband; James fully intended to surround himself with Scots in his bedchamber, to the exclusion of Englishmen, and thus apparently had decided to infringe upon his wife's customary rights in order to placate his disgruntled new subjects by stressing a continuity between the late queen regnant's and the new queen consort's households. Anna, however, left Berwick with her own people very much around her.

In a repeat of James's trip southwards, the new queen found herself feted and celebrated. At York, she and her children were presented with pageants and silver cups filled with gold angels. At Worksop, they were entertained by the 7th Earl of Shrewsbury, and Anna bestowed favour on Cecil's young son (who, according to the custom of the day, was being raised in another household), allowing him to dance with Princess Elizabeth. Onwards they rode, to Holme Pierrepont Hall; to Nottingham (where pastoral festivities were laid

on, involving huntsmen in gold and silver coats, and mock shep-
herds and shepherdesses throwing flowers); to Ashby-de-la-Zouche;
to Leicester (where more silver cups of gold were given them); to
Dingley Hall. Throughout, the royal party swelled, until it num-
bered in the thousands, with courtiers flocking to present themselves
to the family and catch sight of something very few of them could
ever have seen: an acknowledged royal mother and heir. Holdenby
House and Althorp followed, at the latter of which Ben Jonson (a
client of Lucy, Lady Bedford, who had endeared herself to Anna by
coming into Scotland to meet her) presented his *Satyr*, and thereby
established himself in the queen's favour. Delighted with it, a passion
was born in Anna for elaborate, interactive royal entertainments.

After moving on to Easton Neston and lodging with Sir George
Fermor, the party was reunited with its patriarch, who had left the
environs of London to join them. The enormous crowds could now
bear witness not only to a royal mother and son, but to a king,
queen, and heir (Princess Elizabeth had been despatched with Lady
Bedford to visit what would be her future home, Coombe Abbey).
The family and its train of courtiers, servants, hangers-on, and
followers thus wound onwards, to Grafton and thence to Salden
House, by which time the queen had embraced into the fold those
sisters of the late Earl of Essex, Penelope Devereux, Lady Rich,
and Dorothy, Countess of Northumberland, as well as their cousin
Elizabeth, Countess of Southampton, whose imprisoned husband
had been Essex's co-conspirator (and whom James was determined
to rehabilitate).

The ultimate destination was England's ancient Windsor Castle,
one of the primary royal seats, and, on arrival, James was keen to
complete the image of his perfect family. He lifted up the Princess
Elizabeth, who had rejoined them, and said, 'She is not an ill-
favoured wench and may outshine her mother one of these days.'
His attempt at bluff bonhomie was true enough. Elizabeth showed
every indication of inheriting her mother and her grandmother Mary
Stuart's willowy height and beauty. The obsequious Southampton,
who had been released from the Tower and was intent on making the

most of his wife's new connection to Anna, retorted, 'If she equals her Majesty some years hence, it will be more, I will be bold to say, than any other princess upon earth will do.'[18]

The image of domestic harmony and dynastic stability was, however, a cloak for a number of issues, not least the question of religion. James and Anna had, after all, been making free with Catholic hopes to ensure their smooth succession; England's war with Spain was still ongoing; and throughout the country, rumours were pouring in that Jesuits were proclaiming the Infanta of Spain and her husband King and Queen of England. The solution was to legitimise the new regime – and the new royal family. This James did firstly by holding the traditional English Garter ceremony; in July, Prince Henry was invested into the order along with the absentee Christian IV, Lennox, and the Earls of Mar, Southampton, and Pembroke. The king's approach was, as it always would be, pacific.

Unfortunately, this policy was not universally popular. Southampton, despite his recent release, return to favour, and smooth tongue, immediately caused problems. The former Essexian remained wedded to the late earl's ideals of chivalry and honour. Accordingly, he could not help but resume his old feud with the anti-Essex Lord Grey of Wilton. When Queen Anna criticised Essex, Southampton bristled, saying in her hearing that 'if her Majesty made herself a party against the friends of Essex, of course, they were bound to submit, but none of their private enemies durst thus have expressed themselves'.[19] This was bold and impertinent talk for a man who had only narrowly avoided the block for his actions in the previous reign, but it was typical of him. The affront raised Anna's ire, but so too did it cause Lord Grey to spring to her defence; ultimately, she had to intervene to stop them coming to blows, calling for the palace guard to remove them from her presence. James, likely against his inclination, had both men briefly imprisoned in the Tower.

More troubling to the king was the discovery of a pair of tenuously linked plots – the Main Plot and the subsidiary Bye (or By) Plot – which Cecil uncovered. Upon investigation, these were deemed to be the brainchildren of the priest William Watson, Sir Griffin Markham, Lord Grey (again causing trouble), Henry Brooke, 11th Lord Cobham, his brother George, and Sir Walter Raleigh. The purported aim was to prevent the new king and queen from being crowned and to substitute them – with Spanish support – with James's cousin, the daughter of Darnley's brother Charles, Lady Arbella Stuart. Both plots were hare-brained and swiftly subdued, but they are useful in explaining the king's later distrust of Arbella (though she was innocent of any knowledge of the schemes) and they raise interesting questions about Raleigh (whom James already detested, and whom historians largely agree intended only to act as a double agent and to reveal all himself – only to be beaten to the 'discovery' by Cecil). Thankfully, for the moment, James's antipathy towards Raleigh was shared by many, as the fellow had been widely condemned as arrogant; scurrilous libels called him 'Wily Wat' and held him responsible for the popular Essex's death.[20] Raleigh's unpopularity made it easy for him to be tried at Winchester, found guilty, sentenced to death, and imprisoned in the Tower.

When the agents of the plots were dealt with (Watson, the perfidious George Brooke, and a priest named Clarke were executed and the others locked up), the problem of establishing the new peace policy remained. Central to this was a continuation of the king's even-handedness to Catholics whom, though they were a minority, he wished to accept his kingship. The problem was that the Elizabethan recusancy fines had made the outlawed faith functionally legal for the rich: those Catholics who remained committed to their religion were, therefore, often powerful, wealthy, and needed careful handling.

The downside of the king's seeming tolerance was two-fold: it encouraged rumours that both he and Anna were crypto-Catholics, and it excited the agitation of Puritans (a loose grouping of reforming Protestants who had already made their expectations clear by delivering their 'Millenary Petition', which laid out their grievances and was so-called because it allegedly had the support of 1,000 men). Throughout the year, reports landed on Cecil's desk of seditious claims that 'our Queen is a Catholic in heart'; 'with the King's consent, the mass was sometimes secretly celebrated for her'; and 'before he [James] came hither both he and the Queen were papists, and so afterwards [he] would prove a rank papist and his Queen too'.[21] If one bases a belief in Anna's conversion to Catholicism on the grounds that there is no smoke without fire, it seems that James, too, would have been burnt to a crisp. It was all pure rumour and mischief-making, but it was the natural product of the king and queen's manoeuvres. Not helping matters was that, moreover, James was personally intolerant of extremes of any stripe. In matters of faith, he was, and remained, a moderate Calvinist who sought – by careful management of competing interests – a loyal evangelical ministry. Universal conformity, he knew, could not be achieved overnight nor by anything other than gentle pushing (with the occasional hard shove of Catholics or Puritans when opportunity knocked – as in the fiery executions for heresy of the nonconformists Bartholomew Legate and Edward Wightman in 1612). There is no doubt, however, that for all his machinations, and thanks to his long experience of religious and civil strife, peaceful Christian unity was his ultimate, elusive dream. It was to that end that he engaged in correspondence with the Catholic jurist Jacques-Auguste de Thou in December 1603, promising to promote universal peace.

Yet that policy of toleration had to remain in play as long as the throne was unsecured. What James sought, along with his wife and Cecil, was a coronation. Traditionally, these ceremonies marked the inalienable investiture of the sovereign, and they were carried out in tandem with a triumphal entry through London. Unfortunately, plague continued to rage through the city. The solution thus alighted upon was to hold a truncated ceremony in Westminster Abbey first, and to delay the progress through London until the bodies had stopped piling up.[22]

Prince Henry and Princess Elizabeth were despatched well away from danger – to Oatlands in Surrey – whilst James and Anna took up residence at Hampton Court. Eschewing the traditional night in the Tower's royal apartments, they moved on to St James's Palace, where the king held an *ad hoc* ceremony to dub his new Knights of the Bath. On 25 July, amid pouring rain which thundered down on canopies and the abbey roof, the bells of Westminster chimed. King and queen were rowed along the swelling Thames to Westminster, thereafter walking to the abbey.

The ceremony itself followed the traditions laid out in the *Liber regalis*, with the interior of the abbey provided with a curtained 'pulpit' (or stage), two thrones of estate (James's being set higher). and makeshift tiring (or dressing) rooms erected in St Edward's chapel. The three parts of the ceremony – the Election, the Consecration, and the Enthronement – were conducted by John Whitgift, Archbishop of Canterbury, and Thomas Bilson, Bishop of Winchester. Throughout, the reduced number of noble attendees were able to view their monarch. James remained, at this stage in his life, vigorous and healthy. Gone, however, was the fresh-faced young man who had travelled to Norway and Denmark. After years of riding at the chase in sunshine and rain, his once neat features had started growing florid, his clear complexion turning weathered and rosy. For all he admired elaborate fashions draped over other men, still he was immune to decking himself in the elaborate weeds of the English nobility except on special occasions – and his coronation provided one of them. However, he was no slouch when it came to crafting his own image. On James's arrival in England, the Venetian ambassador Scaramelli acidly remarked that 'from his dress he would have been taken for the meanest among his courtiers'.[23] However, the king would soon remedy this and outspend Queen Elizabeth, quadrupling her Wardrobe expenditure in the early years of his reign by buying gems to decorate otherwise understated clothing (his signature being jewelled and feathered hats).

Rather than being concerned with his appearance, the king showed himself more interested in the attractions of his new subjects. During the ceremonial acts of homage, the young Philip Herbert, son of the 2nd Earl of Pembroke and Mary Sidney, defied convention by stepping forward and kissing the king. James, rather than being offended, appeared delighted at the handsome young

man's apparently compulsive act of affection. He had been immediately attracted to Herbert on their first meeting, and already he
had appointed the fellow a place in his privy chamber and dubbed
him a Knight of the Bath. Soon the young man would be the only
Englishman allowed into the bedchamber. A pattern, last seen prior
to the king's marriage, had been re-established. From henceforth,
James was unable or unwilling to rein in his bisexual urges. With the
crown secure on his head and his heirs waiting to succeed him, he
no longer saw any need. How far exactly he went with individuals is,
of course, unknowable, but to critics it hardly mattered – it was all
perceived as lascivious, dissolute, and therefore fit material to rebuke
the king and court.

As the ceremony wore on, another piece of theatre caught the
attention of those present. At the moment of Communion – administered, naturally, according to the rites of the English Church – the
queen refused. This, of course, led to increased speculation that she
had turned Catholic, and that is probably what both she and James
expected. Still, their mutual policy was one of tolerance, and it helped
more than hindered that approach if there was dubiety surrounding
her faith. In truth, the public refusal was unlikely to have been an
independent display of Catholic defiance. For one thing, neither
James nor Cecil evinced any chagrin, and the latter – a tireless hunter
of Catholic plots – revised his opinion of the queen, turning from
a suspicious potential enemy to a genuine friend (so much so that
James could not resist joking that the secretary had fallen for her).
Moreover, Anna could refuse Communion perfectly well as a devout
Lutheran, given that that faith prized the words of the ceremony over
the Eucharist. Of course, few would excuse her refusal on the grounds
of her native Lutheranism, whilst plenty would choose to view her
as a Catholic convert (a boon to those of that faith but an ominous
sign to the Puritans, whom James intended to deal with directly soon
enough). In fact, the traditional reading of the episode, in which
the queen publicly demurs from the Anglican sacrament in spirited
defence of her secret Catholic faith, is problematic in that it would
have been out of character for a woman who was never a doctrinaire.

We might thus view Anna and James, likely with Cecil's acceptance, as working together to keep English and continental Catholics from stirring up dissent against their sovereignty, using the 'wink and nudge' Catholic sympathies of the queen as their tool (the queen, after all, was genuinely sympathetic to the faith, even if not a convert, and thus far more effective than the fervently Protestant James in convincing Catholics of royal support).

If this was the case, it worked. Soon enough, a papal nuncio was writing directly to the king: 'Moreover, his Holiness has made good offices with the Most Christian and Most Catholic Kings and other Princes for peace and a good understanding with you. This good will of the Pope has always been growing, so that I know he will not cease to strive to make it more apparent to you and will secure as far as humanly possible that no harm befalls you from Catholics. He will remove from these countries all who are turbulent and mutinous and chastise the disobedient and seditious not only with ecclesiastical but also with temporal pains. He has already ordered all Catholics to revere and obey you.'[24] Neither James nor Anna could have asked for more.

After the ceremony, the royal party moved on to the banqueting hall to draw the festivities to a close. Thereafter they went to Woodstock where, in September, the sceptical James was persuaded to offer the royal touch as a cure for 'The King's Evil' (scrofula). This no way warmed his increasingly snooty heart to the idea of physical proximity to his lowlier subjects. Henceforth, he would, wherever possible, delegate duties which involved touching the poor – such as the traditional Easter-time Maundy Thursday services, in which royals would wash poor people's feet – to his Archbishops of Canterbury (old Whitgift being replaced by Richard Bancroft in 1604, followed by George Abbot in 1611). When the distasteful practice was over, the royal couple embarked on a tour of the southern counties, there to impress themselves on the localities with all the presence and majesty of the late queen's progresses.

The Stuart dynasty had arrived, and its king and queen had been crowned. The family, moreover, had, if appearances were to be believed, won the hearts of their new subjects, who were delighted by the bloodlessness of the succession, and who could look forward to a reign lacking the perennial instability of a childless woman's regime. Yet, soon enough, the unusual relationships within this seemingly blessed new family would become apparent. The king was still seeking love.

15

Secrets of a Successful Marriage

Upon the establishment of her husband's reign, chief amongst the new queen's concerns were which property rights pertained to her as part of her jointure as an English consort. Lord Treasurer Buckhurst was given the unenviable task of discovering the landholdings which were – ideally – to cover the wages, apparel, and annuities of her servants. As Anna was a sovereign's daughter, the decision was made to model her inheritance on the last king's daughter to sit at the side of a sovereign husband. Buckhurst wrote to Cecil that he had 'not slacked' in his efforts and had gone through the records until landing upon Katherine of Aragon's historical properties as those best suited to the new royal-in-her-own-right consort.[1]

Anna was delighted. She wrote to her brother, who had intervened from Denmark to ensure she was being treated appropriately, thanking him for 'the care you have had concerning our jointure . . . [which was such as] King Henry the Eighth, King of England, gave to Queen Katherine, daughter of Spain, in which we have not only had our desire to imitate her that was born a king's daughter, but his Majesty hath ordained in all other things thereunto belonging so as we are satisfied in the point of honour to be used according to our rank'.[2]

In time, her list of properties would include Somerset House, Nonsuch Palace, Pontefract Castle and Havering-atte-Bower. Yet the queen was required to follow Katherine of Aragon in domestic matters too. As that consort had closed her eyes to her husband's infidelities – at least until Henry VIII's desire to possess Anne Boleyn forced them open – Anna would show herself willing to tolerate

240

James's handsome young hunting companions, with whom he would disappear for days or weeks for, as he called it, his 'necessary recreation'.[3] Soon enough, his penchant for taking himself off 'with eight or ten of his favourites' was matter for diplomatic comment; and in December of 1604, disgruntled subjects kidnapped one of his hunting hounds, Jowler, returning the dog the following day with a note attached to his collar: 'Good Mr Jowler, we pray you speak to the King (for he hears you every day and so doth he not us) that it will please his Majesty to go back to London.'[4] James laughed the incident off, but the truth was that the amount of time he was spending away from his capital was raising eyebrows, not likely to be lowered by his claims that his time was better spent at the chase than 'going . . . to whores' nor that 'manlike and active recreations' were justification for his frequent rustication with favourites.

It is sometimes suggested that, on securing the English Crown, James and Anna moved on to lead largely separate lives. This is not the case. Yet they did pursue separate interests. James continued to exercise a conjugal relationship with his wife for some years, but so too did he revert to his old habit of developing passionate interests in attractive men – always younger – and in the process advancing their careers. For the moment, however, these relationships were not founded on emotional attachments. Those fellows involved provided attractive and welcome diversions; they flattered their sovereign shamelessly, and they shared his sporting and leisure interests. Rapidly, James began to show himself willing to either marry such men off when they ceased to excite him, or allow them to marry if they wished, so long as they continued to dance attendance on their needy monarch.

In the August following their coronation, the king and queen visited Loseley Park, Farnham Castle, Thruxton House, and Wilton, at the latter of which they lodged with the 3rd Earl of Pembroke (brother to Philip Herbert, who had kissed the king so precipitately at the coronation). Their tour continued on through Tottenham House, Wadley House, and Burford Priory; thereafter, Anna took up residence at Basing House, whilst James moved on. Still, they kept up their correspondence. When the elderly Charles Howard, by now 1st Earl of Nottingham and Lord Steward of James's household, began paying court to one of her ladies, young Margaret Stewart (daughter of the Earl of Moray, whom Huntly had murdered in 1592), the queen wrote,

> Your Majesty's letter was welcome to me. I have been as glad of the fair weather as yourself and the last part of your letter, you have guessed right that I would laugh – who would not laugh – both at the persons and the subject but the more at so well chosen Mercury between Mars and Venus? You know that women can hardly keep counsel. I humbly desire your Majesty to tell me how it is possible that I should keep this secret that have already told it and shall tell it to as many as I speak with, and if I were a poet I would make a song of it and sing it to the tune of *Three Fools Well Met*.[5]

Anna, certainly, was joking about being unable to keep her mouth shut (if she were being honest, her true religious views would certainly be clearer), but love was definitely in the air. James was spoiled for choice. Not only was Philip Herbert exercising his considerable powers of attraction over the king, but so too was a twenty-three-year-old Scotsman, James Hay, son of Sir James Hay of Fingask and Margaret Murray, who had already won his way into the bedchamber and was being recognised as a favourite.

Favourites, in England, had by this time acquired quite as much opprobrium as they had in Scotland. Queen Elizabeth had all but formalised the position, using it as a means of advancing men outside the usual channels of reward. Men whom she found attractive or witty, or whose rapid elevation offered some political capital, could thus leapfrog the laborious path of providing years of state service in order to earn favour. Yet, given her sex and the language of courtly love which prevailed at her court, 'favourite' had become a sneering, bawdy byword for lovers, confidants, sycophants, and flatterers. As a female ruler outnumbered by male courtiers, Elizabeth had made favouritism a path to patronage, professionalising it and making it a key part of her domestic polity. This legacy James had inherited. His favourites could no longer be shuffled out of public life with payoffs alone; they had to be rewarded with power and positions – something the generous king was quite willing to do. What he did not do – yet – was to parade his men, whose attractions were chiefly physical, before his wife; and Anna, for her part, appears to have accepted them. Her husband, after all, continued to need her both sexually and in the pursuit of his policy of universal appeal. Presumably, what happened on his innumerable hunting expeditions stayed in the country.

The royal couple were reunited, along with Prince Henry and Princess Elizabeth, in Winchester in September. Delighted, the queen was eager to display her tentative new role as a patroness of the arts – a pleasant thing, given that the royal family was resident in Winchester to oversee Raleigh's trial. She had, on her long journey southwards, become enamoured of the world of English literature and the concomitant display and lyricism with which men like Ben Jonson were then investing it. As she did not yet speak English, and as she had to counter the xenophobic view that she was a doubly for-eign consort, she threw herself into learning and helping elevate the language with a zeal not seen in any previous queen (nor matched by any future one).

Unfortunately, Anna did not yet have at her disposal the literary talents she would later employ. In just over a fortnight, she was thus compelled to put together a somewhat lacklustre masque, entitled *Prince Henry's Welcome at Winchester*, which was universally criticised as rustic and unrefined: an amateur performance more fitting for a bourgeois family gathering than as a piece of public theatre, which royal masques were. Joining the family in this celebration – and as critical of the masque as anyone – was another family member, Lady Arbella Stuart. In her late twenties and still barred from taking a husband, the bookish Arbella derided the queen's entertainments as childish and ridiculous. Not surprisingly, the lady did not endear herself particularly to the royal family. In fact, despite James's deep interest in the Stuart dynasty, it is curious that he never developed anything beyond a detached show of affection towards (and ultimately a deep-rooted suspicion of) Arbella. Nor is it surprising. In truth, this erudite lady could be every bit as pompous and intellectually snobbish as her royal cousin, and this the king did not appreciate. Though he was not entirely against educated and intelligent women – as his patronage of the Scottish poet Christian Lindsay attests – he was certainly averse to any who stood close to his throne. The unfortunate Arbella, who was deeply devoted to classical education, had spent much of her life in virtual imprisonment under her grandmother, Bess of Hardwick, and thus had little taste for extravagant courtly entertainments. Nor did she bear any love for her relatives, whom she knew no better than they knew her.

If Anna was upset by the negative reaction to her masque, there is little record of it – and we can discount as teenage hyperbole the diary of Lady Anne Clifford, which noted that 'there is much talk of a masque the Queen had at Winchester and how all the ladies about the court had gotten such ill-names that it was grown a scandalous place, and the Queen herself [has] much fallen from her former greatness and reputation she had in the world'.[6] Nor is there evidence that she was perturbed by the departure of Elizabeth for Coombe Abbey, where she was to be raised by Lord and Lady Harington (her original governess, Lady Kildare, having gradually lost credit after her husband, Lord Cobham, had been disgraced and locked up for his part in the Main Plot). It was, after all, the custom for English royal children to be raised in high estate by suitably aristocratic guardians.

The first Yuletide festivities for the royal couple were far more ambitious. In October, Anna instituted a programme of serious dramatic production. In doing so, she was reconnecting also with her husband; in December, James's acting troupe, the King's Men (formerly the Lord Chamberlain's Men), best known for including William Shakespeare, performed before the royal couple at Wilton.[7] During the Christmas Revels at Hampton Court, both James and Anna spent prodigiously, with productions of *The Masque of Indian and China Knights* (in which Philip Herbert performed alongside Lennox and his brother), *Robin Goodfellow*, and *The Vision of the Twelve Goddesses*. In the latter – a masque composed by the playwright Samuel Daniel – Anna herself took to the stage, performing as Pallas. In a symbolic move, historic dresses of the late queen were dissected to provide costumes: a sign, if one were needed, that the old reign was over and a new one had begun. Soon enough, foreign ambassadors were jostling for places at the new queen's masques, recognising them for what they were: opportunities for the king and queen to enact their monarchical agenda onstage and for guests to demonstrate their favour – and the favour bestowed on their home nations – by gaining plum positions in the audience.

In the new year, the royal pair were required also to face the consequences of another of their shared enterprises, when the spy Anthony Standen was caught attempting to smuggle beads and other Catholic items into the country, supposedly for the queen. Standen, who had enjoyed a chequered career and could name amongst his previous employers Margaret Douglas, Lord Darnley, Mary Queen of Scots, Philip II, Francis Walsingham, and the 2nd Earl of Essex, appears to have served himself foremost. Yet in 1603, James had despatched him to Florence and Venice to announce the Union of the Crowns; the spy, however, travelled to Rome, where he promised to work at reconciling Anna to the Catholic faith (a job which would hardly have been necessary had she already converted). Evidently he was unsure of his mission and of the queen – writing to Father Persons, he noted that she was 'very assyduous at [Anglican] sermons, so that I am in a stagger what shall become of my tokens'.[8] When he was arrested and imprisoned on his arrival back in England, his Catholic trinkets were sent to Paris, there to be returned to Rome by the papal nuncio. In the opinion of the French ambassador, Beaumont, the hapless spy had been a tool of the royal couple, who simply wished for papal approval of their English inheritance (and for the Pope to therefore quieten English Catholics). Probably Beaumont was right. At any rate, Cecil (who had confronted the spy) was mollified, and Standen sought and was given release. Thereafter, James left it to Anna to divest England of the embarrassing agent. The queen, always eager to play her role as the king's conscience, would in 1606 recommend him to Christina of Lorraine, Grand Duchess of Tuscany, and Standen would depart for the continent.

But Catholics and Catholic chicanery were not the most pressing problem. The Puritans who had assailed James on the road south had not gone away, and neither had their desire for the new reign to bring about a general reformation of the Church been met. Indeed, the king openly stated that he was blessed beyond his predecessors in coming to the throne and finding no need to make religious alterations either in the state or in the private worship he enjoyed in Elizabeth's old Chapels Royal – which was not what those reformers, who had simply been waiting for the old queen to die so that they might push change in the new reign, wished to hear. James, no more a lover of Puritans (equating them as he did with the Presbyterians of the Kirk) than he was of Catholics, elected to confront the issue of religion head-on. Thus, in January 1604, he opened what became known as the Hampton Court Conference, during which he meant to use his own spiritual authority and considerable theological education to respond to those who were agitating for reform (and who had been increasingly perturbed by the glitter – and perceived sleaze – of the new court). For the first time, a monarch of England was tackling sectarians face-to-face; from James's perspective, he might trounce extremists, whilst the Puritans welcomed a chance to educate their sovereign on the liturgy, worship, and structural problems of his new Church. The latter were to be frustrated.

The king, always a lover of debate, held his own against a delegation of hand-picked Puritans, and the great fruit of the conference was the Authorised Bible which still bears its commissioner's name. On 22 February, James issued a proclamation 'commanding all Jesuits, Seminaries, and other Priests to depart the realm', with another following in March banning lay baptism, adding a little to the catechism, and authorising uniformity under the *Book of Common Prayer*. This was intended to throw a bone to his anti-Catholic subjects by reconfirming the terms of the Jesuits, Etc. Act (1584) which banished Catholic priests under threat of execution for treason (and as a result, Father John Sugar was hanged, drawn, and quartered in July). Indeed, at his first English parliament (which met in March), he told the Commons, members of which had already grumbled about the abuse of the Royal Wardrobe and supposed increases in Catholic conversions, that the Church of Rome was 'our Mother Church, although defiled with some infirmities and corruptions'. His doublespeak allowed him at the same time to dismiss the Pope's 'imperiall civill power over all kings and emperors'.[9] With a stream of biblical allusions, James argued that the Roman Church was, like a mother, subservient to the son – Christ and his reformed religion – who rejected errors and grew out of the teachings of the nursery and into a realm of purer truth. A lifting of anti-Catholic legislation was not, however, on the cards; for one thing, the fines gathered in from recusants were far too lucrative and, despite their suspension in the opening months of the reign, they were quickly reinstituted.

Yet the king went on paying lip service to tolerance of both hard-line Protestants and hopeful Catholics. His goal was, at this point, very much to promote continuity, and he had no intention of allowing what he called the 'augmentation' of his kingship to be viewed as a turning point in the history of either Scotland or England. Just as he had spent his last years in Scotland settling the country so that it might function gubernatorially in his absence, quietly governed by his Privy Council and his own signatures, so too did he intend English religion to carry on as it was. This was all part of his anticipated incorporation of the kingdoms: the less things looked like being wildly altered in either, the more his subjects on either side of the border would swallow a quiet but comprehensive union. Indeed, James would, soon enough, try to frame union as a minor, natural, and inevitable piece of business: both kingdoms, he claimed, were alike in language, culture, and religion. Nothing was to be altered and religious toleration was to reign. His goal was to establish a new, less combative balance of power in Europe, with Christian continuities prized rather than differences stressed – and unlike his predecessor on the English throne, he had children worth using in the building of multiple continental alliances.

However, his middle-road approach towards England's faith failed to satisfy the extremists, as middle roads seldom will. The insoluble problem was that neither Catholics nor Protestants wanted tolerance; the former wanted no less than the restoration of Catholicism, and the latter wished every vestige of the Roman faith torn out of the guts of the British Isles. Extremists – crusading Jesuits and canting Puritans – were active threats to his dream of renewed Christian unity and non-aggression on both a domestic and international scale. Although the Hampton Court Conference allowed the king to demonstrate his governorship of the English Church, it remained only to be seen which extreme would break first.

*

No doubt bolstered by what he considered the success of his conference, James went on to enjoy a further demonstration of his kingship throughout the course of the session of parliament. Chief amongst his desires was to promote his idea of 'sincere and perfect union' between his kingdoms. It was at this session that he made his famous speech outlining his familiar conception of a unitary Great Britain. 'What God hath conjoined,' he intoned, 'let no man separate. I am the husband, and all the whole isle is my wife. I am the head, and it is my body. I am the shepherd, and it is my flock. I hope therefore that no man will be so unreasonable as to think that I that am a most Christian King under the Gospel should be a polygamist and husband to two wives; that I being the head should have a divided and monstrous body'.[10] The language of family had become almost instinctive, and thus easily inscribed onto his political ideology. As James the man had a wife in Anna, so James the king had a wife in Great Britain. He would have agreed wholeheartedly with contemporary ideals of unity and cosmic concord, and been delighted by the ingratiating view offered by poet Nicholas Breton: 'Subjects all one, under one King, the laws all tending to one end; why should not the nations be all one people?'[11]

Unfortunately, James was over-eager both in his demands and in his self-belief in his role as parliament's master. Unlike Queen Elizabeth, who had known how to manage her MPs with soft words, the new king viewed the ancient institution as an assembly with limited licence to offer counsel, and he determined from the first to nip any presumptuous thoughts of innovation in the bud. Like the Scottish parliament, it post-dated the office of sovereign and was thus inferior to it; its main function, from James's perspective, was to rubber-stamp supply bills which empowered tax collectors to draw subsidies from trade and property owners, and to deliver the revenue into the royal coffers. The Commons, on the other hand, were increasingly jealous of their rights and privileges, and viewed parliaments as an outlet for airing and addressing local and national grievances.

Members' rancour was apparent from the first, when James intervened over the disputed election of the Lower House. Although this was resolved (following ominous threats from the king), it did not presage a healthy atmosphere to begin serious discussion of political union. To James's chagrin, what he saw as a small matter – the abolition of two kingdoms in favour of the creation of one – was unpopular on both sides of the border. His English parliament cavilled particularly over the historic institutions of England (not only their own – parliament itself – but the system of common law), arguing that the formation of a new state might void all existing laws. Even the name 'Britain', which became popular with playwrights like Shakespeare around this time, was considered too redolent of ancient, pagan heresy. In the event, parliament was prorogued in July, and the king simply proclaimed himself the King of Great Britain, Ireland (where the Elizabethan war against rebels – or freedom fighters – had ended in English victory), and France without ratification. It was a paper title with no legal force. Thereafter, he established a commission to engineer his idea of union (a union which, it should be noted, would anglicise Scotland, enforcing the English episcopal Church on the Kirk and spreading English law north of the border). Outside of the Union Flag, the prototype of which he would approve by 1606, James's efforts were in vain. The commissioners appointed to attempt to map out a legal route to political incorporation never got much beyond thrashing out arguments, and though he never truly gave up on trying to knit Scotland and England into one state, he would not achieve it (and, indeed, the eventual Union of 1707 fell short of his goals of establishing one faith and one rule of law across Great Britain). During parliament's later sitting in 1607, the union project was quietly killed off, as members cavilled at the commission's findings and drowned debate in a wave of anti-Scottish obloquy.

At the same time as parliament first sat in 1604, however, the king found a more amenable institution in Convocation (the Church's ruling assembly), which moved to codify new Anglican canons – aimed at tightening Church administration, in defiance of the reformist desires expressed at the Hampton Court Conference – in an attempt to winnow out Puritans who refused to subscribe and could thus be deprived of their ministries. What resulted were brief, intermittent waves of crackdowns on extreme Puritans, as the king elected to settle the religious question in favour of moderate Calvinism under the royal supremacy, with some – as the years passed, more – sympathy to visual and oral display, and without the disputed doctrine of predestination. Utilising Convocation, however, provoked the Commons by publicly exhibiting the power of ecclesiastical bodies over secular ones.

More welcome to the king than arguing with MPs was the chance to display his kingship to the people. This he was also able to do in March 1604, when the decline in plague deaths allowed him to parade his family through London in the ceremonial royal entry. Following a visit to the Royal Exchange, James, Anna, and Prince Henry took up residence in the Tower, where they listened to William Lubbock preach in favour of a union of the crowns, people, and law. On the morning of the 15th, they began their triumphal ride through the carpeted and railed-off city streets.

Pageants were set up at landmarks along the parade route, with actors playing such luminaries as the King of the Britons, the 'Genius' (or spirit) of London, and, in a somewhat on-the-nose spectacle, the united St Andrew and St George. Over the streets were built tall wood-and-canvas arches, each brightly painted and gilded and topped with statuary. Preceding the royal family on the procession were richly clad judges, nobles, clergymen, knights, and ladies, who led the way up Mark Lane, along Gracechurch Street, and through the city towards Whitehall. Prince Henry, who was already becoming a favourite with the populace, rode ahead of his father, with James mounted on a white horse under a canopy held aloft by his gentlemen. Anna rode in a carriage drawn by six white mules – leaning out and saluting spectators on either side – and, in a further display of familial harmony, Arbella Stuart followed her.

Just like the Christmas Revels and the Hampton Court Conference, the royal entry was hugely expensive. Already, it was becoming apparent to the government that the new king was a spendthrift. For James, however, this was necessary expenditure, and his next great project was, anyway, likely to save England a great deal of money. He intended, despite a politic display of anti-Spanish militancy before the French ambassador back in summer 1603, to conclude the Anglo-Spanish war and establish a lasting and money-saving peace, preferably on Britain's terms. As Spain was the world's greatest Catholic power, this represented a move towards renewed relations, with James poised to snatch the role of Christian peacemaker.

The move towards ending the war began in earnest in May, and Juan de Velasco, constable of Castile, arrived in England in the summer with a brief to negotiate a peace treaty. Both James and Anna were eager that this should come to pass, and for similar reasons: both were tentatively interested in a Spanish match for Prince Henry. Evidently, if there was any strain in their marriage as a result of James's infidelity – and there is no evidence that there was – the couple were mature enough to continue operating in tandem in international diplomacy. When the Spanish ambassador Juan de Tassis, 1st Count of Villamediana, requested the use of Somerset House, James 'replied laughing, "The ambassador must ask my wife, who is the mistress."' Anna, very much supportive of her husband's peace policy, 'readily assented'.[12]

251

The Spanish envoys arrived to finalise the treaty in the middle of August, only to find that James had decamped to Royston on one of his hunting trips. Thus, it was Anna and Cecil – now known as Baron Essendon – who united to watch as the Spanish sailed up the Thames to Westminster, and it fell to Suffolk to provide a suitably grand welcoming reception. The ensuing Somerset House Conference, which James returned to London to join, saw Lord Treasurer Buckhurst (newly created 1st Earl of Dorset) leading other nobles (Nottingham, Devonshire, Northampton, and Essendon) in discussion with their opposite numbers, led by de Velasco. The result was the Treaty of London, which formally ended the war that had been depleting the parsimonious Queen Elizabeth's coffers for nearly twenty years. The rewards for the successful conclusion to the war were quick to fall: Cecil went from Baron Essendon to Viscount Cranborne, in addition to receiving a healthy financial gratuity from the Spanish; Anna received a crystal cup shaped like a dragon (this from Velasco); and the prospect of a grand Spanish match for Prince Henry was floated (foundering only when the Spaniards made clear that they expected England's and Scotland's heir to be shipped to Spain and converted to Catholicism).

With this accomplishment secured, promising as it did an end to bloodshed and a boon to trade, the royal family was given a further lick of gold paint by the arrival of Prince Charles. The younger prince was still an underdeveloped child, but the king and queen had been gratified to hear from Scotland that he was able 'to walk like a gallant soldier, all alone'.[13] In August, he was brought south and inspected before being passed into the care of Sir Robert Carey, with James's old tutor Peter Young being installed as chief overseer of the boy's education (Young was, for his long service, knighted in February 1605 and remained in the king's employ until the early 1620s, whereupon he retired to Scotland, where he died in 1628). Still, Charles was tongue-tied, and James expressed a desire to have the string under his tongue cut to improve his speech. This Anna would not allow, and time proved her to be in the right: the prince went on to speak clearly enough. His mobility, though, remained poor – and at his investiture as Duke of York on the following Twelfth Night, he had to be carried by Nottingham.

Further raising the prestige of the new dynasty was a visit from Anna's brother, Duke Ulrik of Holstein, who had visited Scotland in 1598. He remained throughout the Christmas Revels of 1604–05, and thus bore witness to the curious sight of James's inamorato, Philip Herbert, being married off to Susan de Vere, daughter of the 17th Earl of Oxford (who had died six months beforehand). James was happy to marry off his young favourite – a job made easy because, firstly, the match was more political than it was romantic and, secondly, because he, James, had no great emotional bond to the bridegroom. On 27 December, Lady Susan was thus conveyed to the chapel at Whitehall by Ulrik and Prince Henry, with Anna following and James giving the bride away. Following the wedding banquet and supper, the masque *Juno and Hymenaeus* was performed. However, Ulrik soon showed his disagreeable side. On seeing that the Venetian ambassador was to be seated beside the king, whilst Ulrik himself had been placed on Queen Anna's right, he refused to sit at all. This was only a sign of things to come.

Despite this drama of precedence, the second Stuart Christmas looked set to outdo the first in splendour, glamour, and cost. Indeed, the King's Men were soon scrabbling for fresh material to furnish the royal thirst for entertainment, with its lead actor Burbage reduced to offering a revival of Shakespeare's *Love's Labour's Lost*, as there was apparently no other play in the repertoire the queen had not seen. On Twelfth Night, Anna took to the stage herself, this time as Euphoris in Ben Jonson's *The Masque of Blackness*. This controversial performance cost around £3,000, but it was the use of blackface by the queen and her ladies which drew the most comment (not due to any understanding of racial sensitivity, but because, as the courtier Dudley Carleton acidly noted, 'You cannot imagine a more ugly sight than a troop of lean cheek'd Moors.'[14] At any rate, the widespread criticism was more difficult to ignore even than that faced by Anna over her amateur theatrical at Winchester. As a result – and possibly also due to Ben Jonson falling into a brief period of disgrace for his satirical *Eastward Hoe* (a play which mocked Scottish arrivistes) – she refrained from taking further part in masques for some years.

More embarrassing than the words of her critics, however, was the ongoing behaviour of her brother. Ulrik, who was a hard-drinking and short-tempered man, could not help but be outspoken to the point of rudeness. In the end, he offended the queen so much that she banned him from her apartments, upon which his shouts and curses grew only more colourful. In addition to his boorishness, it became clear that his visit to England was not simply to congratulate Anna and James on the expansion of their territories but motivated by his goal of restarting England's military ventures, in the hopes of being able to recruit mercenaries under his own command. This was abhorrent to both king and queen, who had not only so recently secured peace, but who heard stories from the Borders of the sounds of ghostly armies battling in the dark. Such talk was unwelcome to a couple who, in the new year, discovered a fresh royal pregnancy.

Despite his diversions, James had continued to sleep with his wife. Her resultant pregnancy was powerful news not simply because it proved their ongoing fecundity but because it heralded the coming birth of the first child born to a reigning English monarch since Jane Seymour had given birth to the future Edward VI. In the event, Anna gave birth to a baby girl, named Mary, on 8 April at Greenwich.

As welcome as the birth was, it marked yet another round of expenditure. In the short term, £300 worth of clothing was ordered for the christening; more material was required to outfit the god-parents (Ulrik, who had repaired relations with Anna, stood as godfather and Arbella Stuart as godmother); and £20 was required annually for the infant's care and diet. The cost of housing Ulrik had already proven exorbitant, and, after the christening, when he hinted to James that he might extend his visit, the king's stony silence was answer enough; the duke left (with a present of £4,000). It is doubtful that Cecil's elevation to earldom of Salisbury in May did much to cheer him; the tireless secretary was, and would remain, bowed down with the task of trying to find solutions to an unfolding financial crisis.

One ostensible means of saving money, which had proven invaluable to Queen Elizabeth, was to impose upon hosts. Once Ulrik had left the country, the choice of location honoured with hosting the king, queen, and Prince Henry was Oxford. The university had not received a royal visit since that of Queen Elizabeth in 1592, and both town and gown were eager to win favour. In August, the civic authorities rounded up 300 potential dissidents (their offences including the wearing of inappropriate headgear in church) and locked them up. The royal party rode into Oxford on Tuesday the 27th, whereupon the leading townsfolk, with the mayor at their head, attempted to steal a march on the university elite by rushing out to meet the royal party on the road from Woodstock. In response, the Chancellor of Oxford led out his staff with their own gifts and speeches, and, under the noses of their town rivals, they led the king and his family onto the campus.

At St John's College, a pageant depicting three Sybils meeting Banquo (the mythical progenitor of James's royal line) was staged. Following this, a Greek welcoming speech was delivered, at which Anna smiled and, no doubt with an implied wink to her husband (who fancied himself an expert in Greek pronunciation), stated that she had never heard the language spoken so fluently. Husband and wife were then lodged together at Christ Church, whilst the prince was escorted to his own temporary residence at Magdalen College, where he would officially matriculate. Over the course of four days, James relived his time in Denmark, listening to lectures and joining in with disputations (including one on the use of tobacco – a substance of which the king was an early opponent).

Less inclined to academic esoterica was Prince Henry. In fairness, he was only eleven, but time would prove that whilst he was an aspiring athlete and a military and naval enthusiast, he would never share his father's passion for classical learning. When the university dons spoke of conferring a degree on the boy, James stepped in and blocked it, likely because it would have taught Henry to appreciate one of the things *Basilikon Doron* had warned him against: sycophancy. Matriculation would be quite enough.

Nor, in the midst of all the academic activities, was Anna forgotten. A play originally composed for Queen Elizabeth's celebrated 1566 visit was brushed off and performed. Hopelessly out of date as it was, it entertained no one. Nor did the students' efforts on the last night of the royal visit; then, they tried again with a play, which this time resulted in James falling asleep, only to waken – no doubt to the awkwardness of all involved – and tetchily mutter, 'I marvel what they think me to be!'[15] Given that the king was a self-styled poet of solid if not sparkling ability, we can infer that the lost play was another dud. But despite the lacklustre entertainments, the visit was a resounding success, in that the royal party enjoyed their time in Oxford and the strain on the Privy Purse was, for a brief spell, relaxed.

Another strain, however, was at breaking point. James might have congratulated himself on having begun his reign in England in hope. He had been magnanimous; he had been tolerant; he had, he thought, handled religious affairs well, obviating Catholic threats with fair words, pacifying those Puritans who could be pacified and hounding out those who would not; he had begun a parliament which he still believed would effect his dream of union; he and Anna had produced an indisputably English royal baby; he had managed a balance in his household and government which stressed continuity and maintained his status as Scotland's king; and he had even found a means of indulging his romantic dreams without compromising his outward appearance as a doting family man.

Such, at least, were his beliefs. In reality, he was running up enormous debts; he was turning a blind eye to the disillusion his people and ministers were experiencing on discovering that he intended to rule much of the time remotely; he was racking up disaffection by filling his bedchamber with Scots; and, most pressingly, his stopgap measure of paying lip service to tolerance, encouraging Catholic hopes only to deliver nothing, was about to reap its reward. The breaking point had been reached.

16

The Honeymoon Ends

In 1607, a rattled King James stood before his parliament – that same parliament he had called in 1604 – and said, 'For my liberality, I have told you of it heretofore: my three first years were to me as a Christmas – I could not then be miserable [miserly]. Should I have been over-sparing to them [his Scottish subjects]? They might have thought Joseph had forgotten his brethren, or that the King had been drunk with his new kingdom.'[1]

The party, by 1607, was over. So too was the king's honeymoon period – those first three years in which he had thought himself the undisputed master of all he surveyed. When reality had compelled him to go on the defensive, justifying his cash gifts and disbursement of honours, he had been forced to make an account of his early years in England. To those listening, it must have seemed that the new reign, begun with such hope, had simply become more of the same. As the final years of Elizabeth had witnessed increased grievances on the part of parliament, the first years of James had simply added new and unexpected causes for complaint.

The first sign that the Jacobean age was less golden than it appeared was a threatening one. It came in early November 1605, when an anonymous letter was delivered to Baron Monteagle, warning him to stay away from the opening of parliament. Being a loyal subject, Monteagle handed the letter to the authorities. When it reached James, he read the warning – that 'a great blow' should greet the assembled parliament – and interpreted this to mean that gunpowder, the means used in the assassination of his father, was to be employed. A search was thus conducted of Westminster Hall, and in the seldom-used under-croft was found the Yorkshireman Guy Fawkes, assiduously tending thirty-six explosive barrels. On being apprehended, Fawkes gave the unlikely pseudonym of John Johnson. However, Cecil – now Salisbury – was not taken in. Quickly – so quickly that theories have since abounded that he had foreknowledge of the plot and was only waiting for an excuse to reveal it – he got to the truth.

For too long, King James and Queen Anna had been engaged in encouraging malcontent Catholics with false hopes of a far-reaching policy of toleration. In practice, they had delivered nothing substantial, and it was becoming ever more apparent that they never would. What had resulted was a plot masterminded by the charming, Catholic rebel-with-a-cause Robert Catesby, which aimed to remove James and his government in an explosive coup. The reason, as Fawkes admitted under interrogation, was not just to rid England of its Protestant elite, but to 'blow the Scottish beggars back to their native mountains'.[2] Rather than being solely religious in intent, the 'Powder Treason' was thus as much a xenophobic response to what discontented native Englishmen viewed as a takeover by beggarly, blue-capped Scottish upstarts who were pocketing English gold, dominating the squatting Scottish king's bedchamber (which had become a locus for power and influence), and otherwise threatening the inherently English polity which had existed even under the Protestant Elizabeth. Indeed, this was not a new attitude; it had been simmering under the surface since James had arrived in England to claim his second throne. The notion, on the part of discontented Englishmen, was that they had inadvertently gained a Scottish king who was working primarily for Scottish interests. A popular verse libel ran:

> The King hee hawkes, and hunts;
> The lords they gather coyne;
> The Judges doe as they weere wont;
> The lawyers they purloyne.
> The clergie lyes a dyeing;

The commons toll the Bell;
The Scotts gett all by lyeing;
And this is Englands knell.[3]

James's perpetual Christmas had, in effect, stirred up dissent – mainly because the perception was that he played the benevolent monarch mainly to his grasping Scottish favourites, minions, and bedfellows.

When news of the government's foiling of the Powder Treason reached Fawkes's fellow conspirators, they fled. They had intended to kill James and Prince Henry, before quickly capturing Princess Elizabeth at Coombe Abbey and installing her as a puppet monarch – a grand plan but one which sought to capitalise on shock and awe, with little thought, ironically, for how James's home kingdom might react. With the plan unravelling, they ended up at Holbeche House in Staffordshire, where the authorities fired upon them. Catesby and Thomas Percy were killed as they resisted capture, whilst John and Christopher Wright received fatal wounds. Thomas Wintour, Ambrose Rookwood, and John Grant were caught, as were Robert Wintour, Everard Digby, and Thomas Bates. All were investigated – whilst a terrified and paranoid James took to dining privately and closeted himself in his privy lodgings – and eventually executed. With them went England's leading Jesuit, Father Henry Garnet – a kindly, overweight priest who claimed, probably honestly, to have discouraged the plot, but who admitted foreknowledge via the confessional.

As frightening as the prospect of death by explosion must have been, the plot's failure allowed the king to reap the relief-born goodwill of his subjects. Parliament, under Salisbury's guidance, voted in a £400,000 subsidy and henceforth it was possible for the Crown to appropriate the bulk of the estates of wealthy Catholic recusants. In early March 1606, further apparently fortuitous news circulated. Whilst James had been hunting in the country, rumours reached London that he had been murdered, with variations on the theme holding that he had been smothered, stabbed to death, and even set upon by treacherous Scots dressed as women. The reliable Salisbury immediately took steps to secure Prince Henry and Queen Anna at Whitehall, and the Tower's guards were put on alert against riots and unrest.

Happily, James had not been murdered. The rumours had been started by an escaped criminal riding through the countryside, followed by cries of 'treason'. The incident, however, sparked dedicatory verses from Ben Jonson, who was still in the process of demonstrating his goodwill to the Scots following the satirical *Eastward Hoe* (co-authored by John Marston and George Chapman). Nevertheless, James had to ride back from the country to quell what looked like becoming an uproar. A grand procession formed to welcome him, with the prince meeting his father at the city gates and the usual celebratory bonfires lit. It is difficult not to imagine that James, who always saw the political capital inherent in providential escapes from peril, enjoyed the opportunity to once again demonstrate God's favour, even if there had been no actual danger this time. Further public acclaim awaited when, in the same month, the king and queen toured Salisbury's New Exchange – an upmarket shopping centre and bourse on the Strand – eager to show themselves not only survivors but the heads of a mercantile nation. As if in further proof of this new, global England, the king chartered the Plymouth and Virginia Companies in April, with a view to establishing footholds in America (the former would fail but, after an uncertain beginning, the latter succeeded in building up the famous settlement at Jamestown).

All of this jollity and the cheers and acclamation it provoked were, however, propaganda. There remained a crisis over what to do about Catholic extremists, who had now shown their willingness to plan and undertake real attacks. James, clinging to the remnants of his veneer of Catholic sympathy, attempted to point out, fairly, that traitors were a minority in the Catholic community. Yet this cut little ice with those Puritans who rubbed their hands in glee at this latest example of papist perfidy. The ultimate result of the Gunpowder Plot was not a wholesale rooting out of Catholics and Jesuits but a breakdown in the teamwork which had existed between king and queen. The supposed wickedness of the Catholics allowed the sham of tolerance which the royal couple had shared – and perhaps even genuinely hoped for – to come to an end. Rather than the pair continuing to capitalise on Anna's Catholic sympathies in a united, if *ad hoc*, campaign to quell discontent, they chose different paths. The queen continued encouraging the hopes of those inclined to the Roman religion for discrete political purposes (mainly to persuade foreign ambassadors that she shared their faith, as a means of promoting grand marriage alliances for her eldest son); James, on the other hand, trumpeted his eleventh-hour salvation as a sign from God and retreated into his favourite medium. Taking on Catholic writers with his pen, he began a campaign justifying the new Oath of Allegiance to be taken by all recusants, producing *Triplici Nodo, Triplex Cuneus, or an Apologie for the Oath of Allegiance* (1607). The Catholic Cardinal Robert Bellarmine wrote his own *Responio*, and by 1609 James would reissue his *Apologie* with an updated preface, titled *A Premonition to all most Mighty Monarchs, Kings, Free Princes, and States of Christendom.*

The king's extended jaunts into the countryside ceased, for a time, to be solely for pleasure and leisure; for company he closeted himself with divines and fixated upon the collaborative art of polemic. He was determined to avoid the Gunpowder Plot being publicly acknowledged as embracing anti-Scottish sentiment (as to do so might exacerbate opposition to his plans for union); it was instead the opening gambit for a Europe-wide theological debate on the spiritual and secular jurisdiction of independent states. He was not being vainglorious, and he was no dilettante; with his comprehensive education and experience of European religious affairs, he was an expert and well-suited to press for an ecumenical approach to the continent's divisions. He did not share some of his contemporaries' apocalyptic views of the future as a cosmic battle between competing faiths. Following the religious wars of the sixteenth century, it was God's will – and so James's – that the body of Christianity, too long riven, should begin putting itself back together. This world of religious debate was his milieu, and Anna played no part in it. Nor, unfortunately for James, did those Catholic potentates in Europe to whom he sent his papal-sceptic writings show more than a bemused interest – much to his disappointment. Nevertheless, the king continued claiming the moral high ground: no man in England, he insisted, was ever or would ever die for his conscience if he 'break not out into some outward act'. Catholics were executed for treason, not heresy.

In the immediate aftermath of the plot's discovery, the theatre of the world was wider than the kingdom of England. Foreign ambassadors were keen to pass on their congratulations to James and nervous that the investigations would uncover links between them and the plotters. Thus, it was with some relief to all concerned when, in May 1606, examinations 'of the secret negotiations of Guy Fawkes and Robert Wintour with the King of Spain and Constable of Castile, to induce them to support the Catholic cause' found 'that nothing was proved . . . inculpating any foreign prince in the Gunpowder Plot'.[4] James, as much as Philip III, was eager that the averted horrors of the plot should not give rise to an international incident which might undo the peace assured by the 1604 Treaty of London.

Further securing the royal family's position was the news that Anna was again pregnant. On 22 June, she produced another daughter at Greenwich, Princess Sophia. Unfortunately, the child was sickly and died within a few hours of her birth (and hasty baptism). Thereafter, her body was taken by barge to Westminster, where she was interred in a tomb carved in the shape of a cradle. The queen, however, remained immured until she was formally 'churched' (the spiritual ceremony which allowed a new mother's re-entry to society). She was still residing – and mourning – privately at Greenwich when her brother, Christian IV, arrived in England.

It had been a long time since England had played host to a reigning foreign monarch, and preparations had long been in train for Christian's visit. Unlike his brother Ulrik, the Danish king was a friendly and convivial man – too convivial, as time would show. Moreover, he was less inclined to upset his sister, whom he physically resembled, 'in face so like . . . that he who hath seen the one might paint in his fancy the other'.[5] When his ship, *The Three Crowns*, arrived at Gravesend, it was James and Henry who were waiting to meet him. Christian then passed on into the new royal barge – a floating palace of glass and gold, with sun-catching, gilt-tipped pyramids surmounting its turrets – and the whole party sailed to Greenwich. Despite his sister's immurement, Christian immediately proceeded to her apartments, gained entry, and embraced her. Whilst a triumphal entry was planned – at, naturally, enormous expense – the queen was left behind; James took his brother-in-law off to Salisbury's estate at Theobalds (which was, the following May, handed over to the royal family, at James's request, in exchange for Hatfield).

The consequences of the decorous Anna's absence were soon, however, manifest. Left to entertain his guest by himself, James proved singularly unwilling to behave himself. One of the less attractive traits of his personality was that he took a perverse pleasure in being deliberately brash and boorish, safe in the knowledge that no one dared gainsay him. At Theobalds, therefore, a general air of festive licence ruled, with the king giving every encouragement to an orgy of hedonistic indulgence. At one masque, involving the Queen of Sheba (probably a more old-fashioned affair than Anna's grand literary productions), the lady playing the titular queen drunkenly stumbled, 'overset her caskets into his Danish Majesty's lap and fell at his feet though I rather think it was in his face'.[6] On trying to help her, Christian also collapsed in a drunken stupor and had to be carried to his apartments, still splattered with the fruits of the mock-queen's gifts. Even allowing for exaggeration – this account of the event comes from the gossipy John Harington – it is clear that the Stuart court, particularly when Anna was unable to rein it in, was gaining a reputation for decadence, if not indolence. James was responsible, and his own fondness for the bottle, which would eventually verge on the dipsomaniacal, was already giving rise to criticism. One ambassador reported that the king drank so much he 'fell on the table, after having sat at it for five hours', and even the queen had supposedly worried in 1604 that he 'drinks so much and conducts himself so ill in every respect, that I expect an early and evil result'.[7]

More sober, in every sense of the word, was the triumphal entry through London that followed the revels at Theobalds. No doubt hoping to recapture some of the magic woven around James's own entry through his capital, the government laid on spectacular pageants, wherein sea sprites danced through oceans of blue tissue, statues of giants held aloft enormous rocks painted and gilded with the arms of England and Denmark, mock swains and shepherdesses sang verses beside huge golden suns, and a mechanical dragon bore on its back Mulciber, an alias of the Roman Vulcan.

The state visit thereafter passed with more sedate pursuits: Christian attended St Paul's Cathedral and climbed the steps of the steeple (which had lost its spire in a 1561 fire); tilting was arranged at Whitehall; and, in Westminster Abbey, effigies of previous monarchs and consorts were set up, the intent being to confirm James's descent and the glory of England's royal heritage. By 8 August, Anna had rejoined the family and oversaw more dignified performances than that seen at Theobalds, not least of which was a succession of three plays at Hampton Court by Shakespeare's troupe. Two days later – and with his secret mission to recruit James into a proposed league of Protestant princes unfulfilled – Christian was ready to leave.

James, Anna, and Henry all joined him in sailing to Rochester for a formal farewell, before moving on to Chatham, where a banquet aboard the cloth-of-gold-bedecked *Elizabeth Jonas* awaited. The next day, it was Christian's turn to host his sister and her family aboard his own ship. As parting gifts, the queen received her brother's portrait in a diamond-covered frame; James was given a copper cannon (a present unlikely to have given him much delight); and to Henry went the greatest prize, and one calculated to delight the prince: a warship. The Danish king then gave the signal to begin a fireworks display which, unsurprisingly, failed to provide much of a spectacle in broad daylight. An even less entertaining prelude to his departure followed.

In his capacity as Lord High Admiral, Nottingham was aboard *The Three Crowns*. In vain, the old man attempted to warn Christian that the hour had come for the English royal family to leave. However, the language barrier prevented mutual understanding. In trying to make the point that it was only 2 p.m., the Danish king held up two fingers. Nottingham immediately bristled, interpreting Christian's gesture as 'cuckold's horns'. As the earl had married the much younger Margaret Stewart (their courtship being the one Anna had laughingly written to James about in 1603), he was inordinately sensitive to any perceived slights upon his marriage. The queen compounded his burst of anger by laughing at the misunderstanding, and the ensuing battle rumbled on long after Christian had departed England, with Margaret, Countess of Nottingham herself getting involved and writing to Christian's secretary condemning his master's unprincely attitude.

A fresh feud was thus the fruit of the visit, with Anna pressing, unsuccessfully, for James to banish the countess. Her lack of success in persuading her husband to act according to her wishes was ominous. The queen's response was to strengthen her relationship with her son, thereby making him her political partisan. Soon, the prince was dutifully writing to Arbella, at his mother's instruction, requesting that the lady give up one of her musicians and despatch him as, essentially, a gift to Christian (who had admired the fellow's lute playing).

The state visit had done nothing to help lessen spiralling royal expenditure, for all Christian's presence had added some glitter to the court. Another token gesture of economy followed, with the king bowing to political pressure by allowing the Cecil and Howard families to foot the bill for the festivities when his favourite, James, Lord Hay (later Earl of Carlisle), was married off to Honora Denny (a granddaughter of Thomas Cecil, Lord Burghley). Unfortunately, this was a marriage which would soon cost political capital, as it gave rise to scandal when the bride was accused of infidelity.

The pretence of economy was soon given the lie when, the next month, James and Anna funded the wedding and masque of Sir John

Ramsay (of the Gowrie affair, and by now Viscount Haddington) to the daughter of the 5th Earl of Sussex. This was all part of their longstanding policy of promoting cross-border marriages as a means of uniting the subjects of both kingdoms. Worse still, James had got into the habit of paying off his lovers' debts; in 1606 and 1607 alone, he had used the Privy Purse to offset the gambling losses run up by Philip Herbert. Unsurprisingly, the country was neither mollified nor convinced by James's assurances to parliament that he would reform his lavish ways. Nor did great displays of royal splendour in London do much to dazzle those in the Midlands, who rose under one John 'Captain Pouch' Reynolds in what would be the only revolt of James's reign (and, in truth, a comparatively minor skirmish compared to the uprisings faced by each of the Tudor monarchs), in April 1607. The rioters' grievances centred on illegal land enclosures undertaken by unscrupulous landlords – another perennial Tudor problem which the new king had not done enough to monitor – and in June over forty men were killed as the local government cracked down on protestors.

What must have seemed clear to those suffering from enclosure was that the royal court had become as corrupt, licentious, and dissolute as any of the foreign courts lambasted as venal in the London playhouses. The Jacobean court was, already, a world away from Elizabeth's; it was a place in which elaborate, wasteful, and expensive fashions were the norm, and the king, at its centre, promoted men like Lord Hay, whose contributions to public life included the 'double supper': 'the manner of which was to have the board [dining table] covered at the first entrance of the guests with dishes as tall as a man could well reach, filled with the choicest and dearest viands sea or land could afford. And all this, once seen . . . was in a manner thrown away, and fresh set on the same height.'[8]

Queen Anna might have been sensitive to public opinion and eager to provide a more majestic counterpoint to her husband, but her hold over him, which was already loosening, was about to suffer a major breach. James had never held any deep passion for her; what had developed instead was an indulgent affection born of long companionship and regular contact, both sexual and otherwise. This freed him to look elsewhere for emotional support, thereby leaving her almost entirely to her own pursuits. The cause of their coming difficulties, however, must have seemed innocuous enough at first. King James fell in love.

17

At Long Last Love

James knew the young man, by sight at least. His name was Robert Kerr, though he had anglicised it to Carr; he was a member of the prominent Borders family, the Kerrs of Ferniehirst. Carr had been, briefly, a page in the Scottish court – a post from which, according to legend, he had been dismissed when his butchering of a Latin speech had shown him up as a young nincompoop. This reason for dismissal was probably an embroidery, with the truth being that he had, like many well-born Scots, been sent by his family to France (there to learn polished manners) before joining the court as a great man's servant with hopes of advancement.

The great man which Carr had attached himself to was no less than James's favourite, Lord Hay, who had, only months before, been honourably married off, as Philip Herbert had been before him. At the 1607 King's Day jousts, held at Whitehall on 24 March (in commemoration of the king's accession), the twenty-year-old Carr's job was to ride with his master, bearing Hay's shield (with its painted *impresa* and motto). James, who still liked Hay well enough, watched with detached interest. Then, suddenly, the regular hoof-beats faltered. The young shield-bearer's horse shied, breaking the neat regularity which marked tiltyard processions. As beast and rider passed the king, who sat on his own canopied dais with a good view of proceedings, Carr toppled to the ground, the horse falling with him.

James rose. What he saw was a 'straight-limbed, well-favoured, strong-shouldered and smooth-faced' young man, crumpled in pain, one of those straight limbs – some sources say an arm, others a leg – broken.[1] The king's heart swelled. His paternalistic instincts, always strong, soared. Immediately, he called for the youth to be conveyed to the house of one Mr Rider in Charing Cross, there to be attended by the royal physicians. That night, James himself visited, ostensibly to see how the patient fared. It would not be the last time.

The news of the king's interest in the young man could scarcely be hidden; James's life was a public one. Wryly, courtiers began to follow suit in paying court to what they assumed was another Philip Herbert (who had been elevated by this time to the earldom of Montgomery) or a Lord Hay in the making. This, very probably, was also Queen Anna's initial reading of the situation. They were all wrong. Here was no minor favourite to be pawed and played with, and who could then be bought off with titles, grand marriages, and handouts from the Privy Purse. Love, always an unaccountable and often an unreasonable emotion, had been sparked in the king.

His choice – if one can ascribe choice in these matters – is difficult to fathom. Carr was, as he would later appear to acknowledge and, to his credit, take steps to mitigate, a man of no particular intelligence, wit, or political ability. Yet James seems to have found in him exactly what he had been looking for during his entire adult life: willing clay ready to be moulded. One of the hallmarks of his relationships had always been his desire to be seen as a quasi-parental or schoolmasterly figure to his partners. This had only grown more marked. He was, by this time, growing flabby and his features were coarsening – the product of his increasing proclivity for good food and copious amounts of alcohol. It seems his needs were not simply sexual, but born of a desire to nurture and provide, to teach and promote. In Carr, he found an empty vessel, not in the sense that the young man was eager to learn, but in that he had a bottomless ambition. That passion was also present seems obvious. In a sense, James had come full circle. As he had first been seduced by an older man in Esmé Stuart, now he had become Esmé. Much to his credit, of course, the object of his affection was no callow thirteen-year-old boy but a young man old enough to reciprocate without being

269

abused or manipulated. The only question was whether Carr would return the king's love.

For his part, the young fellow was probably overwhelmed by his instantaneous rise to favour. Each day of his recovery, the king would visit him, kiss him, enquire as to his health, and garrulously instruct him in Latin. Carr cannot have failed to realise either what James wanted or what his own acquiescence might reap in terms of reward. There is no reason to believe he was reluctant; it is, however, unlikely that Carr ever had any romantic feelings for his sovereign. Instead, as the totality of his career suggests, he was willing to trade on his good looks and exploit any interest shown by anyone who might advance him. No one was better placed to do that than James.

There thus formed a love triangle comprising James, Carr, and Anna, although only one member was actually in the throes of passion. Exactly when the queen realised that her husband's new inamorato was more than just another pretty face is impossible to guess – it is significant, however, that following James's infatuation, there were no more royal pregnancies. It is unlikely that this troubled Anna; her marriage had already proven its worth and her husband's new lover could certainly not displace her, in the way that mistresses had displaced previous consorts. What she would in time find intolerable, though, was that Carr's ascendance coincided with her own political influence being side-lined, ignored, and scorned.

Notable in Carr's rise to prominence is not its speed but its steadiness. By the end of 1607, he had been knighted, and given a position as Gentleman of the King's Bedchamber. Soon enough, it was being noted that James could not bear to have the young man out of his sight and, as usual, the lascivious public embraces and kisses were continual. Supporting Carr in what looked like being a long career was one Thomas Overbury – an Englishman whom the new favourite had first met in Edinburgh (when Overbury had visited in 1601 and Carr had been a page in Lord Hay's household). It is possible that Overbury had himself conducted a homosexual relationship with Carr – one from which the young Scot reaped material benefits.[2] Whatever the nature of their friendship, the favourite was soon relying on the far more intelligent Overbury to guide him along the glittering path of the king's affections.

Whilst to Anna, Carr was an irritant, Carr and Overbury together held some dark potential. She was further disheartened by another domestic tragedy, which struck in September 1607. Princess Mary had for some time been ailing, and it became apparent that she was dying. One of the girl's chaplains reported, with what seems exaggeration given the child's age, that 'for the space of twelve or fourteen hours at the least, there was no sound of any word heard breaking from her lips; yet when it sensibly appeared that she would soon make a peaceful end of a troublesome life, she sighed out these words, "I go, I go!" and when, not long after, there was something to be ministered unto her . . . again she repeated "Away, I go!" And yet, a third time, almost immediately before she offered up herself, a sweet virgin sacrifice unto Him that made her, faintly cried "I go, I go!"'[3]

The news of her daughter's death was brought to the queen at Hampton Court by the Earl of Worcester, George Carew, and Robert Sidney. With remarkable courage, she bid them carry it to the king, whilst she held an audience with Salisbury (who came with his condolences), arranged a post-mortem, and handled the funeral arrangements. The infant followed her sister Sophia into the Lady Chapel at Westminster.

Their shared loss did little to return James's attention to his wife. In the absence of his affection, she upheld her political position by returning to the stage. Her role now was to be, in effect, the PR wing of the monarchy, and to establish the court as a centre for English artistic development and patronage, which was reaching new heights in literature, poetics, and baroque visual display. Thus, she took part in her first masque since the objectionable *Masque of Blackness*, performing this time in Jonson's sequel, *The Masque of Beauty*, in a purpose-built hall. The masque certainly allowed her to underline her political credentials and the importance of her royal role. When the Spanish and Venetian ambassadors received invitations, the uninvited French envoy threw a fit. He blamed Anna and all but accused her of being an hispanophile (particularly as she had, again, indicated a preference for Henry to marry the Spanish Infanta). The diplomatic fracas required James's intercession; in an attempt to make peace, he invited the ambassador to dine with himself and the queen. This was refused. James, accordingly, rode off to Royston immediately following the performance, without speaking to Anna – a cheap public stunt which enabled him to retain the goodwill of France.

Yet it drew everyone's attention to the queen's desire to continue playing a central role. She exhibited her attitude towards the rising favourite in the dance – titled *The Queen's Masque* – which followed *Beauty*. The Venetian ambassador, Zorzi Giustinian, noted that this was 'so well composed and ordered' that 'it is evident the mind of her Majesty, the authoress of the whole, is gifted no less highly than her person'.[4] Carr might have been in the ascendant, but Anna was determined that the Stuart court would retain a semblance of regal decorum in counterpoint to the king's public lavishing of attention, affection, and reward on the favourite. As the 'Great Frost' of winter 1607–08 took hold, turning the North Sea coasts into sheets of ice and giving rise to the first 'Frost Fair' on the Thames, relations within the royal marriage appeared to have caught the chill.

If James cared anything for his wife's chagrin, he did little to assuage it. On the contrary, where Carr was concerned, nothing was too much. There were, in fact, shades of Anne Boleyn and Henry VIII in the affair: the young object of desire was again younger, attractive, and veneered with French manners; and the process of advancement was slow and thus more worrying, for it suggested that the love affair would be for the long haul. Carr's behaviour might even have resembled the scholarly consensus on Anne's; it is possible he refused to yield sexually until a future role was assured (though arguing against this is his comparative lack of wit and his more naked desire for gain). Curiously enough, like Anne Boleyn's rise, Carr's was to take several years to reach its zenith. Hers had been replacing Katherine of Aragon, whereas his – with replacing a royal wife obviously out of the question – would be gaining an earldom.

The tyrannical obsession of the pursuer and the intelligence of the pursued were missing – but, like the earlier royal affair, this one was to be handled with little discretion by the king.

Throughout 1608, not only Carr but his friends were showered with gifts. Whilst the favourite received a tablet of gold set with the king's image, Overbury received a knighthood in June, becoming a servitor-in-ordinary. Thereafter, he was allowed – possibly because James did not wish a rival – to travel on the continent, where he would remain until August 1609. In January of that year, despite his mentor's absence, Carr received Sir Walter Raleigh's estate of Sherborne – this in spite of Anna joining forces with her son in attempting to gain sympathy for Raleigh, who remained in the Tower following his perceived involvement in the Main Plot. Yet again, it appeared to the queen that her wishes paled in her husband's eyes in comparison to Carr's. When Lady Raleigh (who, with her husband, wanted the estate for their son) gained an audience with James and begged on her knees that Sherborne might be retained for her family, the king announced, 'I maun have the land – I maun have it for Carr.'[5] Raleigh's attempts at using the courts to retain ownership were dismissed, and his plea to Carr for justice went unheard; James had already purchased the interest by which his 1604 charter had assured Lady Raleigh the use of the estate in her husband's lifetime. Sherborne was his to dispose of. The best the unfortunate lady received was a compensatory payment of £8,000 and a £400 per annum pension – a small return for an estate which yielded £5,000 annually. These were paltry sums indeed, given that, as the court commentator John Chamberlain reported, on Twelfth Night 1608, gamblers were not admitted to court unless they had £300 on them, and in the course of the gaming, Montgomery won £750 for the king, Monteagle lost the queen £400, Sir Robert Carey lost Prince Henry £300, and Salisbury the same sum. For all his promises of economy, James was not simply overseeing a court in which prodigious spending was the norm – he was throwing away money himself.

Once again, Anna registered her autonomy and her opposition

by taking to the stage – this time in February 1609, in Jonson's *The Masque of Queens*. Pointedly, she played the role of Bel-Anna in a performance in which eleven ladies paraded as virtuous historical queens (whilst professional actors read the script). The theme was female power, exemplified via imagery of procreation. The implied comparison was with the inherently un-procreative relationship upon which James had embarked. Anna, as she was fond of pointing out both baldly and through her favourite medium, was a sovereign's daughter and would be a sovereign's mother. Carr, by contrast, was an upstart whose relationship with the king would provide for no one but himself. Unfortunately, the masque did little to improve her standing with her husband. When, the month following the masque, her old friend Henrietta Stuart, by now Marchioness of Huntly, wrote south requesting the queen's intercession on behalf of her husband (who had been briefly imprisoned for hearing the mass), James wrote back himself, telling the lady that his wife had no power to sway him. His old fascination with Huntly (who lived on until 1636) had long since dimmed.

Thwarted, Anna redoubled her efforts by capitalising on her relationship with her son, in the hopes that, in time, he would rectify the public neglect she was enduring at the hands of her smitten husband. Prince Henry was, by this stage, developing firm ideas of his own. Although he has gained a reputation as a golden prince, portraits of Prince Henry suggest that rather than being an inordinately attractive and fair youth, he was strong-featured. Yet, those artists who captured his likeness knew their subject well: in Robert Peake the Elder's image, the youthful prince stands dressed in hunting green in a pose of action, one hand already drawing his sword and his pale face turned to the viewer in challenge. In the famous equestrian painting, he is clad in armour, mounted, his whip hand raised to strike. This was how the boy everyone anticipated as being Henry IX wished to be seen. He was, in all ways, an athletic military enthusiast.

So too was he developing an almost priggish sense of honour and morality – according to his later treasurer, Sir Charles Cornwallis, he was very possibly the inventor of the 'swear box', having given instructions 'to have boxes kept at his three standing houses, St James's, Richmond, and Nonsuch, causing all those who did swear in his hearing to pay moneys to the same, which were duly after given to the poor'.[6] It was his moral rectitude and his militaristic view of Protestantism which endeared him to those of a Puritan bent; increasingly, James's peace policy was coming to be associated with the 'effeminacy' of his court, and there were calls for a warlike champion to inspire Englishmen to shed their blood in defence of European Protestantism. Whilst not everyone clamoured for war, those who shouted loudest in favour of aggression clothed themselves in righteous moral rectitude. Their voices would only grow shriller.

Moreover, rumours re-emerged of the king's old pro-Catholic manoeuvres; it was in 1609 that James Elphinstone, 1st Lord Balmerino, Scotland's secretary (and a former financial aide to Anna), was sentenced to death for supposedly having forged James's signature on letters to Pope Clement VIII back in 1599. Unfortunately, James had encouraged these letters when he had been courting Catholic powers. Knowing this, Anna – probably exercising the traditional role of intercessor with James's approval – spoke up for Balmerino, who had only been acting on orders and who was also related to her lady, Jean Drummond. Balmerino's sentence was commuted to imprisonment – but again James appeared a poor figure to blow the horn for Protestantism, especially in comparison to his pious son. Where the king was a slippery Machiavel, more fond of books and peace than war, the prince was an honest and militant son of the Church. Although in April 1609 Henry had been bequeathed the prodigious library of Lord Lumley, the prince did not aim to be a man of letters and political theory, but a soldier-sovereign. Accordingly, from 1607, Salisbury was busily sending him dispatches out of Ireland (where the policy of plantation had begun), 'the reading whereof will every day prove more proper . . . than Aristotle or Cicero': a sentiment with which James would have disagreed.[7] It was hoped that Henry would also cut a less duplicitous figure than his father, who in September 1609 gave an audience at Wanstead to the Venetian ambassador, Correr, before privately denouncing the fellow as a 'pantalone', or comical money-grubber.

From his mother, Henry had learned the value of political theatre. He put it into effect for the first time on Twelfth Night 1610, holding an indoor tournament at Whitehall titled *The Prince's Barriers*. James's thoughts on this are difficult to imagine; here was his son, anticipating a future beyond his lifetime, and winning accolades all round, including from his doting mother. It could hardly have escaped the king's attention that he was now in the position Queen Elizabeth had once occupied, when James had been the coming man and she the fading sun. Henry was giving every appearance of being a beloved English monarch-in-waiting; meanwhile, he, James, was still being castigated as a foreigner surrounded by foreigners. Indeed, later that same year, Sir John Holles, a Gentleman of the Privy Chamber who would become Henry's comptroller, complained that 'the Scottish monopolise [James's] princely person, standing like a mountain betwixt the beams of his Grace and us'. By contrast, Henry was being fashioned as an English hero, who would one day lend an ear to his warlike subjects rather than distancing himself from them.

The prince's growth into a premier player in English politics put yet more strain on royal finances, and so, once again, James was required to recall parliament (this being the same one he had summoned in 1604). At this stage, Carr, for all the king loved him, had not achieved anything like political supremacy. Salisbury remained England's great statesman. Indeed, in 1608 he had been given the position his father had held under Elizabeth, and which under James represented more burden than honour (given its previous holder, Dorset, dropped dead over the council table): Lord High Treasurer.[8] He had, throughout the reign, attempted to increase Crown revenue, by means of impositions (duties on trade over and above customs duties), cost cutting, and the revival of old fines – but these measures brought only temporary bouts of relief which were soon undone by the king's spending. Something more lasting and comprehensive was needed.

With his customary indefatigability, Salisbury devised an ambitious project known as the Great Contract that would, at a stroke, alleviate some of the Commons' grievances (by ceding royal control over purveyance – the process by which the court could set cheap prices on goods and thereby cheat local producers – and wardships) and in return net an annual income of £200,000. There were, naturally, issues of distrust on both sides, with the Commons wary of making James independent of their power to vote for subsidies, and the king probably rightly pointing out that inflation would soon render £200,000 insufficient. He did nothing to help his case, of course, when, in May, he grandly announced – in a show of hauteur worthy of any of his Tudor predecessors – that 'I was born to be begged of, not to beg'. To the same men he expressed his sincere view that monarchs, though ideally they would act according to the law and to the benefit of the people, were gods on earth and accountable to none but God. This was conventional thinking, but it was tactless at a moment when parliament was seeking to work collaboratively in finding solutions to the problems besetting the reign. Rumours that he had endorsed a book by one Dr John Cowell – the legal dictionary *The Interpreter* – which insisted that English kings might make laws and impose impositions as they saw fit, and that parliament enjoyed no liberties beyond what the sovereign graciously granted, did not help (this despite the king moving to suppress the book). Yet, had either James or his parliament refined the contract in mutual good faith, it might have served. Unfortunately, it came to nothing. Though the sparsely attended sitting approved Henry's elevation as Prince of Wales and voted through a single subsidy, the Great Contract was dead in the water. The parliament was prorogued but never recalled, with James later formally dissolving it. Thereafter, Salisbury found his grip on power loosening, rendering him powerless to halt Carr's rise even if he had wished to. A chance had been lost. As James was unable to rein in his spending, his debts would only rise.

*

What the king and queen still shared were their children's futures and, most importantly, the question of those children's marriages. In March 1610, Anna's nephew (the son of her sister Elizabeth) Frederick Ulrich, future Duke of Brunswick-Lüneburg, arrived, hoping to win the hand of Princess Elizabeth. He was to be unsuccessful, as both James and Anna hoped for a more prestigious match. Still, family was family, and king, queen, and prince were happy to play host to a visiting member. Frederick Ulrich was thus still in England when, in June, Henry was invested as Prince of Wales.

The hallmarks of the ceremony were expense and the need for security, both of which were high. The previous month, Europe had been shaken by the news that Henry IV of France had been stabbed to death in Paris by a Catholic fanatic, François Ravaillac – a worrying turn of events not only for crowned heads across the continent but especially for a monarch who had faced the Gunpowder Plot. Consequently, the prince was denied a triumphal ride to Westminster and was instead escorted on foot within a heavily armed phalanx of men, including Nottingham and Northampton. Inside the Parliament House, the robed Henry bowed three times to James, with the king then touching him with the sword of state before putting a ring on his finger and a coronet on his head. In a mirror of Queen Elizabeth tickling her favourite Leicester's chin in an apparent moment of instinctive familiarity, James leant forward and pinched his son's cheek. Although it has since been claimed that the king was jealous and suspicious of Henry's popularity, this gesture gives that assessment the lie. James was a proud and affectionate father.

The ceremony was followed by three days of celebration, not least of which was 'London's Love to Prince Henry': a water pageant on the Thames. On 5 June an elaborate marine-themed masque was staged: Samuel Daniel's *Tethys' Festival*, in which James himself featured as the King of the Ocean. In the anti-masque (an innovation which provided a comic or light-hearted accompaniment to the masque proper, pioneered by Anna in *The Masque of Queens*), the queen appeared as the sea goddess Tethys, and Prince Charles, sporting fairy wings, played Zephyrus. The stage on which the royals performed was turned into a representation of Milford Haven, with artificial waves flanked by statues of Nereus and Neptune. In the masque proper, Princess Elizabeth appeared as the nymph of the Thames; Arbella Stuart – who was even then plotting a secret marriage to the Tudor-blooded William Seymour, Lord Beauchamp, for which she would suffer house arrest – represented the Trent; Elizabeth Grey was the Medway; and Lady Anne Clifford, Countess of Dorset, was the River Ayr. Perhaps the most beautiful performer, however, was the daughter of Suffolk, Frances, Countess of Essex – a vivacious twenty-year-old who would, soon enough, turn the love triangle existing between king, queen, and Robert Carr into a square.

The new Prince of Wales, emboldened by his explosion onto the public stage, began to take a more active role in affairs from his base at St James's Palace, where he would build up a private menagerie and art collection. He was in all ways presenting as – or being presented as – a Protestant champion-in-waiting: the solution to the problems of muscular European Catholicism and the ongoing difficulties of making Ireland Protestant via colonisation. Again, this was a far cry from his father who, later in the year, would flaunt his *via media* credentials by inviting the centrist scholar Isaac Casaubon to England for learned theological discussions. In September, Henry took his mother, sister, and brother to the launch of his new ship, the *Prince Royal*. Unfortunately, however, adverse weather caused the vessel to become stuck in the silt, and by the time it could be re-floated – in the middle of the night – only the prince was willing to return. On New Year's Day 1611, he followed in his mother's footsteps by producing his first masque, Jonson's *Oberon, the Faery Prince*, which featured a prophetic Silenus stating that Oberon would come to rule Great Britain. At this point Henry, playing the fairy prince, was drawn onto the stage in a chariot pulled by two white bears, whilst a song was sung:

> Melt earth to sea, sea flow to air,
> And air fly into fire,

Whilst we, in tunes, to Arthur's chair
Bear Oberon's desire;
Than which there nothing can be higher
Save James to whom it flies;
But he the wonder is of tongues, of ears, of eyes.[9]

In a subsequent performance, entitled *Love Freed from Ignorance*, Anna appeared as the Queen of the Orient and danced with her son. To those present, the message of the season was clear: if James continued overseeing a disorderly court (which the continental publication of the scurrilous *Ecclesiasticus* implied), his dreams of union would come to nothing.[10] They might, however, see fruition under the future monarch – and that future monarch was clearly his mother's son. As evidence of her influence over Henry, in February, the Tuscan agent Ottaviano Lotti was quick to seek an audience with Anna on the subject of the prince's marriage.

Nor were the other royal children forgotten. In March, the Count of Cartignano arrived as Savoyard ambassador, empowered to negotiate a double match for Princess Elizabeth (who would get the Prince of Piedmont) and Prince Henry (who would get Maria, daughter of Savoy's King Charles Emmanuel). Though Cartignano brought gifts – four horses and, for James, a new pet leopard which had been trained to hunt hares and follow the king like a tame dog – the mooted marriage alliances would founder on the rocks of Savoy's Catholicism. In the same month, the king and queen were at Windsor for the Garter ceremony, at which Charles was invested. The king, however, remained very much in thrall to his lover. Carr, too, received the honour, and thus continued his upwards trajectory. The previous day, indeed, the favourite had gained more: he had been granted property in Scotland (which Anna had been campaigning to be given to the Scottish chancellor, her supporter Alexander Seton, formerly Lord Fyvie and now Earl of Dunfermline) and had been elevated to the viscountcy of Rochester. As a viscountcy was not amongst the top tier of the peerage, this meant that higher honours might follow.

James had become increasingly dependent on the company of Carr – or Rochester, as he was now known. The young man represented an escape from a wife and son united in their disapproval; endless financial worries; increasing disappointment in the once reliable and now ailing Salisbury; and a wider family that was giving cause for concern. The latter was exemplified by Lady Arbella, who had remained under arrest since the previous year. James had never much liked or trusted his cousin, which was unfair, but he was quite correct in scenting suspicion in her clandestine marriage to Lord Beauchamp, who was descended from Henry VII's daughter, Mary. As ominously convenient as it must have seemed, the marriage between the older Arbella and the younger Beauchamp (she was thirteen years his senior) was probably a love match, at least on her part. Yet, given that both were potential heirs to the throne, it needed royal approval, which was unlikely to have been forthcoming, and it certainly gave the appearance of having some dark design behind it.

In June, Arbella and her husband (who had been warded in the Tower for his clandestine marriage) hatched a plot to reunite and live abroad. She disguised herself as a man and boldly set off for the coast, whilst he managed to escape the fortress and follow. The plan was that they should rendezvous on the road, but their timings were as poor as their escapes were daring. In the end, Arbella set out to sea, unsure where her husband was. Her ship was still in the Channel when James was alerted. Admiral William Monson was swiftly despatched on the *Adventure*, which had little trouble capturing the errant lady's vessel. The jig was up, and Arbella surrendered. Ironically enough, her husband managed to slip the net, and he thereafter decamped to Ostend whilst she was locked in the Tower, where she lived on until 1615, dying a sad and lonely death brought on by a hunger strike.

Yet, as much as his family might vex him, James also found trouble brewing in the relationship which had become his chief source of joy. The problem, in a word, was Overbury. Rochester's guiding light had returned to England and resumed his pivotal position as the favourite's secretary. However, he was, by anyone's measure, growing intolerably arrogant. Chief amongst his enemies was Anna, who considered him the hated favourite's even more crooked right hand. During the summer, she looked out from a window at Greenwich and saw Rochester and Overbury in the gardens. 'There,' she remarked, 'go Carr and his governor.'[11] Overbury consequently offended her by turning round and laughing.

This the queen would not tolerate. In a fury, she flew to James, passionately stating that she would sooner return to Denmark than remain in England to be mocked by such a man. James, who was no lover of Overbury himself, was in a quandary. He could not honourably allow the queen to be treated with scorn, but neither did he wish in any way to upset his lover. Accordingly, and rather sheepishly, he promised that his council would consider the case. This proved hollow, however, and nothing was done.

Unwilling to let the slight pass, Anna gained the support of Prince Henry, before attempting to enlist Salisbury. She wrote, 'The King hath told me that he will advise with you and some other four or five of the Council of that fellow [meaning Overbury]. I can say no more, either to make you understand the matter or my mind, than I said this other day. Only I recommend to your care how public the matter is now both in Court and city and how far I have reason in that respect. I refer the rest to this bearer and myself to your love.'[12]

She was not the only one willing to cultivate Salisbury. Whether James had tipped Rochester off or not is unknown, but soon Overbury was asking the Lord Treasurer to be a 'witness of submission . . . To the Queen's mercy . . . because as I understand, her Majesty is not fully satisfied of the integrity of my intent that way'.[13]

In reality, both parties were behind the times in suing for Salisbury's support. The failure of the Great Contract had left him somewhat directionless, and he had never fully recovered James's trust. Moreover, his years of serving Queen Elizabeth, then organising the succession, and then attempting the Herculean task of ensuring some measure of financial sense prevailed in the new regime, had left him utterly broken in body if not spirit. It was increasingly apparent that he was mortally ill. A man inherently loyal to the Crown, his main desire was to please his sovereign, and so he said what he assumed – probably rightly – James wished to hear: Overbury and Carr had not been laughing at the queen but at some private joke – they had not seen Anna nor heard her remark, and neither man had intended any offence. This delighted James, who simply wanted the whole ugly episode to go away.

Anna, who was beginning to experience ill health herself, let the matter drop. This she was loath to do, but she had no choice. Her husband, it was clear, was so deeply in love with Rochester that her attempts at intervening could only redound to her discredit. What she no doubt hoped, of course, was that, in time, Prince Henry would gain in strength; indeed, when James died, the favourite might then go the way of Raleigh, being swiftly despatched out of sight by the new king. But, unfortunately, and to the shock of the king, the queen, and all of James's subjects, the ailing Salisbury was not the only one for whom death was coming.

18

The End of an Era

In the spring and summer of 1612, scurrilous verses found their way from hand to hand, to be chortled over, sung, and spread, despite the legal prohibition on such epigrams. One ran,

> O Ladies, ladies howle & cry,
> For you have lost your Salisbury.
> He that of late was your protection,
> He is now dead by your infection.
> Come with your teares bedew his lockes,
> Death kild him not; it was the pockes.
> . . .
> Soe shall the King, & state be blest,
> And subjects all shall live in rest,
> All which long time have been abused
> By tricks, which divellish whores have used.
> But now the cheife is gone before,
> I hope to see the end of more.[1]

The victim, obviously, was Lord Treasurer Salisbury, the veteran statesman of Queen Elizabeth and architect of the Stuart succession. The sickly Salisbury had long been suffering pains, which precipitated a visit to the healing waters at Bath. What was troubling him, however, was not the pox (as wags, aware of his taste for women, claimed) but cancer. He died in considerable pain of body and mind at Marlborough on 24 May. His enemies – of whom there were many – were quick to express their relief, cruelly making sport of his curved spine:

At Hattfeilde neere Hartforde there lyes in a coffin
A harte griping Harpie; of shape like a Dolphin.[2]

As ever in the period, a disabled physical body was equated with
inner corruption:

The divell now hath fetcht the Ape
Of crooked manners, crooked shape.
Great were his infirmities,
But greater his enormities
Oppression, lechery, blood, & pride
He liv'd in; & like Herod died.[3]

All of this was deeply unfair. Cecil had been devious, but he had
also been brilliant, and every bit the equal of his late father. On two
counts, however, he had failed. The first – his attempts to render
the Crown solvent – was hardly his fault. His second certainly was:
he had not reared up a successor to the multiplicity of roles he had
played as James's chief man of state.

The king, at first, appeared disinclined to choose one. Although
Queen Anna and Prince Henry sought to advance Sir Henry Wotton
(last seen parading around Edinburgh in the guise of Ottavio Baldi),
Rochester opposed them – and the favourite's opinion counted for
more. Blithely, James announced that he was an experienced enough
monarch to handle the onerous duties of Principal Secretary by himself; as for the treasury, that was to pass to a commission comprising
Northampton, Worcester, and Suffolk, as well as Wotton, Zouche,
and Sir Julius Caesar. Given that the royal debt which Salisbury had
occasionally managed to bring down had actually increased, their
job would be no sinecure.

James, for all he flattered himself – with good reason – that he
was a ruler of considerable experience, was – like Henry VIII in the
days of Wolsey and Cromwell – more inclined to apply his mind to
pet projects, ecclesiastical matters, and international affairs than to
the daily grind of government. What his personal handling of the

secretaryship therefore meant was that Rochester was to take on the burdensome duties which had once accrued to Salisbury. In essence, the royal lover, by now a Privy Councillor, had moved from being the king's confidant and bedfellow to sitting at the heart of English government.

The loss of Salisbury (and gain of Rochester) was a further blow to Queen Anna. Yet in one sphere she retained an indisputable level of influence. As she had carefully nurtured her relationship with Prince Henry and maintained a positive one with Princess Elizabeth, she was still able to unite with James over the question of their marriages. Elizabeth's glittering array of suitors had included the widowed Philip III of Spain; King Gustavus Adolphus of Sweden (vetoed by Anna); Frederick, Elector Palatine (the Palatinate being a Calvinist state on the Rhine), leader of the Evangelical Union; the Prince of Nassau; the Prince of Anhalt; and the son of the Landgrave of Hesse-Kassel. Yet king and queen clashed over the victor, with Anna favouring the highest-ranking candidate and James primarily interested in securing a Protestant husband for his daughter (to counterbalance what he hoped would be a Catholic princess for Prince Henry). It was the king who had his way, and only two days after Salisbury's death, a contract was signed between Princess Elizabeth and Frederick Casimir, the Elector Palatine.

This meant that his corresponding goal of a Catholic marriage for Prince Henry could go forward. On this, James and Anna could agree, although their favoured Spanish match had been ruined when, the previous year, the French regent (and widow of Henry IV) Marie de Medici had matched her daughter Elisabeth and son Louis with the two eldest Spanish royal children. Henry, who was developing ideas of his own, was not especially keen on marriage to a Catholic, but that counted for little. Cynically, though, he viewed his father's attempts to marry him off as being financially motivated. According to the Venetian ambassador, the prince had complained that 'the large dower which is offered would not come into his hands nor be applied for the good of the Crown but would very soon be scattered by the King's profusion, besides which he thinks he need have no difficulty in finding money, as he is heir to so many crowns'.[4]

Henry's grievance was honest enough: he knew well that if he was sold in marriage in return for an enormous dowry, the cash would end up in the pockets of his father's favourites, whether as gifts or to pay off their gambling debts. As far as his own attitude to money went, Henry was able to maintain a suitable standard of living largely within his means (those means being income from the duchy of Cornwall and the earldom of Chester). On the subject of favourites, the prince was likewise unequivocal, protesting that 'neither fantasy nor flattery should move him to confer upon any a superlative place in his favour, but [he] would do to the uttermost of his understanding measure unto all according to the merit of their services, as holding it not just to yield unto affections'.[5] He did not name Rochester, but it was clear enough who was the prime target of his implicit criticism of his father's behaviour. In all, Henry looked like a young man of promise.

By contrast, James and his court were looking grubby. Indeed, in spring, the gossips had more than just the death of Salisbury and the primacy of Rochester to work with: a Scottish diplomat and peer, Robert Crichton, 8th Lord of Sanquhar, was accused of encouraging his followers to murder a fencing master called John Turner (who had once wounded Sanquhar's eye). The result was a public display of infamy, with accusations flying that the peer had in fact solicited various men to commit murder. After being caught and tried, Sanquhar was hanged at the end of June in Westminster Palace Yard, declaring his Catholicism at the last. It was small wonder that the reputation of the Jacobean court as a place of outward glitter and inner decay was growing.

Relations between James and his son were not, however, frosty. The king had, in fact, handed over the royal manor of Woodstock, in Oxfordshire, to Henry, and in the summer of 1612, the prince set about renovating it. To show off his achievements in turning what had once been Queen Elizabeth's prison into a pleasure palace, Henry then invited his mother and father to an entertainment there, at which he hoped to preside as host. Unfortunately, however, the stress of the building project, the turmoil rising over his future marriage, and his own unforgiving exercise regime conspired to lay low his immune system. As the Woodstock entertainments were going on, Henry began complaining of 'a giddy lumpish heaviness in his forehead, the pain of which obliged him to stroke up his brow and forehead with his hand before he put on his hat'; soon, his nose was bleeding profusely.[6] Rather than resting, however, the prince elected to exercise harder, in the mistaken belief that pushing his body further would render him in fit shape to receive his sister's fiancé, who was due to arrive in October.

On the 16th of that month, Frederick appeared in England and was conveyed to Whitehall, where James cheerfully declared, 'Suffice it that I am anxious to testify to you by deeds that you are welcome.'[7] Anna, however, was not yet reconciled to the match, and sat in stony silence. For once, Henry sided with his father over his mother. It was apparent to him that the sullen, serious young suitor was genuinely attracted to Elizabeth and she to him (in a mirror of the bride's parents in their youth, the pair could correspond happily in French). Thus, the prince invited the new couple to his palace at St James's, where he again intended to play host. Unfortunately, this round of activity proved too much. As the autumn had approached, he had given up his exercise regime. Still, he suffered 'continual headaches, laziness, and indisposition', which manifested in 'dead, sunk eyes'.[8] Whilst entertaining Elizabeth and Frederick, he collapsed.

By now, it was clear that something was really wrong with Henry. His parents, alarmed, assigned Anna's personal physician to the case. The Genevan doctor, Théodore de Mayerne, was what would in later generations be known as a society doctor. Obese, self-important, and highly educated in contemporary medical theory, his remedies were often as colourful as they were horrifying. On examining Henry, he diagnosed a tertian fever (characterised by recurrence at intervals). His solution was to bleed the prince, which achieved nothing other than further weakening him. Mayerne therefore decided that the condition could be improved if Henry's head was shaved, live fowl sliced up the spine and, still warm and gushing blood, applied to his scalp. Unsurprisingly, given he was likely suffering from typhoid, this effected no cure. Nor did enemas, medicines containing rhubarb and senna (these causing only agonising diarrhoea), powdered unicorn horn, or the 'bone' of a stag's heart.

Anna, in desperation, wrote to Sir Walter Raleigh, who had set up a laboratory in the Tower, in which he was known to concoct his own efficacious medicines. The pair had corresponded in 1611 over Raleigh's belief in riches in the Americas, and in truth the imprisoned Elizabethan favourite was as eager to see Henry (who admired him) live as was his frantic mother. He thus made up and despatched his cordial of 'pearl, musk, hartshorn, bezoar stone, mint, borage, gentian, mace, sugar, aloes, and spirit of wine' for the prince's use.[9] Amazingly, when this was administered, Henry did in fact seem to rally. It was, however, false hope. Shortly afterwards, he collapsed again. The combined talents of the physicians, by this time comprising Drs Mayerne, Hamond, Butler, Giffard, Atkins, and Palmer, availed nothing. On 6 November, he died at eighteen, reputedly asking, 'Where is my dear sister?' Princess Elizabeth, sadly, had been denied access to her dying brother.

Both James and Anna were distraught. Yet the loss did not bring them together. The queen locked herself away at Somerset House, whilst the king consoled himself with Rochester at Theobalds. Whilst they mourned privately, England and Scotland did so publicly. What people wanted to know, though, was how such a seemingly healthy and active young man had died so suddenly. It was not long before whispers of poison (the most cruel and unfair of which blamed James) were heard – in addition to claims that Mayerne was guilty of malpractice. The post-mortem, however, declared the death natural.

The immediate results of Prince Henry's death were that an appropriate funeral had to be arranged, and the planned marriage between Elizabeth and Frederick, for decency's sake, had to be postponed. For four weeks, the prince's body lay in state at St James's, whilst his household maintained a solemn vigil. This macabre scene was, however, enlivened by the appearance of a madman, who somehow gained access to the apartments, stripped naked, and ran around screeching that he was Henry's ghost.

Thankfully, the funeral, held on 7 December, was free of such ghoulishness. Hundreds of mourners, including Frederick, formed a procession to Westminster Abbey, led by Prince Charles – the new heir – as chief mourner. Charles had, throughout his young life, hero-worshipped his brother, who had embodied all the ideals of militant masculinity so prized in the period. Henceforth, international interest would be focused on this previously overlooked prince, and he became both the cynosure of his mother's life and, increasingly, an object of devoted and sentimental affection to his father.

Not in attendance at the funeral were the king and queen, as was usual when an heir was laid to rest. They thus did not witness the prince being interred next to his grandmother, Mary Queen of Scots, who had been recently reinterred in the south aisle of the Lady Chapel in a splendid new tomb designed by Cornelius Cure and completed by his son. James's fascination with his prestigious family had not passed. He and Anna would, however, soon have to look towards the Stuarts' new future.

*

At Christmas 1612, the court held its breath, watching with anticipation as the king emerged from his privy apartments. James did not disappoint them. He strode into the public gaze, giving every appearance of good humour – not out of callousness, but because he was aware of having to take the lead in a country which was undergoing a period of national gloom. This he managed despite suffering an illness of his own: he had been forced to bed 'with a sore toe, but [he] will not have it called the gout'. Anna, suffering herself, was unable to join him at Hampton Court when the marriage between Elizabeth and Frederick was solemnised, because she too had 'a fit of the gout'.[10] Although they were not, by modern standards, old, both king and queen were beginning to settle into what passed in the period for late middle age, and the frequency of health complaints

290

would only multiply (with Anna's recurrent attacks of 'gout' likely being, in reality, the onset of osteoarthritis).

Her illness probably did not help her mood. As the date for the marriage proper drew closer, the queen remained obdurate. Decades later, it would be remembered that she had referred to her daughter as 'Goodwife Palsgrave' (a Palsgrave being a Count Palatine). The joke was that in marrying Frederick, Elizabeth was, in her mother's eyes, going down in the world. It was not particularly funny, and it might have been dangerous, given it risked upsetting a foreign power. Yet the young couple were comfortable enough in their relationship to let it pass, and Elizabeth was supposedly able to counter that she would 'rather be the Palsgrave's wife than the greatest papist Queen in Christendom'.[11]

Duly, and with outward happiness restored throughout the family, the marriage went ahead at Whitehall's Chapel Royal on Valentine's Day 1613. Frederick shone in cloth-of-silver as he walked to the chapel in the company of sixteen single men (representing each of his sixteen years). Elizabeth, too, wore silver, and her loose hair was dressed with pearls; she, too, had sixteen attendants. Anna was decked in white and weighted down with £400,000 worth of jewels. James rose to the occasion himself. Whilst he was still not habitually an elaborate dresser, he remained a lover of gemstones: over his black suit and Spanish cape, he dazzled in £600,000 of jewels, including 'the fair great pearl pendant called the Brethren, the Portugal Diamond, and the great table diamond set in gold called the Mirror of France'.[12] The pressure on the Privy Purse (especially when one takes into account Elizabeth's £40,000 dowry) scarcely needs mentioning. The royal family were, in effect, parading around in England's Crown Jewels whilst the nation's finances were in the red.

The young bride could barely contain her giggles, but the Archbishop of Canterbury, George Abbot, managed to conduct the ceremony with appropriate solemnity. Revelry followed, in the form of the designer Inigo Jones (a favourite of Anna's, who collaborated for a time with Ben Jonson) and writer Thomas Campion's *The Lords*

Masque. Unfortunately, at least one commentator found the show 'very long and tedious'; certainly, James appeared to agree, falling asleep as he did during it.[13] Better received was Shakespeare's *The Tempest*, which found analogues for Frederick and Elizabeth in Ferdinand and Miranda. The following morning, James visited the couple to confirm that the marriage had been irrevocably sealed by consummation; Frederick then further displayed his virility – and martial prowess – by riding out to the tiltyard. Throughout, the ongoing festivities hinged on two themes: England (or Great Britain) was now a major colonialist power, and in the new golden couple, the spirit of militant Protestantism would be reborn.

Without Salisbury's attempts at financial guidance, James fell back on what had always been his own nebulous sense of economy. His strategy involved granting Prince Charles 'just twenty-five of Henry's original household of 250 followers', thereby slashing spending – a move that infuriated Anna.[14] More immediately, on realising that he was haemorrhaging money on his new son-in-law's English household, the king decided to disband it. Elizabeth, unconscious of the expense, was furious at what she perceived as a slight, and so she and her husband decided to leave for Frederick's seat of Heidelberg in the Lower Palatinate. This they did in April, with Anna accompanying her daughter by barge firstly to Greenwich and then to Rochester, to the salute of cannon and guns from the palaces which dotted the Thames.

All did not go smoothly. Anna's old nemesis, bad weather, raised such a tumult (thankfully without anyone blaming witches) that she was forced to wait whilst her daughter, along with her attendants Lady Harington and the Countess of Arundel, embarked and disembarked repeatedly. At this stage, Rochester became involved. He had little respect for the queen, but he did not wish that widely known. Affecting an air of sympathetic friendliness, he invited the royal party to dine with him at Rochester Castle: an invitation which Anna could hardly refuse. It was thus from her husband's lover's house that the queen said her last goodbye to her daughter, when an improvement in sailing conditions at last allowed her to depart.

Elizabeth did not return to England in her parents' lifetimes, but her marriage – always one of genuine passion – would come to give the king more headaches than it was worth.

No doubt James was delighted by his lover's show of hospitality to his wife and daughter, and no doubt Anna was vexed. Rochester had, since Salisbury's death, been attending his new duties using Overbury as his secretary (and, in truth, his brain). It seems, however, that the love on display at the royal marriage had fired something in the favourite, who thus far had remained unmarried and at the beck and call of his sovereign. Rochester had fallen in love himself.

The object of his desire was Frances, Countess of Essex and daughter of Suffolk, who had appeared in *Tethys' Festival* as the representation of the River Lea. Yet Frances already had a husband: the 3rd Earl of Essex (son to the more famous late Elizabethan Essex). James himself had encouraged this marriage, which neither of the young people had much wanted, for political reasons (chiefly the reconciliation of the warring Howards and Devereux) in January 1606. It had been a grand spectacle, with Jonson's Romanesque *Hymenaei* performed and marriage advocated by Truth in a mock combat titled the *Barriers*. Yet for all the glitter, success had not ensued. Essex had left England to tour Europe in 1607 and remained abroad until 1609; on his return, he had found no more liking for his bride – nor she for him – than when he had left.

Essex was, in short, an unsatisfactory husband. Rochester, on the other hand, was glamorous, attractive, and in high favour with the king. Frances and her fellow Howards (comprising the powerful Suffolk, Nottingham, and Northampton) therefore saw every reason to undo the Essex marriage and promote a match with Rochester. Happily, they did not have to reckon with Queen Anna, who would no doubt have understood exactly what was going on and thrown her weight against the dissolution of the Essex marriage; the queen's illness had worsened to such an extent that she required medical attention and, despite the fact that the waters had done nothing for Salisbury, Mayerne's guidance was that she decamp to Bath. Accordingly, in April, she parted from James at Hampton Court and rode off on a grand spring progress. She was away for five weeks, followed by a return visit to the waters in August, during which time the affair between Rochester and Frances continued apace, whilst the Howards plotted how best to free up the pretty countess.

Yet it was not entirely smooth sailing for the young lovers. For one thing, Overbury put his foot down, proving himself the chief spanner in the works by counselling Rochester against marrying Frances, whom he detested. For another, and despite her illness, the queen too remained a force to be reckoned with. On her return from Bath, and somewhat restored in health, Anna joined her husband at Theobalds, where the king was relaxing amongst his courtiers and pets (amongst them his beloved armadillo, which had by this time been appointed its own keeper). There, during a hunt, she shot – quite by accident – one of James's favourite dogs, Jewel. Far from being angry, the king assured his upset wife that he would 'love her never the worse'.[15] He meant it. As his own age was beginning to show and as her health was beginning to worsen, James found himself more and more appreciative of his relationship with the queen. He surprised her with a diamond valued at £2,000, which he charmingly claimed was Jewel's legacy. As John Chamberlain noted, 'love and kindnes increases dayly between' Anna and James, who 'were never in better termes'.[16] Yet the king's generosity was, as usual, built on a shaky foundation. Chamberlain archly noted in the same letter that, at the time of the gift, London's aldermen were being 'pressed to lend £2000 each to the King'. Even now, the queen's potential hostility, by virtue of her good relationship with James, might make the Howards' (and Rochester's) schemes more difficult.

Curiously, when the king discovered that Rochester wished to take a wife, he was enthusiastic. This is not because he had tired of his lover, but rather because he believed that Rochester was in love with him, and that marriage would no more separate them than had the reality of his own marriage to Anna. James was quite willing to encourage his lovers to marry, even at the height of his relationships with them, provided the wives were unloved objects who did not interfere with their husbands' attendance in the royal bedchamber.

On hearing of Overbury's interference, James was thus happy to support Rochester. When, in April (during Anna's parting from Princess Elizabeth), it was suggested that the favourite's mentor be placed in an overseas post – with Russia mooted – the king agreed. He had long disliked his favourite having another man in his life – and particularly one who was infringing on James's own coveted role as wise elder. Overbury, however, played for time, eventually flatly refusing the posting. Foolishly, he relied on Rochester to protect him from the consequences.

The high-handed royal response – one which was, as later recognised, out of all proportion to the offence – was to clap Overbury in the Tower for resisting the king's command. With him safely locked away, matters proceeded more smoothly. The Howards had landed on the idea of using Essex's alleged impotence, and Frances's consequent virginity, as the means of dissolving the marriage. James had no problem with this; he had seen impotence used as a reason for dissolving a marriage back in 1581, when his old minister Arran had secured his lover the Countess of March's divorce from her husband.

The nullity suit was passed to a commission, made up of a quiver of politicians and divines. They met in June 1613 and listened to the ostensible facts of the case as reported by Frances and Essex: he confirmed that he had, indeed, not touched his wife sexually, but that his incapacity was strictly limited to her. She echoed the lack of consummation but blamed witchcraft for Essex's impotence. This odd suggestion served only to complicate matters, as a more critical quorum was chosen to test the validity of claims of sorcery. Archbishop Abbot, throughout, was utterly opposed, no doubt seeing with some acuity that the nullity suit was simply a means of freeing up Frances so that she might wed the king's lover: it was, from his perspective, a shameless and shameful debacle being engineered by the troublesome Howards.

James, however, was adamant. Along with Suffolk, he set about fixing the outcome. This was easy enough to do, given that the majority of commissioners were willing to please the king. Yet Abbot remained steadfast. On his knees, he appealed to James's intellect, pointing out that witchcraft had never been proven to cause impotence. This was entirely the wrong tack; the king had demonstrated in his own writings that witches could do just that. For all his principled stance, the archbishop was fighting a losing battle. Having lost patience, James simply packed the commission with extra members to ensure the outcome he – and Rochester – sought. The decision was taken that the marriage could be dissolved pending a prurient investigation of the countess's private parts by selected noblewomen. In the event, a veiled woman – who may or may not have been a substitute – submitted herself to this appalling treatment and Frances was thereafter a free agent. The Essex marriage was declared void by majority in September, and her remarriage could take place.

The most vocal opponent, Overbury, heard of proceedings from the Tower, from which he had – unsuccessfully – attempted to gain Queen Anna's support. If he planned on making any further protests, however, he was given no opportunity. Even as his former friend was preparing to marry his legally proven virgin bride, the unfortunate prisoner died after a bout of painful illness. He went sadly un-mourned by all but his family. He would not, though, be forgotten.

Burying news of Overbury's mysterious death was the king's showering of honours on Rochester; he was raised to the pinnacle of his titular elevation as Earl of Somerset, before being appointed Scotland's treasurer. The day after Christmas, he and Frances were wed by the Dean of the Chapel Royal at Whitehall, James Montague, Bishop of Bath and Wells – the same man who had wed Frances to Essex at the same location. The only difference was the bridegroom. The king, for his part, was cock-a-hoop not only at being able to give Somerset what he wanted but at having won the right to do so despite opposition.

To pay for the celebrations, James sold off Crown lands. He gave the groom a golden sword, and he showered the bride with jewels to weave through her hair (which she wore loose, to display her virginity). In order to secure the queen's attendance and thus approbation (Anna initially having intended to ignore the marriage), the king aided her in a property dispute over Greenwich lands. He then induced her to play a role in the wedding masque penned by Campion. Given Anna's past collaboration with the writer, it is difficult not to see her hand in the following lines:

> Some friendship between man and man prefer,
> But I, th'affection between man and wife.[17]

Beyond the square of James, Anna, Somerset, and the new countess, the country watched this latest episode of courtly scandal with jaundiced eyes. Once again, libellers had a field day. Playing on Henry VIII's (platonic) relationship with his favourite Charles Brandon, who had married that king's sister, one ran:

> Henry raised Brandon
> James, Carr, upon my life
> The one married the King's sister,
> The other Essex's wife.[18]

More bawdily, another mocked the bride's chastity and Somerset's elevation:

> Essex's bird hath flown her cage,
> And gone to Court to lie with a page.
> She was a lady fine of late,
> She could not be entered, she was so straight;
> But now, with use, she is so wide,
> A Carr may enter on every side.[19]

Somerset, still referred to contemptuously as mere 'Carr', was far from popular, and neither was his marriage, for all its splendour. It is small wonder that, after the Christmas Revels of 1613–14, James swiftly escaped his hated capital (a city which, a couple of years later, he would call 'a general nuisance to the whole kingdom') for the hunting grounds at Newmarket.

The problem, to many English observers, was that Somerset epitomised the phenomenon of the over-promoted Scot whose relationship with the king was both scandal in itself and the cause of the moral decay infecting the court. Where these critics were correct was that Somerset's good fortune derived solely from James's love. That love, however, was beginning to burn out. As the king would soon realise, he had not married his lover off to a submissive woman whose new husband might ignore her, but to a headstrong lady who did not intend on sharing her lovestruck husband's body with the monarch. Others, soon enough, would have much worse to say about the enigmatic new Countess of Somerset.

19

Fall and Rise of a Favourite

Raucous merrymaking spilled over the Christmas Revels. Following Rochester's marriage, in January 1614, news arrived of another successful coupling; Princess Elizabeth had delivered Frederick a son, named Henry Frederick (after the late Prince of Wales). Thankfully, James was not required to pay for his first grandson's household – a fact that undoubtedly made the news even more joyous. Whilst Queen Anna was happily occupied with the weddings and festivities of her ladies (Jean Drummond became Lady Roxburgh in February, and Frances Southwell became Lady Rodney, both sets of nuptials taking place at Somerset House), James was desperately seeking financial assistance.

The early part of 1614 was taken up with the calling of the reign's second parliament. The king was no lover of parliaments, yet he was bound by the English constitution's insistence that, without them, funds could not be granted him. Indeed, in December 1612, it had been noted that the requirement for a parliament was successfully avoided when '£20,000 was found to relieve the King's necessities'.[1] On his taking up the post of Lord Treasurer in 1608, Salisbury had attempted to raise money by alternative means, from the grudging sale of Crown lands, to imposing fines for ancient misdemeanours, to claiming feudal rights (or 'aids') on ceremonial occasions (with subjects required to hand over cash on, for example, Prince Henry's elevation). Money had even been raised by the selling of baronetcies, beginning in 1611 – including to Catholics.[2] By 1614, however, there was nothing to be found down the backs of settles, and cash was needed. The king bowed to the inevitable. But the old dog – who had often struggled with his Scottish Estates – had no intention of learning new tricks when it came to managing the ancient English system.

The writs of election summoning MPs were issued in February, in a move supported by the up-and-coming Attorney General – and cousin of the late Salisbury – Sir Francis Bacon. Opposing the move were the Howards – understandably, given that their monopolies were likely to come under scrutiny – with the clan only coming round to the idea when Northampton realised he might engineer a failure of the session.[3] In response to rumours that he was considering finding a pro-Catholic appointee for the secretaryship, James was also finally induced to fill Salisbury's vacant role ahead of the parliament. The job went to Sir Ralph Winwood, who had been Master of Requests since 1609. Despite gossip, this was probably not at Somerset's suggestion or insistence. James was not a fool. He had allowed Somerset ever greater power as a means of controlling his lover. He was not, however, a lovestruck dupe. Winwood, with his 'upright and sincere carriage', might have lacked the wiles and experience of Salisbury, but he was a capable pair of hands, and he had the benefit – to Protestant observers – of being virulently anti-Spanish and anti-Catholic.

Although the king claimed to want a 'Parliament of love', the Commons were in no mood to be conciliatory. Indeed, the session opened amid dark rumours that the Crown had sought to flood the Lower House with royal lackeys – rumours which were investigated and found to be overblown. When business opened, the Commons' primary complaint was the use of impositions – those duties on trade over and above customs duties – which Salisbury had exploited in 1606 by securing them for the king's lifetime. The threat perceived by MPs was that the Crown was intruding on property law, but a wider anxiety had been in the background since James's succession: the question of whether it was the king's duty to uphold the existing law (and legal rights to property) or his right to trample laws as he saw fit. On this question there could be no agreement, any more than on the subject of royal spending, or on parliament's antagonism

300

to what they considered spendthrift and beggarly Scottish courtiers. James's attempts to bend the Commons to his will failed, and efforts to bounce them into voting him financial subsidies only turned them further against him. In June, he dissolved what became known as the 'Addled' parliament, locking up some of its more belligerent members in the Tower.[4] No legislation had been passed, nor had any cash been voted into the royal coffers. The Crown was reduced to cajoling, begging, and bullying private citizens into handing over voluntary benefices – with a predictable lack of success.

This has been seen as a triumph of the crypto-Catholic Lord Privy Seal, Northampton (the cleverest and most able of the Howard faction), who had advised against summoning parliament and then counselled the king to dissolve it. Yet it was a pyrrhic victory, as Northampton promptly dropped dead on 15 June, leaving James to contemplate seeking Spanish support in what was becoming a battle with his English subjects. As a parting shot, the old earl had demanded that 'the Earl of Pembroke and Lord Lisle, his enemies, might not have any of his offices', and so they went instead to Somerset, his new kinsman by marriage.[5]

James, without his subsidies, had to beg a £100,000 loan from the city. Later in the year he launched a project by which Alderman William Cockayne would have the monopoly on an English dyeing industry (rather than sending cheap, undyed cloths abroad, as had been the custom). The hope was that, by this means, £40,000 would flow annually into the English Exchequer from the duties on imported dyestuffs. James, of course, had little understanding of trade, and less interest. The venture would falter, fail, and be abandoned entirely over the course of the next two years – thanks to a Dutch ban on English cloth imports and the incompetence of Cockayne – and the cloth trade, so long a vital part of England's economy, would suffer the after-effects. Needless to say, no cash injection came from the scheme.

That the king was increasingly pro-Spanish was not in doubt, as unpopular as that position was. He had struck up a positive working relationship with the Spanish ambassador, Diego Sarmiento de

301

Acuña, later 1st Count of Gondomar: a polished Castilian aristocrat who was exceedingly good at his job, and whose strategy was to appeal to the king's outgoing nature and intellectual vanity. Nor was the Spanish course without merit. For one thing, only Prince Charles remained on the international marriage market, making it critical – if the king wished to maintain his policy of balancing Princess Elizabeth's Protestant match with a Catholic one for his son – that Spain remained in the running. For another, Queen Anna was still in favour of it; she retained a sneaking admiration for the Spanish court's strict formality. Money also mattered, of course. Spain was the richest kingdom in Europe and, with a suitably large dowry, Maria Anna of Spain's marriage to Charles could, at a stroke, nullify the need to call troublesome parliaments for the foreseeable future.

Into the midst of all this regard for Catholic Spain, however, came a reminder of the king and queen's Protestant relations. Anna was in residence at Somerset House in July when her page, Pierre Hugon, announced that her brother, King Christian, had arrived. Naturally, the queen did not believe him. It was only when the Danish king's retinue caused a ruckus that she sprang up, and 'with great difficulty she only managed to receive him at the door'.[6] He had landed unannounced at Great Yarmouth with a tiny retinue, insisting that his visit 'was only one of kindness'.[7] No one believed this, and they were right. He had recently won the Kalmar War between Denmark-Norway and Sweden, but the Swedes remained recalcitrant. His true mission was swift to emerge: Christian wanted English support in maintaining control of the beaten nation.

James had been out of town when the Danish king arrived, but the unannounced visit forced him to return to London to institute – and pay for – the usual round of 'hunting, bear baiting, fencing, and other amusements'.[8] What he would not do was betray his policy of keeping English swords sheathed. He had, in fact, been using Scottish soldiery to support Sweden before the outbreak of conflict, and thereafter employed Sir James Spens to help negotiate an end to the Kalmar War and ensure ongoing peace. Further, for years he had been encouraging Protestant unity with a view to forming a bloc which might proceed to an accord with the Catholic Church – indeed, the year's Synod of Tonneins, to which James had sent an emissary, was in the process of trying to minimise sectarian conflict between Protestant faiths. Thus, Christian remained for only a few days, achieving nothing other than cheering up his sister (though not helping her in her ongoing struggles against Somerset's supremacy). After a fireworks display, James and Charles escorted the Danish sovereign to Woolwich, where they abandoned him to his ship.

If Anna was dismayed at the apparently unstoppable favour falling upon Somerset, she was not alone. As the favourite had married into the Howard family, it was to be expected that other noble houses would balk at the power accruing to him and his. The primary malcontents were James's old plaything, Philip Herbert (now Earl of Montgomery), his brother the Earl of Pembroke, and the Earls of Hertford and Bedford, who, together, decided enough was enough. Symbolically, they threw dirt at a portrait of Somerset; practically, they began plotting. It is possible that they saw Somerset's marriage as an opportunity. It was clear to all that the king's lover had committed the cardinal sin of falling in love with his own wife.

Nor had this escaped James's notice. In fact, with dawning horror he realised that the man he had fallen for, and for whom he had provided a wife – a necessary evil for the production of heirs, from the king's perspective – did not love him back. Worst of all, Somerset lacked the wit to mask his passion for his new countess; rather, his attention became focused on her, whilst with James he grew surly, short, and disinterested. For both James and the plotting earls, the time was ripe to push the favourite aside and substitute him with a younger, more willing model.

Somerset was quick to sense that factional politics were ranging against him. His unfortunate response, however, was to act as Anne Boleyn reputedly had when, married to Henry VIII, she sensed her husband was straying; rather than closing his eyes, the earl reproved his sovereign in a series of unedifying displays of anger and jealousy, born of fear. Ultimately, he put pen to paper and set down his grievances towards his perceived enemies at court. James replied, in what has become one of his most revelatory missives: 'First, I take God, the searcher of all hearts, to record that, in all the time past of idle talk, I never knew, nor could, out of any observation of mine, find any appearance of any such Court faction as you have apprehended . . . Next, I take the same God to record, that never man, of any degree, did directly or indirectly let fall to me anything that might be interpreted for the lessening of your credit with me.'⁹

His goal, clearly, was to put Somerset's mind at rest. He was, however, being disingenuous. As the letter grew more passionate, the essential conflict between the two became apparent:

> I am far from thinking of any possibility of any man ever to come within many degrees of your trust with me, as I must ingenuously confess you have deserved more trust and confidence of me than ever man did – in secrecy above all flesh.

> And in those points I never saw any come towards your merit: I mean in the points of inwardly trusty friend and servant. But as a piece of ground cannot be so fertile, but if either by the own natural rankness of evil manuring thereof it becomes also fertile of strong and noisome weeds, it then proves useless and altogether unprofitable; even so, these before rehearsed rich and rare parts and merits of yours have been of so long time, but especially of late, since the strange frenzy took you, so powdered and mixed with strange seams of unquietness, passion, fury, and insolent pride, and (which is worst of all) with a settled kind of induced obstinacy, as it chokes and obscures all these excellent and good parts that God hath bestowed upon you.

If it were not clear enough that James's complaint was an age-old one – 'you have changed towards me' – his subsequent paralepsis leaves no doubt: 'I leave out of this reckoning your long creeping back and withdrawing yourself from lying in my chamber, notwithstanding my many hundred times earnestly soliciting you to the contrary.'

Whatever James had been accustomed to getting from Somerset – whether pure emotional dedication or sexual contact in any degree – it is clear the younger man had ceased to give it. The king closed what was essentially an aggrieved farewell letter by expressing his hope that the two might still be friends and attempting a sweetener by insisting that any future man in his life would 'rise' only if Somerset gave his approval. The truth was that James was fed up with his lover – and there was already a man at court being groomed for the job.

Originally, George Villiers, son of a knight, was a protégé of the Scottish courtier and privy chamber man, Sir John Graham, who had earmarked the young Villiers – about to turn twenty-two – not because he was especially bright or highly born, but because he was exceptionally physically attractive and inherently good-natured. Later, he would be described as 'the handsomest-bodied man in all of England; his limbs so well compacted, and his conversation so pleasing, and of so sweet a disposition'.[10] His 'especially effeminate' face drew appreciative glances and one overcome observer gushed that 'from the nails of his fingers – nay – from the sole of his foot to the crown of his head, there was no blemish in him. And yet his carriage and every stoop of his deportment, more than his excellent form, were the beauty of his beauty.'[11] Villiers had long been cherished by his mother, Mary, who had paid for him to spend time in France, learning the arts of fencing and enough of the language to sound cultured. Graham, sensing a real find, had had the young paragon brought before the king at Apethorpe as a prospective cupbearer, but the pair met with little appreciable success in winning James's attention; for all his physical charm and French manners, Villiers was lacking a final polish.

What the young man needed were backers to instruct him in courtly etiquette and swap his black and worn suit for more fashionable weeds: fine manners and clothes, certainly, would draw the king's eye. Thus began a Pygmalion-like campaign of beautification. More and more, Villiers appeared at court functions, dancing to display his finely turned calves. At Twelfth Night 1615, Jonson's *Mercury Vindicated from the Alchemists* was reputedly staged especially to show him off. James, however, was curiously slow to respond. Having had his fingers burned, and with the sad end of his affair with Somerset fresh in his mind, he was disinclined to launch immediately into a new relationship. Not helping matters was that the fallen favourite remained on the scene. Though the king's love for him had cooled, Somerset intended to hold him to his promise of starting no new affair unless he, Somerset, was the furtherer and approver of the candidate. When the new earl – justifiably paranoid – sensed what was going on and remonstrated with the king, he found James truculent.

At some point, the earls backing Villiers' candidacy as the king's bedfellow became frustrated at their lack of success. They realised that it was not, as in the past, a matter of replacing a royal wife. Indeed, Queen Anna hated Somerset as much as they did. Accordingly, they sought her support. If this might seem awkward – asking a woman to help promote a man all the way into her husband's bed – then James himself was the alleged cause. Later, Bishop Goodman would claim that the king openly stated that he required his wife to approve his men, so that she would be unable later to complain about them.[12] If James indeed ran his private life in this way, he did not do so consistently, as the example of Somerset, of whom Anna never approved, clearly shows.

The plotter chosen to approach the queen was Pembroke, who found her walking her miniature greyhounds at Greenwich. At first, she demurred; they had more success in enlisting George Abbot, Archbishop of Canterbury, whose hatred for Somerset derived from the favourite's links to the pro-Catholic Howards and, of course, from simmering resentment over the nullity suit. Abbot provided another voice in the queen's ear, and this seems to have persuaded her. She agreed to do what she could to put Villiers in her husband's bedchamber. However, she issued a warning to the plotters: 'Neither you nor your friends know what you desire. I know your master [the king] better than you all; if Villiers get once into his favour, those who shall have most contributed to his preferment will be the first sufferers by him. I shall be no more spared than the rest. The King will teach him himself to despise us and to treat us with pride and scorn. The young, proud favourite will fancy that he is obliged to nobody for his preferment.'[13]

Anna, quite simply, had seen it all before; she knew well enough that James had learned no lessons from the Somerset affair, and that Villiers might end up growing in arrogance, pride, and unpopularity. She might, too, find herself as shut out from James's counsel as she had been under the old favourite.

Nevertheless, having given her consent, the queen threw herself – ill again as she was – into the breach. She had, by now, replaced the former bond she had enjoyed with Prince Henry with a new one with Prince Charles (whom, in a move as illustrative as it is saccharine, she had nicknamed her 'little servant'). In April, she and Charles united in pushing James into promoting Villiers.

St George's Day was chosen as a propitious occasion and, with his wife's encouragement, James elected to honour the new man with the coveted position of Gentleman of the Bedchamber in a ceremony organised by Anna at her own Somerset House. Somerset, who had retained his post as Lord Chamberlain, got wind of this, however, and sent a note to the king requesting him to bestow only the inferior position of Groom. At this point, Abbot intervened, writing his own hasty note warning the queen of what the old favourite was about and asking her to 'perfect' her work. This she did, insisting on the better position. James capitulated.

As Villiers bowed before the royal couple, Anna did indeed perfect her work. Turning to Prince Charles, she requested his sword. This Charles gave her, and she turned with it to the king – upon which James made a jesting show of being frightened of his armed wife. When the presumably awkward silence which followed had passed, the king accepted the sword, whilst Anna asked him to use it to knight the new man. Again, James acceded to her request – already, betting on Villiers was proving useful in restoring the queen's ability to gain favours – and the honour was duly given.

To his credit, the new knight was not hostile to the old favourite. Rather, Villiers hoped to win Somerset's approval, thereby delighting the king by allowing James to keep his promise. Somerset, however, was by now volatile and terrified for his own position. On receiving Villiers' friendly letter, which offered service and warm feelings, from the courtier Sir Humphrey May (who was already eyeing the new man as a patron), the cast-out favourite retorted, 'I will none of your service and you shall none of my favour. I will, if I can, break your neck.'[14] Once again, his hot temper harmed more than healed. James detested violence and violent speeches more with each passing year, and he might well have recalled the heartless (and certainly biased) words written about Henry VIII's move from Anne Boleyn to Jane Seymour: 'The King hath come out of hell and into heaven for the gentleness in this and the cursedness and unhappiness in the other.'[15] Though the ambassador who recorded these words several reigns before could not have known it, they would apply better to James's situation than to Henry's.

As James was by nature a peacemaker, so too – at this stage – was Villiers. The new man, astutely reading his sovereign's character (or being coached on it) made every effort to give the king what he wanted. Chief amongst this was love, not just between the two of them, but throughout the family. He thus cultivated Anna in ways that Somerset had not; rather than treating her with scorn as the forgotten and unimportant wife, he established a friendship, treating her with scrupulous deference and respect and uniting with her in an almost touching campaign to reform the king's manners – or to 'lug the sow's ears', as they called it in their joking notes to one another. To James, he provided that other valuable attribute: a genuine willingness to learn. This was no act, and, unlike Somerset, Villiers had a nascent talent for statecraft in both its public performance and its backroom machinations – to the king's delight, this handsome youth truly desired to learn at the feet of an experienced elder.

With both James and Anna, the new favourite affectionately termed himself 'your dog'. One note from Anna thus read,

My kind dog,

I have received your letter which is very welcome to me. You do very well in lugging the sow's ear and I thank you for it and would have you do so still upon condition that you continue a watchful dog to him and be always true to him. So, wishing you all happiness.

ANNA R[16]

Likely, the queen was relieved more than anything – firstly, that Somerset had fallen and, secondly, that the new favourite was a positive force in her family and in her husband's life. If there were to be three people in her marriage, it was, from her perspective, far better that the third be a man who owed his position to her and who treated her as his sovereign lady.

Soon enough, it was clear that Villiers, nicknamed 'Steenie' by James for his resemblance to the supposedly beautiful St Stephen, was high in favour – whilst Somerset still haunted the political stage by dint of his array of titles and positions. At court functions, the king's former and new lover were forced to stare one another down. Most awkwardly of all, the old favourite clung harder than ever to his *de facto* secretaryship, to the chagrin of the real Secretary of State, Sir Ralph Winwood. It was evident throughout the court that a reckoning would come, and both men and women were quick to attach themselves to the rising sun. Sensing trouble ahead, although probably unsure of the shocking form it would take, Somerset sought a general pardon for unspecified crimes he claimed might be alleged against him.

The queen, unfortunately, was again sorely troubled by health issues, which necessitated a return visit to Bath. Though only forty, she had begun what would be a steady decline. If it seems curious that she should have been so ill at so young an age, it should be remembered that she had experienced repeated and traumatic pregnancies and miscarriages, she had a fondness for sweets, and Théodore de Mayerne was her principal physician. Her illness, however, did not stop her from counselling James against granting Somerset his general pardon (which was certainly opposed by Lord Chancellor Ellesmere), nor did it prohibit the king from engaging on his summer progress, during the climax of which, at Farnham Castle, he consummated his new relationship. Our evidence for this comes from a letter Villiers wrote years later, in which he lovingly recalled their first night at Farnham, 'when the bed's head could not be found between the master and his dog'.[17]

One figure left out in the cold by the royal ménage-à-trois was Prince Charles, whose proposed marriage still proved a hot topic throughout 1615 (with Anna pivoting towards France, and James still inclined to Spain). Indeed, the question of his 'Spanish match', later to loom so large, reached its first state of limbo when, in May, the Spaniards' demands were issued: any children of Charles and any Spanish Infanta must be baptised Catholics; their religious instruction was to be overseen by their mother; if they remained Catholics, there was to be no prejudice to their succession rights; any Spanish Queen of England was to worship publicly in a Catholic chapel with Catholic servants; and the penal laws against English Catholics would have to be lifted. Unsurprisingly, the negotiations simply dragged on.

At this stage, Charles was keen to emulate his strictly Protestant late brother, not just in matters of religion but, importantly, in his hatred of their father's favourites. Thus, the young prince misbehaved, stealing Villiers' ring and earning James's rebuke. In May, the prince also deliberately diverted a stream of water from a fountain at Greenwich, soaking the new favourite; for this, he received a cuff round the ear from his father. The young Charles, however, was a born follower, at the mercy of stronger personalities. Villiers recognised this and set out to become the lad's new mentor, friend, and surrogate brother-figure. In time, he would prove supremely successful; Charles would abandon his pretence of playing Henry and simply substitute his heroic lost brother with the golden-haired, immaculately dressed favourite.

Not so easy to convince was the wider public. As James was

disinclined to hide his relationships, they had become common currency, to be bandied about by scandalmongers at home and abroad. A serious attack came in the form of a text titled *Corona Regia*, falsely attributed to Isaac Casaubon and printed at Louvain. This saucy pamphlet pulled no punches. It mercilessly attacked James's character (in terms of his scholarly pursuits, his supposedly effeminate pacifism, and his flexible sexuality) and his court, which was reviled as a place in which men would rather dress up to the nines than make ready to butcher Catholics. The king, moreover, was comically hideous outwardly as well as inwardly: his 'body indeed [did] depart from the rules of nature' and he advanced 'the prettiest little boys'. Worse, James sought to hide under a 'veil of piety . . . [to cover up] every manner of vice'.[18] Those vices were not limited to the supposedly misshapen king feeding his 'eyes with drunken delight at banquets' but included the arousal of 'lust by the forwardness of your words, to pinch cheeks, slobber kisses, and, as it were, to burst forth in flame from this smoke, a flame you may extinguish in private'. Whilst Queen Elizabeth's body, even in old age, was frequently represented as an object of veneration, James's, by contrast, became an object of ridicule. Strong efforts were made to track down the author of the pamphlet, and Anna, always eager to prove her political worth and to defend Stuart honour, involved herself, urging the Dutch ambassador to suppress the text and punish a professor at Louvain for his part in its publication. As James was an utterly unselfconscious man, confident – too confident – in his status and uncaring of what people thought of him (provided they did not physically threaten him), her intervention was valuable.

If *Corona Regia* lampooned what it claimed was a rotten court full of favourites advanced for their sex appeal rather than their moral rectitude, its salacious gossip appeared to be on the point of vindication. A scandal was about to erupt which would make the virulent rumours more believable. For all he had clung on doggedly to the vestiges of his former glory, Somerset was about to be cast out of court as well as cast down in fortune. The skeleton of the unhappy Sir Thomas Overbury was ready to claw its way out of the closet.

*

Sir Ralph Winwood had a justifiable grudge against Somerset, whom he knew to be holding on to diplomatic packets which were, by rights, the business of the Secretary of State. He was thus delighted when news arrived from the continent that an apothecary's boy – later named as William Reeve, but, curiously, never sought out for questioning by the English government – had made a frank and startling confession. The lad had, he supposedly claimed, been servant to the respected Dr Paul Lobell, who had attended Overbury in the Tower. In that capacity, he had administered a poisonous clyster (enema) to the unfortunate patient. Lobell's instructions had, apparently, been received from the Countess of Somerset.

Winwood immediately turned detective. Throughout the late summer, he undertook a meticulous investigation, intent not only on destroying Lady Somerset but her husband too. The sensational news could hardly be kept under wraps; the questioning of Gervase Helwys, Lieutenant of the Tower, buried even the news of the sad death of Arbella Stuart within its walls. Helwys, a political stooge over-promoted by the late Northampton, sang like a canary – although his revelations were not about Lobell. He had, he claimed, discovered that Overbury's own manservant, Richard Weston, had been 'intending to poison Overbury, [which] so terrified him that he had [Weston] deceive those who sent the poisons, by pretending to administer them, but not doing so. At length Overbury being ill, Weston confessed that the apothecary's servant was corrupted to poison him with a glister [clyster].' Helwys further claimed to know 'none but Weston and Mrs Turner who were actors' in the murder plot.[19]

Mrs Anne Turner was a friend of Lady Somerset, in addition to being a wealthy widow, a reputed brothel keeper, the mistress of Sir Arthur Mainwaring (a carver to the late Prince Henry), and the inventor of a means of dying ruffs a fashionable golden yellow. Upon her arrest, Mrs Turner confessed that the glamorous young countess had expressed a desire to see Overbury die and promised to reward any who helped him on his way. Accordingly, she, Mrs

Turner, had procured poison from a Dr Franklin, and the countess had tried by various means to deliver poisoned tarts to Weston, that he might pass them on to Overbury. The unfortunate victim, if all these stories were true, was thus being poisoned from all sides: with the wealthy countess having given the word, it was off to the races for every would-be assassin in London. Here was an explanation for Overbury's last days and hours and the appalling condition of his corpse. The unfortunate Helwys (who had probably done nothing more than try to keep Overbury alive without offending those powerful figures who wished him dead), Mrs Turner, Dr Franklin, and Richard Weston were rapidly tried and executed.

But what, people wanted to know, would happen to the countess and her husband, who had apparently engineered the murder? And, more importantly, what did King James know of all that had been happening? It suddenly looked exceedingly suspicious that the sovereign had imprisoned the victim for the minor infraction of refusing to be posted abroad. James himself was aware of how peculiar it all looked. So was Somerset, who, along with his wife, was arraigned for trial. Stories emerged of the last meeting between the king and his fallen lover, the most sensationalist attributed to Sir Anthony Weldon. In his account, James 'hung about [Somerset's] neck, slabbering his cheeks, saying, "For God's sake, when shall I see thee again? On my soul, I shall neither eat nor sleep until you come again!"' In this version, the king gulled the young earl into believing he was protected before showing his true colours and announcing, 'I shall never see his face again.'[20] This was an attempt to portray James as a dissembler, and its veracity is doubtful.

Whatever the nature of the last parting between the pair, the Christmas period of 1615–16 was of as much anxiety to the king and his family as it was of prurient delight to the masses: here was a scandal which surpassed any that had come before, and which affirmed all the criticism to which the Jacobean court had been subjected. It was imperative that the royal family should be seen to publicly distance themselves from the infamous couple, and their method was typically ostentatious. On 1 January 1616, Ben Jonson staged *The Golden Age Restored*, which celebrated the downfall of the Somersets and the restoration of order at court; on Twelfth Night, James ordered it performed again. For his efforts, Jonson would soon receive a royal pension of 100 marks (an English mark being two-thirds of a pound sterling). The king was intent on presenting a revitalised court and was aided by Villiers, who received the plum position of Master of the Horse, followed in April by membership of the Order of the Garter. When the Somersets came to trial in May 1616, rumours flew that the former favourite refused to appear or to plead; that he had threatened the king with revelations irreparably damaging to the Crown; that, when he did appear, it was only with armed men surrounding him, ready to muzzle him if he misspoke.

In the event, the trial went smoothly, and the verdict was a fore-gone conclusion. The countess, who was by now pregnant, made a full confession and was found guilty, with Lord Ellesmere passing the death sentence. She was probably telling the truth. The next day, Somerset pled not guilty but received the same verdict and sentence. In all probability (at least at the time of the murder) he was unaware of his wife's scheme to bring about his old friend's death. As everyone expected, however, James commuted the sentences to life imprison-ment, with the countess being held under house arrest until she gave birth to her daughter, whom she called 'Anne' (likely hoping the queen's favour, given Anna's sympathy towards the couple when it became clear they would be found guilty). James's leniency infuri-ated the people of London, for whom the case had become a *cause célèbre*: it seemed that justice was meted out unflinchingly against the lower orders whilst courtly creatures were showered with royal mercy. A furious crowd caught sight of Anna's carriage after the trial and chased after it, only realising that it did not contain the wicked countess when it approached Whitehall. The mob were, arguably, justified in their belief that justice had not been done – furthermore, both Somerset and his countess would be freed from the Tower in 1622 and allowed to live under house arrest thereafter.

James, no doubt, breathed a sigh of relief on multiple counts. The disagreeable Somerset, who had given him such trouble since marrying his countess and being displaced by Villiers, was gone, and in the end had gone quietly, making no accusations (which, it should be stressed, would certainly have been false; the king was no poisoner). Most pleasing of all, however, was that whatever was being said or written about him – and he continued to care little for public opinion – he had finally achieved his domestic ideal: his affectionate wife was, for the first time, in open camaraderie with his exciting, attractive lover, and that lover was making strong efforts to win over his son. Genuinely happy, the king waxed nostalgic and grew misty-eyed. Having got what he wanted, his thoughts returned to the first time he had really been in love: in Scotland, with the long-dead Esmé Stuart. With these sentiments growing, he decided it was time to visit his home.

20

The Return of the King

What prevented James from making any immediate homecoming plans was, as usual, the question of financing them. Plans had begun for the return visit in February 1616, when orders had been issued north that the hunting of game should be halted to allow stocks to rebuild ahead of the king's arrival, and in May the Scottish parliament passed an Act approving the refurbishment of Holyroodhouse, Stirling Castle's palace, and Falkland, and clearing 'masterful beggars, counterfeit bards, and fools' from Edinburgh. However, preparations for the progress stagnated. There were swiftly found to be 'difficulties in raising a loan of £100,000 from [London's] Aldermen upon security of the royal jewels, and the like sum from the Farmers of the Customs'; the financing of the trip was thus at the root of its deferral.[1]

The problem was that James was still living wildly beyond his means. The price of elevating Villiers alone was a drain on his coffers – but it was one he would not avoid or delay. The sale of peerages, which began in earnest in the summer, did little to offset the costs incurred in September when, in the presence of James, Anna, and Charles, the favourite became Baron Whaddon, Viscount Villiers. Nor was expense spared in sending the old favourite Lord Hay to France to negotiate (unsuccessfully) a match between Prince Charles and the Princess Christina; Hay complained that French fashions had altered and that he must have a new wardrobe. Expensive, too, was the formal investiture of Prince Charles as Prince of Wales in November. Against a backdrop of poor finances, poor weather, and the prince's own ill health, this ceremony was a muted one. Although

James's attendance was critical, Anna – ill herself – stayed away, 'lest she should renew her grief for the late prince'.[2] This proved to be a wise decision. During the service, the Bishop of Ely flubbed his lines, solemnly commanding those present to 'pray for the Prince of Wales, Prince Henry'.

Charles was, by now, not only rapidly reconciling himself to Villiers, but displaying a willingness to join his mother in political agitation – even when their efforts flew in the face of the king's will. Recently, James's fury had been rekindled against a longstanding nuisance: Lord Chief Justice of the King's Bench, Sir Edward Coke. Yet Anna favoured the intelligent lawyer and had rewarded him with a diamond for his opposition to the Somersets. The problem was that Coke had long been a stalwart defender of the common law as an historic institution independent of royal interference: a position which could only raise the king's hackles. The conflict reached a head when James used the writ of *in commendam* to gift ecclesiastical property to Richard Neile, Bishop of Lincoln, despite Neile having no intention of performing ecclesiastical duties there. Coke's response was to activate the courts against the king, subsequently issuing a formal criticism of James's actions. In a fit of royal temper, James tore up the complaint in the presence of a delegation of judges, declaring, 'I well know the true and ancient Common Law to be the most favourable to kings of any law in the world, to which law I do advise you, my judges, to apply your studies.'[3] Coke was adamant and refused to back down. On advice from Sir Francis Bacon (who had been Coke's enemy and rival since Elizabeth's reign), James dismissed the lawyer-judge from his post and the Privy Council. Anna and Charles were well aware of the strength of public feeling in Coke's favour and campaigned, unsuccessfully, to have the king relent and elevate the fallen lawyer to the peerage.

Defeated, Anna's health declined further – a situation which kept her at Somerset House over Christmas and prevented her from attending another spectacular – and costly – court event: James's raising of Villiers to the earldom of Buckingham on 1 January. Accompanying this title was a miniature of the king, painted holding a heart in his open palm. The political implications were clear; the new earl was also appointed a place on the Privy Council. To defend the rapid elevation, James delivered a speech: 'I . . . am,' he said, 'neither a god nor an angel, but a man like any other. Therefore, I act like a man, and confess to loving those dear to me more than other men. You may be sure that I love the Earl of Buckingham . . . more than you who are here assembled . . . I wish . . . not to have it thought a defect, for Jesus Christ did the same . . . Christ had His John and I have my George.'[4] By this, he did not mean to imply that Christ and John the Apostle had been lovers, but rather to justify the emotional bond, which he posited as existing separately from the sexual imperative. James, certainly, would not have identified himself as 'bisexual', the term not then existing – but he would have recognised that he had attained a marital and extramarital settlement which allowed for the provision of heirs and obviated the desire to take mistresses. Further, he had found a scriptural basis for his love of men. In any case, the period was not troubled by discrete sexual identities nor liberated by fluid ones. Above all else, James recognised himself as king, and by making a comparison to Christ, he was probably not thinking of sex at all.

Like his wife, 'the man like any other' was becoming prey to advancing age and concomitant illness. The popular image of the disabled James with the twisted foot and halting gait was by now taking shape. Mayerne later reported that 'pains many years since have invaded first the right foot, which had an odd twist when walking, and from a wrong habit of steps [James's riders' gait] had a less right position than the other and grew weaker . . . Afterwards occurred various bruises from . . . frequent falls from horseback, from the rubbing graves and stirrups and other external causes which the King ingeniously discovered . . . in the year 1616, this weakness continued for more than four months with oedematous swelling of the whole skin of both feet.'[5]

In the new year, James was wasting no time. In contrast to Somerset's steady elevation, it was apparent that the new favourite enjoyed 'rather a flight than a growth'.[6]

In the early months of 1617, a potential solution to the king's financial woes seemed tangible. After years of being encouraged to do so by his family, James was finally willing to listen to the lofty assurances of Sir Walter Raleigh, who had languished in the Tower until 1616. Raleigh's contention was that a rich seam of gold lay under the ground, ripe for the taking, beside the Spanish-controlled Orinoco, and that he should lead an expedition to claim it. This seemed plausible. Gold from the Americas was keeping Spain wealthy, and England was keen on its share of the New World. In the latter part of 1616, the native Princess Pocahontas, with her husband John Rolfe, had been entertained to great acclaim at court during the festive period (where she watched Jonson's *The Vision of Delight*). Further, a native American youth had been converted to the English faith and christened 'Peter' at a ceremony attended by the Privy Council and members of the East India Company. Here was an opportunity for England to establish more lucrative American links than the Plymouth and Virginia Companies had managed.

James, however, made conditions. His relationship – and thus his country's relationship – with Spain was still warm, and he insisted that, if Raleigh were released to embark on his expedition, the old adventurer must not, on pain of death, threaten Anglo-Spanish relations. Delighted at the prospect of freedom and with all the confidence of his hey-day, Raleigh agreed. He was freed to begin preparations in March.

*

With this potential American windfall, James embarked on his Scottish progress. Early in 1617, Captain David Murray sailed from Scotland to London on the *Charles*, with instructions to gather appropriate furnishings with which to decorate the king's Scottish residences. Murray called also for the Scottish royal robes to be despatched south and inspected, to ensure that they were in fit condition for James's use (and, in the event, James inspected them himself).

The progress was scheduled to begin in March. Anna remained behind, and with good reason. Given the elevation of two of Henry

VIII's wives during his absences abroad, she was said to 'aim at the Regency if the King goes to Scotland'.[7] If she was disappointed at not being offered the job, she raised no grievance. In truth, the governance of England was a poisoned chalice. The Lord Chancellor, Thomas Egerton, 1st Viscount Brackley, died in the middle of the month and there was immediate backbiting over his replacement. In the event, it was not until the following year that Sir Francis Bacon was appointed; in the meantime, the question of who would govern as regent remained. James chose Bacon, who soon drew criticism – not least from Secretary Winwood, who remained in England – for holding court as a pseudo-king. Wisely, the queen kept out of the fray.

At any rate, Anna displayed no hard feelings at being passed over for the regency. Indeed, James dined with his wife at Somerset House, which was thereafter formally rechristened Denmark House, before setting off from Whitehall. His journey – a slow one – took him north via Theobalds, Lincoln, York, Durham, and Newcastle, through Bothall, and on to Alnwick, before returning to Scottish soil. With him were Villiers – now Buckingham – Lennox, Arundel, Southampton, and his old flame Montgomery. With what might be termed malice aforethought, the king had also brought a quiver of ecclesiastics, including Lancelot Andrewes, Bishop of Ely; James Montague, Bishop of Winchester; and Richard Neile, Bishop of Lincoln (lately behind the latest breach with Sir Edward Coke). His goal was obvious: he hoped to anglicise the Scottish Kirk, bolstering his case with arguments from his English clergy. The king had for years continued to support Scottish episcopacy (and he had gone as far as summoning the old firebrand Andrew Melvill south in 1606, only to imprison and then banish him in 1611); now was the chance to take direct action. His reasons were plain. His oft-quoted maxim, expressed in 1604, was 'no Bishop, no King' – he foresaw the reduction of one authority as pulling at a house of cards.

From Berwick, James went to the Earl of Home's seat at Dunglass, before moving on to the opulent Seton Palace. Here, the poet William Drummond of Hawthornden presented his laudatory *Forth*

Feasting, a Panegyric to the King's Most Excellent Majesty, in which the River Forth and its sprites awaken to the sounds of joy and acclamation attendant on the return of a sovereign (who had once promised to visit at least every three years).

James met that acclamation on his return to Edinburgh, where he was heralded as 'our true phoenix, the bright star of our northern firmament'; 'so loving a Prince – a King second to no other ... matchless in birth and royal descent but more in heroical and amazing virtues'.[8] The burgesses welcomed him, in scarlet velvet robes and gold chains and backed up by musket-bearing soldiery arrayed in white satin doublets. To the king's delight, Edinburgh then showed its pleasure at his return with a gift of 10,000 gold marks.

The joy with which he was received was, however, soon soured. At Holyroodhouse, James attended religious services in the manner to which he had become accustomed in England. Though obviously Protestant, the English Church retained the use of surplices and both organ and choral music. In keeping with the king's taste for ceremonial, one of Whitehall's organs had been shipped north for the visit and preparations had been made – but were cancelled – to install gilt statues in Holyroodhouse's Chapel Royal. Kirk ministers found this intolerable, particularly as the king evidently wished these colourful additions to be permanently introduced north of the border. As one observer wryly put it, 'The organs were come before, and after comes the mass!'[9] This was an exaggeration, but Presbyterians saw in these innovations a creeping Arminianism: that brand of reformed, scripturally based Protestantism which welcomed beautified churches and accepted free will and redemption rather than the hard Calvinist doctrine of predestination. To the established Kirk, it all looked a little too Catholic.

Probably wisely, James decamped to his old hunting grounds at Falkland, before going on a tour of his nation which took in Kinnaird, Dundee, and Dalkeith. Yet he needed to make the politico-religious goals of his visit clear. On returning to Edinburgh, he opened a session of the Scottish parliament, where he delivered a scathing rebuke to the people he had abandoned. He chided Scots for what he considered their barbarous ways (in failing to show him appropriate deference as their sovereign lord) and exhorted them to follow the English not, as they had been doing, in smoking and dressing ostentatiously, but in displaying obsequious respect for their betters. Though he worked with the Lords of the Articles to frame the agenda, pressure from Kirk ministers ensured that suspicion about royal motives reigned – and it was well-founded.

James's real objective was to persuade Scots to embrace the supremacy of their sovereign in spiritual affairs, and thus recognise that his innovations were good and proper. Gradual convergence with English practice had long been his policy, enacted skilfully through remote management of religious and parliamentary affairs. Nor did he wish to leave doubt as to his intentions; at St Andrews, he convened an ecclesiastical conference, the main purpose of which was to gauge reaction to what would become known as 'the Five Articles of Perth'. These insisted that Holy Communion should be received on bended knee; that Scotland should reintroduce religious holidays and festivals; that confirmation should be introduced and administered by bishops; and that private delivery of the sacraments by ministers was permissible when the recipients were gravely ill. When his Articles received a frosty reception, James agreed to refer them to the General Assembly. The following year, after an initial refusal and royal threats of wrath, a specially convened Assembly at Perth accepted them, although in practice individual parishes had considerable leeway. To his credit, James did not insist on rigorous enforcement, both in light of potential opposition and because he believed that the Kirk would, in time, incline naturally towards English practices. Instead, the Articles were ratified by the Scottish parliament in 1621, on a reputedly thundery day – and the cause of Presbyterianism was given a fillip which outlasted King James.

As was often the case on James's visits, his hosts were aware of his intellectual and academic bent – and not for no reason had James once remarked, on visiting the Bodleian Library at Oxford, 'Were I not a King, I would be a university man.' Thus, at Stirling, he took part in a Latin disputation organised by Henry Charteris, principal of

Edinburgh University (who was worried about the king's rumoured intention to suppress the institution in a bid to reduce Scotland's number of universities). At Linlithgow, he was treated to the sight and sound of the burgh's schoolmaster encased in a painted plaster lion – the 'King of Beasts' welcoming the 'King of Men'. He went on to Glasgow (where he was lauded as 'that great peacemaker . . . the man who . . . united two [of] the most warlike nations of the world') and the neighbouring abbey burgh of Paisley.[10] Towards the summer's end, he was in Dumfries, where he handed civic authorities a miniature piece of solid silver ordinance to mark the investiture of an annual 'wapinschaw' (or military inspection). Accompanied by a bevy of Scottish counsellors, he then proceeded south towards Carlisle, leaving his home kingdom behind him forever.

*

James left Carlisle at the start of August, taking in those north-western counties never visited by Queen Elizabeth and progressing through the Midlands. The route was engineered to allow the sovereign to be seen and appreciated – and it worked. In Lancashire, the king responded to a popular petition against local Puritan Justices (who had been forbidding entirely legal fun on the Sabbath) by penning his *Declaration of Sports*, which endorsed legal recreations and was reissued nationwide the following year (though, unfortunately, his commandment that the book be read in churches was rescinded as soon as it was realised that it inflamed tensions between local laity and clergy).

James was in a sporting mood himself. However, though he spent his journey southwards hunting, the usual sea of trouble – which had been neatly adumbrated by Chamberlain in July – awaited him: 'The weather wet and great floods . . . Quarrel between the Earl of Montgomery and Lord Walden, and between Winwood and the Lord Keeper [Bacon]. The merchants backward in the loan. Sir Walter Raleigh's fleet scattered by a storm . . . Quarrel between Sir John and Lady Packington.'[11]

Worrying, too, was the arrest of a Scotsman in the King's Guard named George Carr, who 'in his drink threatened to kill

Buckingham, as the cause of Somerset's fall'.[12] Yet even the cheering news that Princess Elizabeth, Electress Palatine, was again pregnant did little to counter what was the most persistent problem on the journey: money, or the lack of it. Soon, James was complaining that he received no answers from the treasurer or chancellor in response to his pleas for cash – despite making it clear that his 'household and hunt are in want'.[13]

The reasons for the delay in getting money into the king's pocket were made manifest by the Privy Council in September:

> His [James's] revenue was proved nearly equal to his ordinary expenditure ... but his great extraordinaries have interrupted all. The 100,000*l* to be borrowed of the farmers of customs, by 25,000*l* a year for payment of his debts, fails, because the sale of woods, from which the farmers were to be repaid, proves so injurious that they dare not pursue it. The 120,000*l* borrowed from the city and merchant strangers, which was to have gone towards the debts, will almost all be swallowed up in extraordinaries since [before] Christmas; viz., gifts on his departure, provision for the journey, enlarging of Theobalds Park, charges of ambassadors, and the accounts from Christmas to Lady Day [25 March]. The total debt is now 726,000*l*; 114,000*l* is provided for by sale of forests; for the rest, the ways are left to his Majesty's best judgement.[14]

James's best judgement was, in money matters, a dangerous thing on which to rely. The king had returned to England in reportedly good health, though it was noted that he had grown too corpulent to easily mount his horses. He was merely irritated by the reality of his financial situation and certainly had no intention of reining in his 'extraordinary' expenses.

In October, another of them arose. For some time, Buckingham had been lobbying to find a wife for his mentally ill brother, John, whom it was well known experienced bouts of insanity. James was only too happy to comply. The bride chosen was Frances, the daughter of Sir Edward Coke, and the groom was elevated to the viscountcy of Purbeck. Coke's wife, Lady Hatton (who retained the more exalted title from her first marriage), however, had no desire to see her daughter married to the favourite's unstable brother; she and Frances absconded, only to be tracked down by Coke himself. It was optimistically reported too that 'Lady Hatton has produced a contract between the Earl of Oxford and her daughter, which will spoil her husband's game'.[15] The perception was that Coke was inclined towards the match, as a means of repairing his poor relationship with the king (although he held back on confirming the size of the dowry). At least, in September, he was recalled to the council.

Most passionate of all in the matter, though, was Buckingham's mother, Mary Villiers, who intended to make the most of her glamorous son's relationship with James. Mary knew the value of marriage. She had, immediately following the 1606 death of George's father (by whom she had produced John, George, Kit, and Susan), gone on to marry the eighty-year-old Sir William Rayner (who died that same year) and finally, in 1616, she had wed one Thomas Compton, a son of Henry Compton, 1st Baron Compton. Despite the reluctance of the bride and her mother, the combined efforts of Mary, Sir Edward, Buckingham, and the king rendered the match unstoppable. It went ahead, with James, Anna, and Charles in attendance – and the bride reputedly crying throughout the ceremony. The general air of enforced festivity was only dulled when, in late October, Secretary Winwood – who had not only been fighting with Bacon, but secretly encouraging Raleigh to ignore James's orders and attack the Spanish in the New World – dropped dead of a fever. His physician had been Mayerne: a fact which led Chamberlain to laconically note that 'Mayerne [is] generally unfortunate with his patients'.[16]

The loss of Winwood was disastrous, not necessarily because he had been central to government (and in any case he had been assisted in his role by Sir Thomas Lake since 1616), but because it was soon realised that James – and his wife – were visibly fading. Although both were far younger than Queen Elizabeth had been, they were experiencing the kind of perennial losses that she had faced: experienced ministers were dropping like flies, only adding to the general headache of government. Naturally, Buckingham, who was understandably keen to involve his appointees and family members in every aspect of government, leapt on the post (with Bacon's support), the better to safeguard his own future. Bacon, who was always ambitious and all too aware of how the world and its governments worked, had by now insinuated himself into the earl's graces and become his confidential adviser.

By the end of 1617, James had acceded to Buckingham's request that his friend Sir Robert Naunton should be appointed secretary – a necessary move as the remaining secretary, Sir Thomas Lake, was in the midst of an unfolding and very public family scandal involving land disputes and slander, which would ultimately cost him his job. As payment, Buckingham was able to induce Naunton to name the favourite's brother Kit Villiers as his heir and to surrender £500 per annum into Buckingham's coffers. Corruption in the court was by now endemic, and with money so scarce everyone who was anyone fought for their share. Already, the favourite was being viewed as the chief beneficiary, surrounded not only by grasping family members but by men like Giles Mompesson, knighted in 1616 and, in 1617, hard at work exploiting positions Bacon and Buckingham had achieved for him as a commissioner overseeing licences for inns, and profiting from the sale of royal woodlands. It was said, sourly, that men could 'obtain no grace except they vow and beseech at the shrine of the great one [Buckingham]'.

The king appears to have been curiously detached from the changes in his government. Most likely is that he viewed the new man as just another tool; he knew Naunton to have been a loyal nephew, secretary, and protégé in intelligence work to William Ashby, resident English ambassador in Scotland back in the Armada days. James probably never questioned whether the new appointee would prove his instrument or Buckingham's; every secretary was *de facto* the king's servant. The following year, he would ennoble the Villiers clan still further by making its matriarch, Mary, the Countess of Buckingham in her own right. Her daughter Susan's husband, William Feilding, would be created Baron and Viscount Feilding in 1620 (and raised to the earldom of Denbigh in September 1622, making Susan a countess). Buckingham himself would rise from an earldom to a marquessate, in addition to being appointed Lord High Admiral. Most likely, James was looking for a quiet life – an understandable desire given his own health had taken another turn for the worse in the wake of the Scottish trip.

Touchingly, Anna and James appear to have been brought together by their illnesses (with the queen reported as having 'an ill habit of body') and mutual desire for quietness. With Prince Charles in tow, they escaped to the splendour of Theobalds to convalesce. As always, the country air worked wonders for the king, who was able to travel on to Newmarket. The queen, however, remained so unwell over Christmas that she had to cancel the planned *Masque of Ladies*. Even news of Princess Elizabeth's second-born son, Charles, provoked no recovery. Whilst the new baby's namesake, Prince Charles, staged Jonson's *Pleasure Reconciled to a Virtue* on Twelfth Night, Anna remained on her sickbed. Loath as she always was to miss out on family events, she might have drawn some comfort from the fact that the masque was reputed a dud: according to the wit Nathaniel Brent, 'The masque of Twelfth Night was so dull that people say the poet [Ben Jonson] should return to his old trade of brickmaking' – a dig he appears to have filched from *The Return from Parnassus*.[17]

James's quiet life, however, proved chimeric. The remnants of the Howard faction – led by Suffolk, who had not fallen from grace with his daughter – remained active against Buckingham. Their plan was to do what had been done to them: to displace the king's lover with a fresh-faced new model. The young man being pimped was a son of Admiral William Monson (who had successfully prevented Arbella Stuart escaping to the continent). Suffolk and his followers set about 'tricking and pranking' the poor lad up: they dressed him carefully and washed his face 'every day with posset curd' to ensure a bright and clear complexion. Their timing, however, was off. Buckingham had been able to supplant Somerset because Somerset had been drawing back from James's touch; no new man could hope to push out Buckingham when the favourite was still riding high in the king's affections. It was one of Buckingham's original benefactors, Pembroke, the Lord Chamberlain, who gloated to the unfortunate Monson that 'the King did not like of his forwardness and presenting himself continually about him'.[18] Although James later showed Monson some sympathy, refusing to have him sent abroad and denying that he was barred from his person, the king was not interested.

The sense of calm between the king and his wife was also soon put under strain. Throughout March, they were visiting regularly to commiserate over one another's pains, but April brought news that set them once again at odds. Raleigh, it seemed, had not only failed to find an endless supply of gold, but, worse, his crew had attacked a Spanish settlement. In fairness, this was not his fault. Whilst Raleigh was lying ill, his headstrong son, Wat, disobeyed orders from his father's second-in-command, Lawrence Keymis, and was killed whilst leading a raid on Santo Tomé de Guayana.

James had no sympathy. All he saw was that his express command had been broken by a man he had been right to distrust from the start. Moreover, Buckingham reported that with the connivance of their minion Sir John Bingley, Lord Treasurer Suffolk and his wife – when they were not busy freshening the complexion of handsome youths – had been using the treasury as their own private purse, thereby increasing the royal debt to £900,000. For this, Suffolk was dismissed from office in July and the following year he and his countess were tried in the Star Chamber and sentenced to imprisonment and a fine of £30,000 – which James reduced to £7,000, probably because he had more chance of receiving the smaller sum. In comparison to the debt, this and the loan of £20,000 the king secured (and would never repay) from the East India Company (in recompense for its opposition to the establishment of a Scottish rival company) was small beer.

Raleigh's failure to locate the promised bonanza could not have been more poorly timed. His actions, it was soon reported, were 'disliked by the King, and contrary to his instructions to preserve amity'.[19] The smooth Spanish ambassador, Gondomar, was quick to point out that James had pledged to treat Raleigh as a pirate if he offended the Spanish. For his part, the king was eager to listen; indeed, he offered to humour Gondomar and send Queen Elizabeth's old favourite to Spain for execution. This suggestion was sensibly refused by King Philip, who was as sensitive to public opinion as James was eager to see Raleigh killed by someone else's hand. James, in a bind, put on a politic display of exasperation at Gondomar's insistence on immediate execution, declaring that justice was not meted out arbitrarily in England. His solution was to dress the affair in legality; he appointed a special commission of Privy Councillors to investigate. It duly found that Raleigh deserved to have his old death sentence carried out.

Despite early thoughts of escaping his fate by fleeing to France, Raleigh accepted that he had gambled and lost, and returned to England to submit to the law. Probably to his own surprise, he found that he had become something of a national hero in his years of captivity – he was a living reminder of the glories of Elizabeth's reign, which was being overlaid with nostalgia and compared favourably to the extravagant excess of James's court.

Anna, more than her husband, was sensitive to this. Moreover, she recalled Raleigh's kindness in mixing up a cordial for the late Prince Henry, which had – albeit briefly – brought about a revival. As she had little credit with Gondomar, who continued to play on the king's anger, she wrote to Buckingham:

My kind dog,

If I have any power or credit with you, I earnestly pray you let me have a trial of it at this time, in dealing sincerely and earnestly with the King that Sir Walter Raleigh's life may not be called in question if you do it so, that your success answer my expectation, assure yourself that I will take it extraordinarily kindly at your hands.[20]

Buckingham, however, knew on which side his bread was buttered. Like James, he was pro-Spanish, and not just for the king's sake: he naturally expected to outlive both Anna and James, and thus had to keep an eye on the future. The prevailing direction of travel for Prince Charles's marriage – which remained the critical issue in British politics – was a Spanish match. Buckingham remained unwilling to risk offending Spain and ranging himself against Charles's future for the sake of either the queen or an old man left over from the previous reign.

On the matter of Raleigh's execution, James was implacable. Though the king lacked the sociopathic ruthlessness of Henry VIII (who could, without a hint of remorse or regret, cheerfully see former friends, wives, and long-standing servants cut off or cut up), he was merciful – historically too merciful – only to those with whom he had developed a personal affinity. For those whom he did not know or care to know, he could act with detached callousness.

Anna thus failed in what would be her final attempt at swaying royal policy. At the end of October 1618, Raleigh was led out to the scaffold in the Old Palace Yard at Westminster. There, he knelt, and the axe carried out the death sentence originally passed on him back in 1603. The remnants of the Elizabethan age went with him. As in 1612, however, death would not be content with just one member of the court.

21

Death and Taxes

The winter of 1618–19 was another with little cheer, thanks chiefly to the queen's absence. So ill was she that, when James visited Theobalds, she could not join him – medical advice was that she remain at Denmark House. In early January, a slight improvement – probably caused by the news of Princess Elizabeth being safely delivered of her third child, a daughter named Elisabeth – was reported. Whilst a general sense of gloom pervaded the court – not helped by the portentous sight of a fire burning down the Banqueting House – Anna recovered sufficiently to be moved to Hampton Court, which had long been one of her favourite residences, with her companion Elizabeth Stanley, Countess of Derby. This lift in her spirits, however, was brief. The pains which affected her limbs, resulting in swollen, ulcerated legs – likely caused by tuberculosis – returned treble-fold.

With Yuletide over, it became clear that she was desperately ill: and her condition was worsened rather than remedied by Mayerne's advice that she take an axe and begin wood-chopping in the privy gardens. James, Buckingham, and Charles visited her, the latter installing himself in apartments adjoining his mother's. Chamberlain, always close to court gossip, noted that 'danger is apprehended; the courtiers already plot for the leases of her lands, the keeping of Somerset [now Denmark] House, etc.'.[1]

Anna was aware of her condition. Summoning Sir Edward Coke, in whose legal knowledge she trusted, she made clear her intentions (although she did not go so far as to make a will). Above all, she expressed her anxiety 'that the Prince should grow up in virtue and honour'.[2] Not only does this reveal her embarrassment at her husband's lax attitude towards maintaining regal decorum, but it betrays an underlying current of concern regarding Buckingham's growing influence over the prince.

Mixed news continued to emanate from the palace: the queen was getting better; she might recover; she was ill again. Her brother, Christian IV, wrote expressing his concern, and Anna asked for James. However, this wish was not granted. The king had not forgotten his sick wife – he was in bed at Newmarket, about to experience the most serious illness of his own life. Her chief comfort remained her son, who did not leave her side. Charles loved his mother deeply, but his bid to get her to write a will, when it reached James's ears, resulted only in tawdry scenes of suspicion. Unfairly, the king believed his son was trying to line his own pockets at his dying mother's expense. When he heard of his father's suspicions, Charles was quick to explain himself to Buckingham, writing, 'My meaning was never to claim anything as of right, but to submit myself well in this as in all other things to the King's pleasure.'[3]

At the beginning of March, the doors to Anna's chambers were locked, with even the Countess of Derby turned out. Only the dying woman and a maid, Anna (likely Anna Rumler, the wife of the page Pierre Hugon, though sometimes claimed to be Anna Sophia Kaas, last seen departing Scotland in 1591) remained inside. The official 'good death' story, recounted by Chamberlain, held that, at 2 a.m. on the 2nd, Queen Anna realised that she might not survive the night. She thus activated a pre-arranged plan to have the Archbishop of Canterbury, the Bishop of London, and Prince Charles with her at the end. Tragically, she could know them only by sound and touch; she had gone blind. Charles asked whether she intended that he should take charge of her estates and discharge her debts, to which she murmured assent. At the behest of the clergymen, she agreed to die a good Protestant. To counter this narrative, the Catholics whom she had long courted produced their own accounts of her end, which involved secret visits by priests in the days before her death. Whatever the truth, she passed away in the company of her son, leaving everyone guessing – then and since – about her true faith. In all likelihood, she remained a liberal Lutheran with sneaking (and politically advantageous) Catholic sympathies: an unfocused, middle-ground position which pleased neither Catholics (who wanted a militant convert) nor Puritans and Calvinists (who wanted a rabid anti-papist).

When James learned of the news, he was grief-stricken. He returned to his pen, using a comet (believed to be harbingers of the death of famous personages) lately seen as his inspiration:

Thee to invite, the great God sent His star,
Whose friends and nearest kin good princes are,
Who, though they run the race of men and die,
Death serves but to refine their majesty.
So did my Queen from hence her Court remove
And left off earth to be enthroned above.
She's changed, not dead, for sure no good prince dies,
But, as the sun, sets, only for to rise.[4]

These are not words of lost passion but of sorrow at the loss of a woman – probably the only woman – the king had ever loved in a lasting, meaningful sense. If Anna had long since ceased to be a sexual object to him, she had become a person he respected and cared for deeply. Moreover, although biographers tend to identify her activities in later life – her masques and public performances – as separate from his, the truth is that these were often adjuncts of the king's policy. The queen, as outspoken as she often was, had been his defender, the protector of their family's reputation, and, as much as she could, the guardian and patroness of Stuart prestige despite her husband's (and his court's) lackadaisical sense of propriety. She had been family.

News of her death provoked a general appreciation of her role. Sir Gerard Herbert noted that 'the Queen is much lamented, having benefitted many and injured none; she died most willingly, and was more comely in death then [than] ever in life'.[5] What everyone wanted to know, though, was the fate of her estates. It was said that she 'postponed settling her affairs; she answered yea to a question whether the Prince should inherit all, after paying her debts and relieving her servants, but it is not thought the King will consent, her property in goods, jewels, &c. being worth 200,000*l*'. Sir Edward Harwood wrote that 'she verbally left all to the Prince, but the King thinks he himself ought to be heir, as nearest to her, and the Prince is willing to yield, if the wish comes only from his father'.[6] This was true. For all James mourned her, he wanted and needed every penny he could grasp.

For with Anna's death arose yet another cost; her funeral, the king decided, must be grander even than Queen Elizabeth's. Indeed, he demanded thrice the cost of the old queen's interment be expended on his wife's. The problem was that there was no money. Worse still, for eight days James was stricken with 'pain in his joints and nephritis with thick sand . . . [continuing with] fever, bilious diarrhoea . . . fainting, sighing, dread, incredible sadness, intermittent pulse'.[7] Kidney problems, which had plagued him for years, worsened, and his doctors went into action despite his protests. From 1619 onwards, he would be forced to undergo regular bleedings, via leeches attached to his haemorrhoids, and – less disgustingly – through blistering cups. He was more right than he knew when he complained, according to Mayerne, that physicians were useless, and that their treatments rested on 'conjectures, which were uncertain and therefore invalid'. His slow recovery sapped him of the energy and wit to gather cash, and so the queen's embalmed corpse remained uninterred. On being taken to Denmark House, the body was given round-the-clock attendance by her black-clad women. This was usual enough for a short period, but the macabre ritual stretched first into weeks and then into months, during which the playhouses were closed and all festivity in London banned.

It was April before James was able to 'sit up a short time, but he does little business, and packets a month old lie unopened'; and it was mid-May before the funeral could take place.[8] As was customary, the king did not attend. Thus, he did not witness the sight of what Chamberlain dismissively reported as a parade of nobles in black 'laggering all along', the ladies in twelve yards of broadcloth each and the countesses wearing sixteen.[9] The Countess of Arundel acted as chief mourner, having won out over Lady Nottingham. Beside her walked Lennox and the 2nd Marquess of Hamilton. Behind this group (who were themselves preceded by 280 female commoners and sundry servants) came Prince Charles, marching ahead of the hearse, which bore a wax effigy of the queen. Following the body was Anna's Master of Horse and numerous other nobles and clergymen. When the procession reached Westminster Abbey, the Earls of Pembroke, Oxford, and Arundel lifted the coffin and bore it inside, laying it to rest under a catafalque designed by Maximilian Colt. In the company of several of her lost children, the queen was laid to rest.

*

Following her burial, interest remained fixed on Anna's property. It soon emerged that she had left a casket of jewels worth £30,000, with the intention that they be sent to her daughter, Princess Elizabeth. However, the casket had disappeared. Investigations found that, at the end, she had been robbed by Pierre Hugon and one 'Dutch Anna'. This was almost certainly Hugon's wife, Anna Rumler, who was actually German. The pair were apprehended, whereupon Hugon claimed that he had been handed the casket – now also comprising Catholic devotional objects – by the late queen with instructions that he take it to France and use the jewels to found a monastery. This was likely bunkum – but it has certainly served to further muddy the waters of Anna's faith.

The playing up of Catholic hopes, which the queen had managed since her earliest days in Scotland, took on a new significance without her. In June, James reappeared in public, restored to health. Evidently, he had decided to put an official end to the extended period of mourning (and to signal his own recovery) by riding into London clad in pale blue satin and wearing a jaunty hat bearing blue and white feathers. This might well have been a nod to the arms of Christian IV, which featured three pale blue, crowned lions passant; however, it was a miscalculation. James's arrival coincided with the visit of twenty-four black-clad Frenchmen on an embassy from the Duke of Lorraine, who were shocked and embarrassed by the king's jolly weeds. This was an inauspicious start to his return to the political stage, and for his life without Anna.

For all James craved a peaceful life, three issues were about to collide in spectacular and unwelcome fashion. Europe was on the brink of a war precipitated by his daughter and son-in-law; Charles had to be married into the continent – preferably Spain – and swiftly; and James was in such desperate need of money that, if no dowry from a bride for his son could be found, he would have to go cap in hand to a new parliament. To a man who had just lost his wife and recovered from a painful and dangerous illness, these were daunting challenges. Unsurprisingly, he turned to his pen and to Buckingham: his *Meditation on the Lord's Prayer* (dedicated to the favourite) outlined his hopes for peace and – in his usual familial language – lamented English Puritanism as fathering sectarian division; but his attachment to Buckingham was more interesting. Now that Anna was gone, James's dependence grew into something deeper and more complex. The favourite became not just a lover with an anomalous place in the family, but both surrogate wife and son.

The problems centring on Elizabeth and Frederick were not of their making but rooted in the disputed sovereignty of Bohemia (a kingdom which today forms much of the Czech Republic). Bohemia was, like many European nations, comprised of conflicting faith groups, each of which sought either control of the state or the right to practise their religion. In 1617, the Catholic Holy Roman Emperor Matthias, who held the throne of Bohemia, argued for – and won – the right to make his cousin, Archduke Ferdinand of Styria, his successor as Bohemian king. His goal was to keep the country in Catholic Habsburg hands – and he cheerfully assured the Protestants in Bohemia of toleration to secure their agreement. Ferdinand was duly crowned in June 1617, to his cousin's delight. However, the reality of another Habsburg soon began to pall on his new subjects – and, in addition to throwing Imperial ministers from a window (and into a dungheap) in May 1618, the Bohemian Protestants began canvassing support from their coreligionists throughout Europe to rebel against Ferdinand and Matthias. Happy to respond were the Elector Palatine and his wife, who sent an army under Ernst von Mansfeld. In February, during Queen Anna's illness, James had been invited by the Spanish – who were close kin to the Imperial Habsburgs – to arbitrate. He was only too happy to do so; peaceful outcomes on his mind. Towards the end of 1618, the Synod of Dort began at Dordrecht, and British representatives were instructed to secure the Dutch Provinces and press, as ever, the case for Protestant unity as a prelude to a more universal religious peace. Gleeful at the chance of again showing his peacekeeping credentials, the king despatched Lord Hay, who had been elevated to the viscountcy of Doncaster, in February 1619. Doncaster, however, quickly appreciated the deteriorating continental situation and warned James to prepare for a crisis by allying himself resolutely with his daughter and son-in-law.

James vacillated. Frederick and Elizabeth's actions, however, soon forced him to take a stance. In March 1619, Emperor Matthias died, and Ferdinand II of Bohemia challenged his Protestant rebels more aggressively. In response, a confederation of the Bohemian Estates decided to depose him, offering the crown to Frederick in hopes that, when the inevitable Imperial response was received, he could and would mobilise his allies: the princely members of the Evangelical Union and, of course, King James. To his credit, Frederick did not immediately accept the Bohemian crown. Rather, he despatched an ambassador to England to beg his father-in-law's advice. James was horrified by the turn of events. Horror turned to fury, however, when he discovered that Frederick had not waited for his reply; probably with Elizabeth's encouragement, the Elector Palatine had accepted the crown on offer. Coldly, James told the ambassador that his daughter and son-in-law were on their own, for he would not 'embark them in an unjust and needless quarrel'.[10] This was to prove more hope than resolution.

Frederick and Elizabeth, the new rulers of Bohemia – or so they hoped – arrived in their capital of Prague to widespread Protestant joy. Together, the young couple tossed largesse in the form of newly minted coins struck with the words, 'God and the Estates gave me the crown'. When Elizabeth gave birth to a third son (later known to history as Prince Rupert of the Rhine), she had him dubbed Duke of Lusatia – a Bohemian territory.

James, of course, was aghast and horrified at what he considered his son-in-law's usurpation of someone else's throne. However, the English people did not share his view that Elizabeth and Frederick had embarked on a dangerous folly that might – and, in fact, would – result in one of the bloodiest wars in European history. Rather, many of the people of England perceived in the young couple everything they felt their king lacked: manliness, courage, and a warlike zeal for the Protestant faith. The King and Queen of Bohemia made hay for some time, enjoying their acclamation, but time soon enough proved James right.

Emperor Ferdinand II, furious that an upstart and his wife had taken his throne, began planning a multi-pronged attack on the pair. Frederick and Elizabeth's rapturous delight at their welcome soon turned to fear as Ferdinand's allies, Maximilian of Bavaria and the general Ambrogio Spinola, began mustering forces against them: the former intending to assault Bohemia, and the latter making ready to invade Frederick's home of the Lower Palatinate. Of more immediate consequence to James, the emperor also prevailed upon Philip III of Spain to despatch Gondomar back to England to muddy the waters. The ambassador arrived in March 1620, whereupon the king attempted another one of his jokes (quipping that the new arrival looked just like his old friend, the Count of Gondomar – but could not be because that fellow had abandoned him). Naturally, Gondomar's presence only complicated matters; his goal, shared by his master Philip III and Emperor Ferdinand, was to keep James's hopes of a Spanish match alive – without committing to one or settling a dowry – purely to prevent the king from letting England join the war against his daughter's enemies.

Gondomar was able to lift the king's spirits, but James was also cheered by domestic news. He had, by this time, become an old man. Outside the problems of international affairs, which were forced upon him, he took pleasure almost entirely in Buckingham and Prince Charles; in essence, he still sought a measure of harmony at home. Thus, when Buckingham's mother began promoting a marriage between her son and the fabulously wealthy Katherine Manners, the daughter (and heir) of the 6th Earl of Rutland, he was happy to consider it. This was a far cry from the passionate love match Somerset had made, and the king had no anxieties concerning his favourite taking a wife. Buckingham would be marrying for money – and, moreover, Katherine was a plain young woman who excited no jealousy. More importantly, she was also shrewd, tolerant, and discreet. The only obstacles were her Catholicism and her father's opposition. The first, which James had to make a politic display of cavilling over, was overcome by a show of conversion. It was the old countess who adroitly overcame the second. Lady Buckingham invited Katherine to supper with herself and her son. After illness forced the lady to spend the night, she found that her father had imperiously declared her scandalous and forbade her his house, insisting that the man who had kept her overnight wed her immediately. After a show of refusal – aimed at safeguarding these attacks on Katherine's honour – Buckingham, with the king's blessing, married her in May, without any particular sexual or emotional passion driving him.

To James, his family – which had been reduced to Buckingham and Charles – was simply expanded. He wrote to Katherine after the wedding, addressing her as his 'only sweet and dear child . . . and also his daughter' and expressing his desire that 'the lord of Heaven send you a sweet and bright wakening, all kind of comfort in your sanctified bed, and bless the fruits thereof, that I might have sweet bedchamber boys to play with me'.[11] The semi-incestuous overtones (mirrored in his letters to Buckingham, which labelled him both 'wife' and 'son') are difficult to dismiss, as is the prurient interest in what his lover and that lover's new wife might have been doing; however, James had by this time appropriated the role of doting, grandfatherly patriarch to all whom he drew to him – and it seems likely that his increasing frailty had by this time ended the sexual dimension of his relationship with his favourite.[12] Thereafter, and with increasingly pathetic dependence, the king relied on Buckingham's new wife as a kind of replacement for what Anna had become in her later years: a gentle lady (with creeping Catholic sympathies) with whom he could share domestic gossip.

Gentle chatter was, in fact, a welcome diversion from the packets of European news rapidly mounting up. Thanks to the range of supporters upon whom he could call, Emperor Ferdinand II was escalating the usurpation of Bohemia into a large-scale European war on multiple fronts. As soon as James heard about Spinola's intended infringements on the Palatinate, he was incensed. Although he had disapproved of what Frederick had done in taking someone else's crown, he considered any attack on the Palatinate to be just as bad. His response was, however, cautious; in mid-1620, he despatched a force of English volunteers to fight in defence of his daughter, son-in-law, and grandchildren's home. This was not a full commitment to English involvement in the war but, as James intended it to be, a warning.

As the battles continued throughout the autumn, the tide gradually turned against Elizabeth and Frederick. First, the Palatinate fell to Spinola, and thereafter Maximilian of Bavaria and his army rode into Bohemia. Frederick's forces were laid low at the battle of White Hill. He and Elizabeth were thus compelled to flee Prague with their children, having held it for just over a year, to seek refuge in The Hague. When the news reached London, libels were scattered about the streets condemning the king for his inertness. James, for his part, closeted himself at Newmarket, reportedly 'very sad and grieved' at Elizabeth's plight. Yet he would do nothing materially, despite the entreaties of Prince Charles; indeed, the French ambassador reported that 'the intelligence of this king hath diminished. His timidity increases day by day as old age carries him into apprehension, and vices diminish his intelligence.'[13] This was not fair and almost certainly sprang from a French attempt to explain away James's pro-Spanish proclivities. In reality, Elizabeth and Frederick had placed the king in an impossible situation, which demanded he either defend their rights for honour's sake and thereby lose the goodwill of the Holy Roman Emperor and the Spanish; retain Habsburg goodwill and give up his daughter's rights; attempt some *via media*; or hope that the situation would improve of its own accord (his favoured stance). What complicated matters and confused James's already overworn mind was Gondomar counselling non-intervention by offering the carrot of a Spanish match, whilst Elizabeth was busily writing to Buckingham to persuade him to go to war.

Due to the short nature of her husband's reign, Elizabeth was thereafter known as the 'Winter Queen': a sobriquet whose charm to modern ears is belied by the insult it implied against Frederick, no less than from the horror and violence of the events which gave rise to it. With what would become the Thirty Years War now in full swing, the Imperial conquest of Bohemia would not be the end of the affair.

Events on the continent presented James with a double-edged sword. He had been given an excuse – the potential need to fund a war – to induce a parliament to raise him subsidies via taxation; but he continued to distrust the institution. It was, to his mind, a nest of Puritanical agitators like the war-hungry character depicted with ass's ears he laughed at in a play in December. His mood therefore matched that of England, which witnessed a winter so extreme that the Thames froze over twice, and huge snow drifts piled up 'like rocks and mountains'.[14] Nevertheless, the writs were issued in November, and the disagreeable Commons were called to London on 16 January 1621. The king attended the opening himself, though, due to another bout of illness, he had to be carried in a chair, with observers – to whom he made a point of smiling and chatting – doubting that he would ever walk again. He would, but Daniel Mytens' portrait, which dates from around this time, certainly indicates that the king appeared physically spent.

James's man in parliament was Sir Francis Bacon, who had been acting as Buckingham's mentor. Unfortunately for all three men, the

Commons were in a truculent mood – likely because they felt that opportunities to air grievances, which had only intensified, had been thwarted by James's dissolution of the 1614 parliament and subsequent attempts to rule without recourse to the institution. Their primary complaint regarded monopolies – those patents which allowed favoured individuals to bleed the country dry in the name of personal enrichment – and both the men who brokered and those who held them. These had been a problem exciting parliaments well before James's reign. Corruption, indeed, had always been endemic in the political system. As has been the case throughout history, however, there are moments when tipping points are reached, and when recognition of, and opposition to, venality coalesce and cannot be ignored. This was such a moment.

Chosen to lead the Commons in their complaints was none other than Bacon's enemy, Sir Edward Coke. The esteemed judge and jurist was, despite his daughter's marriage to John Villiers, eager to make the most of his time in the spotlight. He immediately began a campaign against Buckingham's friend, the avaricious Sir Giles Mompesson, and Sir Francis Mitchell. These unfortunate chancers, who had been lining their pockets merrily at public – and royal – expense for years, were now threatened with arrest. Mitchell capitulated, having his sword broken over his head before his imprisonment. To avoid a similar fate, Mompesson fled to the continent.

This was, in a way, good news for James and Buckingham. Although the king had personally approved the patent that gave Mompesson the right to exploit the licensing of inns, the man's flight allowed James and his favourite to cast themselves as dupes of a scheming trickster. With crocodile tears, the king was able to feign shock at the actions of a character who had 'injured, molested, vexed . . . [and] oppressed' his people.[15]

Unfortunately, parliament was unsatisfied. Its members knew the king was desperate to raise taxes, and they decided to take maximum advantage. Their next target was Buckingham's half-brother, Sir Edward, who had been awarded a monopoly on the manufacture of gold and silver thread. In a panic, the favourite attempted to persuade James to dismiss parliament – a request he would not have granted. The king believed that he himself might calm the mood of the nation and its representatives via a personal address (this having been a tactic much resorted to by Queen Elizabeth).

James had intuited that the real target for opprobrium was his lover. Thus, in the House of Lords, he delivered an impassioned speech in favour of Buckingham, saying, 'I desire you not to look of [at] him as adorned with these honours as Marquess of Buckingham, Admiral of England, Master of my Horse, Gentleman of my Bedchamber, a Privy Councillor, and Knight of the Garter, but as he was when he came to me as poor George Villiers, and if he prove not himself a white crow, he shall be called a black crow.'[16]

In response, Buckingham knelt before the king – and the astonished lords – and announced his intention to be cleared of all charges of corruption or else embrace the odious reputation of a 'black crow'. To reinforce this piece of theatre, the favourite then expressed to both Houses his willingness to be investigated.

However, James's intervention had worked. Rather than pursuing Buckingham directly, parliament set its sights on a more accessible victim: Sir Francis Bacon. The intelligent lawyer immediately realised what was afoot and attempted to gain the favourite's support. Unfortunately, although Buckingham continued to feign friendship – he visited Bacon when he fell ill soon after – the truth was that he and James had decided to let parliament claim a scalp. As accusations of corruption mounted, Bacon found himself cut adrift politically and left prey to the feeding frenzy. Only when the Lords' final vote on his fate came did Buckingham make the token gesture of refusing to vote in favour of his guilt. His was a lone voice. Bacon was stripped of the chancellorship, fined £40,000, and locked in the Tower before being exiled to his estate at Gorhambury, his public career in ruins. His replacement as Lord Keeper, John Williams, Bishop of Lincoln, an ecclesiastic without the customary legal training, marked the first time the office had fallen into ecclesiastical hands since the reign of Mary I. Yet, with parliament assuaged, it voted in two subsidies amounting in total to £145,000 – small beer, in comparison to the royal debt and the cost of rearmament – before being adjourned. Its members' last word was that they would vote further subsidies if the Palatinate were not restored: a warning that the loudest were waxing warlike and expected their king to act accordingly if he wanted money. More to James's taste would be news out of Scotland, the parliament of which, thanks to bullying and fancy footwork, ratified his Five Articles of Perth and agreed to taxation.

Although he sympathised with Bacon, James was still caught in an unenviable situation. Given his daughter's struggles against the Imperial Habsburgs and their Spanish allies, he was rapidly losing hope of a Spanish match for Charles (and its Exchequer-saving dowry), despite Gondomar's continual entertaining of his hopes and the accession and seeming friendliness of the teenage Philip IV (whose father had died in Madrid during the course of the English parliament's anti-corruption frenzy). James was thus dependent on parliament for money. Yet he remained hopeful that some peaceful means could be found of rectifying continental affairs and solving domestic financial woes. Indeed, it was the financial situation which led him to accept Buckingham's suggestion – and a good suggestion it was – of appointing Lionel Cranfield as Lord High Treasurer in September. Cranfield, who had been Surveyor-General of the Customs, a Master of Requests, Keeper of the Great Wardrobe, and Master of the Court of Wards and Liveries, was a safe pair of hands. He would not, in the coming years, succeed in restoring James's finances to the black, but he would manage to keep the monarchy afloat.

In October, the diplomat John Digby returned to England following a failed attempt to broker a settlement with Ferdinand II. His views were not encouraging. In the presence of the king and Privy Council, he advised James to take up arms in support of Frederick and Elizabeth. The king agreed to both recall parliament and send £40,000 to enable his daughter and her husband to live in appropriate state in exile. However, war remained anathema. He had to concoct a solution which would result in parliament being bested, Elizabeth and Frederick receiving support, Charles receiving a Spanish bride, the royal coffers gaining a large dowry, and himself winning golden opinions as Solomon the peacemaker. This was audacious, at least – but could he pull it off?

22

But Where Are My Twa Bonnie Boys?

The king's plan was ingenious in its simplicity. Firstly, as Philip III of Spain had died reputedly apologising to his daughter with the words, 'I am sorry that I must die before I have married you [found you a husband],' James would redouble his efforts for a Spanish match.[1] With that accomplished, his son, in his capacity as brother-in-law to Philip IV, could persuade his new Habsburg relatives to reach an accord with Elizabeth and Frederick over the Palatinate. Nevertheless, he would warn parliament of the imminent danger of war, hoodwinking its members into voting grants of taxation even as the Spanish match – the solution to all – was progressing apace. The institution could, of course, be dissolved once the marriage was secured.

The problems, of course, were legion. It was unclear, despite Gondomar's warm assurances, whether Philip IV was really interested in matching his sister with Prince Charles (it was whispered that he had promised his father to make her an empress). Even if this marriage could be achieved, there was no evidence that the Habsburgs would take any notice of Charles's pleas on behalf of his sister and brother-in-law. Finally, and most pressingly, the success of the plan depended on MPs' gullibility.

This came to the test when parliament was recalled in November 1621. The king called on Sir John Digby to explain the need to place England on a war footing. Despite his pro-Spanish inclinations, Digby remained antagonistic towards the Imperial Habsburgs. In venting his anger before MPs, the diplomat took no prisoners in his denunciation of the craft and perfidy of Ferdinand II. The choice before the House, he said, was simple: abandon a much-loved daughter of England or vote in £900,000 in preparation for war.

Needless to say, this was a war James did not intend to fight. Indeed, he confided in Gondomar that the entire performance had been stage-managed: a means of directing the parliamentarians' anger away from the Spanish sovereign and towards the Holy Roman Emperor. The parliament, he assured his Spanish friend, would be dissolved if it grew too rambunctious – and, better yet, James would keep his hands clean by decamping to Newmarket with Buckingham and leaving the popular Prince Charles to manage the session.

James's plans seemed vindicated when secret letters were intercepted which indicated that relations between Philip IV and Ferdinand II were cooling. The king immediately sought to capitalise on this. With Buckingham's aid, he instructed the MP Sir George Goring to draw up a 'protestation' by which the House petitioned the king to pledge war if Philip did not cease his support for Ferdinand. By this means, he thought to widen the breach exposed by the letters between Spain and the Holy Roman Empire. The plan, however, backfired. In addition to being suspicious that Goring was one of Buckingham's agents, the MPs unleashed a fury against Spain and all things Spanish which James had neither intended nor foreseen. This resulted in a slew of anti-Catholic amendments to the proposal which had the unintended result of damaging Charles's Spanish marriage prospects.

The prince was woefully ill-equipped for dealing with this. To his fury, he watched as the Commons began openly discussing his marriage and demanding that he wed a Protestant. In Charles's caustic judgement, MPs were 'seditious fellows' for infringing on the *arcana imperii* – secret state matters.[2] James shared his son's attitude. His plan was already unravelling. His response was to accuse members of the Lower House of touching on 'matters far beyond their reach and capacity'.[3] In doing so, he was not being arbitrary or acting without precedent; Queen Elizabeth, in admittedly rare moments of conflict, had clamped down as regally on MPs who dared touch on the question of her marriage. However, times had changed.

347

The English parliament was – and had been – growing aware of its strength, at least in part because its constitutional role had been elevated by the Tudors, who had involved it in furthering both the Reformation and, under Henry VIII, the succession. Indeed, in the very first session of James's reign, its members had drafted but not published an *Apologie* which stated that they had delayed acting to their full potential under the old queen only out of respect for her age and sex. Now, they refused to be quieted. Freedom of speech, they declared, was their 'ancient and undoubted right'. James countered that it was not; they enjoyed it only by his liberality. Soon, the Commons were at work attempting to codify their perceived rights once and for all. An infuriated James personally ripped the record out of the Commons' *Journal*, before dissolving parliament. A greater conflict was thus averted, or postponed; indeed, the king's performances were, as so often, characterised by theatrical displays of superiority which fell short of causing constitutional crises. Yet his two subsidies would not be collected and subsequent attempts at gathering voluntary benevolences – even with browbeating applied – would yield little.

The manipulation of parliament had manifestly failed. James was not, however, put off from seeing through his remaining objectives.

*

James was disappointed, but he was not bereft. With part of his plan a dead letter, he threw himself into securing a Spanish match for Charles. By salvaging this, he might still provide Frederick and Elizabeth with peaceful, diplomatic support.

As 1622 dawned, things looked more hopeful. Digby, still of use given his history of diplomatic missions in Spain (which had been centred on marriage negotiations), was sent to Madrid. A request for Gondomar's recall then came from Philip IV. This James agreed to; although he prized the affable ambassador's company, he believed that Gondomar could be trusted to forward Charles's mooted marriage at home. At a farewell dinner at Greenwich, both king and prince gifted diamond rings (tokens and reminders of constancy) to Gondomar, asking that he come to England again. Afterwards, privately, Charles told the ambassador that he would be willing – indeed, he was eager – to travel to Spain personally, wearing a disguise. In this, he was acting independently; but he had learned the means of courtly wooing and hazarding dangers in person from the stories of his mother and father's first meeting. It was not his fault that the golden age of chivalry had passed.

Prince Charles was, by this time, a graceful, energetic, quiet, and well-educated young man: a far cry from the weak child who had looked likely to require his tongue being cut to aid his development. In behaviour, he resembled more his mother than his father. Like Anna, he was devoted not only to the arts but to the art of monarchy as an institution predicated on established codes of honour and elaborate behaviour. From James, however, he had learned a high estimation of his status and a deep distrust of anyone or anything which threatened it. Physically, he was lean and his eyes, like his father's, were heavy lidded, so that in appearance he resembled the king at his youthful peak.

Gondomar appeared flattered if somewhat bemused by Charles's confidence; but optimistically, he misinterpreted it as a sign that the prince was willing to convert to Catholicism (a Spanish demand that had been hampering proposed Spanish matches since Prince Henry's day). This it was not. In reality, Charles was simply in need of a bride. His high moral character naturally precluded brothels and he had shown no inclination towards anything other than strict heterosexuality (it is questionable whether he even knew the nature of the relationship between his father and Buckingham – probably, like most people, he preferred not to think of either parent having a sex life at all). He simply wanted a wife to establish his own status and propagate the dynasty. As a measure of his desire, when Digby assented to his demands for a portrait of his intended and sent one over, Charles professed himself to be in love with the Infanta Maria Anna – a pleasing enough lady, though possessed of the distinctive, prominent Habsburg jaw. Filling the prince's head, too, with glowing reports of her beauty was Buckingham's man in Spain, Endymion

Porter, who provocatively described her to Charles as 'a likely lady to make you happy'.[4]

To please James, Buckingham worked tirelessly in favour of the Spanish match. But so too had he been busy with his wife: in 1622, he and Katherine produced their first child, a girl, whom they named Mary (after Buckingham's mother). James immediately and affectionately nicknamed the infant Mal, and soon he was doting on her (as he would dote on the children that followed). It appeared, indeed, that a desire to provide parental affection was suddenly unloosed in the king: an affection which separate households had hitherto prevented him displaying with his own children. In his final years, this sentimentality became almost a mania, distracting and shielding him from the world's unpleasant realities.

Throughout 1622, however, his objective was to put the world to rights. James was bent on saving Europe from its descent into violence and conflict. In August he issued his *Directions Concerning Preachers* in a bid to quieten rabble-rousing Puritanical pulpits, whilst at the same time – in the interests of the Spanish match – he relaxed harsh treatment of lay Catholics (despite expulsion orders against crusading priests remaining in force). In a climate of European war, international marriage negotiation, and domestic agitation, James's balancing act – which had long comprised occasional blind eyes turned, spasmodic moves now against Catholics, now against Puritans, and gradual movement towards Calvinist conformity with increased ceremonial – was becoming harder to maintain.

Peace and balance were simply not popular. Soon enough, an anonymously authored seditious manuscript, titled *Tom Tell Troth*, appeared in London. Supposedly, it represented the views of the people, and it complained that 'they wish Queen Elizabeth were alive again, who (they say) would never have suffered the enemies of their religion to have unbalanced Christendom as they have done within these few years'.[5] The idea being promulgated was that James was less of a man – and less of a monarch – than his female predecessor had been. Erased from history was the old queen's distaste for war and the fact that she had had to be dragged into it against her will. Blamed were both James and his relationship with Buckingham; his whole history of male lovers, indeed, was condemned: '[In his bedchamber] he may kiss his minions without shame & make his grooms his companions without danger . . . because they are acquainted with his secret sins.'[6] The homophobia, which equated homosexuality with pacificism, increased still further elsewhere. The French Count of Tillières implied in his despatches that James's affection for Mal, Buckingham's daughter, and for one of the favourite's nieces, made him effectively a child molester, it being then supposed that one 'vice' – physical relations between men – was of a piece with others.

None of this vitriol – the latter of which was as absurd as it was disgustingly prejudiced – mattered to the king in his quest for peace. Seeking out like-minded leaders amongst the continental fraternity – most of whom had their own dogs in the fight – he landed upon Pope Gregory XV, whom he addressed as the 'Holy Father', and to whom he wrote, 'Your Holiness will perhaps marvel that we, differing from you in point of religion, should now first salute you with letters. Howbeit, such is the trouble of our minds for these calamitous discords and bloodsheds, which for these years bypast have so miserably rent the Christian world; and so our great care and daily solicitude [is] to stop the course of these growing evils . . . we break this silence [i.e., his previous lack of direct communication with Gregory] to move your Holiness . . . that you would be pleased, together with us, to put your hand to so pious a work . . .'[7]

James had not lost his diplomatic flair. The sad reality was, however, that neither he nor the Pope – nor their combined efforts – could do anything to stop the war. Somewhat like the much later outbreak of the First World War, too many vested interests and complex networks of treaties and alliances were involved; and, like the later Edward VII – another peace-making, hedonistic sovereign who ultimately failed to ensure lasting tranquillity – James was unable to stop forces already in motion.

Very much in motion were Prince Charles and Buckingham. By 1623, the pair had elected to make good on the prince's desire to travel into Spain and thereby bring to fruition James's plan of marriage. The motivation to make the trip was not born in a vacuum. Rather, Endymion Porter – after an eventful trip – returned safely to England with news that his mission to Madrid had been promising. Philip IV, he claimed, seemed willing to match his sister with Charles and, better still, he had shown himself amenable to brokering an accord between Frederick and Elizabeth and Ferdinand II. Gondomar, too, wrote Buckingham a bawdy letter claiming that 'the decision [over the Spanish match] has already been made . . . the Prince of Wales should mount Spain'.[8] It was thus Buckingham who brought before the king the proposal that he and Charles should go to Spain to fetch the bride, sweetening it with the idea that the pair should travel with Endymion Porter and Sir Francis Cottington, who had served as an envoy at the Spanish court. James at first cavilled, out of a terror of losing Buckingham and the son he had taken, in the infantilising language that had become his norm, to calling 'Baby Charles'.

Buckingham wished the nature of the trip kept from the pair of suggested travelling partners until the point of departure, but an anxious James revealed all to Cottington. The envoy was horrified. On being summoned to James and Buckingham's presence, he pointed out that not only was such a venture hazardous, but it was a minefield of diplomatic dangers. Once Charles was effectively in Spanish hands, the English advantage would be lost; the prince might become a hostage until James agreed to whatever demands Philip IV and his chief minister, the devious Gaspar de Guzmán, Count-Duke of Olivares, insisted upon.

Buckingham was furious, and he directed his anger at Cottington, whom he claimed had only been suggested as an escort because he had some knowledge of the condition of the roads. At this James intervened, trying to take the unfortunate Cottington's part. Yet, despite the king's now-heightened worries, Buckingham roundly insisted that the trip be approved. James played for time again, before pouring his heart out in writing to his favourite, complaining that 'I do nothing but weep and mourn . . . and the tears [are] trickling down my cheeks . . . [so] that I can scarcely see to write'.[9]

These tears cut no ice with Buckingham or Charles. Not even the offer of a dukedom, which James made before the trip (and which Buckingham refused, lest it should further excite his enemies) was enough to sway the favourite and the prince from their plans. In the end, they had their way, and their lachrymose 'old Dad' relented.

The trip – on which Buckingham and Charles were to travel incognito, wearing false beards and calling themselves, implausibly, Jack and Tom Smith – was launched on Monday 17 February 1623. Leaving Theobalds, the prince and favourite travelled to Buckingham's New Hall with another escort, Sir Richard Graham, where they hosted a dinner. The following morning, they donned their disguises and rode for Gravesend, where they crossed the Thames *en route* to Dover. Unfortunately, their attempts at subterfuge appeared doomed from the start. The wherryman who rowed them across the water grew alarmed on being paid in gold, and reported the two suspicious characters to the local authorities. An immediate alert was raised. This caught up with them at Canterbury, where the mayor halted and attempted to arrest them – a farcical scene made more so when Buckingham was forced to yank off his false beard, reveal his true identity, and claim that in his capacity as Lord Admiral he was on a secret mission to inspect the fleet. Cowed, the mayor let the implausible party ride on. Undermining their game still further, the porter charged with conveying their coffers of luggage separately to Dover also guessed the pair's true identities; Buckingham had to pay him to keep his mouth shut.

At last, however, they reached the port, where Cottington and Endymion Porter (who had not officially been told of the plot) awaited them. Together, the group crossed the Channel to Boulogne. The plan thereafter was to travel through France via Paris. The danger of recognition, though, remained strong; indeed, as fate would have it, a party of German travellers was also on the road. These men had not only visited England but had seen Buckingham and Charles at Newmarket, and they were quick to make their obeisance. This time, Sir Richard Graham took the initiative, denying the men's identities and pointing out how unlikely it was that the Lord Admiral of

England and the Prince of Wales should be wandering the road to Paris. This worked.

In Paris itself, lodgings had been arranged on the Rue St Jacques for the 'brothers' Tom and Jack. When the party arrived, however, they found a treacly letter from James, sent by a speedier English messenger:

> My Sweet Boys and dear venturous knights, worthy to be put in a new romanso . . . alas, I think it not possible that you can be many hours undiscovered, for your parting was so blown abroad that day ye came to Dover . . . I sent Doncaster to the French king . . . to acquaint him with my son's passing, unknown, through his country; and this I have done for fear that, upon the first rumour of your passing, he should take a pretext to stop you; and therefore, Baby Charles, ye shall do well how soon ye come to Spain [i.e., James hoped to both speed up and make safer their passage by his actions] . . . Your poor old Dad is lamer than ever he was and writes all this out of his naked bed [i.e., he was too desolate to get up and be dressed]. God Almighty bless you both, my sweet boys, and send you a safe, happy return.[10]

The 'dear venturous knights' were not inclined to listen to this good advice. Rather, they decided to retain their disguises, tour the ancient capital of France, and enjoy its refined and sophisticated sights. As the French king held court in the same style as Scottish sovereigns – that is, allowing the public to see how he lived at close hand – they were even able to glimpse Louis XIII relaxing in the Tuileries and watch his sister Henriette Marie dance (though the young lady drew no comment from Charles at the time). Later, colourful, romanticised, and unlikely stories would emerge concerning Buckingham's supposedly taking the opportunity, disguised in a wig, to seduce Louis's wife, Queen Anne (whose beauty Charles did note). These were almost certainly nonsense, but they neatly display the kind of scurrility which was to dog the favourite.

Thereafter, the adventurous pair rode hard through difficult, icy countryside, intent on evading suspicious local notables. Before they could pass the Pyrenees, they crossed paths with Sir John Digby's steward, Gresley, who was making the opposite journey with despatches from Spain. Boldly, Buckingham took these and read them, only to find that, whilst most were ciphered, the gist seemed to be that the Spanish were seeking to back out of the match by raising the necessity of a papal dispensation for their Infanta to wed a heretic. Sensing how this news might affect James, the Lord Admiral elected to ask Gresley to retrace his steps as their guide (an offer he could hardly refuse). The remaining journey thus proved easier. From Irun, they wrote to James of their safe arrival in Spain, signing themselves your 'obedient son and servant' and 'your humble slave and dog, Steenie'. Gresley was sent back towards England with this letter – and without his original despatches.

If the steward had been shocked at meeting the Prince of Wales and Lord Admiral on the road, it was nothing compared to the reaction of Digby himself. The ambassador was, frankly, furious at this unannounced and unexpected arrival, which threatened to render moot all his careful diplomatic work. He managed, however, to hide both his astonishment and his anger. In the face of Buckingham's demands that Philip IV be immediately alerted to Charles's arrival, Digby elected to write to Gondomar saying only that Buckingham had turned up. When Gondomar arrived at the English embassy the next day, though, knowledge of the prince's presence had already reached him by other means; he had been able to prepare an appropriately warm and deferential welcome.

This was just as well. Gondomar was in a state of panic. Hastily, he wrote to Olivares, and the chief minister took the reins, meeting privately with Buckingham and communicating via an interpreter, Sir Walter Aston (a permanent resident of the embassy). This resulted in Buckingham conferring privately with the seventeen-year-old Philip IV, and the meeting passed off smoothly. Gondomar was invited to play a lead role in negotiating the marriage, and Charles was to be allowed a brief glimpse of his intended – from a distance, through a crack in a curtain hung on his coach when the Infanta was driven by. This was a political rebuke as much as it was an example of Spanish royal reserve. Charles's actions were considered impetuous, rash, and not how things were done in the etiquette-driven court of Spain. Now that he had arrived, he was obliged to live as Spanish royalty did – a life of heightened decorum.

It was enough. Charles professed himself in love. His next step was to meet Philip IV, which he did in another venture (in which the Spanish king passed through the streets in disguise and leapt into Buckingham's coach, which was then driven to the Prado promenade, where Charles was waiting). Diplomatic conversation passed between them (with Endymion Porter this time translating), but nothing was settled regarding the marriage. Nevertheless, Buckingham believed that it was a good sign; ambassadors such as Digby, he said, were to be 'condemned' for emphasising the difficulties of the negotiations. He and Charles, he thought, had cut the Gordian knot.

There followed lavish public displays and, in March, a cere- monial entry into Madrid, designed to amaze the English guests with the splendour and riches of Spain. What was to be kept from Buckingham and Charles, however, was that this had necessitated a lifting of a general ban on Spanish court festivities, which had been in place to try to remedy Spain's parlous finances. Rich, too, were the apartments in the Royal Alcázar of Madrid, in which the prince was to spend his time.

James, back in England, was relieved beyond measure at his son and lover's safe arrival in Spain. It was even rumoured that, in a fit of joy, he was to make 'Baby' Charles appear more illustrious by arbi- trarily naming him 'King of Scotland or Ireland'.[11] Certainly, in a letter to King Philip, James arbitrarily titled his son 'Sworn King of Scotland', with recourse to the law. Whilst the young gallants were being hosted and toasted in Madrid, an increasingly lonely James found solace in condoling with Katherine, Countess of Buckingham, over the absence of their mutual wife whilst dandling little Mal on his lap. Although he attempted to take his mind off the absentees by visiting Cambridge in March, the play performed, *Loyola*, did not appreciably improve his spirits or health. Instead, he sought comfort in penning constant, touching letters, in an attempt to reconstruct the presence of his absent addressees: 'My Sweet Boys, I write this now, my seventh letter . . . I have sent you, my Baby, two of your chaplains . . . I send you also the jewels as I promised . . . As for thee, my sweet gossip, I send thee a fair table diamond . . . for wearing in thy hat or where thou pleases . . . thus you see how, as long as I want the comfort of my sweet boys' conversation, I am forced, yea, and delight, to converse with them by long letters.'[12]

Rather sweetly, he also sent his son a mirror, with instructions that he should present it to the Infanta along with a claim that it was enchanted, and that when she looked into it, she should see 'the fairest lady that either her brother or your father's dominions can afford'. In return, the king received gratifying letters from Buckingham, in which the favourite expressed his hopes that James would soon be 'marching on your well-shaped legs again'.[13] One romantically expressed a desire to 'kiss your dirty hands' – an unsubtle reminder of their bonding sessions at the hunt, when James would claim first blood. In another, the favourite saucily promised his royal master that 'once I get hold of your bedpost again, never [will I] quit it'.

What neither James nor his two boys realised was that their combined efforts at wooing were to no avail. Philip IV, who was busily entertaining the so-called 'King of Scotland', had no intention of allowing the marriage to go ahead. Certainly, he had written to the Pope for a dispensation – but so too had he sent a secret message asking the Pontiff not to grant it. His objection was on religious grounds. When Charles had arrived, Philip – probably fairly – believed, as Gondomar had, that this was tacit admittance that the prince would convert. The chaplains (Mawe and Wren) James had despatched to Spain, though, had been instructed to stretch the Anglican manner of worship as far as they might without conceding to papistry – with a view, as always, to stressing Christian continuities. With the realisation that the prince was to remain a heretic, neither Philip nor the prospective bride would countenance the match and it was, in effect, a dead letter. But this could not be admitted openly. The truth was that only the Spanish government knew the extent of the country's financial difficulties – difficulties which meant that it could not afford war with England, either over the Palatinate or over offence caused by outright refusal of the marriage.

Complicating matters, the papal dispensation had already been sent to Spain before Philip's secret message arrived at the Vatican. This, however, did nothing to encourage the match, filled as it was with impossible requirements. In addition to existing Spanish demands, the Pope insisted that the Infanta, on becoming Queen of England, be allowed not only a strictly Spanish and Catholic household, but that she bring to her new kingdom a bishop and twenty-four priests, who were to be exempt from English law. Further, the Catholic queen's chapel was to be open to any English worshippers who inclined towards the Roman religion. Addended to these exactions – already enough to make Englishmen balk – were secret clauses, which required James to enshrine perpetual toleration of his Catholic subjects' religion; to permit them to worship as they wished in their own homes; to refrain from passing any punitive laws against them; to force his parliament to repeal any such existing laws; and to refuse to give Royal Assent to any measures that parliament might attempt against them in the future.

This should have been enough to allow Philip to cancel the proposed match without appearing to be the cause of its failure. The stumbling block was Charles, who believed himself in love with the Infanta (despite having only caught rare glimpses of her) yet remained constant in the English reformed faith. James, too, remained staunchly in favour of the match; indeed, he had broken off diplomatic contact with Ferdinand II, and thus all the eggs he hoped would hatch into European doves of peace were now in this Spanish basket. Even Katherine became involved, jokingly sending Buckingham 'spy glasses' with a note suggesting that he and Charles use them to get a closer look at the Infanta to speed the marriage. It was to no avail. Even when the prince was permitted to kiss his putative bride's hand, she coldly stared into the distance, appearing unmoved by the interpreter's version of Charles's affectionate words.

In April, Philip increased his efforts to back out of the match. He formed a commission of divines to provide what he hoped were intolerable conditions he might fairly insist upon as insurance that James would honour both the Spanish and papal contractual demands. The theologians first interviewed Charles in one of Philip's chambers but found him resolute in his faith. On realising that they aimed at conversion, Buckingham threw his hat to the floor and stomped on it. An impasse had been reached already. Yet still the prince refused to relinquish his proposed marriage. Indeed, in an attempt to win the Infanta's support and banish the gathering theological clouds, he and Porter scaled a wall and invaded her private orchard, only for the lady to scream in terror and flee indoors. Charles and Porter, their mission having failed, were thrown out.

This bizarre state of affairs stretched on towards the summer of 1623 – and the time it was taking ought to have alerted everyone to its futility. The English royal family was in danger of becoming a laughing stock; indeed, in July, Duke Christian of Brunswick-Lüneburg (a son of Anna's sister Elizabeth) turned the air blue with a diatribe against James's inaction over the Palatinate crisis, decrying his uncle as 'the old pants shitter, the old English bed-wetter – because of his stupidity, [he] is the greatest ass in the world!' Injurious words closer to home were more dangerous – and they were getting out of hand, leading to a proclamation against seditious printing.

At home, too, the king was still lonely. To cheer himself up, he insisted on conferring the dukedom Buckingham had earlier refused, sending the papers to Madrid. James left no doubt as to his reasons for the elevation: Buckingham was informed in an accompanying letter that 'his Majesty is most constant, and in some degrees more enflamed in his affections to your Grace than formerly'.[14] Buckingham was now the only non-royal English duke: a member of the family in title if not in fact. The official reason for the promotion to the royal title, however, was that Buckingham deserved to treat with his opposite number, the Count-Duke of Olivares, on equal terms. In reality, absence had made the king's heart grow fonder.

The elevation, unfortunately, rather hindered than helped. The new Duke of Buckingham grew proud – and worse, to Spanish eyes, he behaved with appalling familiarity and jocularity with the prince, lounging around Charles's chambers half-dressed and accompanying his superior on their trips to purchase artworks and exotic animals (James would, in fact, receive five camels and an elephant from the Spanish government, whose king was not to be outdone by the upstart duke). The report of the commission appointed by Philip to investigate the religious issues, however, brought both Buckingham and Charles back down to earth.

In June, it appeared the Spanish had found a way out of the match. Their strategy was to call England's bluff. The theologians stated that, yes, the marriage should go ahead – indeed, the betrothal should be immediate. But the wedding proper – and with it the consummation – should be delayed by a year, during which James would be expected to demonstrate his commitment to the demands made of him by instituting a policy of toleration of Catholic worship in his kingdoms. This appalled Buckingham and Charles, who, despite their lavish spending, found themselves virtual prisoners of the Spanish court, being reported on and monitored constantly. Sir Francis Cottington conveyed the news back to England, along with a letter from the prince and duke. James, who was at Greenwich, was horrified. Immediately, he burnt the letter from his son and favourite and took up his pen.

My Sweet Boys,

Your letter by Cottington hath stricken me dead; I fear it shall very much shorten my days, and I am the more perplexed that I know not how to satisfy the people's expectation here, neither know I what to say to the Council . . . My advice and directions that ye crave . . . [are] to come speedily away, and if ye can get leave, give over all treaty. And this I speak without respect of any security they can offer you, except ye never look to see your old Dad again, whom I fear ye shall never see, if you see him not before winter. Alas, I now repent me sore that I ever suffered ye to go away. I care not for match nor nothing, so I may once have you in my arms again. God grant it, God grant it, God grant it; amen, amen, amen![15]

James's fear – a fear which he had borne since before the venture was even put in train – was that he might really lose his son and his lover to Spanish wiles. His advice that the pair 'give over all treaty' was taken. Charles agreed to the outrageous conditions set by Philip, the Pope, and the ecclesiastical commission – all to gain leave to return home. In July, he made a formal acknowledgement of his acceptance to the Spanish monarch. The bluffer had been bluffed, and Philip was forced to appear delighted. What Charles and James had done, however, was box themselves into a corner; in the same month, the English king had to solemnise the match at Whitehall and swear to abide by the conditions made upon him to the Spanish ambassador (Gondomar's replacement, the Marquis of Inojosa). A feast followed at the new Banqueting House, constructed to Inigo Jones's design; but it is unlikely James enjoyed the delectables served up on solid gold plates. He knew, well enough, that he was in a tight spot: either the marriage would go ahead – which he wished – and he would be forced to face his subjects, having sold England's reformed faith short; or it would not, in which case the people would clamour more loudly for war. Still, he wrote the requisite note of introduction to the Infanta, informing her that 'the celebrity of your virtues has not only attracted, in the capacity of a lover, my very dear son to come from afar to see you, but has inspired me also with an ardent desire of having the happiness of your presence, and of enjoying the pleasure of embracing such a Princess in the quality of a daughter'.[16] The bright side was the projected expansion of his family unit.

Meanwhile, Charles and Buckingham (who was by now suddenly repentant and fearful over the consequences of the disastrous Spanish mission) made ready to flee. Before they could go, however, the prince was forced to undergo one last act of humiliation: he had to formally swear that he would listen to the learned arguments of his bride's Catholic theologians, and 'hearken to them willingly . . . laying aside all excuse'.[17] In other words, he had sworn to open his ears to attempts at conversion. He also signed the requisite proxy document, which Digby, still England's ambassador to Spain, was expected to hand over to Philip once the Pope had ratified the match. This document was intended to play the groom, allowing a legal marriage to be formalised in Spain in Charles's absence. But the prince was not totally in thrall. By this time, he had turned against the marriage, having been disillusioned not only by the Infanta's evident lack of interest but by the protracted and unpleasant experience of Spanish negotiations. Moreover, he had come to realise that his marriage with Spain would not guarantee Spanish backing over his sister and brother-in-law's restoration to the Palatinate (on this, Olivares had been clear). Before he left, laden down with gifts, Charles was unequivocal: Digby was not to hand over the proxy. The marriage, therefore, was not to go ahead.

If James's spirits were low due to the significant domestic political cost of achieving the Spanish match, they were soon to be lifted. Despite the unforgiving conditions, one part of his initial plan to secure European peace had seemingly succeeded, although there was no guarantee that it would improve the lot of his daughter and her husband. For the moment, that did not matter. His 'Sweet Boys' were coming home and would soon enough be in his arms. The pair departed Spain in September, having travelled via the Escorial to the port of Santander. However, when they arrived in England in October, to tumultuous public rejoicing, their doting sovereign would find both men as emotionally and politically distant as when they had been abroad. This sad parting of the ways set the stage for the final year of the king's life – and for the strange circumstances of his death.

23

Death's Triumphing Dart

The sky over London was choked with the smoke of celebratory bon-fires – more than 300 between Whitehall and Temple Bar, according to the observer Simonds D'Ewes. Song and the music of tabours and fifes rose above crooked rooftops to meet it. The occasion was news of the prince's homecoming, which, on his arrival at Portsmouth, had torn through the country to a general rapture.

James, who had become severely ill again, was at Royston. Nevertheless, when Charles and Buckingham rode into the court-yard, he descended the stairs to embrace them: he 'fell on their necks and they all wept together'.[1] Thereafter, the trio retired to a private chamber in which the boys could unfold their experiences of Spanish diplomacy and guile. Tellingly, when James emerged, he publicly announced that he would not assent to 'marry his son with a por-tion of his daughter's tears'.[2] Clearly, Charles had warned him that if the Spanish match went ahead, it would not improve Elizabeth's lot, given Philip IV's alliance with Ferdinand II. This provided an honourable English excuse to back away.

Confusion now reigned throughout court, council, and country. No one knew quite what was intended, nor whether the Spanish match, so recently celebrated at Whitehall, was on or off. Not help-ing matters was the council's official line that it remained on; some intuited that there would simply be a delay. The Spanish ambas-sador, Inojosa, was as baffled as anyone when, on attempting to approach the royal household, he found himself ordered to lodge at an inn and await further instructions. Soon after, it was rumoured that James had returned to London for a secret conference with

Spanish representatives, with a view to pardoning imprisoned Jesuit missionaries.

The king seemed content to encourage and exacerbate the general confusion, promoting mixed messages in a play for time. He was, in truth, in a state of political paralysis, awaiting public reaction as to whether the match should go ahead or not, and hoping that antagonism to the extreme conditions would be less than he feared.

When it became apparent that James continued to favour the marriage, despite what they had told him about the reality of the situation, Charles and Buckingham were united in their anger. James, meanwhile, clung doggedly to his view, desperately insisting that he knew best, no matter what they had heard from Olivares regarding Spain's dedication to the Imperial cause. He ordered splendid formal receptions for incoming Spanish envoys and ambassadors, begging Buckingham to lay on lavish entertainments. This the duke did, albeit grudgingly. Charles, too, remained intransigently cool, despite his father's entreaties that he warmly accept their letters from Philip.

Increasingly, it was obvious that the duke and prince had the majority of English opinion on their side, and James, clinging to the remnants of a failed policy, lacked support. Buckingham felt newly empowered, not only by his dukedom but by the reception he had received on his return to England – he had been feted as a noble escapee from the devious Spanish rather than the corrupt minion which the previous parliament had tried to make of him. Henceforth, he eschewed full meetings of the Privy Council in favour of committees and so-called 'Cabinet Councils' packed with malleable fellows, including the new secretary Sir Edward Conway (who at the start of 1623 had succeeded Naunton in the role). Charles, too, had come into his own; he saw no honour in his father's peace policy, which he suspected was more founded in a desire for dowry money than a moralistic means of securing Spanish support for Elizabeth and Frederick.

Divided politically from the younger men, James was keen to make amends. He listened seriously when Buckingham came to him with a new proposal: the summoning of a fresh parliament. This had not been the duke's idea; it had come from a voice from the past – Buckingham's old friend and adviser, the much-maligned Sir Francis Bacon. Bacon well knew the power of parliament, given the circumstances of his fall. He knew also that its prevailing anti-Spanish mood aligned perfectly with Buckingham's – and against the king's.

Buckingham (who had, notwithstanding, continued corresponding with Philip IV at James's behest) now joined with Charles in counselling a decisive end to all idea of Anglo-Spanish amity. James greeted this with tears, querulously asking, 'Do you want me to go to war, in my twilight years, and force me to break with Spain?'[3] This was exactly what the pair wanted. Nor were they alone. They had set about creating a populist war party, which included Pembroke, Southampton, and Oxford (with whom the duke reconciled following a public quarrel). Meanwhile, Spanish representatives resident in England (and those English politicians who favoured them) had not been inactive. Their countermeasure was to embark on a whispering campaign against Buckingham, including scandalous accusations that he had attempted to seduce Olivares's wife when in Spain, hoping thereby to win James away from his favourite. Although the duke and prince attempted to isolate the king from them, one Don Francesco managed to arrange a secret meeting with him at Theobalds. Unfortunately, this failed to deliver any miraculous resolution to the Spanish problem or to the Palatinate. Rather, Francesco revealed that Buckingham – without James's knowledge – was treating for a match with a French princess: Henriette Marie, better known by the italianised Henrietta Maria, which English tongues found easier. The Spaniard's clear intention was to turn James against his favourite.

It was in this inert climate – caught as he was between Spain on one hand and his son and favourite on the other – that James agreed to summon a parliament. The idea had considerable merit. Rather than locking horns with members, he might build a mutual, conciliar approach to the seemingly insoluble issues of the Spanish match and the European battleground. In this way, he could neutralise parliamentary gripes about supposedly ancient rights to free speech by inviting members to have an active voice in matters pertaining to the royal prerogative. Then, whatever the outcome, he could take or leave their advice. Taking it would score a domestic win – and if this were unpopular abroad, it could be projected as being the will of the English people rather than their sovereign.

The parliament called to sit in early February 1624 got off to a poor start. Its initial opening was postponed due to inclement weather (another freezing winter having tightened its grip on London). When James was being robed for its rescheduled opening, news reached him that his cousin Lennox, who had been at his side since 1583 and recently been his High Steward (in charge of organising ceremonial events), had dropped dead. James was shaken. He was, indeed, unable to proceed.

It was thus not until 19 February that the king was conveyed, in a velvet-draped chariot, to Westminster, with Charles riding behind him. In his opening speech, the king, as was so often the case, fell into – this time somewhat confused – familial imagery, announcing that he was the husband, parliament was his wife, and the Commons his children. There was a reason for this. It formed the prelude to inviting MPs to discourse on the Spanish match – a royal prerogative which he hitherto would have insisted was none of their business. Although he had been encouraged to call parliament by Buckingham, James intended to win its members over by presenting himself as their natural ally, and thereby to disincline them to support his favourite's and his son's war party. 'Consider with yourselves,' he said, 'the state of Christendom, my children, and this my own kingdom. Consider of these, and upon all give me your advice.'4

Parliament's advice, however, proved in the majority to be as bellicose as Buckingham and Charles. James maintained, throughout, that he could only countenance war if its goal were simply the recovery of the Palatinate for Elizabeth and Frederick – but the Commons were disinclined to codify limits in the text of their subsidy bill (which they knew the king needed). In response, James wrote the condition in himself.

The king's cautious approach proved far less beguiling than Buckingham's stirring speeches, which were tailored to excite an already war-hungry body. The duke had wisely elected not to try to persuade MPs, but, having read the prevailing mood, to pander. He insisted that the war would pay for itself, and that it would recall the glory days of Queen Elizabeth, when Englishmen had fought Spain on land and at sea, profiting by the fruits of English seamanship. Not surprisingly, when they were persuaded to vote in three subsidies, the Commons insisted that the money raised be spent chiefly on fitting out Buckingham's navy. Nevertheless, this was a drop in the ocean compared to what the duke and Charles would actually spend on military preparations. Inadequate, too, was the £10,000 apiece for Buckingham and James which the king chiselled out of the East India Company (which he had long patronised on the basis of its continued profitability), as part of the pair's share of its piratical capture of the Portuguese settlement at Ormuz back in 1622.

For the moment, Buckingham remained parliament's golden boy, well able to manage opposition. When his old friend and client Lionel Cranfield – who had by now been created the 1st Earl of Middlesex, and who had remained in the thankless post of Lord High Treasurer since 1618 – dared speak out against war, the duke bristled. Middlesex, he decided, was an ingrate. Buckingham had not only sponsored the man's career but encouraged a marriage between Middlesex and his cousin, Anne Brett; in return, the treasurer first attempted a Suffolk-esque plot of supplanting him with a handsome youth (in 1622, Anne's brother, Arthur, had been 'set up as a new idol or darling' – and now, ominously, Arthur was back at court). Now, Middlesex was openly opposing him in parliament. It was not to be borne.

Cunningly, Buckingham marshalled the parliamentarians' anger in his enemy's direction, just as Coke had once directed it towards Mompesson and Bacon. Investigations were set up into goings-on at the treasury, and the idea of impeachment was raised. This ancient means of prosecuting royal servants accused of committing misdeeds in the Crown's name had, prior to James's reign, fallen into disuse.

It involved the arrest and trial of nobles by their peers in the Lords – and the premier lord, the Duke of Buckingham, was united with Prince Charles in seeking its use against the hapless Middlesex. James was both furious and forward-looking. He warned Charles, with remarkable foresight, that by agitating a parliament into seeking to throw down the high-born, he was 'making a rod with which you will be scourged yourself'.[5]

This warning fell on deaf ears. In April, Middlesex was impeached on charges of corruption. His fate followed that of Suffolk – he was tried, dismissed from his post, imprisoned (though James commuted this to exile beyond the verge of court), and fined £50,000. As the subsidies had been voted in, the king saw no reason to continue entertaining his favourite and his son's malicious antics nor their pugnacious posturing. To his great sadness, he was now openly at odds with his lover, who was holding sway over his son. Throughout the year, Spanish agents in London and their friends in government – not least the Lord Keeper, Bishop John Williams – did what they could to widen the breach. James, his mind as ravaged as his body, was in turmoil, unsure who to trust. He was induced, eventually, to launch an investigation into his entire council, though he handed Buckingham an advance copy of the questions to be put to each man. Charles, worried for his friend, wrote, 'Steenie . . . my advice to you is that you do not oppose, or show yourself discontented, at the King's course herein.'[6] Buckingham alerted his mother to his potential loss of the king's favour and the fact that a campaign was being mounted by the pro-Spanish, anti-war party against him. As he prepared to go to Theobalds for his examination, he said to her that he might return 'as he was born' – that is, stripped of every title and office.

This did not happen. Reports vary as to how angry James showed himself towards Buckingham; what seems clear, however, is that his investigation into his councillors produced no evidence of any treacherous intent. Nevertheless, Buckingham was shaken – so much so that he fell ill in the middle of May. The trusty Théodore de Mayerne was called for and, after giving the same diagnosis he had passed on the late Prince Henry – a tertian fever – he prescribed bleeding. James, always sensitive to illnesses in those he loved, was in a swoon. Immediately, his hard feelings towards his lover were forgotten, and he bombarded Buckingham with gifts: cherries (a treat James enjoyed), sweetmeats, and – oddly enough – the testicles of a deer, which were thought to give strength when eaten. The pair restarted their old, warm correspondence, with the king writing that he looked forward to the time when his 'sweetheart' and 'thy cunts [James's vulgar term from his favourite's womenfolk: a bawdy pun on "countesses"] may see me hunt the buck'.[7] All of the king's paternal, sexual, and romantic instincts bubbled over in reaction to his lover's ill health – soon enough, Buckingham was restored to favour. When Arthur Brett, that kinsman of the fallen Middlesex who had hoped to catch the king's eye, made a more vigorous attempt to thrust himself into royal favour, James was 'much offended' and had the unfortunate lad clapped in gaol.

At the end of May, James prorogued parliament, assuring members that they would be recalled in the winter. It had not gone as he had hoped, its members were beginning to encroach on ecclesiastical affairs, and the subsidies voted in offered him nothing for personal use – but it had very much suited Buckingham and Prince Charles. In the following month, the favourite returned to court, restored to health. Thereafter, the mood of the nation only increased in its anti-Spanish hostility. In August, the playwright Thomas Middleton's satirical *A Game at Chess* debuted at the Globe; in it, the House of White (the Stuarts) is set in opposition to the House of Black (the Habsburgs). Stirring up trouble are the Black Duke (an allegorical representation of Olivares) and the Black Knight (Gondomar). The play lasted little over a week before the government cracked down. By that time, of course, everyone who was anyone had seen it – in some cases more than once.

James, increasingly feeble and once again in Buckingham's power, acceded to the dismissal of Inojosa, and thereafter the duke took charge of arrangements for the new French match. He managed this with far more efficacy than he had the Spanish suit, whilst the king remained aloof, occasionally sending gently chiding notes – one reading, 'Where is your glorious match with France?'[8] By winter, he had his answer: the duke, to Charles's delight, had pulled it off, and the marriage treaty looked set to be concluded, with James having agreed to Catholic toleration in September. Moreover, throughout the summer, English troops were marshalled with a view to going to war over the Palatinate under the leadership of the German mercenary Count Mansfeld – news which sent Elizabeth and Frederick into paroxysms of joy. James attempted to temper this by warning Mansfeld that he would lose his position if he employed his new English troops for any conflict on the continent other than recovering the Palatinate – but in truth, the king was a spent force. Indeed, when the time came to sign the treaty for the French match, it had to be stamped; James's fingers were so swollen and painful that he could not hold a pen. Nor could he entertain the French ambassadors. Charles, instead, stepped into the breach.

Illness also prevented the king from attending the annual Christmas Revels. Instead, he dictated a poignant note to his favourite, addressing him as 'My only sweet and dear child':

> Notwithstanding of your desiring me to write yesterday, yet I had written in the evening, if at my coming in out of the park such a drowsiness had not comed [sic] upon me, as I was forced to sit and sleep in my chair half an hour. And yet I cannot content myself without sending you this billet, praying God that I may have a joyful and comfortable meeting with you, and that we make at this Christenmass a new marriage, ever to be kept hereafter for God so to love me, as I desire to live only to live in this world for your sake, and that I had rather live banished in any part of the earth with you than live a sorrowful widow-life without you. And so God bless you, my sweet child and wife, and grant that ye may ever be a comfort to your dear Dad and husband.[9]

In the king's suffering, Buckingham and Prince Charles were *de facto* kings. However, as the new year dawned, their successes of the second half of 1624 looked to be under threat. Mansfeld's mission, comprising a gaggle of pressed men, got off to a poor start. Even before leaving, the English conscripts wrought havoc in the countryside. Once abroad, poor communication, a lack of direction, and bad organisation spelled failure. Soon, icy weather, disease, and shortages of food and money took their toll, and the army was decimated before it could launch any assault. Not helping this were the king's restrictions on mobilisation. Though Buckingham and Charles pressed him to allow Mansfeld to relieve the town of Breda, which had fallen to Spinola and the Spanish, James demurred. As far as he was concerned, the troops had been raised purely to recover the Palatinate. Not only did this attitude irritate his son and favourite, but it baffled his putative Dutch allies. Worse, he replied to demands that his army intercede at Breda by issuing his own: he wanted compensation from the Dutch over the deaths of English merchants at the hands of the Dutch East India Company, and a £20,000 loan for the payment of his troops. In short, James was looking for a way out of firm military commitment that might result in England falling into full-scale war. Instead, he received reports of an ill-organised and aimless troop, which was doing little other than starving to death.

Ill as he was, James was angry. Nor was he mollified when the papal dispensation for the French match arrived. Like that for the Spanish marriage, it contained numerous conditions regarding Catholic toleration. Why, then, had his Spanish match been exchanged for one which offered neither political support over the Palatinate nor conditions any more palatable to the English people? The king imperiously told Effiat, the French ambassador, that he might reject his son's French match entirely. Buckingham began to sense that James was moving again towards Spain – a notion not helped by rumours that Gondomar was likely to darken England's doorway again.

Whatever James's intentions, he looked increasingly unlikely to see them through. In February, he was conveyed to Theobalds via Newmarket, Chesterfield, and Royston, where the country air had always been a tonic. Responding to a request to join him, and revealing again the extraordinary emotional proximity between servant and royal master, Buckingham wrote, 'Dear Dad, I cannot come tonight . . . tomorrow, without fail, I will wait of [on] you.' Attending to the king's doting affections had, likely, begun to pall now that he was handling affairs of state and, moreover, now that he had to try to handle the diplomatic dangers which James's ongoing partiality towards Spain was causing.

The king, however, needed attention. When he received news that Lennox's successor as Lord High Steward, the 2nd Marquess of Hamilton, had died, he sank into a depression and retired to his bed. This latest loss only heightened his fear that death was approaching. Pain was now his constant companion, swelling his joints and gripping his bones. Like many a sick person throughout history, he began cursing his doctors, who were acting according to written instructions left by the senior royal physician Mayerne (who was, probably mercifully, abroad at the time). In early March, the medical team fell upon their absent master's favourite diagnosis: the king was suffering a tertian fever. The ostensible causes included the eating of unripe fruit, and this certainly was a habit of James, who had lost most of his teeth but not his appetite: later, Bishop Goodman recalled that when the Master of the Spicery 'did present him with the first strawberries, cherries, and other fruits, and, kneeling to the King, had some speech ready . . . [James] never had patience to hear him one word, but his hand was in the basket'.[10] As the fever was considered a manageable illness, which could even cast out ill humours, the medical men were not greatly concerned, and an old adage did the rounds: 'A tertian in spring is physic to a king.'

Two people were, however, unwilling to leave the king to his existing physicians. These were Buckingham and his mother, who had her own painful experience of death, having lost two husbands. They proposed a new man, whom the countess swore by, named Remington: an obscure Essex doctor with no official qualifications. By this time, Henry Atkins, the president of the College of Physicians, had taken over the king's case, and his prescription was for round-the-clock attendance, with special treatments given when

James's fever rose. When it fell, James appeared better – he was well enough, in fact, to play cards with Buckingham, who had moved into a private room adjoining the royal bedchamber, on 11 March. Plans were even begun for a move from Theobalds to Hampton Court. The royal physicians continued to monitor the king, whose bouts of fever seemed to be growing less serious with each cyclical attack. In one of his better moments – at which point Buckingham had returned to London for a spell – James was even able to receive the gift of a book from John Murray, 1st Earl of Annandale. By the time the duke returned, the king was up and walking, albeit only for short distances.

At this juncture, Remington was called upon by Buckingham to administer his own remedy: a modern version of mithridate, a semi-mythical cure-all said to contain up to sixty-five secret ingredients. To the confusion of the other assembled physicians, Buckingham and his mother produced a batch. Dr Lister, part of the official medical team, spoke up against the treatment, where-upon Buckingham administered it himself. James took the syrup and was slathered with the poultice, whereupon a violent reaction ensued, throwing the royal physicians into a panic. One of them, Dr Craig, remonstrated with the duke and countess directly – the fault, the medical men believed, was that it had been the wrong time to administer medicine (the belief being that tertian fever had times for medication and times for being left well enough alone). In the middle of the night, James requested that one of his bedchamber men, Henry Gibb, remove plaster.

The next day, 22 March, the king lay in a deep sleep. He woke in the evening, at which point Communion was given, and thereafter two royal doctors, Chambers and Ramsey, were left in attendance. Chambers later claimed that the king had said Buckingham's syrup had made him 'burn and roast'. James was now in mortal danger, and the physicians oversaw several more days of unremitting diarrhoea, discoloured urine, loss of speech, and gasping cries of thirst. Immediately, people began looking at Buckingham, and it was reported that Dr Craig went so far as to suggest that he had

administered poison: an accusation which led the duke to supposedly threaten a slander suit. It was also said that Buckingham had
used the excuse of the king's infirmity to stamp a warrant barring
Gondomar from coming to England. Both Craig and Gibb were
gaoled for having been loose-tongued over the king's attitude
towards the syrup. The proof of innocence of poisoning seemed
assured, however, when the royal physicians themselves sampled the
syrup – and the plaster – and received no ill effects. This supported
later – admittedly shakier – testimony that Buckingham's man Baker
had also tested the stuff, and that Sir James Palmer, a groom, had
actually been cured of his own ague by it.

In the midst of all this, James continued to decline. On the 24th,
he took a serious turn for the worse – likely, he was experiencing a
series of mini-strokes ahead of a final, fatal one. The following day, it
was clear he did not have long left and, on the 26th, the physicians
relinquished their charge to the clergymen, Archbishop Abbot and
John Williams, the Lord Keeper and Bishop of Lincoln. The room
filled with divines, each adding to the chorus of prayers intended
to see their sovereign out of the world. 'Come, Lord Jesu,' chanted
Williams, 'come quickly.' In the late morning of Sunday the 27th,
King James died.

*

Immediately, members of the Privy Council rushed to proclaim
Charles sovereign. As quickly, Buckingham fell ill, swooning and
dissolving into fits of tears. When these post-death dramas were over,
arrangements for the royal funeral began. James's body was conveyed by torchlight – despite damp weather – to Denmark House,
where it lay in state until the 5,000-strong funeral procession to
Westminster Abbey could be arranged. Only after miles of ruinously
expensive black cloth had been found to outfit the mourners could
this go ahead. Casting aside protocol, Charles, flanked by noblemen,
marched behind the hearse and its finely carved and dressed effigy.
This display of deference was a necessary antidote to the fact that the
new king's first actions had been to ramp up war preparations and

undo his late father's restrictions on the English army's movements abroad. Buckingham, as Master of the Horse, followed King Charles.

The funeral took place on the 7 May 1625 and, again, Bishop Williams was prevailed upon to deliver the sermon. His theme was the long-standing identification of James as Solomon. 'I dare say,' he intoned, 'you never read in your lives of two kings more fully paralleled amongst themselves, and better distinguished from all other kings.' The theme was well chosen, although it contained a measure of criticism of the new monarch's martial fervour. James had been, at heart, a peace-loving man. Ironically, this was one of the planks of his policy (in addition to his profligacy, for which there can be little excuse) which drew so much criticism, and yet which makes him seem more attractive nowadays.

James had, undoubtedly, successfully and skilfully – and over time – brought Scotland to something like obedience to its monarch. His perception of England, however, was that it was already a compliant nation which craved peace and simply required a new leader. What he did not realise was that he had taken possession of a realm which was growing less governable, partly due to its increasing population and competing internal interests, and partly due to an ongoing distrust in a foreign ruler who was thought to have divided loyalties. He might justly have congratulated himself for governing Scotland in challenging times – but that exhausting and hard-won success had left him self-congratulatory and complacent when, in middle age, he began a new reign in a new kingdom. His mistake was assuming that England was settled and that he need concern himself only with approving its existing religious settlement whilst – equally to his taste – enjoying the role of an aloof, continental leader.

In terms of international relations, James was, if anything, a good king at the wrong time. His people, increasingly, were thirsty for war, seeing it nostalgically as manlike and redolent of a mythologised past. He, to his credit, resisted conflict. Where he failed was in his flagrant spending habits and, perhaps more dangerously for the future, in his over-reliance on the men he loved and his desire to rule parliament in a manner that had been archaic even during

Elizabeth's reign. James had, throughout his life, entertained lofty ideals and correspondingly idealistic visions for everything: family, the monarchy, international relations, and the ease of union between his kingdoms. But he had not lived in an ideal world. He was guilty, too, of being highly personal in his judgements and attitudes, which led to many of his policies and political actions being based on his own likes and dislikes of the players involved. This only makes him all the more endearing to modern eyes, but in practice it meant that he often lacked the sangfroid prized in early modern sovereigns.

James's surviving son inherited – from his mother and deceased brother – a passion for aesthetics and visual splendour which led him to begin building Britain's Royal Collection of artworks. From his father, Charles inherited a desire to return to a time when parliament was more tractable, and he also developed a high idea of his own station and a preference for High Church aesthetics rather than dour Puritanism and Presbyterianism. This would culminate in the Wars of the Three Kingdoms and Charles's own gruesome end on the block, after trial by the men of his parliament.

James's other surviving child – the beautiful, tragic Elizabeth, along with her husband Frederick – would never regain the Palatinate, although her son Charles Louis did (her eldest, Henry Frederick, having died in 1629). She continued producing children in exile until 1632. When Frederick died in that same year, Charles invited her to return to England. This she refused. Instead, she remained in The Hague, following in her mother's footsteps by fostering the arts and arranging matches for her dwindling band of children. Horrified by the civil wars which drenched the British Isles in blood (and in which her sons Rupert and Maurice fought), she returned to England on the restoration of the Stuart line. But years of fighting had taken their toll; her youthful beauty had faded and she had come to strongly resemble her father in his dotage. She died in Leicester House in 1662.

Politically, Buckingham was not unduly troubled by James's death, for the accession of Charles I meant his position was secure. The great favourite had, very likely, come to love the old king – ironically enough, in the way James had come to love Anna: more in terms of deep affection than passion, despite their sexual history. But he had become a serious statesman – a road he had been on since his return from Spain. However, his popularity did not last, as criticism of his corruption and military blunders mounted up. His assassination in 1628 left Charles bereft.

Yet a question mark has long hung over the king's last – and greatest – lover's part in those curious events in March 1625. It is true that the deaths of notables in the period habitually encouraged accusations of poison; but not all accusations were born equal. Some, like the claim Anne Boleyn poisoned Katherine of Aragon, or that James had poisoned Prince Henry, had limited shelf lives and little to commend them. Others lasted longer and require more attention.

Charles's complicity in a Buckingham-led regicide was a charge levelled against him at the time of his downfall, when contemporaries recalled the circumstances of the old king's death (although, importantly, they had political axes to grind). Nevertheless, it is not disputed that the duke administered his mother's syrup and poultice. Recently, Benjamin Woolley, and, separately, Alastair Bellany and Thomas Cogswell, have revived and deeply investigated this curious royal death. The latter have comprehensively deconstructed the events of James's last hours, days, and weeks, exposing the welter of political propaganda which appeared then and was embroidered later. The former asked the late John Henry, an expert toxicologist, to review the medical records and documentary evidence still extant. Henry's conclusion was apparently unequivocal: James was poisoned with aconite, derived from wolfsbane or monkshood. There are, naturally, always reservations in dealing with cold – extremely cold – cases, but the strange sequence of events, as recorded, certainly provide rich loam for claims of foul play. Woolley therefore concludes that Buckingham, with Charles's connivance, killed the king to prevent him from reactivating his pro-Spanish policy and dashing their own plans for the future of England.

This is unlikely. For one thing, Charles never had the character of a murderer, and certainly not a regicide (his belief in the sanctity of monarchs being one of the things his own eventual enemies were keen to disabuse him of, with an axe as their teaching tool). For those keen to push the criminal narrative, Buckingham, newly energised, could have deliberately administered poison, perhaps in an effort to usher in the new reign. Alternatively, the motive might have been one of mercy – the king, as we have seen, was rapidly declining well before his final illness in the late winter and early spring of 1625. However, even this seems unlikely. The duke was well aware that there was a whispering campaign against him, and that any odd medical intervention on his part would invite suspicion. This is, indeed, what happened.

The moment James's last breath faded, his death became a political football, tossed between pro-Spanish Catholic commentators (who were keen to destabilise the new regime and Buckingham's position in it) and militant Protestants (who were keen to present an image of a noble death in the reformed faith). The former had only to question the actions of the Countess of Buckingham and her son. Suddenly, the medications they had peremptorily administered took on a conveniently sinister complexion. As Bellany and Cosgwell have demonstrated, the accusations only grew bolder and more colourful. In 1626, the affair of the syrup and poultice came to public notice when Dr George Eglisham, a royal physician, printed his *The Forerunner of Revenge*, which openly accused the duke of murder. At Charles's first parliament, when any excuse was being sought to remove the seemingly untouchable favourite from government, James's doctors were questioned by a select committee, which found that Buckingham had administered a putative cure 'no better than poison'. Charles then dissolved the parliament before impeachment of the duke could take place, thereby inviting later accusations of his own complicity.

If the king's death were a genuine murder mystery, there was one obvious 'dark horse' suspect: Mary Villiers, Countess of Buckingham. It was she who called upon a mysterious doctor from outside the circle of royal physicians, and it was she who recommended unauthorised remedies. Her guiding motive throughout her life was feathering the Villiers' family nest – and only months before, her son had come to her with a warning that he might lose credit with the king and be reduced to the state in which he had been born. Notably, however, it was not she but her son, and then the prince, who faced the lion's share of accusations. This is not surprising. Not only was the countess a less politically useful target, but she had converted to Catholicism at some point in 1622 (the announcement of her intentions having prompted James to organise a three-day religious conference extolling the virtues of Protestantism).[11] There was thus little motivation on the parts of those who first pushed the murder narrative – those pro-Spanish agents who had been active against Buckingham even before James's death – to bother with her. The comparative lack of accusation levelled against her should lead us to doubt the welter of rumour and innuendo which circulated against her son (and, consequently, Charles). The barrage of invective against the favourite is, therefore, more useful as a demonstration of just how effective scurrilous rumour had become as a means of political weaponry in the early seventeenth century than it is as evidence of murder.

Ultimately, then, we are left with the most reasonable conclusion. There was no need to murder James, who was already dying. On the contrary, Buckingham knew that if he could save the king's life, even if only for a matter of weeks or months, his credit would never be higher. Further, he was aware that there were pro-Habsburg elements engaged in what would now be called a propaganda war against him, and that those enemies would (and they did) work up a failed attempt to cure James into murder. The affair of the poultice and syrup, therefore, was likely a gamble, genuinely intended to effect a cure. It simply did not pay off. If the king did not die a wholly natural death, it is possible that the medicines given him – those from the royal physicians and the concoctions from the Buckinghams – combined to do more harm than good to an already failing body (indeed, one wonders how many during this period died due to cures administered with the best of intentions). The absolute truth of what went on within his weakened body will never, of course, be known.

What is known, however, is that King James, so often overlooked, reigned in sybaritic splendour over two of the most colourful and tumultuous courts in British history. It is fitting that he is remembered not simply as the 'wisest fool in Christendom' but as a man who loved deeply, sought peace assiduously, joked terribly, and sought a sense of family which seemed always just beyond his reach.

Primary Sources

Abbreviations:

Acts and Proceedings of the General Assemblies of the Kirk of Scotland, 1560–1618 (*Acts and Proceedings*)

Bodleian Library Manuscripts (*Bodleian MSS*)

British Library Manuscripts (*BL MSS*)

Calendar of State Papers Foreign: Elizabeth (*CSP, Elizabeth*)

Calendar of State Papers Relating to English Affairs in the Archives of Venice (*CSP, Venice*)

Calendar of State Papers, Domestic: James I (*CSP, James*)

Calendar of State Papers, Scotland (*CSP, Scotland*)

Calendar of State Papers, Spain (Simancas) (*CSP, Simancas*)

Calendar of the Manuscripts of the Most Honourable the Marquess of Salisbury (*Salisbury MSS*)

City of Chester Record Office Manuscripts (*CCRO MSS*)

Norfolk Record Office (*NRO*)

The Border Papers: Calendar of Letters and Papers Relating to the Affairs of the Borders of England and Scotland (*LP, Borders*)

Printed Sources

Akrigg, G.P.V. (1984) *Letters of King James VI & I*. Oxford: University of California Press.

Ashley, M. (1965) *The Stuarts in Love*. London: Macmillan.

Ashton, R. (1969) *James I by his Contemporaries*. London: Hutchinson.

Barclay, W. (2004) *The Revelation of John*, II. Louisville: Westminster John Knox Press.

Bath, M. (2012) 'Rare Shewes, the Stirling Baptism of Prince Henry', *Journal of the Northern Renaissance, 4*. <http://northern renaissance.org/rare-shewes-and-singular-inventions-the-stirling-baptism-of-prince-henry/> Accessed 24 January 2022.

Bell, I. (2016) *Elizabeth I: The Voice of a Monarch*. London: Palgrave Macmillan.

Bellany, A. (2002) *The Politics of Court Scandal in Early Modern England*. Cambridge: CUP.

Bellany, A., and Cogswell, T. (2015) *The Murder of King James*. New Haven: Yale University Press.

Beresford Chancellor, E. (1886) *The Life of Charles I, 1600–1625*. London: George Bell & Sons.

Bergeron, D.M. (1985) *Royal Family, Royal Lovers*. Missouri: University of Missouri Press.

Bergeron, D.M. (2002) *King James and Letters of Homoerotic Desire*. Iowa: University of Iowa Press.

Bingham, C. (1969) *The Making of a King*. London: Collins.

Bingham, C. (1979) *James VI of Scotland*. London: Weidenfeld and Nicolson.

Bingham, C. (1981) *James I of England*. London: Weidenfeld and Nicolson.

Birch, T. (1760) *The Life of Henry, Prince of Wales, Eldest Son of King James I*. Dublin: G. Faulkner.

Bourne, H. (1736) *The History of Newcastle Upon Tyne*. Newcastle: John White.

Breton, N. (1879) [1607]. 'A Murmurer' in A.B. Grosart (ed.) *The Works in Verse and Prose of Nicholas Breton, II*. Edinburgh: Edinburgh University Press.

Brotton, J. (2007) *The Sale of the Late King's Goods: Charles I and His Art Collection*. London: Pan Books.

Bruce, J. (1849) *Letters of Queen Elizabeth and King James VI of Scotland*. London: J.B. Nichols & Son.

Bruce, J. (1867) *Papers Relating to William, First Earl of Gowrie, and Patrick Ruthven, His Fifth and Last Surviving Son*. London: J.E. Taylor & Co.

Burel, J. (1828) 'Poems' in J.T. Gibson (ed.) *Papers Relative to the Marriage of King James the Sixth of Scotland with the Princess Anna of Denmark*. Edinburgh: Bannatyne.

Calderwood, D. (1678) *The True History of the Church of Scotland*. Folio.

Calderwood, D. (1842) *The History of the Kirk of Scotland*, III. Edinburgh: Wodrow.

Calderwood, D. (1844) *The History of the Kirk of Scotland*, V. Edinburgh: Wodrow.

Campbell, B. (1874) *The Lives of the Chief Justices of England*, I. London: Cockcroft.

Carnegie, D., & Gunby, D. (2007) 'The Progeny of Prince James: Sources and States', *Print Quarterly*, 23 (3), pp. 238–254.

Cassell, J. (1859) *Illustrated History of England*, III. London: W. Kent and Co.

Chamberlain, J. (1939) *The Letters of John Chamberlain*, Volume 1. Philadelphia: The American Philosophical Society.

Chambers, R. (1835) *A Biographical Dictionary of Eminent Scotsmen*, I. Glasgow: Blackie & Son.

Chambers, R. (1858) *Domestic Annals of Scotland*, I. Edinburgh: W & R Chambers.

Church of Scotland. (1870) *The Scottish Kirk: Its History and Present Position*. London: The Society for the Liberation of Religion from State Patronage and Control.

Clayton, J.W. (1859) *Personal Memoirs of Charles the Second,* I. London: Skeet.

Clifford, A. (1992) *The Diary of The Lady Anne Clifford.* D.J.H. Clifford (ed.). Stroud: The History Press.

Coke, R. (1697) *A Detection of the Court and State of England.* London: Andrew Bell.

Colville, J. (1858) *Original Letters of John Colville, 1582–1603: to which is Added His Palinode, 1600: with a Memoir of the Author.* Edinburgh: John Hughes.

Cornwallis, C. (1641) *The life and death of our late most incomparable and heroique prince, Henry Prince of Wales A prince (for valour and vertue) fit to be imitated in succeeding times. Written by Sir Charles Cornvvallis knight, treasurer of his Highnesse household.* London: John Dawson.

Croft, P. (2002) *King James.* London: Macmillan.

Cust, R. (2014) *Charles I.* London: Routledge.

D'Ewes, S. (1845) *The Autobiography and Correspondence of Sir Simonds D'Ewes,* II. London: Richard Bentley.

Daurignac, J.M.S. (1865) *History of the Society of Jesus from its Foundation to the Present Time,* I. Cincinnati: John P. Walsh.

Davenport, R.A. (1827) *New Elegant Extracts, V.* Chiswick: C. Whittingham.

Dawson, J.E.A. (2007) *Scotland Re-formed, 1488–1587.* Edinburgh: Edinburgh University Press.

Donaldson, I. (2012) *Ben Jonson: A Life.* Oxford: OUP.

Drake, N. (1838) *Shakespeare and His Times.* Paris: Baudry's European Library.

Dryden, J. (1808) *The Works of John Dryden,* VIII. London: William Miller.

Dunham, W.H., and Pargellis, S.M. (1968) *Complaint and Reform in England, 1436–1714.* New York: Octagon Books.

Dutton, R. (2016) *Shakespeare, Court Dramatist.* Oxford: Oxford University Press.

Elizabeth I. (2002) *Collected Works.* L.S. Marcus, J. Mueller, and M.B. Rose (eds.). Chicago: University of Chicago Press.

Everett Green, M.A. (1855) *Lives of the Princesses of England, VI.* London: Henry Colburn.

Folkestone Williams, R. (1848) *The Court and Times of James the First, I.* London: Henry Colburn.

Fraser, A. (1969) *Mary Queen of Scots*. London: Weidenfeld and Nicolson.

Fraser, A. (1977) *King James VI of Scotland, I of England*. London: Sphere.

Fraser, W. (1889) *Memorials of the Earls of Haddington*, II. Edinburgh: T&A Constable.

Goodare, J. (1988) 'Queen Mary's Catholic Interlude' in M. Lynch (ed.) *Mary Stewart: Queen in Three Kingdoms*. Oxford: Blackwell.

Goodman, G. (1839) [c.1650]. *The Court of King James the First*, Volume II. London: Samuel Bentley.

Grierson, J. (1833) *Delineations of St. Andrews: being a particular account of everything remarkable in the history and present state of the city and ruins, the university, etc.* Cupar: G.S. Tullis.

Guenther, G. (2012) *Magical Imaginations: Instrumental Aesthetics in the English Renaissance*. Toronto: University of Toronto Press.

Halliwell-Phillips, J.O. (1846) *Letters of the Kings of England*, II. London: Henry Colburn.

Handover, P.M. (1959) *The Second Cecil*. London: Eyre and Spottiswoode.

Harris, A. (1879) *The Œconomy of the Fleete*. Westminster: Camden.

Harris-Wilson, D. (1956) *King James VI and I*. New York: Cape.

Harwicke, Earl of. (1778) *Miscellaneous State Papers*, I. London: W. Strahan & T. Cadell.

Hayward, M. (2020) *Stuart Style: Monarchy, Dress and the Scottish Male Elite*. New Haven: Yale University Press.

Hepworth Dixon, W. (1869) *Her Majesty's Tower*, I. Leipzig: Berhnard Tauchnitz.

Herman, P.C. (2010) *Royal Poetrie: Monarchic Verse and the Political Imaginary of Early Modern England*. Ithaca: Cornell University Press.

Herries, J.M. (1836) *Historical Memoirs of the Reign of Mary Queen of Scots*. Edinburgh: Edinburgh Printing Company.

Hill Burton, J. (1875) *The History of Scotland from Agricola's Invasion to the Extinction of the Last Jacobite Insurrection*, VI. New York: Scribner, Welford, and Armstrong.

Holmes, F. (2005) *The Sickly Stuarts: The Medical Downfall of a Dynasty*. Stroud: Sutton.

Houston, S.J. (2014) *James I*. London: Routledge.

Howitt, M.B. (1851) *Biographical Sketches of the Queens of Great Britain*. London: Henry G. Bohn.

Hume-Brown, P. (1911) *History of Scotland to the Present Time*, I. Cambridge: CUP.

Irving, E. (1831) *The Confessions of Faith and the Books of Discipline of the Church of Scotland*. London: Baldwin and Cradock.

James VI and I. *Basilikon Doron*. (1887) [1599]. London: Wertheimer, Lea & Co.

Jesse, J.H. (1857) *Memoirs of the Court of England During the Reign of the Stuarts, Including the Protectorate. By John Heneage Jesse*, I. London: Henry G. Bohn.

Journal of the House of Commons, 1, 1547–1629. 1802. London: His Majesty's Stationery Office.

Kenyon, J.P. (1990) *Stuart England*. London: Penguin.

Kinney, A.F., Dutcher, J.M., & Lake Prescott, A. (2008) *Renaissance Historicisms*. Newark: University of Delaware Press.

Kittridge True, C. (1881) *The Life and Times of Sir Walter Raleigh*. London: Wesleyan.

Knight, C. (1857) *The Popular History of England*, III. London: Bradbury & Evans.

Krag, N. (1823) [1599]. 'Relation om sit gesandskab til England 1598–1599', *Nye Danske Magazin*, 4 (3.6).

Laffan, B.J. (1880) *Kensington*. Edinburgh: John Menzies.

Laing, H. (1850) *Descriptive Catalogue of Impressions from Ancient Scottish Seals, Royal, Baronial, Ecclesiastical, and Municipal, Embracing a Period from A.D. 1094 to the Commonwealth, Taken from Original Charters and Other Deeds Preserved in Public and Private Archives*. Edinburgh: T. Constable.

Lee, M. (1959) *John Maitland of Thirlestane and the Foundation of Stewart Despotism*. New Jersey: Princeton University Press.

Lehman, H.E. (2011) *Lives of England's Reigning Consorts and Queens*. Chapel Hill: AUTHORHOUSE.

Levack, B.P. (2008) *Witch-Hunting in Scotland: Law, Politics and Religion*. London: Routledge.

Limon, J. (1990) *The Masque of Stuart Culture*. Newark: University of Delaware Press.

Lindsay, A.C. (1849) *Lives of the Lindsays: Or, A Memoir of the Houses of Crawford and Balcarres*, I. London: John Murray.

Lockyer, R. (2014) *Buckingham*. London: Routledge.

Longueville, T. (1894) *A Life of Archbishop Laud*. London: Kegan Paul.

Loomie, A.J. (1971) 'King James I's Catholic Consort', *Huntington Library Quarterly* 34 (4), pp. 303–316.

MacCunn, F.A. (1905) *Mary Stuart*. London: Methuen.

Marcus, L., Mueller, J., & Rose, M.B. (2000) *Elizabeth I: Collected Works*. Chicago: University of Chicago Press.

Marshall, R.K. (1997) *The Winter Queen: The Life of Elizabeth of Bohemia*. Edinburgh: Scottish National Portrait Gallery.

Marshall, R.K. (2019) *Scottish Queens, 1031–1714*. Edinburgh: Birlinn.

Mayer, J. (2004) *The Struggle for the Succession in Late Elizabethan England: Politics, Polemics and Cultural Representations*. Montpellier: Université Paul-Valéry Montpellier.

McManus, C. (2002) *Women on the Renaissance Stage: Anna of Denmark and Female Masquing in the Stuart Court (1590–1619)*. Manchester: Manchester University Press.

Meikle, M. (1999) '"Holde her at the Oeconomicke rule of the House": Anna of Denmark and Scottish Court Finances, 1589–1603' in E. Ewan, and M. Meikle (eds.) *Women in Scotland: c1100–c1750*. East Linton: Tuckwell Press.

Melville, J. (1973) *Memoirs of his own life by Sir James Melville of Halhill. M.D.XLIX.–M.D.XCIII. From the original manuscript*. New York: AMS Press.

Montrose, L. (2006) *The Subject of Elizabeth: Authority, Gender, and Representation*. Chicago: University of Chicago Press.

Mosley, A. (2000) 'Astronomical Books and Courtly Communication' in M. Frasca-Spada, and N. Jardine (eds.) *Books and the Sciences in History*. Cambridge: Cambridge University Press.

Moysie, D. (1830) *Memoirs of the Affairs of Scotland*. Edinburgh: Bannatyne.

Mumby, F.A. (1921) *The Fall of Mary Stuart*. London: Constable.

Nichols, J. (1828) *The Progresses, Processions, and Magnificent Festivities, of King James the First, His Royal Consort, Family, and Court*, II. London: J.B. Nichols.

Nichols, J. (1828) *The Progresses, Processions, and Magnificent Festivities, of King James the First, His Royal Consort, Family, and Court*, III. London: J.B. Nichols.

Parry, G. (1981) *The Golden Age Restor'd*. Manchester: Manchester University Press.

Paton, H. (1904) *Report on the Manuscripts of the Earl of Mar and Kellie*. London: H.M. Stationery Office.

Peters, T., Garrard, P., Ganesan, V., & Stephenson, J. (2012) 'The nature of King James VI/I's medical conditions: new approaches to the diagnosis', *History of Psychiatry*, 23 (3), pp. 277–290.

Pitcairn, R. (1842) *The Autobiography and Diary of Mr James Melville*. Edinburgh: Wodrow.

Pitcairn, S. (1929) *The Journal Guide to Dunfermline*. Dunfermline: Journal Printing Works.

Potter, H. (2002) *Blood Feud: The Murrays and Gordons at War in the Age of Mary Queen of Scots*. Stroud: Tempus.

Pritchard, R.E. (2021) *Sex, Love, and Marriage in the Elizabethan Age*. Barnsley: Pen and Sword.

Questier, M. (2019) *Dynastic Politics and the British Reformations, 1558–1630*. Oxford: OUP.

Rait, R.S. (1927) *King James's Secret*. London: Nisbet.

Rawson Gardiner, S. (1869) *Prince Charles and the Spanish Marriage, II*. London: Hurst and Blackett.

Rawson Gardiner, S. (1895) *History of England From the Accession of James I, II*. London: Longmans, Green, & Co.

Rawson Gardiner, S. (1895) *History of England From the Accession of James I, III*. London: Longmans, Green, & Co.

Rawson Gardiner, S. (2011) *History of England From the Accession of James I, IV*. Cambridge: CUP.

Redworth, G. (2003) *The Prince and the Infanta*. New Haven: Yale University Press.

Robertson, W. (1759) *The History of Scotland, During the Reigns of Queen Mary and of King James VI*. London: A. Millar.

Ross Williamson, H. (1940) *George Villiers, First Duke of Buckingham*. London: Duckworth.

Roughead, W. (1936) *The Riddle of the Ruthvens and Other Studies*. Edinburgh: Moray Press.

Ruigh, R.E. (1971) *The Parliament of 1624*. Cambridge: Harvard University Press.

Rymer, T. (1727) *Fœdera*. London: Tonson.

Scottish Historical Review, 10. (1913) Glasgow: Maclehouse & Sons.

Shapiro, H. (1970) *Scotland in the Days of James VI.* London: Longman.

Somerset, A. (1998) *Unnatural Murder.* Phoenix Press.

Spottiswood, J. (1851) *History of the Church of Scotland,* II. Edinburgh: Oliver & Boyd.

Stair-Kerr, E. (1913) *Stirling Castle: Its Place in Scottish History.* Glasgow: Maclehouse & Sons.

Stedall, R. (2014) *The Survival of the Crown.* Sussex: Book Guild Publishing.

Steeholm, C. and Steeholm, H. (1938) *James I of England.* New York: Covici-Friede.

Stewart, A. (2004) *The Cradle King: The Life of James VI and I.* London: Pimlico.

Strickland, A. (1844) *Lives of the Queens of England,* VII. Philadelphia: Lea and Blanchard.

Strickland, A. (1848) *Lives of the Queens of England,* VI. Philadelphia: Lea and Blanchard.

Sully, Duke of. (1891) *Memoirs of the Duke of Sully, Prime-Minister to Henry the Great,* III. Sligo: Hardpress.

Teems, D. (2010) *Majestie.* Dallas: Thomas Nelson.

Thomson, A.T. (1860) *The Life and Times of George Villiers, Duke of Buckingham,* 1. London: Hurst and Blackett.

Tokson, E.H. (1982) *The Popular Image of the Black Man in English Drama, 1550–1688.* Boston: Hall.

Turner, S. (1829) *The Modern History of England, Part the Second,* IV. London: Longham, Rees, Orme, Brown, and Green.

Tytler, P.F. (1837) *History of Scotland,* 6. Edinburgh: William Tait.

Tytler, P.F. (1842) *History of Scotland,* 7. Edinburgh: William Tait.

Tytler, P.F. (1842) *History of Scotland,* 8. Edinburgh: William Tait.

Vaughan, R. (1867) *Revolutions in English History,* III. London: Longmans, Green, & Co.

Von Raumer, F. (1836) *Contributions to Modern History from the British Museum and the State Paper Office.* London: Charles Knight & Co.

Wade, M.R. (2010) 'Scandinavia Triumphans' in J.R. Mulryne, H. Watanabe-O'Kelly, M. Shewring, E. Goldring, and S. Knight (eds.) *Europa Triumphans.* Farnham: Ashgate.

Warner Ellis, H. (1863) *Denmark and Her Missions.* London: Seeley, Jackson, and Halliday.

Weir, A. (2008) *Mary Queen of Scots and the Murder of Lord Darnley.* London: Vintage.

Weldon, A. (1817) [1651]. *The Court and Character of King James.* London: R.I.

Wells, S. and Spencer, T.J. (1980) *A Book of Masques.* Cambridge: Cambridge University Press.

Williams, C. (2008) *James I.* Eugene: Wipf & Stock.

Williams, E.C. (1970) *Anne of Denmark.* London: Longmans.

Wooding, L. (2015) *Henry VIII.* London: Routledge.

Woolley, B. (2017) *The King's Assassin: The Fatal Affair of George Villiers and James I.* London: St Martin's Press.

Wright, T. (1852) *The History of Scotland,* II. London: London Printing and Publishing Co.

Notes

Introduction: *Triumphus Jacobi*

1 David Carnegie and David Gunby suggest that the earliest version of *The Progeny dates from the period between Charles I's betrothal to Henrietta Maria and James's death. See Carnegie and Gunby, 'The Progeny of Prince James'*, pp. 238–254.

2 Weldon, *The Court and Character of King James,* pp. 55–56.

3 The description is often attributed to Henry IV of France, but without evidence; it is first found in Weldon's *Court and Character.*

4 Peters *et al, 'The Nature of King James VI/I's medical conditions'.*

5 It's often reported that Weldon had been sacked for his xenophobic writings and thus had a vendetta against James. However, this has been disputed, and – given publication came later – even Weldon's authorship is debatable. We can safely say that the source is highly coloured and depicts a vision of James – however true or untrue – in his later years.

6 Montrose, *The Subject*, p. 212.

7 James VI and I, *Basilikon Doron*, pp. 97–98.

8 Somerset, *Unnatural Murder*, p. 44; Teems, *Majestie*, p. 102.

9 Wright, *The History*, p. 370.

10 Lockyer, *Buckingham*, p. 233.

Chapter 1: Baptism of Fire

1 A special tax was agreed by the Privy Council in October, with £6,000 to be gathered from the Kirk, £4,000 from landowners, and £2,000 from the burghs.

2 Herries, *Memoirs*, pp. 73–74.

3 Mumby, *The Fall*, p. 86.

4   The queen did occasionally express a desire to restore Catholicism. See Goodare, 'Queen Mary's Catholic Interlude'.
5   *CSP, Elizabeth*, 8, 1226.
6   Steeholm, *James I*, p. 43.

Chapter 2: Coming of Age

1   Paton, *Report*, p. 22.
2   This short parliament was followed early the next month by a Convention of Estates.
3   Ashton, *James VI*, p. 27.
4   It is sometimes claimed that the hole was in the roof of the building – but this seems less likely to have been noticed by a child sitting under a canopy of estate.
5   Melville, *Memoirs*, p. 249.
6   Akrigg, *Letters*, p. 41.
7   Stewart, *The Cradle King*, p. 40.
8   Kirkcaldy of Grange, a former opponent of Mary, had been won to her cause following her ignoble treatment after the battle of Carberry Hill; he would be hanged. Maitland of Lethington, formerly the queen's Principal Secretary, later her enemy, and then a born-again supporter, died – possibly by suicide, though he was likely dying already – in the castle.
9   Chambers, *A Biographical Dictionary*, I, p. 407.
10 Stair-Kerr, *Stirling Castle*, p. 84.
11 *CSP, Elizabeth*, 10, 1481.
12 *CSP, Scotland*, 2, 317.
13 *CSP, Scotland*, 5, 135.
14 Stedall, *Survival of the Crown*, pp. 169–170.

Chapter 3: Man and Boy

1   Pritchard, *Sex, Love, and Marriage*, p. 130.
2   Chambers, *Domestic Annals*, I, p. 131.
3   Fraser, *King James*, p. 37.
4   Hume Brown, *History*, I, p. 137.
5   Today, at Stirling, one can visit the recreated royal apartments and view both the semi-public bedchamber with its state bed

and the private staircase hidden behind it, which leads up to the intimate bedchamber where the monarch actually slept.

6 Harris Wilson, *King James*, p. 36; Bingham, *James VI*, p. 55.
7 Lee, *John Maitland*, p. 39.
8 Moysie, *Memoirs*, p. 26.
9 *LP, Borders*, I, 77–86; Pitcairn, *Autobiography*, p. 76.
10 Calderwood, *History*, p. 649.
11 *CSP, Scotland*, 6, 51–52.
12 The twentieth century saw this collection of writers named 'the Castalians', a sobriquet derived from the Castalian Spring at Delphi, which Roman poets mythologised as a source of inspiration. One of James's 1590s sonnets explicitly refers to 'Castalia's fountaine cleare'. However, there is no contemporary record of such a name being used.
13 Bingham, *James VI*, p. 79.
14 *CSP, Scotland*, 1, 95.
15 *LP, Borders*, May 1582.
16 Herman, *Royal Poetrie*, p. 175.
17 Bingham, *The Making of a King*, p. 130.

Chapter 4: The End of the Affair

1 Fraser, *Mary Queen of Scots*, p. 498.
2 Irving, *The Confessions*, p. 134.
3 Chambers, *Domestic Annals*, p. 127; *CSP Scotland*, 28, 74.
4 Calderwood, *True History*, p. 111.
5 Melville, *Memoirs*, pp. 119–20.
6 *CSP, Scotland*, 29, 62.
7 *CSP, Scotland*, 30, 22, 24.
8 *CSP, Scotland*, 30, 1.
9 David Calderwood lists the Earls of Mar and Gowrie, the Master of Glamis, the Laird of Easter-Wemyss, Lewis Bellenden, Lord Boyd, Lord Lindsay, the Abbot of Dunfermline, David Erskine, Commendator of Dryburgh, the Abbot of Paisley, the Prior of Pittenweem, and the Constable of Dundee as the chief movers. Bothwell, Glencairn, and the master of Oliphant joined the main 'Ruthven Raiders' at Stirling.
10 *CSP, Scotland*, 30, 26.

11   *Acts and Proceedings*, 1582, October.
12   *CSP, Scotland*, 30, 33.
13   Bergeron, *King James*, pp. 49–50.
14   Bruce, *Papers*, p. 14.
15   *CSP, Simancas*, 3, 311.
16   Stewart, *The Cradle King*, p. 69.

Chapter 5: Madame and Mother

1   Melville, *Memoirs*, p. 287.
2   Tytler, *History*, 6, p. 404.
3   Bell, *Elizabeth I*, p. 63. *The chronicler Camden embroidered this speech to add maternal rhetoric.*
4   *CSP, Scotland*, 6, 603.
5   Ashton, *James I*, p. 2.
6   Laffan, *Kensington*, p. 41.
7   Melville, *Memoirs*, pp. 119–120.
8   Lee, *John Maitland*, p. 81.
9   Stedall, *Survival of the Crown*, p. 198.
10   Tytler, *History*, 8, p. 197.
11   Bruce, *Letters*, p. 16.
12   Weir, *Mary Queen of Scots*, p. 506.

Chapter 6: The Serpent Slain

1   Bruce, *Letters*, pp. 20–21.
2   *CSP, Scotland*, 8, 536.
3   Elizabeth I, *Collected Works*, p. 261.
4   Kinney, *Renaissance Historicisms*, p. 209.
5   Tytler, *History*, 7, p. 95.
6   MacCunn, *Mary Stuart*, p. 301.
7   Halliwell-Phillips, *Letters*, II, p. 73.
8   *Salisbury MSS*, 3, 402.
9   Halliwell-Phillips, *Letters*, II, p. 77.
10   Halliwell-Phillips, *Letters*, II, p. 78.
11   Stewart, *The Cradle King*, p. 83.
12   Williams, *James I*, p. 80.
13   Gray to James, 12 January 1587, London.

14 Robertson, *History*, p. 90.
15 Von Raumer, *Contributions*, p. 415.
16 Turner, *Modern History of England* 2, IV, p. 468.
17 Calderwood, *True History*, p. 611.
18 Rait, *King James's Secret*, p. 191.
19 Dawson, *Scotland Re-formed*, p. 318.
20 Marcus, *Collected Works*, p. 197.
21 Stedall, *Survival of the Crown*, p. 275.

Chapter 7: The Marriage Game

1 James VI, 'A Satire'.
2 Ashley, *Stuarts in Love*, p. 107.
3 Stewart, *The Cradle King*, p. 91.
4 Potter, *Blood Feud*, p. 128.
5 Potter, *Blood Feud*, p. 138.
6 Bingham, *James VI*, p. 104.
7 *CSP, Scotland*, 10, 19.
8 Halliwell-Phillips, *Letters*, II, p. 81.
9 *Salisbury MSS*, 3, 210–211.

Chapter 8: The Second-best Bedfellow

1 Warner Ellis, *Denmark and Her Missions*, p. 33.
2 Wade, 'Scandinavia Triumphans', p. 241.
3 Strickland, *Lives*, VII, p. 239.
4 Lee, *John Maitland*, p. 182.
5 Colville, *Letters*, p. 91.
6 *CSP, Scotland*, 10, 69–70.
7 Strickland, *Lives*, VII, p. 249.
8 *Salisbury MSS*, 3, 421.
9 *CSP, Scotland*, 10, 118.
10 Williams, *Anne of Denmark*, p. 14.
11 *CSP, Scotland*, 10, 176.
12 *CSP, Scotland*, 10, 164.
13 Shapiro, *Scotland*, p. 27.

Chapter 9: 'Tis Thou Maun Bring Her Hame

1   *CSP, Scotland*, 10, 224.
2   *CSP, Scotland*, 10, 236.
3   *CSP, Scotland*, 10, 238.
4   *Salisbury MSS*, 3, 438.
5   *CSP, Scotland*, 10, 218.
6   Moysie, *Memoirs*, p. 80.
7   Strickland, *Lives*, VII, p. 249. *In his Lives of the Lindsays, Alexander Crawford Lindsay claims Spynie did travel to Denmark. However, James's letter back to him in Scotland, quoted later, implies that he either did not go or, at least, was sent home prior to James's time at Kronborg.*
8   Ashley, *Stuarts in Love*, p. 99.
9   Strickland, *Lives*, VI, p. 184.
10 Crawford Lindsay, *Lives of the Lindsays*, I, p. 318.
11 Moysie, *Memoirs*, p. 81.
12 A twentieth-century source claims that four young black men were forced to dance in the snow to entertain the king and queen, and that the quartet thereafter died of pneumonia. This was almost certainly invented out of whole cloth; no contemporary account makes any mention of such a tragedy.
13 Lee, *John Maitland*, p. 209.
14 Stewart, *The Cradle King*, p. 114.
15 Mosley, 'Astronomical books', p. 121.

Chapter 10: His Will Revealed

1   Steeholm, *James I*, p. 134.
2   Williams, *Anne of Denmark*, pp. 28–29.
3   Strickland, *Lives*, VII, p. 260.
4   Croft, *King James*, p. 111.
5   Strickland, *Lives*, VII, pp. 262–263.
6   Strickland, *Lives*, VII, p. 263.
7   Burel, *Papers Relative*, p. vi.
8   McManus, *Women on the Renaissance Stage*, p. 76.
9   Burel, *Papers Relative*, p. v.
10 Laing, *Descriptive Catalogue*, p. 17.
11 This jewel had, in fact, been James's property, but he had pawned

it to the city in exchange for a £4,000 Scots loan; the city's gift was therefore the king's.

12 Calderwood, *History,* 5, p. 98.
13 Strickland, *Lives,* VII, p. 265.
14 Strickland, *Lives,* VII, p. 265.
15 Pitcairn, *The Journal,* p. 48.
16 Melville had helped rescue James from the Ruthven raiders and thus retained a sterling reputation for loyalty to the Crown.
17 Melville, *Memoirs,* pp. 393–395.
18 Meikle, 'Hold her at the Oeconomicke rule', pp. 106–107.
19 The English monarchs had ceased taking their dinners in their more public chambers under Henry VIII.

Chapter 11: Toil and Trouble

1 Meville, *Memoirs,* p. 389.
2 Melville, *Memoirs,* p. 389.
3 Levack, *Witch-hunting,* p. 37.
4 *CSP, Scotland,* 10, 276.
5 Guenther, *Magical Imaginations,* p. 140.
6 Stewart, *The Cradle King,* p. 126.
7 *CSP, Scotland,* 10, 612.
8 *Ibid.*
9 Chambers, *Domestic Annals,* I, p. 201.
10 *CSP, Scotland,* 10, 652.
11 Melville, *Memoirs,* p. 415.

Chapter 12: Disillusion

1 *CSP, Scotland,* 11, 148.
2 *CSP, Scotland,* 11, 175.
3 Williams, *Anne of Denmark,* p. 109.
4 *CSP, Scotland,* 11, 175.
5 *CSP, Scotland,* 11, 185.
6 *CSP, Scotland,* 11, 248.
7 *Ibid.*
8 *CSP, Scotland,* 11, 300.

9   Inflation obviously played a role in the difference in sums but only to an extent.
10 Williams, *Anne of Denmark*, pp. 51–52.
11 Bath, 'Rare shewes', p. 103.
12 *CSP, Scotland*, 10, 533.
13 *CSP, Scotland*, 11, 545.
14 Spottiswood, *History*, p. 463.

Chapter 13: All Things to All Men

1   *Salisbury MSS*, 6, 31.
2   Loomie, 'King James I's Catholic Consort', p. 305.
3   Mayer, *The Struggle*, p. 8.
4   Williams, *Anne of Denmark*, p. 200.
5   Church of Scotland, *The Scottish Kirk*, p. 29.
6   Grierson, *St Andrews*, p. 30.
7   I am indebted to Julian Goodare for drawing my attention to the importance of this event, often called a riot. See Goodare, 'The Attempted Scottish Coup'.
8   Stewart, *The Cradle King*, p. 145.
9   Krag, 'Relation', p. 187.
10 James VI and I, *Basilikon Doron*, pp. 97–98.
11 Strickland, *Lives*, VII, p. 285.
12 Strickland, *Lives*, VII, p. 288.
13 Roughead, *The Riddle of the Ruthvens*, p. 22.
14 *CSP, Scotland*, 13, 55.

Chapter 14: Succession

1   Stewart, *The Cradle King*, p. 168.
2   Bingham, *James I*, p. 11.
3   Handover, *The Second Cecil*, p. 300.
4   Montrose, *The Subject*, p. 212.
5   Croft, *King James*, p. 41.
6   Folkestone Williams, *The Court*, p. 3.
7   Hayward, *Stuart Style*, p. 60.
8   Bowes, that useful commentator on Scottish affairs throughout the 1590s, had died in 1597.

9   *Salisbury MSS*, 23, 97–124.
10 *Ibid.*
11 Strickland, *Lives,* VII, p. 296.
12 Fraser, *Memorials,* II, p. 211.
13 Strickland, *Lives,* VII, p. 298.
14 Hill Burton, *The History of Scotland,* 6, p. 170.
15 *Ibid.*
16 The French Duke of Sully reported that she rode out with the foetus of her miscarried son in a casket, thereby hoping to counter rumours that she had been feigning her pregnancy and illness. In this account, the casket was carried all the way into England. However, there are no contemporary Scottish accounts of this, nor any records of burial in England. See Sully, *Memoirs,* 3, p. 112.
17 *Salisbury MSS*, 15, 13.
18 Marshall, *Scottish Queens*, p. 13.
19 Strickland, *Lives, VII*, p. 311.
20 *BL Add. MS,* 22601, fol. 63r.
21 *Salisbury MSS*, 15, 187, 127.
22 Strict limits were imposed on the numbers of guests, with earls allowed sixteen attendants and bishops and lords ten.
23 Hayward, *Stuart Style*, p. 204.
24 *Salisbury MSS*, 15, 243–253.

Chapter 15: Secrets of a Successful Marriage

1   *Salisbury MSS*, 15, 225–243.
2   *Salisbury, MSS*, 15, 345–398.
3   *CSP, James*, 12, 13, 71.
4   Dryden, *Dramatic Works*, VIII, p. 452.
5   Howitt, *Biographical Sketches*, p. 431.
6   Clifford, *Diaries*, p. 27.
7   The play performed is often named as being *As You Like It, but this is mere tradition.*
8   *CSP, James*, 5, Addenda, pp. 433–435.
9   *Journal of the House of Commons*, 1, pp. 142–149.
10 Williams, *James I*, p. 247.
11 Breton, *A Murmurer*, p. 13.

12 *CSP, Venice*, 10, 207.
13 Bergeron, *Royal Family*, p. 117.
14 Tokson, *The Popular Image*, p. 7.
15 Dutton, *Shakespeare*, p. 86.

Chapter 16: The Honeymoon Ends

1 Knight, *Popular History*, III, p. 341.
2 Daurignac, *History of the Society of Jesus*, 1, p. 279.
3 *Bodleian MS Malone*, 23, p. 121.
4 *CSP, James*, 21, 6.
5 Nichols, *Progresses*, II, p. 53.
6 Parry, *The Golden Age*, p. 59.
7 Vaughan, *Revolutions*, III, p. 16.
8 Drake, *Shakespeare*, p. 408.

Chapter 17: At Long Last Love

1 Bellany, *Politics of Court Scandal*, p. 31.
2 Anne Somerset notes that Carr was described as both 'minion' and 'bedfellow' to Overbury (who was a few years older), whilst Francis Bacon, who was either homosexual or bisexual himself, recorded an 'excess' of friendship between the two men. See Somerset, *Unnatural Murder*, pp. 62–63.
3 Everett Green, *Lives of the Princesses of England*, VI, pp. 94–95.
4 *CSP, Venice*, 11, 154.
5 Rawson Gardiner, *History*, 2, p. 46.
6 Cornwallis, *The Life and Death*, p. 249.
7 Birch, *Henry*, p. 104.
8 Thomas Sackville, 1st Earl of Dorset, had been the Lord Buckhurst retained as treasurer in 1603.
9 Jonson's *Faery Prince* in Donaldson, *Ben Jonson*, p. 277.
10 *Ecclesiasticus auctoritati Jacobi regis oppositus (1611)*, by the Catholic Caspar Schoppe, attributed to Sir Henry Wotton the quip that an ambassador was an 'honest man sent to lie abroad for the good of his country'. Wotton would endure a period of disgrace as a result.
11 D'Ewes, *Autobiography*, II, p. 335.
12 *Salisbury MSS*, 21, 134, 153.

13 Goodman, *The Court of King James I*, II, p. 144.

Chapter 18: The End of an Era

1 *Bodleian MS, Tanner* 299, fols. 11v–12r.
2 *BL MS, Egerton* 2230, fol. 34r–v.
3 *Bodleian MS,* Tanner 299, fol. 11r.
4 *CSP, Venice*, 12, 447.
5 Cornwallis, *Life and Character*, p. 21.
6 Birch, *Henry, Prince of Wales*, p. 249.
7 Marshall, *The Winter Queen*, p. 29.
8 Birch, *Henry*, p. 257.
9 Hepworth Dixon, *Her Majesty's Tower*, I, p. 260.
10 *CSP, James*, 71, 69.
11 Coke, *A Detection*, p. 68. *The first mention of the joke comes in a remembrance written in the late 1600s. It was evidently intended to glorify Elizabeth via recording her supposed retort; Anna's disdain, however, chimes with contemporary accounts of her attitude.*
12 Bingham, *James I*, p. 117.
13 Wells and Spencer, *A Book of Masques*, p. 102.
14 Brotton, *The Sale*, p. 53.
15 Chamberlain, *Letters*, I, p. 469.
16 *CSP, James*, 74, 49.
17 Campion in Limon, *The Masque*, p. 177.
18 *CCRO MS*, CR 63/2/19, fol. 11r.
19 *Bodleian MS*, Rawl. Poet. 26, fol. 17v.

Chapter 19: Fall and Rise of a Favourite

1 *CSP, James*, 71, 51.
2 Croft, *King James*, p. 81.
3 In April, complaints were made by MPs 'against the patent [for wine licences] granted to the Lord Admiral [Nottingham] and his son the Lord of Effingham'. See *CSP, James*, 77, 14.
4 Winwood noted that four MPs, 'Sir Walter Chute, Christopher Neville, Hoskins, and Wentworth, are sent to prison, and Sir Charles Cornwallis and Dr Lionel Sharp are to go'. See *CSP, James*, 77, 236–240.

5   *CSP, James*, 77, 53.
6   *CSP, Venice*, 13, 348.
7   *CSP, James*, 77, 70.
8   *CSP, James*, 77, 75.
9   Halliwell-Phillips, *Letters*, II, p. 126.
10 Goodman, *The Court*, pp. 225–226.
11 Hackett in Goodman, *The Court*, p. 226.
12 Nichols, *Progresses*, III, pp. 81–82.
13 Frederick Smith, *John Cassell's Illustrated History*, 3, p. 57.
14 Thomson, *Life and Times*, I, p. 89.
15 Wooding, *Henry VIII*, p. 216.
16 Heneage Jesse, *Memoirs*, 1, p. 109.
17 Ross Williamson, *George Villiers*, p. 59.
18 *Corona Regia, translation provided by the University of Birmingham.*
19 *CSP, James*, 81, 86.
20 Clayton, *Personal Memoirs*, I, pp. 7–8.

Chapter 20: The Return of the King

1   *CSP, James*, 90, 25.
2   *CSP, James*, 89, 17.
3   Campbell, *Lives*, I, p. 286.
4   Rawson Gardiner, *History*, III, p. 98.
5   Holmes, *The Sickly Stuarts*, pp. 46–47.
6   Longueville, *Archbishop Laud*, p. 67.
7   *CSP, James*, 90, 8.
8   *Scottish Historical Review*, 10, p. 26.
9   Bourne, *The History*, p. 228.
10 Bingham, *James I*, p. 164.
11 *CSP, James*, 92, 88.
12 *CSP, James*, 92, 3.
13 *CSP, James*, 93, 25.
14 *CSP, James*, 93, 99.
15 *CSP, James*, 93, 33.
16 *CSP, James*, 93, 158.
17 *CSP, James*, 95, 12.
18 Nichols, *Progresses*, III, p. 469.
19 *CSP, James*, 97, 98.

20 Kittridge True, *The Life and Times of Sir Walter Raleigh*, p. 189.

Chapter 21: Death and Taxes

1 *CSP, James*, 105, 2.
2 *CSP, James*, 105, 54.
3 Chancellor, *The Life of Charles I*, p. 47.
4 Lehman, *Lives of England's Reigning and Consort Queens*, p. 441.
5 *CSP, James*, 107, 37.
6 *CSP, James*, 107, 38, 41.
7 Holmes, *The Sickly Stuarts*, p. 48.
8 *CSP, James*, 108, 50.
9 *CSP, James*, 109, 32.
10 Questier, *Dynastic Politics*, p. 289.
11 Halliwell-Phillips, *Letters*, II, p. 156.
12 Interestingly, there exists at Apethorpe a secret passage linking the king's bedchamber to Buckingham's apartments. This has been dated to the early 1620s and used, since its discovery, as proof of the pair's sexual entanglement. It would be a matter of historical and scholarly irony if it was, in fact, used simply for close contact and was constructed after they had ceased having a sexual relationship.
13 Houston, *James I*, p. 75.
14 Harris, *The Œconomy of the Fleete*, p. 191.
15 *De Proclamatione Regia in Rymer, Fœdera*, p. 289.
16 Lockyer, *Buckingham*, p. 94.

Chapter 22: But Where Are My Two Bonnie Boys?

1 Rawson Gardiner, *History*, p. 189.
2 Cust, *Charles I*, p. 9.
3 Kenyon, *Stuart England*, p. 94.
4 Redworth, *The Prince and the Infanta*, p. 64.
5 *NRO*, AYL/192, ff. [1r]–[14r].
6 Dunham and Pargellis, *Complaint and Reform*, p. 503.
7 Halliwell-Phillips, *Letters*, II, p. 159.
8 Brotton, *The Sale*, p. 85.
9 Halliwell-Phillips, *Letters*, II, p. 232.

10 Chancellor, *The Life of Charles I*, p. 87.
11 *CSP, James*, 145, 593.
12 Halliwell-Phillips, *Letters*, II, p. 182.
13 Bergeron, *King James*, p. 135.
14 Woolley, *The King's Assassin*, p. 125.
15 Davenport, *New Elegant Extracts*, 5, pp. 61–62.
16 Halliwell-Phillips, *Letters*, II, p. 227.
17 Rawson Gardiner, *Prince Charles*, II, p. 383.

Chapter 23: Death's Triumphing Dart

1 Thomson, *Life and Times*, I, p. 25.
2 Nichols, *Progresses*, III, Appendix, p. 1120.
3 Stewart, *The Cradle King*, p. 330.
4 Ruigh, *The Parliament*, p. 155.
5 Ruigh, *The Parliament*, p. 336.
6 Earl of Hardwicke, *Miscellaneous State Papers*, 1, p. 456.
7 Bergeron, *King James*, p. 175.
8 Lockyer, *Buckingham*, p. 232.
9 Bergeron, *King James*, p. 138.
10 Goodman, *The Court*, p. 409.
11 Questier, *Stuart Dynastic Policy*, p. 30.

Index